The Flatbush Journal of Jewish Law and Thought

Volume 28 / Spring 2020

A publication of
Hakirah, Inc.
www.Hakirah.org

Ḥakirah

The Flatbush Journal of Jewish Law and Thought

Volume 28 / Spring 2020

11 | Letters to the Editor

JEWISH THOUGHT

15 | Amalek from Generation to Generation
Asher Benzion Buchman

35 | An "Even Better" Judaism? Progressivism and Orthodox Judaism
Steven Kessler

HISTORY OF HALAKHAH

49 | Siddur Avodat HaLev:
A New Siddur and Insights on the Old
Aton Holzer and Arie Folger

83 | "David Melech Yisrael Chai VeKayam":
Kiddush HaLevanah, Midrash, Archeology and Redemption
Nachman Levine

101 | A Positive Light on the Nations:
R. Moshe Isserles' Revisionistic Views on Christianity
Asher Turin

129 | The Code of Esther: A Counter-Investigation
Emmanuel Bloch

HALAKHAH

147 | Loving the Convert Prior to a Completed Conversion:
With a Test Case Application of Inviting Conversion
Candidates to Pesach Seder and Yom Tov Meals
Michael J. Broyde and Benjamin J. Samuels

TALMUD TORAH

187 | Idle Chatter or Vital Chat? A Janus-Faced Talmudic Dictum
David Nimmer

223 | The Original Understanding of Sea Sponges in mShabbat 21:3
Steven H. Adams

253 | On the Meaning of the Word Ḥem'ah in Biblical Hebrew
Yisroel Asher Coleman

TORAH AND MEDICINE

257 | BRCA Testing for All Ashkenazi Women: A Halakhic Inquiry
Sharon Galper Grossman

HISTORY

285 | Outlawed Visitors on al-Haram al-Sharif:
Jews on the Temple Mount during the Ottoman and
British rule of Jerusalem, 1517–1967
F. M. Loewenberg

MINHAG

301 | Tehillat Hashem and Other Verses Before Birkat Ha-Mazon
Zvi Ron

ה | סרבנות גט: המצב באירופה בכלל ובצרפת בפרט.
הצעה לקיצור זמן העיגון של מסורבות גט
יוסף יצחק איידלר

כג | "כבד פה וכבד לשון" – הצעות להסבר
אבנר טלר

Introduction

Before the appearance of the coronavirus, the most pressing concern of the American Jewish community was the recent rise in antisemitism. And in the midst of the ravages of the virus, as has so often been the case in the past, it too became a reason for antisemitism in some circles. Our opening article, "Amalek from Generation to Generation," traces the history of antisemitism to *Kabbalat Ha-Torah* and seeks to explain its root cause, concluding that Amalek's hatred is for Judaism more than for the Jews themselves. Other articles in *Ḥakirah* 28 are related to this theme as they deal with Israel's relationship to the nations of the world. The second article in the *Jewish Thought* section, "An 'Ever Better' Judaism? Progressivism & Orthodox Judaism," argues that modern left-wing thought is in opposition to the eternal teachings of the Torah. An article in the *History of Halakhah* section, "A Positive Light on the Nations: R. Isserles' Revisionistic Views on Christianity," examines the predominant negative view of the Ba'alei Tosefot towards Christianity and compares it with the more positive assessment of Rama generations later. An article in the *Jewish Law* section, "Loving the Convert Prior to a Completed Conversion: With a Test Case Application of Inviting Conversion Candidates to Pesach Seder and Yom Tov Meals," suggests that the mitzvah of loving the *ger* applies even before the final conversion has taken place.

Antisemitism is also relevant in an article titled "The Code of Esther: A Counter-Investigation," where the author investigates the claim that there is a hint in *Megillat Esther* linking the most prominent antisemite of ancient times to the Nazis of the modern era. Other articles highlight Israel's determination to overcome persecution and return to their land. In "Outlawed Visitors on al-Haram al-Sharif: Jews on the Temple Mount during the Ottoman and British rule of Jerusalem, 1517–1967" we see that despite an Arab ban and halakhic issues with ascending the Temple Mount, individuals still managed to ascend over the centuries. In our *Minhag* section, "*Tehillat Hashem* and Other Verses Before *Birkat Ha-Mazon*" traces the development of the custom to say certain Psalms and verses before *Birkat Ha-Mazon* and the practice of some people to add a few additional verses after *Shir Hama'alot.* Here, too, the motivation behind the choice of these texts shows the yearning of Israel to return to Eretz Yisrael. And in an article in our *Talmud Torah* section, "'David Melech Yisrael Chai VeKayam': Kiddush HaLevanah, Midrash, Archeology, and Redemption," we see how halakhah, *minhag*, midrash, history, archeology, and iconography interface to reveal how the Rabbis perceived *kiddush ha-levanah* as a means of maintaining Jewish sovereignty in their land.

Other articles in our *Talmud Torah* section also show how modern discoveries and insights can be used to shed light on ancient texts and practices. In "The Original Understanding of Sea Sponges in mShabbat 21:3," the author studies *girsaos* and history to attempt to prove that a later layer, added after the completion of the Talmud, introduces a new halakhic prohibition. In "On the Meaning of the Word Ḥem'ah in Biblical Hebrew," the author researches ancient and medieval sources and applies logic to reevaluate the translation of a word in the Bible. In "Idle Chatter or Vital Chat? A Janus-Faced Talmudic Dictum," the author sheds light on Aggadic passages dealing with the completeness of the Torah and shows that "the same slogan [is] deployed by champions of particularism to support their viewpoint no less than by champions of universalism to support their contrary position." And in a Hebrew article on the *"kevad peh kevad lashon"* of Moshe Rabbenu, the author uses many methods of Biblical analysis, including modern medicine, to suggest the meaning of this term.

Two important articles deal with contemporary issues affecting women. In a Hebrew article the author explains the unique problems involved with the *agunah* situation in Europe because of the governments' intrusive regulations. In our *Torah and Medicine* section, the essay "BRCA Testing for All Ashkenazi Women: A Halachic Inquiry" explores medical and halakhic issues regarding whether a potentially life-saving procedure should be performed. Some of the issues weighed—possible medical benefit that comes with the knowledge of greater statistical susceptibility versus the psychological and life-style harm caused by this knowledge—are relevant to the precautions that have been almost universally accepted to stem the spread of the coronavirus.

In "A New Siddur and Insights on the Old," contributing editors for the new RCA siddur explain issues and considerations in the production of a new siddur to enhance performance of the eternal *mitzvah* of *tefillah* in the 21st century.

Our opening article on Amalek contends that just as there is an external Amalek, there is also an Amalek within the human psyche, and that Israel is only harmed by the external Amalek when it has given an opening to the internal Amalek. The internal Amalek convinces man of his own centrality and invincibility. The pain and the fear that the coronavirus has generated throughout the world should spark the realization of how vulnerable mankind really is, and how dependent we are upon our Creator. Our community was slow to recognize the danger and was particularly hard hit by this pandemic, but then quickly became integrally involved in combatting it. Many amongst us demonstrated both great courage and faith. It is incumbent upon us to evaluate our actions and understand our strengths and weaknesses. As the Biblical text implies and the Mishnah explicitly states, the response to the ravages caused by Amalek is turning our hearts to G-d.

Special thanks to all those who worked hard to make this edition of *Ḥakirah* a reality, including Ari Bornstein, Nina Ackerman Indig, Mindy Schaper, and Sorelle Weinstein, copy-editing; Tuvia Ganz, cover design and production; and Chaim Lam, design and maintenance of our Web page, www.Hakirah.org.

It is our continuing hope that the articles in this journal will stimulate thought, study and discussion, and inspire other members of the public to contribute their own insights. The articles we print thus reflect a wide range of opinion and do not necessarily represent the views of our editorial board.

Stay safe and healthy. ☙

Instructions for Contributors

Ḥakirah, The Flatbush Journal of Jewish Law and Thought, publishes original, interesting, well-researched and well-organized manuscripts that provide new or profound insights into areas of Jewish *halakhah* and *hashkafah.*

Manuscripts should be in Microsoft Word format and sent as an email attachment to HakirahFlatbush@msn.com. Short references—for example, to a Biblical verse or to a page within the Talmud—should be embedded directly into the text of the manuscript. Longer references should be inserted electronically as footnotes, rather than endnotes.

The author's name should not appear on the manuscript, as it is the Journal's policy to forward the articles for evaluation without disclosing the author's identity. On a separate cover sheet include your name, a short bio, an abstract of your article, your telephone number, fax number, and e-mail address.

After reviewing and accepting your manuscript, we are likely to request clarification of certain points. A revised electronic copy of your manuscript will then be required.

To encourage a wide variety of contributors, the Journal accepts articles employing the Hebrew transliteration style of either *Encyclopedia Judaica* or *ArtScroll.* If you have no preference we suggest you follow the pronunciation rules used by the *Encyclopedia Judaica.* Words in languages other than English should always be italicized, unless the foreign words have become part of the English language.

For more information about writing an article for *Ḥakirah* see <www.Hakirah.org\HakirahGuideToWriting.pdf>. ☙

We Listen to the Coronavirus Experts

By: HESHEY ZELCER

The following poem was written on April 23, 2020. Two short weeks later my brother-in-law succumbed to Covid-19. Less than a week after that my father-in-law passed away from the same disease.

My dear brother-in-law, R. Yechiel Yosef ben Zvi Bezalel Bornstein, z"l, was taken from us on 12 Iyyar 5780. Born in Yerushalayim to a ḥareidi family, he joined the Israeli Defense Forces. During the Six-Day War he served in a tank battalion protecting the State of Israel. Following his discharge, he moved to the United States and found employment in the diamond industry. Saving his money, he brought his parents over and helped settle them in Borough Park. With his charm, personality, and constant smile, he won over and married my sister, Chanie. Yossie was loved by everyone he met and helped those in need. He loved learning Torah and teaching Nakh. The last few years of his life he served as president of Anshei Sfard of Borough Park (the Sfardishe Shul), where he worked tirelessly attending to the needs of the congregation and its members. Yossie is survived by his wife, his three children Rivi, Ari and Toby, numerous grandchildren, and a great-granddaughter.

My dear father-in-law, R. Avraham ben Nechemia Yisrael Solomon, z"l passed away just a few days later on Lag Ba-Omer. Born in Kirhaus, Czechoslovakia he spent the war years as a forced laborer. After the liberation he was taken to Föhrenwald DP Camp where he was privileged to hear the Klausenberger rebbeh whose words lifted his spirit. With his faith intact, and anxious to rebuild his life, he relocated to the United States where he was introduced to Rivka, a young woman whom he remembered from Kirhaus. They married, settled in Borough Park and raised four wonderful children. He was kind to everyone, scrupulous in his business dealings, and beloved by family, friends and neighbors. His passion for davening and Torah study remained with him until his final days. After marrying off their children they moved to Flatbush near Hisachdis Yirieim Veretzky (R. Landau's Shul) where they were warmly embraced by its previous rebbeh ztz"l and afterwards by its current rebbeh shlit"a. He is survived by his four children Temy, Nechemia, Shia and Zisha, numerous grandchildren and great-grandchildren.

May their memories be a blessing.

Heshey Zelcer is on the editorial board of *Ḥakirah* and has published books and articles on Jewish law, philosophy, history and liturgy.

We Listen to the Coronavirus Experts

We close our houses of worship—
God will understand
We send our employees home—
Finances will work themselves out.

We separate old from young
High-risk from low
Family from friends.

We have it all worked out
We keep our social distance
Don our masks and gloves
We will live forever.

In my naiveté I imagine an ideal life
At home, sipping coffee
Chatting leisurely with my dear wife.

But yesterday, as night approached, sadness descended
It is seven weeks since I hugged my children
Seven weeks since I kissed my grandkids' cheeks.

I awake at night and obsess
Are my hands clean?
Did I touch my face?
Is my cough the start of that dreaded disease?

I try to go back to sleep
But I see loved ones fighting for their lives
Close friends of whom I now speak in the past tense
Fitfully I fall asleep.

I awake in the morning
The sky is brightening
Better days are sure to come.

May God spread His protective shield over us all.

☙

LETTERS TO THE EDITOR

Yashar Prenuptial

THE *Yashar Prenuptial Agreement*, described in "A Prenuptial Agreement by and for the Ḥaredi Community" (*Ḥakirah* 27), includes a number of features worthy of wider adoption. However, its paragraph 37, as written, is problematic. This paragraph (summarized as point 11 in the "Highlights" section of the article) reads as follows: 'The parties agree not to resort to *Heter Meah Rabonim*, *Heter Nisuin* or *Bitul Kedushin* [annulment of the marriage] if the wife is willing and able to accept a *get* [a Jewish divorce].' Even a person who is not learned in the fine points of the Laws of Marriage and Divorce can see at once that this clause has an internal inconsistency.

If the three Hebrew terms listed all refer to remedies that only a husband could ever employ, then there is no need for the wife to waive the option of using them; having her do so is a pointless exercise. On the other hand, if one or more of them could be used by the wife in some set of circumstances, then why would she ever voluntarily commit herself not to do so in the situation where she *is* willing and able to accept a *get*, but her husband is *not* willing and able to give one?

Whether *bitul kedushin b'ilas mekach ta'us machmas mum ba-baal* is, under any circumstances, 'a thing,' as the current popular idiom puts it, is far too broad a topic to discuss in a letter. But whether it is or whether it is not, in neither case does having the *kallah* waive it, in advance and unconditionally, promote the goal of preventing *iggun*. I personally would advise a *kallah* against signing the *Yashar Prenuptial Agreement* unless either the subject of Clause 37 is amended to refer to the husband alone, or its final condition is amended to refer to the cooperation of both parties in giving and receiving a *get*.

David Hoffman
Jerusalem

ON P. 96, HESHEY ZELCER reports that R. Elazar Muskin stated that R. Shmuel Fuerst 'now supports signing the RCA prenuptial.' Alas, this is a false report. What Rabbi Muskin actually stated is that Rabbi Fuerst supports signing **a** prenuptial, but in no way has Rabbi Muskin ever claimed that Rabbi Fuerst endorses the particular prenuptial popularized by the RCA.

On pp. 97-98, Zelcer cites *Iggerot Moshe, Even ha-Ezer* IV, no. 107 as a precedent for his *Yashar Prenuptial Agreement*. Alas, Zelcer fails to take into account the two variant versions of this *Iggerot Moshe* responsum, and the halakhic ramification that may emerge from this discrepancy. See Section R of my online essay for elucidation.

On p. 98, Zelcer claims that the *Yashar Prenuptial Agreement* stipulates that 'within its first session, Beit Din will set an interim payment amount that the husband must pay the wife for the continuation of the household, and for the children to continue to attend *yeshivot.*' Alas, this is a complete fabrication. Nowhere in the *Yashar Prenuptial Agreement* is such a financial penalty on the husband ever stipulated.

Shalom C. Spira
Montreal

Heshey Zelcer responds:

I thank David Hoffman and Shalom Spira for their thoughtful and articulate comments.

Regarding David Hoffman's critique of paragraph 37 of the *Yashar Agreement* (actually paragraph 36 in the current version), it was inserted at the insistence of a *rav* who helped formulate the *Yashar Prenuptial Agreement* and who gave his approbation. I do not and cannot speak for the *rav* but I assume his intent was to avoid using extreme halakhic solutions, and instead commit the couple to negotiate the dissolution of their marriage—as quickly and painlessly as possible—within the context of a Beth Din they had both chosen. Without a prenuptial agreement it can take months for the parties to agree upon a venue.

David Hoffman is correct that by signing the *Yashar Prenuptial Agreement* the *kallah* gives up her ability to utilize *Bitul Kedushin* to dissolve their marriage. *Bitul Kedushin*, however, also has its dark side. When granted by a Beth Din based on subjective criteria, it could leave the woman vulnerable—even many years later—to charges by a vengeful ex-husband that she was not really a *penuah*, a single woman, when she remarried.

Regarding Shalom Spira's comment concerning Rabbi Shmuel Fuerst's view of the *RCA Prenuptial Agreement*: While the quoted article may be ambiguous as to which prenuptial agreement Rabbi Shmuel Fuerst is referring, there is nothing ambiguous about Rabbi Fuerst's position regarding the *RCA Prenuptial Agreement.* On December 15, 2019, Rabbi Fuerst spoke at K'hal Ner L-Meiah in Flatbush at the invitation of its Rav, Rabbi Baruch Goldstein. In front of approximately one hundred people, Rabbi Fuerst declared clearly and forcefully that he supports the *RCA Prenuptial Agreement.* He was less enthusiastic about the *Yashar Prenuptial Agreement* as he felt it was not as forceful as the *RCA Prenuptial Agreement* in compelling the husband to provide substantial financial support for his family.[1]

---

[1] Rabbi Shmuel Fuerst's complete lecture can be heard at https://www.torahanytime.com/#/lectures?v=90435 (beginning 03:45).

Rabbi Moshe Feinstein's *teshuva* (*Even ha-Ezer* IV, no. 107) cited in my article—as an example of 'A *hareidi* precedent in the US for a prenuptial agreement'—is a faithful translation of the *teshuva* as printed in *Iggerot Moshe*.

I am puzzled why R. Spira refers to financial support undertaken by the husband as a 'penalty'. As for his charge of 'complete fabrication' of a non-existent statement in the *Yashar Prenuptial Agreement*, see paragraph 16 of the *Yashar Prenuptial Agreement* which states: 'At the initial session, Beth Din shall outline the issues between the Parties and make a determination of the interim payments necessary to ensure that the lifestyle of the un-emancipated children of the household (if any) can be maintained, and that they can continue to attend yeshiva.'

ᘓ

Amalek from Generation to Generation

By: ASHER BENZION BUCHMAN

Mitzvos upon Entering the Land

Rambam begins *Hilchos Melachim* by listing three mitzvos that Israel was commanded to fulfill upon entering their land.

> א שלוש מצוות נצטוו ישראל בשעת כניסתן לארץ: למנות להם מלך שנאמר "שום תשים עליך מלך" (דברים יז,טו), ולהכרית זרעו של עמלק שנאמר "תמחה את זכר עמלק" (דברים כה,יט), ולבנות להם בית הבחירה שנאמר "לשכנו תדרשו, ובאת שמה" (דברים יב,ה). מינוי מלך קודם למלחמת עמלק, שנאמר "אותי שלח ה' למשוחך למלך... ועתה לך והכית את עמלק" (שמואל א טו,א-ג). והכרתת זרע עמלק קודמת לבניין הבית, שנאמר "ויהי, כי ישב המלך בביתו; וה' הניח לו מסביב, מכל אויביו. ויאמר המלך, אל נתן הנביא, ראה... אנוכי יושב בבית ארזים..." (שמואל ב ז,א-ב).

> Israel was commanded to fulfill three mitzvos upon entering the Promised Land: To choose a king, as Deuteronomy (17:15) states: "Appoint a king over yourselves"; To wipe out the descendants of Amalek, as Deuteronomy (25:19) states: "Erase the memory of Amalek"; To build G-d's chosen house, as Deuteronomy (12:5) states: "Seek out His Presence and go there." The appointment of a king should precede the war against Amalek. This is evident from Samuel's charge to King Saul (I Samuel 15: 1-3): "G-d sent me to anoint you as king ... Now, go and smite Amalek." Amalek's seed should be annihilated before the construction of the Temple, as II Samuel (7:1-2) states: "And it came to pass, when the king dwelled in his palace, and G-d gave him peace from all his enemies who surrounded him, the king said to Nathan, the prophet: 'Look! I am dwelling in a house of cedar...but the ark of G-d dwells within curtains.'"[1]

These were all commands to the people, and although the appointment of a government would be the first step in organizing the nation to

---

[1] Even though the mitzvah of building the *Mikdash* based on the verse of ועשו לי מקדש is brought in *Hilchos Bais HaBechirah*, it is here based on לשכנו תדרשו, referring to the permanent sanctuary that was to be the central feature of the Jewish Nation.

Asher Benzion Buchman is the author of *Encountering the Creator: Divine Providence and Prayer in the Works of Rambam* (Targum, 2004) and *Rambam and Redemption* (Targum, 2005). He is the editor-in-chief of *Ḥakirah.*

fulfill the other two mitzvos, Rambam is nevertheless explicit that all three mitzvos are incumbent on the community as a whole,[2] not solely on the king. The individual must contribute what he is able towards a goal that can only be accomplished by the nation as a whole. We have discussed all three mitzvos and how they comprise three steps in fulfilling Israel's purpose as a nation elsewhere.[3] Here, however, we will concentrate on better understanding the command to "annihilate Amalek."

Amalek is the nation which attacked Israel immediately after they left Egypt, and thus it follows that they represent those who threaten Israel's security. Aside from the fact that this is what is implied by the Torah narrative, this also emerges from Rambam's explanation for the reason this mitzvah precedes building the Beis HaMikdash:

> והכרתת זרע עמלק קודמת לבניין הבית, שנאמר "ויהי, כי ישב המלך בביתו; וה' הניח לו מסביב, מכל אויביו. ויאמר המלך, אל נתן הנביא, ראה... אנוכי יושב בבית ארזים...
>
> Amalek's seed should be annihilated before the construction of the Temple, as II Samuel (7:1-2) states: "And it came to pass, when the king dwelled in his palace, and G-d gave him peace from all his enemies who surrounded him, the king said to Nathan, the prophet: 'Look! I am dwelling in a house of cedar...but the ark of G-d dwells within curtains.'"

Although this verse in Shmuel does not speak of Amalek, *Chazal* understand it to be referring to Amalek since the Torah itself links the war against Amalek with battles for security.

> וְהָיָה בְּהָנִיחַ ה אֱלֹהֶיךָ לְךָ מִכָּל-אֹיְבֶיךָ מִסָּבִיב, בָּאָרֶץ אֲשֶׁר ה- אֱלֹהֶיךָ נֹתֵן לְךָ נַחֲלָה לְרִשְׁתָּהּ--תִּמְחֶה אֶת-זֵכֶר עֲמָלֵק, מִתַּחַת הַשָּׁמָיִם; לֹא תִּשְׁכָּח.

---

2 See *Sefer HaMitzvos*, at the end of the *Mitzvos Aseh*. Ramban (*Ramban al HaTorah, BeMidbar* 16:21-22) says the sin of Israel which was the reason for the plague in the days of David was that Israel did not build the *Mikdash* independently all the years after the first conquest. The people need not have waited for a king. It would seem that Rambam would disagree, and that the means for fulfilling the latter two mitzvos was first appointing a king. Nevertheless, Rambam would agree with Ramban's premise that these *mitzvos* are obligations on the nation, with each individual expected to do his part. The Gemara (*Sanhedrin* 20b) brings the verse יד על כס קה as a proof that there must be a king for the mitzvah of destroying Amalek to apply. Rambam implies that this is not a requirement for the obligation in the mitzvah to begin but merely an explanation of what order the mitzvos are to proceed in initially.

3 See *Hakirah* 25 pp 55ff, "Rambam's Missing Mitzvah."

> When G-d will give you ease from all your surrounding enemies, in the Land which G-d Your G-d has given to you as an inheritance, erase the memory of Amalek from beneath the Heavens. Do not forget.

The *Smag* (163), based on this verse,[4] says it follows that all other enemies are to be destroyed, then Amalek, then the Beis HaMikdash can be rebuilt. Although it is not considered a "surrounding enemy," even at a distance it remains a threat to Israel's security.

Identifying Amalek, מלחמה לה' בעמלק מדור דור

The *Aruch HaShulchan*[5] states that from the fact that the defeat of Amalek must precede the building of the Beis HaMikdash, and that Amalek strikes Israel for no apparent reason, it appears that Amalek is an ideological foe who opposes Judaism. He then stops himself, fearing that he is veering away from Halachah and lapsing into homiletics.[6] Yet this cannot be avoided, and it is the Briskers[7] especially who felt compelled to develop this idea. Rav Soloveitchik, *zt"l*,[8] quotes in the name of his father an understanding of Amalek as those who seek the destruction of the Jewish people even if they are not biological descendants of Amalek. He suggests this as Rambam's source for counting עזרת ישראל מצר שבא עליהם, "saving Israel from an enemy who rises against them," (*Hilchos Melachim* 5:1) as a category of *milchemes mitzvah,* an obligatory war.

Rambam writes[9] that while the war against the seven Canaanite na-

4 Which is brought in TB *Sanhedrin* 20b.

5 *Aruch HaShulchan HaAsid, Hilchos Melachim, siman* 71.

6 דרוש.

7 The ultimate halachists.

8 In a footnote in the 10th section of *Kol Dodi Dofek.*

9 *Mitzvas Aseh* 187. Despite his absolute clarity on this point, I have seen him misquoted by those who equate this battle against *avodah zarah* with the war against Amalek. The fact that in the *Moreh*, Rambam explains that the Torah details the lineage of Amalek to make clear that only a part of Esau is to be destroyed, is no evidence for the exclusively biological definition of Amalek. On the contrary, Rambam's point is that the war against Amalek is not a war against Esau. Esau symbolically represents secular civilization. They are not our arch-enemy.

tions was completed by King David, it nevertheless is considered an eternal mitzvah and is to be counted amongst the *Taryag*[10] because the command is eternal, and the inability to perform it does not detract from its permanent nature.[11] He compares this with the mitzvah of warring against Amalek, which remains applicable until *Melech HaMashiach* completes it. And though he will, it is of course an eternal mitzvah. Clearly he believes זרע עמלק, "the seed of Amalek," still exists and the assumption of בא סנחריב ובלבל האומות, "Sancherib intermixed all the nations" or that there is some kind of בטול "annulment" on the remnant of a destroyed nation, that Rambam applies to the Canaanite nations, was not applied to Amalek. Indeed, the Torah is explicit מדור דור "from generation to generation," that this would be a never-ending challenge to the Jewish people. The conclusion is inescapable—Amalek transcends biology and refers to ideology.

Rambam[12] refers to the seven Canaanite nations that must be destroyed as עיקר ע"ז "the essence of *avodah zarah*" and this helps explain why he says David destroyed them even though some of their genetic descendants survived and were mixed among the nations.[13] The mitzvah only applies with regard to those who still maintain the identity of the original people and what they stood for. Perhaps this identity is rooted in all the תועבות "abominations" that the Torah associates with their idol worship, so in the modern world, enlightened by science and the influence of monotheism, this quality has been sufficiently diluted so that the identity of Canaan is lost. Likewise, with Amalek, we are not concerned with genetics but with the nation and what it stood for. Just as Rambam codifies that a convert from Amalek becomes a Jew[14] and sheds his Amalekite identity, those who adopt Amalek's ideology become Amalek. Apparently this ideology and its proponents are alive and well.

The Rogatchover Gaon[15] also takes this approach, describing Amalek as those who deny G-d's *hashgachah* (Divine Providence). He apparently says this based on the words of the Torah in describing their motivation

---

10 613 mitzvos. In *Shoresh* 3 of *Sefer HaMitzvos* he explains that mitzvos that were not לדורות (eternal) are not to be counted.

11 He also explains that the war against the Canaanites was a battle against עיקר ע"ז, "the essence of idol worship," and this fight has been won, as the seven nations and what they stood for were destroyed. We will return to this idea, later.

12 *Sefer HaMitzvos,* ibid.

13 Thus we can contend that the Canaanites also represent an ideology.

14 See *Hilchos Issurei Biah* 12:17; *Hilchos Sanhedrin* 18:6. Some argue on this point.

15 In his commentary on the *Chumash* on *Parashas Beshalach* and *Balak*.

for attacking, לא ירא אלקים, "They did not fear G-d." He contrasts Bilaam's description ראשית גוים עמלק, "Amalek is the first of nations," with Israel's גוי אחד בארץ[16], "the unique nation on the earth" (Shmuel II 7:23), saying there are only two nation-ideologies, neither of which is subject to being annulled (בטול), and he refers to Amalek as a species (מין). Having set up Israel and Amalek as opposing nations and ideologies, this subset of Esau is the ideological opponent of Israel and so the two are constantly competing for dominance of the world. In the *Moreh Nevuchim* (III, 50) Rambam explains that the Torah details the lineage of Esau to make clear that only a part of Esau is to be destroyed. In the *Sefer HaMitzvos* this is also explicit.

הציווי שנצטווינו להכרית זרע עמלק בלבד מכל שאר זרע עשו (מ"ע קפח)

> There is a commandment to destroy the seed of Amalek alone of the seed of Esau

What follows directly from this point is that the war against Amalek is not a war against Esau. Esau symbolically represents secular civilization, most specifically Western civilization.[17] But though we are in constant competition with them, as Yitzchak states in his blessing to Yaakov (*Bereishis* 27), they are not our archenemy. One opinion amongst *Chazal* is that at their fateful meeting, Esau embraced Yaakov with all his heart[18] and, undoubtedly, there are many in Christian America who embrace the Jewish people today.[19] But, Amalek, a subset of Esau, seeks Israel's destruction, and we are commanded to oppose them.

The Mitzvah of Fighting Amalek Today

In *Iggeres Teiman*,[20] Rambam describes the eternal battle of attempted annihilation waged against Israel, first by Amalek and others who attempted physical annihilation, and then by the Greeks and Romans who attempted spiritual annihilation. In later generations, different approaches were taken by Christians and Muslims. While Rambam does not explicitly call these later enemies of the Jewish people Amalek, he clearly describes them

---

16 And the *midrash* on the first verse in *Bereishis* בשביל ראשית... ישראל – See Rashi.

17 See Abarbanel to *Yeshayah* chap. 34 and Malbim *Ovadiah* 1:1.

18 See Rashi *Bereishis* 33:4.

19 Still, there is a relationship between Amalek and Rome (the Western world) and we will return to this later.

20 See Rambam & Redemption, pp. 74-80.

as their heirs, and hence we can look at our defensive wars against them as an extension of *milchemes Amalek*.

To avoid the *Aruch HaShulchan*'s fear of lapsing into homiletics, we must formulate the parameters of this mitzvah in pure halachic terms. The strict, explicit mitzvah stated in the Torah is the destruction of the genetic descendants of Amalek. However, Rambam's category of[21] *divrei sofrim* defines non-explicit elements in a mitzvah, largely conceptual derivations from the *mikra,* that are also to be viewed as binding Torah law. Here, it extends the mitzvah to opposition to those who seek our annihilation. As only an extension of the explicit Torah law, it is not subject to all the details of the essential mitzvah, such as that of actually physically killing people. Perhaps, since the mitzvah is extended to those who try to destroy our spiritual values, the reciprocal mitzvah of their annihilation is to defeat their ideals.

A good example of a comparable mitzvah using the principle of *divrei sofrim* is *lav* 57, לא תשחית, the prohibition against "wanton destruction." Rambam explains in the *Sefer HaMitzvos* that the explicit prohibition in the Torah of cutting down trees during war includes all forms of destruction, and there is the Torah punishment of lashes in all cases. But in *Mishneh Torah* he qualifies that, except for fruit trees, the lashes are only מכות מרדות דרבנן, of Rabbinic origin. This causes many commentaries to question whether this extension is Rabbinic or Torah law. In fact, it is of Torah origin but subject to a lower level of punishment because the Torah does not mention it explicitly, and so it is of an auxiliary nature. Rambam applies this principle in many cases, and this is the case with regard to Amalek. The prohibition of לא תשחית and mitzvos regarding Amalek are both in *Hilchos Melachim*, leading some to believe that they are only applicable when the monarchy is functioning in Israel, but in fact the conceptual *divrei sofrim* elements of these mitzvos are of eternal relevance.

The *drush* with which *Aruch HaShulchan* does not want to taint pure halachic methodology should not be avoided. The essence of *lomdus* is conceptualization, and this conceptualization should ideally grow from the simple rendering of the text, פשוטו של מקרא. The Torah presents Amalek as the enemy who attacks Israel for no reason. He is defined as one "who does not fear G-d." The Torah singles him out as the eternal enemy of G-d: מלחמה לה' בעמלק מדר דור, "A war for G-d is to be waged with Amalek from generation to generation." The *halachah* pertaining to Amalek should follow his conceptualization in the Torah. *Midrash Tanchuma*

21 Literally the "words of the scribes." See *Shoresh 2* in *Sefer HaMitzvos.*

(*Parashas Ki Seitzei*) describes Amalek's hatred for Israel and says the etymology of his name is עמלק, עם שבא ללוק דמן של ישראל, "Amalek, the nation that comes to suck the blood of Israel."

Mitzvah of *Zechirah*—Never Forget

While this mitzvah in its literal sense—destroying another nation—is certainly out of favor in the modern civilized world, the Torah doubles down on it. There are two supporting mitzvos to ensure that Israel will fulfill it. There is the mitzvah to remember what Amalek did to us and yet another mitzvah that prohibits us from forgetting it. In *Mishneh Torah* Rambam formulates all three mitzvos very succinctly:

> וכן מצות עשה לאבד זרע עמלק, שנאמר "תמחה את זכר עמלק" (דברים כה,יט) ומצות עשה לזכור תמיד מעשיו הרעים ואריבתו, כדי לעורר איבתו--שנאמר "זכור את אשר עשה לך עמלק" (דברים כה,יז) מפי השמועה למדו, "זכור" בפה; "לא תשכח" (דברים כה,יט) בלב, שאסור לשכוח איבתו ושנאתו. (הל' מלכים ה:ה)
>
> Similarly, it is a positive commandment to destroy the memory of Amalek, as Deuteronomy (25:19) states: "Obliterate the memory of Amalek." It is also a positive commandment to constantly remember their evil deeds and their ambush of Israel to arouse our hatred of them, as it states (ibid:17): "Remember what Amalek did to you." The Oral Tradition teaches: "... Remember," with your mouths; "... Do not forget," in your hearts. For it is forbidden to forget our hatred and enmity for them.

While there is the mitzvah of remembering *yetzias Mitzrayim* and, in fact, many mitzvos exist to help us remember it as it is the source of our nationhood and our special relationship with G-d, there is no mitzvah in the *Taryag*[22] requiring us to not forget. The Briskers[23] and others note, as Rambam's language clearly suggests, these mitzvos of remembering are to ensure that we will fulfill our obligation of warring against Amalek. Again, in *Sefer HaMitzvos*, Rambam is most clear on this point:

> **המצווה הקפ"ט:** הציווי שנצטווינו לזכור את אשר עשה לנו עמלק, שקדם אותנו ברע, שנאמר את זה בכל זמן וזמן ונעורר את הנפשות בדברים להלחם בו, שנקרא את בני האדם לשנאו, כדי **שלא ישכח הדבר ולא תחלש שנאתו ולא תמעט בנפשות במשך הזמן, וזה אמרו יתעלה: "זכור את אשר עשה לך עמלק" (**דברים כה, יז) .ולשון ספרי "זכור את אשר עשה לך עמלק – בפה, ולא תשכח - בלב." כלומר: אמור דברים בפיך שיביאו בני אדם לכך, שלא תסור שנאתו מן

---

22 According to Rambam. Ramban in fact counts as a mitzvah that we not forget *Har Sinai.*

23 See for example at the end of *Chidushei Griz al HaTorah.*

לב. ולשון ספרא "זכור את אשר עשה לך עמלק, יכול בלבבך, כשהוא אומר 'לא תשכח', הרי שכחת הלב אמורה, הא מה אני מקים 'זכור'? - שתהא שונה בפיך." הלא תראה, **איך עשה שמואל הנביא, כשבא לקיים מצווה זו: שהוא זכר תחילה, ואחר כך ציווה להרגם, והוא אמרו "פקדתי את אשר עשה עמלק לישראל" (שמואל-א טו, ב).**[24]

The 189th *mitzvah* is that we are commanded to constantly remember what Amalek did to us, i.e., being the first to attack us [after we were redeemed from Egypt]; and to speak of it constantly; to arouse people to wage war against them and hate them, **in order that it not be forgotten or the hatred towards them lessened with the passage of time. The source of this commandment is G-d's statement (exalted be He), "Remember what Amalek did to you. [Do not forget.]"** The *Sifri* says, "The phrase 'Remember what Amalek did to you' refers to doing so verbally. The phrase 'Do not forget' means in one's heart." This means that one should say verbally words that cause people to keep this hatred in their hearts. The*Sifra*[4] says, "From the verse, 'Remember what Amalek did to you,' you might think it means in your heart. But when it says, 'Do not forget,' that means in your heart! How do we explain the commandment to 'remember'? It means to speak about it verbally." **You can see how the Prophet Shmuel went about fulfilling this commandment: first he remembered them [verbally] and then commanded that they be killed. This was done when he said, "I remember what Amalek did to the Jewish people when they came up from Egypt."**

If we reflect for a moment, we of course make the connection to the slogans that have arisen in response to the Holocaust and that have become associated with Yom HaZikaron and Yom HaShoah; "Never Forget" is meant to ensure "Never Again." As Primo Levi said, "It happened, so it can happen again. That is the essence of what we have to say." It is up to Israel to prevent a recurrence. This war against Amalek and his ideology is the war against antisemitism.

Before we explore this equation, it is important to realize, as the Torah says explicitly, it is actually G-d's war with Amalek in which we are to act as His agents.[25] This mitzvah is a central tenet of our religion—and is the mitzvah that precedes and is necessary for the building of the Beis HaMikdash.

---

24 See also *Lav* 59.

25 Even should one argue that the mitzvah of *Mechiyas Amalek* only applies when there is a Jewish king, certainly these two auxiliary mitzvos apply even today.

Rambam's Account of *Antisemitism*

Let us turn to Rambam's words in *Iggeres Teiman* where he defines the battle against Israel of Amalek and his successors, antisemitism. It sounds as if he is expounding upon the message of the famous words of the Haggadah:

> והיא שעמדה לאבותינו ולנו שלא אחד בלבד עמד עלינו לכלותינו אלא שבכל דור ודור עומדים עלינו לכלותינו והקב"ה מצילנו מידם.
>
> This [the Torah] stood up for our fathers and for us. For not just one arose against us, but in every generation they arise against us to annihilate us, and the Holy One Blessed is He saves us from their hands.

First he explains what the והיא is that makes us special and worthy of salvation—the Torah.

> Know that this Torah is the true teaching of G-d that was given to us by the master of all prophets... And with this Torah He distinguished us from the rest of the world as it says "Only your fathers did G-d desire to love and he chose their descendants after them, from all the nations of the world just as this day" (*Devarim* 10:15). It is not because we were worthy of it that we were chosen, but in the Creator's mercy and goodness, He acted kindly with us because of the conduct of the *Avos* who did special actions in *Avodas Hashem* and in acquiring knowledge of G-d, as it says "Because of G-d's love for you and in keeping the oath that he swore to your fathers."

Then Rambam (*Iggeres Teiman* part 2) explains the reason for the hatred against Israel.

> G-d distinguished us with his laws and statutes, and thus the superiority of our system of conduct over that of all others became evident, as it says, "What nation is so great that it has such righteous rule and laws, like this entire Torah which I am presenting before you today." **Thus all the nations became extremely jealous of our religion.** Their kings then stirred their peoples to hatred towards us. **Their true will is to war against G-d and to quarrel with Him, but who can fight with G-d.**

The nations of the world are like rejected children who see that their father prefers a younger brother. The love for this brother is a result of his superior conduct and adherence to the principles that the father has taught. They could gain that same love by emulating their conduct, but this they refuse to do, for the standards of the father are too demanding. Their true resentment and anger are for the father, but the only way they can hope to take revenge for the feelings of shame and inferiority that envelop them is to strike out at the chosen son.

> In every era, since the Torah was given to us, every idolatrous king or powerful leader has always made as his first priority the overturn of our faith via force, by violence and the sword. This was Amalek, Sisera, Sancheriv, Nebuchadnezzer, Titus and Hadrian and many others like them. These comprise the first of the groups whose aim it is to defeat the Divine will. But the second group is more intelligent and is found in nations such as the Romans, Persians and Greeks. Their intent is also to destroy our religion and our Torah but their vehicle for so doing is the arguments and the questions that they compose. The goal of their writing is the dissolution of the Torah and the removal of all traces of it, similar to what the violent kings wished to accomplish by war. Neither approach will succeed, for the Holy One Blessed Be He announced to us through the prophet Yeshayahu that any oppressor that attempts to destroy our Torah or abolish our religion with military might will find his weapons destroyed by the Creator—which is a metaphor for saying that he will be unsuccessful. Likewise, any who tries to use intellectual arguments and debate to undermine the received wisdom of our religion shall find his arguments undermined and shall lose the debate. This is found in the verse "Any tool created against you shall fail and any tongue that stands against you in law will be invalidated. Such is the inheritance of the servants of G-d, for their righteousness is from Me, says the L-rd."

The attempts "to annihilate us" that the Haggadah speaks of take different forms. ראשית גוים עמלק, Amalek is the first to pour out his hatred to Israel. He and those who succeed him attempt to destroy us physically. Other groups that follow attempt to destroy us spiritually by destroying our beliefs. In these latter cases, the enemy is satisfied merely if the bond between us and G-d be broken. It is this special relationship of chosen son that they are jealous of and wish to destroy. Rambam here defines the eternal phenomenon of antisemitism, the heritage of Amalek. The hatred is to G-d and His servants. The target is really Judaism, G-d's revelation, the Torah.[26] Sometimes it seems desirable to shoot the messenger, but killing the message is the ultimate goal.

> Despite the difficulty these two groups found in their attempt to overthrow our structure they continued in their attempts **and joined in partnership in their effort**.

---

[26] סיני, משם יצא שנאה לעולם.

So important is this goal to the nations of the world that at times the two groups of destroyers, the brutes and the intellectuals, who are natural enemies with different world views, ally together to accomplish this goal. Their only common denominator is their jealousy. Thus the thieves and murderers of the 70 nations sit together with the more civilized and sophisticated Western nations and unanimously[27] condemn Israel for defending itself. And thus the base of the Democratic Party in the United States is made up of the envious lower classes, the Muslims, and the G-dless "intellectuals" who dominate and indoctrinate on our college campuses and in the media. All are driven by jealousy. Feminists and homosexuals coexist in blissful harmony with Muslims, who are for the oppression of women and the murder of homosexuals. Jealousy and its precipitous hatred for the Jews and Judeo-Christian America unite them. Many prosperous people will join in, for as Rambam makes clear to us, the greatest jealousy is of virtue, and even the rich and famous are infested with it.

> Nevertheless, they only found themselves increasing their own toil and pains while the structure remains firm. But the Truth, i.e., the Holy One Blessed Be He, mocks them for their feeble attempts to accomplish the impossible. This is the meaning of King David's statement said with *Ruach HaKodesh* (the holy spirit), "**Let us break off their shackles, and discard their bonds.** He who sits in Heaven mocks and derides them." We have been troubled and tested with these two groups through all the days of our monarchy and part of the days of our *galus*. (*Iggeres Teiman*, ibid.)

"Let us break off their shackles," is their common cry. The values professed by Israel are a burden that hampers their freedom. But what they attempt to do is impossible. Those who impose their rule by the brute force of weapons eventually find themselves deposed by those with greater weapons. And as for dominion gained by ideas, here Rambam explains, G-d's name is truth, and thus the lies they employ in their arguments will fail. The rules of the Torah are the rules which man must follow in order to thrive. The Creator mocks those who try to destroy the Jewish religion in this way. As they are in fact trying to defy the laws of nature, the laws of nature will prove their folly.

> Later, a new group that combined the abilities of the two earlier groups arose, to embitter our lives. It attempted to destroy our nation with a new approach. It conspired to claim a new prophecy,

---

27 With the exception of the United States in most cases.

> revealing a new religion. It claimed both the Torah and this new revelation were from G-d, therefore hoping to sow confusion in our hearts. This plan was initiated by Yeshu the Nazarene. He caused others to believe that he was sent from heaven to explain the unclear parts of the Torah, and that he was the Mashiach promised by the prophet. He explained the Torah in such a way as to nullify it and its mitzvos and to permit what it had prohibited. Sometime later a religion arose, formed by the descendants of Esav, that associated itself with him but which did not reflect his views. Still later, there arose Mohammed who followed in his footsteps, attempting to change our religion. In addition, he sought political power and tried to subjugate us, creating the well-known religion [of Islam]. All these men had but one desire, to equate their religions with the religion of G-d. But the work of man bears no resemblance to that of G-d, except to an infant that does not comprehend either of them. These religions that copy ours are as comparable to ours, as is a mannequin to a human being… in that a fool will look at each and say they look alike but a wise man understands what is inside of each, realizing that the innards of a man has wondrous organs that reflect the wisdom of our blessed Creator. So too the fool, who does not understand the secrets of Holy Writ and internals of the mitzvos will compare our religion to the forgeries. He notes that both have the permitted and the prohibited, and forms of worship, and many commands and warnings bearing reward and punishment. But if he understood what is in the inside, he would see that the true G-dly faith has inner brilliance, and has no command or prohibition that does not bring with it perfection of man both in his character and in his intellect. (*Iggeres Teiman* ibid.)

The nations of the world realized with time that the laws of the Torah bound Israel with G-d, and thus made Israel indestructible. Their only hope to gain advantage over the Jewish people and to tear them away from the Torah was to imitate their practices. They took from the Torah as much as their character would allow and then claimed that their version of the Torah was the actual will of G-d. But in so doing they took only that which appealed to their superficial understanding. In the details of the Torah lies a system that perfects man and makes him a true servant of G-d, and it is this system alone that makes Israel the *am segulah*, the chosen people. They hoped to convince the Jews to join them with argumentation and, when that failed, with the violence of slaughter and forced conversions.

> Often our Rabbis speak of periods of persecutions and *shemad* (forced apostasy) … and then of how G-d nullified the decrees and those that had made them. Thus *Chazal* say *shemad* does not last. And

> The Holy One, Blessed Be He, promised Yaakov Avinu that even though the nations will persecute his descendants, they will survive and triumph over them, and the oppressors will be destroyed – "And your seed will be like the dust of the earth [and you will break forth to the west, east, north, and south]" (*Bereishis* 28:14) meaning that though they will be trampled like dust that is stepped on by all, at the end they will be victorious. And so too in a metaphoric fashion, the dust is eternal and eventually settles on all the people who had trampled it while the tramplers perish... The Creator has informed us through our prophets that we will never be destroyed nor cease to be an important nation. As it is impossible for the Holy One Blessed Be He to cease to exist, so too it is impossible for us to cease from creation for it says "For I am the L-rd, I have not changed, and you are the children of Yaakov, you have not ceased to be" (*Malachi* 3:6). (*Iggeres Teiman*)

As we have seen, Rambam sees the source of Amalek's enmity as jealousy. The rejected son of Yitzchak is not willing to pay the price to acquire Eretz Yisrael. He hates the Jews because he hates Judaism. In their comprehensively researched work on the history of and reasons for antisemitism, *Why the Jews?,* Dennis Prager and Joseph Telushkin come to the same conclusion as Rambam. Antisemitism is not a function of racism, and the claim that this is the case is itself generated by antisemitism. Rambam goes one step deeper in explaining that the real hatred is towards G-d for His creation of a world that requires adherence to the principles of the Torah in order for man to reach meaningful fulfillment and inner happiness.

This same hatred has now been extended to the Judeo-Christian state of America[28] by those, both within and without the country, who wish to undermine the principles upon which it was founded.

Megillas Esther

R. *Eliezer HaModai* (TB *Megillah* 7a) says that in the Torah's command to Moshe and Yehoshua:

> וַיֹּאמֶר ה אֶל־מֹשֶׁה כְּתֹב זֹאת זִכָּרוֹן בַּסֵּפֶר וְשִׂים בְּאָזְנֵי יְהוֹשֻׁעַ כִּי־מָחֹה אֶמְחֶה אֶת־זֵכֶר עֲמָלֵק מִתַּחַת הַשָּׁמָיִם׃
>
> G-d said to Moshe, 'Write this as remembrance in a book and tell it to Yehoshua, that I will erase the memory of Amalek from beneath the Heavens.

---

28 See especially their chapter on "non-Jewish Jews" such as Chomsky and Jerry Rubin.

The book (*sefer*) refers to *Megillas Esther*. *Chazal* tell us that המן האגגי is the descendant of Amalek, king אגג.[29] The story of the *Megillah* is that of classical antisemitism. Achashverosh rules an empire of diverse nations; he emphasizes at a gathering of leaders והשתיה כדת אין אונס, "the drinking is according to everyone's personal taste,"[30] and there is a spirit of freedom and respect for individual rights in his reign. Later he makes the democratic proclamation להיות כל איש שורר בביתו ומדבר כלשון עמו, "every man should be lord of his own house and speak the language of his own nation,"[31] i.e., the Empire grants freedom to the nations under its rule as well as to individual households. And still later, the king makes a commoner queen, chosen from all his servants and all his nations. Yet he is quick to proclaim annihilation for עם אחד מפזר ומפרד... ודתיהם שנות מכל עם ודתי המלך אינם עושים, "One nation spread out everywhere… with laws different from every nation, who do not conform to the laws of the king."[32] Even in the spirit of freedom with which Achashverosh rules his domain, Israel's commitment to the Torah cannot be tolerated. Mordechai "will not bend nor bow," לא יכרע ולא ישתחוה, as his allegiance and subservience both privately and publicly is only to the G-d of Israel.

The Inner Amalek—לא ירא אלקים

Rama, in his commentary on the *Megillah*, מחיר יין, explains that the lessons of the *Megillah* are meant to be understood not only on a literal level, but also metaphorically. He quotes *Moreh Nevuchim* (2:30) to relate המן to the יצר הרע "the evil inclination," and more specifically to סמאל who is the rider (guiding force) of the snake in *Gan Eden*. This force is rooted in man's כח המדמה, his imaginative/emotional nature.

> It is obvious to anyone of understanding that the evil Haman represents סמאל... he is the descendant of Amalek, all of whose actions are twisted. All who follow the forces of דמיונות (imagination) and lusts will eventually be lost, as they were. This is what *Chazal* meant in saying המן מן התורה מנין, המן העץ "Where do we find המן in the Torah? In the phrase "Did you (המן) take from the tree," meaning that Haman was at the "tree" and was the one who seduced you. The king elevates Haman's chair above all others as the snake who is ערום מכל חית השדה "more cunning than all the animals of the field,"

---

29 *Bilaam*, in his blessing, sees how Israel will conquer אגג. See *Targum* on *Megillas Esther* 3:1.

30 *Megillas Esther* 1:5.

31 *Megillas Esther* 1:22.

32 *Megillas Esther* 3:8.

meaning that all the forces of one's soul obey him and bow to him except Mordechai [HaYehudi].

Amalek is not merely an entity outside of Israel seeking his destruction, but it is an entity within human nature, and every Jew must wage the battle against his internal Amalek. *Why the Jews?* has a chapter on "Non-Jewish" Jews, from Marx to Chomsky, as we must acknowledge the phenomenon of biological Jews who are converts from Judaism to the nation of Amalek. But more importantly, we must realize that even as observant and loyal Jews, it is possible and even probable that some elements of Amalek exist within ourselves.

The Rama's analysis of the defining quality of Amalek is that of Rambam's כח המדמה which is imagination, anti-rationalism, and he further identifies this with the יצר הרע. Anti-rationalism, a denial of the laws of nature that the Torah is in harmony with, conforms with the identity that we have been forging for Amalek. But as we have noted, the *mikra* specifically identifies Amalek's motivation as לא ירא אלקים—lacking fear of G-d. In *Parashas Ki Seitzei* we find:

> אֲשֶׁר קָרְךָ בַּדֶּרֶךְ וַיְזַנֵּב בְּךָ כָּל־הַנֶּחֱשָׁלִים אַחֲרֶיךָ וְאַתָּה עָיֵף וְיָגֵעַ וְלֹא יָרֵא אֱלֹקִים.
>
> They encountered you on the road and ambushed all those who were weakened and trailing, as you were tired and weary, and did not fear G-d (*Devarim* 25:18).

Chazal[33] present two interpretations of the final words of the *pasuk*; it is either Amalek or Israel who lacks the fear of G-d. But both the external Amalek, and the internal Amalek that allows the external one to conquer Israel, are identified by this quality, lacking the fear of G-d. Israel is also described as "tired and weary" when Amalek is successful; Israel must be strong and alert in order to prevail. Moshe sends Yehoshua and a select group of soldiers to battle while his hands, uplifted to Heaven, decide the outcome.

> וַיֹּאמֶר מֹשֶׁה אֶל־יְהוֹשֻׁעַ בְּחַר־לָנוּ אֲנָשִׁים וְצֵא הִלָּחֵם בַּעֲמָלֵק מָחָר אָנֹכִי נִצָּב עַל־רֹאשׁ הַגִּבְעָה וּמַטֵּה הָאֱלֹהִים בְּיָדִי:י וַיַּעַשׂ יְהוֹשֻׁעַ כַּאֲשֶׁר אָמַר־לוֹ מֹשֶׁה לְהִלָּחֵם בַּעֲמָלֵק וּמֹשֶׁה אַהֲרֹן וְחוּר עָלוּ רֹאשׁ הַגִּבְעָה: יא וְהָיָה כַּאֲשֶׁר יָרִים מֹשֶׁה יָדוֹ וְגָבַר יִשְׂרָאֵל וְכַאֲשֶׁר יָנִיחַ יָדוֹ וְגָבַר עֲמָלֵק: יב וִידֵי מֹשֶׁה כְּבֵדִים וַיִּקְחוּ־אֶבֶן וַיָּשִׂימוּ תַחְתָּיו וַיֵּשֶׁב עָלֶיהָ וְאַהֲרֹן וְחוּר תָּמְכוּ בְיָדָיו מִזֶּה אֶחָד וּמִזֶּה אֶחָד וַיְהִי יָדָיו אֱמוּנָה עַד־בֹּא הַשָּׁמֶשׁ: יג וַיַּחֲלֹשׁ יְהוֹשֻׁעַ אֶת־עֲמָלֵק וְאֶת־עַמּוֹ לְפִי־חָרֶב.
>
> Moses said to Joshua, "Pick some men for us, and go out and do battle with Amalek. Tomorrow I will station myself on the top of

---

33 See commentaries on this verse.

> the hill, with the rod of G-d in my hand." Joshua did as Moses told him and fought with Amalek, while Moses, Aaron, and Hur went up to the top of the hill. Then, whenever Moses held up his hand, Israel prevailed; but whenever he let down his hand, Amalek prevailed. But Moses' hands grew heavy; so they took a stone and put it under him and he sat on it, while Aaron and Hur, one on each side, supported his hands; thus his hands remained steady until the sun set. And Joshua overwhelmed the people of Amalek with the sword.

In an unusual Aggadic excursion in the Mishnah of *Maseches Rosh HaShanah* (3:8), *Chazal* express the message behind Israel's original battle against Amalek.

> והיה כאשר ירים משה ידו וגבר ישראל (שמות יז יא) וכי ידיו של משה עושות מלחמה או שוברות מלחמה אלא לומר לך כל זמן שהיו ישראל מסתכלים כלפי מעלה ומשעבדין את לבם לאביהם שבשמים היו מתגברים ואם לאו היו נופלין.

> "And it came to pass, when Moses held up his hand Israel prevailed," etc. (*Shemos* 17:1). Did the hands of Moses wage war or break [Israel's ability] to wage war? Rather, this teaches that as long as Israel would look upwards and subject their hearts to their Father in Heaven they prevailed, and if not they fell. (*Shemos* 17:9-13)

Amalek is antithetical to the fear of G-d. As noted earlier, his anger is towards G-d and, were it possible, he would war against G-d Himself, Whom he resents. Israel's task is to make man feel His presence in this world. Amalek's is to keep Him away from human consciousness. Rambam explains the essence of the mitzvah of the fear of G-d in *Hilchos Yesodei HaTorah* after explaining love of G-d:

> והיאך היא הדרך לאהבתו, ויראתו: בשעה שיתבונן האדם במעשיו וברואיו הנפלאים הגדולים, ויראה מהם חכמתו שאין לה ערך ולא קץ--מיד הוא אוהב ומשבח ומפאר ומתאווה תאווה גדולה לידע השם הגדול, כמו שאמר דויד "צמאה נפשי, לאלוקים--לקל חי" (תהילים מב,ג) וכשמחשב בדברים האלו עצמן, מיד הוא נרתע לאחוריו, ויירא ויפחד ויידע שהוא **בריה קטנה שפלה אפלה, עומד בדעת קלה מעוטה לפני תמים דעות**, כמו שאמר דויד "כי אראה שמיך... מה אנוש, כי תזכרנו" (תהילים ח,ד-ה). (הל' יסדה"ת ב:א)

> What is the path [to attain] love and fear of Him? When a person contemplates His wondrous and great deeds and creations and appreciates His infinite wisdom that surpasses all comparison, he will immediately love, praise, and glorify [Him], yearning with tremendous desire to know [G-d's] great name, as David stated: "My soul thirsts for the Lord, for the living G-d" [Psalms 42:3]. When he [continues] to reflect on these same matters, he will immediately recoil in awe and fear, appreciating how he is a tiny, lowly, and dark creature,

standing with his flimsy, limited wisdom before Him Who is of perfect knowledge, as David stated: "When I see Your heavens, the work of Your fingers... [I wonder] what is man that You should recall Him" [Psalms 8:4-5].

Moshe, upon whom victory depends, is defined with only one superlative quality, והאיש משה ענו מאד מכל האדם "The man Moshe is much more modest than all men." Amalek's quest to elevate man above G-d is steeped in arrogance. When we hear someone say, "We are the ones we have been waiting for," we can hear Amalek speak.

Identifying Amalek Today

There are two primary nations, two ideologies—Israel and Amalek. Israel's ideology is a search for G-d within nature, and subservience to Him via adherence to the rules He revealed to man which were the rules by which the world was created הסתכל באורייתא וברא עלמא,[34] "G-d looked into the Torah and created the world." Amalek celebrates man and demands freedom; the freedom he demands is a freedom from G-d.

In their chapter on Nazi antisemitism, Prager and Telushkin discuss the 1899 influential and well-received (by many intellectuals of the day) *Foundations of the Nineteenth Century*. They write, "According to *Foundations*, the future of humanity will be determined by the outcome of the epochal struggle between two races: the Teutonic ("Aryan") and Jewish ("Semitic")." *Why the Jews?* explains that the "real opposition was to the Jews' values and theology, not to their race and biology." The author of *Foundations*, H.W. Chamberlain, writes, "I cannot help shuddering…at the portentous, irremediable mistake the world made in accepting the traditions of this wretched little nation as the basis of its belief." *Why the Jews?* quotes him and explains, "He hated the Jews for their monotheism and moral values which **prevented the natural human being from possessing unrestricted freedom. "The Jew came into our world and spoiled everything with his concept of sin, his law, and his cross."**[35]

Hillary Clinton, the "moderate" Democratic presidential candidate of 2016, addressed the evil she saw in America's Judeo-Christian[36] culture and, had she been elected president, she would have accelerated the march of the Democratic Party to emulate the governments of Europe to uproot

---

34 See *Bereishis Rabah* 1:1; *Zohar* 3:178:1.

35 He saw Christianity and its values as an extension of Judaism.

36 See Torah and Western Thought: Intellectual Portraits of Orthodoxy and Modernity by Meir Y. Soloveichik (2016).

that culture. The *Washington Post* records her words.[37] "In a speech not long before she launched her 2016 presidential campaign, Hillary Clinton made a stunning declaration of war on religious Americans. Speaking to the 2015 Women in the World Summit, Clinton declared that 'deep-seated cultural codes, religious beliefs and structural biases have to be changed.' Religious beliefs have to be changed? This is perhaps the most radical statement against religious liberty ever uttered by someone seeking the presidency. It is also deeply revealing. Clinton believes that, as president, it is her job not to respect the views of religious conservatives but to force them to change their beliefs and bend to her radical agenda favoring taxpayer-funded abortion on demand."

Amalek believes that freedom demands that an inconvenient infant can be killed if it escapes the attempt to kill him in the womb. It believes that freedom demands that one should be able to declare one's gender based on preference rather than biology. It believes that men in a relationship may be declared "married." Indeed, *Chazal* interpret אשר קרך בדרך, "who encountered you on the road," as subjecting the Jews to משכב זכר (homosexual relations). Amalek opposes the limits of the Torah because it opposes the limits that G-d put into nature.

As Rambam explains, this hatred towards G-d and His servants does not allow Amalek to be satisfied to live its deviant life unobstructed. Seeing others committed to the Torah life and even to its offshoot, the Judeo-Christian culture, and thriving because of it, stirs up the jealousy of the rejected son. Amalek cannot bear the happiness in others that comes from a connection with G-d. *Chazal* say of ויזנב בך that he "cut off the מלות", i.e., destroyed the ברית (covenant) between Israel and G-d. The Torah refers to rejection of the *mitzvos* as בחקתי תמאסו and *Chazal* explain מואסים באחרים עושים מצוות, "They are disgusted by others who do the mitzvos."[38]

Pirkei D'Reb Eliezer notes that Amalek strikes after Israel doubts G-d's presence: היש ה' בקרבנו — "Is G-d in our midst?" The Midrash comments that those who are attacked are those who have been rejected by the ענן ("cloud") of G-d's protection.[39] *Chazal* discover Amalek in the Torah in a place where he is not named.

א וַיִּשְׁמַע הַכְּנַעֲנִי מֶלֶךְ-עֲרָד, יֹשֵׁב הַנֶּגֶב, כִּי בָּא יִשְׂרָאֵל, דֶּרֶךְ הָאֲתָרִים; וַיִּלָּחֶם בְּיִשְׂרָאֵל, וַיִּשְׁבְּ מִמֶּנּוּ שֶׁבִי .(במדבר כא:א)

---

37 See Marc Thiessen writing in the *Washington Post* of Oct 13, 2016.

38 See *Rashi* to *Vayikra* 26:15.

39 See *Rashi*, *Shemos*.

> When the Canaanite, king of Arad, who dwelt in the Negev, learned that Israel was coming by the way of Atharim, he engaged Israel in battle and took some of them captive.

Though the Torah says it was the Canaanim who struck, *Chazal*[40] note that both Amalek and Canaan inhabited the south, and it is the way of Amalek to make unprovoked sneak attacks. It was, in fact, Amalek disguised as Canaan who attacked Israel. They disguised themselves so that Israel would not know who they were so that when Israel prayed, as Moshe had demonstrated to them, they would pray to defeat Canaan and not Amalek and thus Israel would remain vulnerable.

Undoubtedly the Rabbis are teaching us a crucial message that we must apply today. We believe the reason for the hatred of the left for Israel is that Israel thwarts their will to fulfill their desires. This is not the case. In fact, as Rambam tells us, *ikkar avodah zarah* has been fundamentally defeated, and even though the remnant is still disbursed amongst the nations as they call out to do every תועבה (abomination) that the Canaanim popularized, mankind has learned and essentially knows in its heart that these things are self-destructive. The intense hatred comes from jealousy towards the chosen people. This cannot be appeased. The Midrash continues that Israel was victorious by being מתפלל סתם, "praying without identifying any enemy," i.e., strengthening our relationship with G-d. This is the preparation needed for the battle, the battle against internal Amalek that prepares us for the battle against the external Amalek.

The mitzvah of *Binyan Beis HaMikdash* awaits the fulfillment of the mitzvah of the destruction of Amalek. It is incumbent on our community to fight this battle. We cannot expect others to do it for us. Achashverosh gave the Jews the right to fight and encouragement, but as is the case in Israel today so too in America, the battle is upon us. We must rely on the hands of Moshe, the Torah he gave us. But Moshe did not participate in the actual battle; he left that up to *Klal Yisrael.* An ideological battle must be waged. Our duty lies before us. ☙

---

40 Quoted by *Rashi.*

An "Ever Better" Judaism? Progressivism and Orthodox Judaism

By: STEVEN KESSLER

The political climate in America is more hostile today than at any other time in recent memory. Many believe the country is headed for a civil war between liberals and conservatives, whose issues are not confined exclusively to the domain of politics. These issues are now penetrating Jewish thought, ritual, and practice.

Essentially, the debate is an ideological clash between two conflicting visions. The liberals, in the vein of their godfather and patron saint, Jean-Jacques Rousseau, believe in the ideology of progressivism, originally known as Meliorism during the Enlightenment (Kessler, 2018). Roughly translated, the Latin adjective Meliora means "ever better."

There are two main tenets to Meliorism. The first is a belief in the natural goodness of Man, corrupted by society. Human beings are born naturally benevolent, and the evil and problems in the world are introduced to us externally from society. By tinkering with society—adjusting our norms and customs—we can eradicate these problems, balance the world, and make everyone healthy and happy.

The second main tenet is a belief in the progress of human nature. The present age is superior to the past, which means that the norms of the past are insufficient for contemporary Man. We must therefore abolish the norms of the past and create new ones to suit today's modern Man.

The opposition to Meliorism is called, "the tragic nature of the human condition" (Kessler, 2018; Sowell, 1987). The tragic nature's counterargument to the first tenet is that human beings are born neither purely good nor evil, but with an ethical dualism raging inside each person. Our evil inclinations are sewn into the very fabric of the human condition. Evil cannot be eradicated from the world, no matter how much tinkering we attempt to apply.

The second rejoinder is that human nature is constant, fixed, and unchanging. We, in the present, are no different than our earliest ances-

---

Steven Kessler is the Edmund Burke Society Fellow at the Russell Kirk Center for Cultural Renewal. He received his doctorate in Higher Education Administration from the University of Rochester.

tors. To those believing in the tragic nature, they believe that, "by definition, human nature is constant. Because of that constancy, men of vision were able to describe the norms, the rules for mankind" (Kirk, 1989, p. 39). These norms are, "an enduring standard… law of nature, which we ignore at our peril" (Kirk, 1989, p. 17). Unlike Meliorism, which believes progress consists in the destruction of old norms and the creation of new ones, the tragic nature believes that, "real progress consists in the movement of mankind towards the understanding of norms, and towards conformity to norms" (Kirk, 1989, p. 20). True progress is not found in the creation of new norms, nor in the destruction of the old ones, but rather in adherence to the old norms.

Liberal progressive values are permeating many spheres of social life and contemporary Orthodox Judaism is not immune from their reach. In this essay, liberal progressive values, their origins, and their counterarguments are explored to determine if they are congruent with traditional Orthodox Judaism. It is important to note that the validity of these issues in contemporary American society are not explored. This conversation is confined exclusively within the domain of traditional Orthodox Judaism, and not society at large. The main source for interpreting liberal progressive values will be Jean-Jacques Rousseau; the counterargument will emanate largely from the work and thought of Edmund Burke, the original conservative.

The first place to start in this assessment is with Rousseau. Progressivism, as an ideology, emanates largely from his philosophical work. The seminal construct in Rousseau's work and thought is quoted below:

> The fundamental principle of all morality, upon which I have reasoned in all my writings and which I developed with all the clarity of which I am capable is that man is a being who is naturally good, loving justice and order; that there is no original perversity in the human heart, and the first movements of nature are always good. (Rousseau, 1762)

By tinkering with society—adjusting our norms, laws, customs, and language—we can eradicate evil. As Arthur Melzer, a scholar of Rousseau, explained: "Evil derives from society rather than from their sinful natures and that it may be cured or ameliorated through human… action" (Melzer, 1990, p. 19). Because evil comes from without and not from within, "then perhaps it could be overcome by reordering society. In principle, Rousseau opens up radical new hopes for politics, utopian, messianic… hopes that it can transform the human condition, bring secular salvation, make all men healthy and happy" (Melzer, 1990, p. 23).

This is the surface explanation of the above referenced quotation. The way Rousseau arrived at this conclusion is subtly alluded to at the end: "There is no original perversity in the human heart." The word "original" is an allusion to the concept of Original-Sin, a doctrine articulated by St. Augustine regarding one of the first biblical stories from the Torah, the story of Adam and Eve eating from the Tree of Knowledge in the Garden of Eden. Due to their first sin, we are all vicarious sinners, and we are all subsequently imperfect and flawed beings due to their actions. As Jews, we do not believe in Original-Sin on a semantic level, but we certainly believe in the validity and truth of the Torah. Orthodox Jews read this story from the Torah literally and believe with reverence that the event occurred as written.

Rousseau invalidated the evil inclination within Man and then transferred it to society. This is at odds with what Ben Zoma asked in Pirkei Avot: "Who is strong? He who conquers his evil inclination" (4:1). As Jews, we believe in an ethical dualism with the figurative angel on one shoulder, known as the "*Yetzer-Tov*," and the figurative devil on the other, known as the "*Yetzer-Hara*." It is through our choices and temperance to our evil inclination that our behavior is adjudicated, not our relationship to society.

In secular terms, Edmund Burke believed Rousseau's notion of the natural goodness of Man was wildly inaccurate. He understood Man's ethical dualism thusly:

> We must soften into a credulity below the milkiness of infancy to think all men virtuous. We must be tainted with a malignity truly diabolical, to believe all the world to be equally wicked and corrupt. Men are in public life as in private, some good, some evil. The elevation of the one, the depression of the other, are the first objects of all true policy. (Burke, 1770)

Human beings can be good, yes, but they can also be evil. Enabling Man's good nature and suppressing his evil inclination is of the utmost importance.

For Rousseau, society was indeed the source of Man's corruption. Again, as he negated Original-Sin, he did not believe in the Torah's creation myth. He had his own origin-story for Mankind. He believed in something he referred to as, "the state of nature."

The state of nature was a fictitious utopia where human beings were naturally equals and were naturally benevolent, and lived free from labor and the judgments of others. Rousseau wrote of the loss of the state of nature in *Discourse on the Origins of Inequality* (1753): "The first man who, having enclosed a piece of ground, bethought himself of saying This is mine, and found people simple enough to believe him, was the real founder of civil society" (1753, p. 23). Once this person acquired private property for himself, society began, and then our ensuing corruption. Rousseau interpreted the causal chain of events in the following way: "The moment one man began to stand in need of the help of another; from the moment it appeared advantageous to any one man to have enough provisions for two, equality disappeared, property was introduced, work became indispensable" (1753, p. 27).

Rousseau discussed a nuanced position in the quote above to which many liberals today adhere: the notion that prior to the corrupting influence of society, human beings were equal. Rousseau truly believed that, "there is in fact in this state of nature an actual and indestructible equality" (Rousseau, 1762).

Traditional Orthodox Judaism does not support the notion of equity. The pith of the Decalogue are authoritative commandments from God to the Jews. Not only are we to obey the word of God, but in the fifth commandment, we must honor our parents. The importance of our surrender to the authority of our parents is an important reminder of the just and natural hierarchies of the world; they necessitate our acceptance. Ben Zoma asked a question that supports this notion: "Who is rich? He who is happy with his portion" (4:1). The reason for this answer is that there will always be someone with more than you. More money, a bigger house, better luck, a more attractive spouse, or a nicer car. It is our job to temper our evil inclination, accept that life is not fair, and accept that we, as human beings, are not equals.

Burke also understood what Ben Zoma did. There are natural hierarchies and just-inequities in the world. Attempting to rectify these just-inequities means that, "those who attempt to level, never equalise… The levellers therefore only change and pervert the natural order of things" (1790, para. 79). These natural inequalities are sewn into the fabric of the human condition and can never be eradicated. Attempting to fix them will only make things worse than had we accepted them in the first place.

The liberal progressives repudiate this notion, and instead believe in the natural equity of Man, corrupted by society. This natural equity of Man corrupted by society is the basis for a major component of progressive ideology (Haidt, 2013). The Meliorist progressivist believes that by fixing society, we can balance the world, and restore the natural equality and natural goodness of Man. This Meliorist premise is implicit in the contemporary iteration of society fixing, an ideological term known as, "social justice."

Social justice is predicated on rectifying societal inequities. According to social justice scholarship, society is an arbitrary social construct—in other words, a complete nonsensical fabrication—that is inequitably structured to favor White, male, able-bodied, cisgendered, heterosexuals. The theory assumes that these people are successful in life because society is structured to favor them, and they use the inequitable structure of society to socially advance by stepping on the heads and shoulders of "people of color" or "others." These others are unsuccessful because White men are stepping on their heads and shoulders to get ahead. Should we fix the inequitable structure of society, we will restore the natural equity of the world. In theory, those at the bottom will rise to the top, and those at the top will sink to a lower social status.

To the social justice scholar, the "big 3" of social justice—racism, privilege, and cultural appropriation—are based on a simple formula: racism, privilege, or cultural appropriation equals prejudice plus power structure. Therefore, only those benefiting from societal power structure—i.e., White men (and, to a lesser extent, those with any of the aforementioned demographic characteristics)—are capable of having privilege, being racist, or appropriating culture (Haidt & Lukianoff, 2018).

The goal of social justice is to rectify the discrepancies caused by society to restore the natural equity of Man. Peggy McIntosh, author of, *White Privilege: Unpacking the Invisible Knapsack* (1989), referred to these discrepancies as either unearned entitlements, unearned privileges, or unearned power. Because these societal entitlements are unearned, they must be taken away from those privileged and in positions of power.

For example, only White people are capable of appropriating culture, so a White person with dreadlocks—a hairstyle not typically associated with Caucasian genetics—is appropriating culture, while a Black woman with blonde highlights—another hairstyle not typically associated with Black genetics—is not. In accordance with social justice ideology, the White person is appropriating culture, and the Black person is not. Those who wish to implement social justice practices in this instance are then endowed with the ability to take the dreadlocks away from the White person without gaining anything in return.

This is the hallmark of the emotion of envy. When it is not about someone rising to the level of another person, but about the lower person yanking the higher person down; when it is not about someone having what another person has, but about the other person not having it altogether; and when it is not about someone winning, but about another losing, we have envy on our hands (Shoeck, 1966; de la Mora, 1987).

Social justice, as an ideology, desires equity. The implicit problem with equity as a moral foundation and goal, something liberals base much of their ideological presumptions on (Nisbet, 1966; Haidt, 2013), is that equity causes envy. As Alexis de Tocqueville, author of the brilliant tome, *Democracy in America*, astutely observed:

> One must not conceal from oneself that democratic institutions develop the sentiment of envy in the human heart to a very high degree. It is not so much because they offer to each the means of becoming equal to others, but because these means constantly fail those who employ them. Democratic institutions awaken and flatter the passion for equality without ever being able to satisfy it entirely. Every day this complete equality eludes the hands of the people at the moment when they believe they have seized it, and it flees... the people become heated in the search for this good, all the more precious as it is near enough to be known, far enough not to be tasted. (1836, p. 189)

Equity breeds envy. The more democratic the institution or ideology, like the United States, or social justice, the greater the arousal of envy.

Envy and its consequences are a major theme in the Torah. Whether it's Cain and Abel, Leah and Rachel, Jacob and Esau, Joseph and his brothers, or Saul and David, the Torah is ripe with examples of envy and its consequences. The 10th commandment is a commandment against the emotion of envy. An ideology that promotes envy should axiomatically be understood as incongruent with traditional Judaism.

Traditional Orthodox Judaism is thousands of years old. The ideology of social justice is a contemporary one first originating from the Enlightenment. The notion that Judaism, a 3,300-year-old religion, conforms to its tenets is far-fetched and arbitrary. Making something fit an arbitrary standard is known as, "the bed of Procrustes." For an example of this, inspect the titles of two articles written by contemporary Rabbis: "Re'eh (5769)—Judaism's Vision for Social Justice," (2009) by Rabbi Jonathan Sacks, former Chief Rabbi of England, and, "Social Justice Lies at the Heart of the Jewish People," (2012) by Rabbi Gideon Sylvester.

Rabbi Sacks made a bold interpretation of the concept of *tzedakah*, traditionally known as charity. To him, the Torah is saying that: "… the laws of *tzedakah*—the word usually translated as 'charity' but which also means 'distributive justice, equity'" (Sacks, 2009, para. 3). Rabbi Sacks equated charity and *tzedakah* with social justice, specifically distributive justice. Here, Sacks attempts to force the notion of *tzedakah* to fit into the bed of Procrustes.

Sacks and Sylvester are not alone in their attempt to shoehorn Meliorism into Orthodox Judaism. Socialism, social justice, progressivism, intersectionality, or whatever form of liberal ideology, are creeping into traditional Orthodox Judaism. On April 5th, 2019, Rabbi Avram Mlotek authored a piece for the *Jewish Telegraph Agency*, titled, "I'm an Orthodox rabbi who is going to start officiating LGBTQ weddings. Here's why" (Mlotek, 2019).

The most compelling rationale for his departure from traditional Orthodoxy is found in the concluding paragraph of his article: "We are long overdue for a new paradigm" (Mlotek, 2019, para. 18). Mlotek believes in the progressive nature of the human condition, and that by his alterations, we can balance the world and eradicate some of the existing Jewish societal inequities. He believes that excluding homosexuals from the Jewish community is, "a painful reminder that LGBTQ Jews still lack the ability to fully participate as equals in all facets of Orthodox life" (Mlotek, 2019, para. 11).

The notion of the progressive nature of the human condition is not corroborated by the scripture in the book of Ecclesiastes: "Generations come and generations go, but the earth remains forever… What has been will be again, what has been done will be done again; there is nothing new under the sun" (1:4, & 1:9). Due to the constancy of the human condition, the present age is no different than previous ages. Because of the constancy of human nature, the human condition moves cyclically. The present constantly repeats the past. We are witnessing a conversation that took place many years ago between Edmund Burke and Rousseau happening again before our eyes.

The Enlightenment was known as, "the age of reason" (Levin, 2000). At that time, people began looking inwards toward their feelings and using these feelings as the basis for facts and social policy, replacing custom, tradition, and prescription (Kessler, 2018). Edmund Burke understood traditions and customs as the accumulated wisdom of our ancestors. It represented the totality of the human condition, and no one person could ever possess sufficient mental capital to look within and decide that he knew best at the expense of the wisdom of our ancestors.

For those unaware of what makes Edmund Burke relevant and his legacy so enduring, I offer the following excerpt, where his oratory brilliance is on full display:

> Because a nation is not an idea only of local extent, and individual momentary aggregation, but it is an idea of continuity, which extends in time as well as in numbers, and in space. And this is a choice not of one day, or one set of people, not a tumultuary and giddy choice; it is a deliberate election of ages and of generations; it

> is a Constitution made by what is ten thousand times better than choice, it is made by the peculiar circumstances, occasions, tempers, dispositions, and moral, civil, and social habitudes of the people, which disclose themselves only in a long space of time. It is a vestment, which accommodates itself to the body. (1782)

Burke's speech related to political decisions, but the concept remains applicable and appropriate in the current context. He concluded, pithy as ever:

> for man is a most unwise, and a most wise, being. The individual is foolish. The multitude, for the moment, is foolish, when they act without deliberation; but the species is wise, and when time is given to it, as a species it almost always acts right. (1782)

The individual is foolish, but the species is wise. When we look inward, we are only using our own personal discretion and capital. When we look toward traditions, customs, and our ancestors, we are using a wisdom that is infinitely greater than any amount of capital a single individual could ever hope to possess.

This is essentially what the Torah *she-be-al peh* is, and why it is still so important today. This is the rationale for why our traditions and customs are so important. They are not arbitrary social constructs, but rather reflect the divinely sanctioned wisdom of our ancestors, bequeathed to us over a long process of trial and error.

This line of thinking, where one looks inward at the expense of tradition, is visible in Mlotek's rationale for his position: "But I also believe that the Torah does not want human beings to live alone, and supports a covenantal relationship between parties as they build a faithful Jewish home" (2019, para. 8). Mlotek is looking inward and making a judgement based on his personal feelings. Essentially, he is doing exactly what Burke feared years ago:

> We are afraid to put men to live and trade each on his own private stock of reason; because we suspect that this stock in each man is small, and that the individuals would do better to avail themselves of the general bank and capital of nations and of ages. (1790, para. 145)

Mlotek means well, and I truly believe his motives are compassion and love for his fellow Jew. His quote below illustrates this position:

> I know that Judaism has, for thousands of years, had a rich understanding of the diversity of gender identities. I know that the Torah affirms the God-endowed dignity of all human beings… The onus of responsibility now rests upon those of us in religious leadership

> positions: to continue to make space, validate, humanize, empathize and support those who have long felt suppressed by our traditions, and not the aggrieved parties themselves. (2019, paras. 8-10)

Looking inward, giving in to our feelings, and following our impulses are hallmarks of liberal ideology, predicated on the natural goodness of Man. Rousseau's natural goodness of Man meant that one only needs to, "give myself to the impression of the moment without resistance and [even] without scruple; for I am perfectly sure that my heart loves only that which is good" (Rousseau, as quoted by Ryn, 1978). Rousseau argued that, "Only the wicked person wants evil and premeditates it, the wicked person alone will be punished" (Rousseau, as quoted by Blum, 1986). Man is naturally good, and therefore, no one person would do anything intentionally evil. Our only requirement as a society is to look inward and follow our feelings, which, again, are naturally benevolent.

In the state of nature, human beings lived, among other things, free of the opinions and judgments of others (Rousseau, 1750). Rousseau lived his life fearing the judgments and opinions of others and wanted to rid our lives of their potential negativity. Read his account of what the judgments and opinions of others does to the psyche of Man:

> One does not dare to appear as what one is. And in this perpetual constraint, men who make up this herd we call society, placed in the same circumstances, will all do the same things, unless more powerful motives prevent them. Thus, one will never know well the person one is dealing with. (1750)

Rousseau wanted to look within, follow his impulses, and free himself from judgment. This is the source of Rousseau's desire to live "authentically" or "sincerely." Arthur Melzer commented on this premise, noting that Rousseau credited "the good as being oneself regardless of what one may be" (Melzer, 1995). Simply be yourself and, "let go and stop trying… I truly find myself when, rejecting all strenuous talk about my higher self, and liberated from shame and guilt, I just freely observe and sincerely acknowledge all that goes on within my soul" (Melzer, 1995).

This is the source of the liberal moral foundation of autonomy, or the ability to be free and choose for ourselves, freed from the constraints of society (Haidt, 2013). The conservative counterpunch to autonomy is authority, meaning normative restraint (Haidt, 2013). To the conservative, the fundamental principle of conservatism is restraint, also known as temperance (Muller, 1997). This is predicated on the fallen nature of Man, and the belief that Man's nature is savage and beastly.

This savage nature of Man necessitates restraints, for when the restraints on Man's unruly passions and appetites are removed, they run amok (Muller, 1997).

Burke too, generations ago, understood this notion. He knew that, "Our physical well-being, our moral worth, our social happiness, our political tranquility, all depend on that control of all our appetites and passions, which the ancients designed by the cardinal virtue of Temperance" (1796). Our well-being, collective, individual, and societal, are tied to Man's ability to control his unruly passions and appetites. This notion, that self-control is the key to our success, has been corroborated by a longitudinal study performed at Stanford University called, "The marshmallow test: mastering self-control" (Mischel, 2014).

To conclude, the examples referenced in the preceding paragraphs check all the liberal philosophical moral foundations: Autonomy, the belief in progress of human nature, the belief that we need to use our feelings as facts, and the natural goodness of Man, corrupted by society. This leads us to ask the question as to whether these values have a place in traditional Orthodox Judaism? We are not asking whether these liberal values have a place in our personal, secular, or political lives, but specifically, if they have a place in traditional Orthodox Judaism?

Is it likely that Orthodox Judaism, a religion roughly a few thousand years old, adheres to the principles of the 1700's, Rousseau, and the other Meliorists who followed him? Is it likely that these liberal values, which are in many ways predicated on invalidating one of the first *mashals* in the Torah, conform to Orthodox Judaism? Is it likely that Judaism, which has 613 commandments, 365 of which are negative commandments that place restraints on our lives, values liberal autonomy? Is it likely that Judaism values a belief that we can make everyone happy?

Remember, the name Israel, when translated to English, means struggle. Why is the name of the Jewish people "struggle"? Because life is a struggle and the human condition is tragic. The history of the Jewish people is, inter alia, one struggle after another. This is exactly what Edmund Burke understood of life and the human condition. Burke knew the human condition was tragic, and that no amount of tinkering by Man could ever truly eradicate that tragic nature:

> I have sometimes been in a good deal more than Doubt, whether the Creator did ever really intend Man for a State of Happiness. He has mixed in his Cup a Number of natural Evils… and every Endeavor which the Art and Policy of Mankind has used from the Beginning of the World to this Day, in order to alleviate, or cure them, has only served to introduce new Mischiefs, or to aggravate and inflame the old. (Burke, 1756, para. 3)

This is the nature of the human condition: tragic, brutal, and savage. The savage and beastly nature of Man necessitates restraints, for when these restraints are removed from our lives, the beastly nature of Man runs amok. To put it more poetically, read Burke's criticism of Rousseau from "Letter to a Member of the National Assembly" (1791):

> Men are qualified for civil liberty in exact proportion to their disposition to put moral chains upon their own appetites… Society cannot exist, unless a controlling power upon will and appetite be placed somewhere; and the less of it there is within, the more there must be without. It is ordained in the eternal constitution of things, that men of intemperate minds cannot be free. Their passions forge their fetters.

This is the meaning of the negative commandments from the Torah: they act as restraints on our savage nature and channel us to walk the "*Mesillat Yesharim*," the path of the just.

Real progress consists not in the creation of new norms, but rather, in adherence to the old ones (Kirk, 1989). In *Sefer Va-Yikra*, the Torah explicitly tells us that homosexuality is forbidden; in *Sefer Devarim*, the Torah tells us that, "A woman must not wear men's clothing, nor a man wear women's clothing, for the Lord your God detests anyone who does this." The point here is not to bash LGBT people and criticize their lifestyles, but rather to acknowledge a simple and basic premise in this discussion: that there is nothing new under the sun. These are not new concepts, nor are they novel; they were an issue when we originally received the Torah at Mt. Sinai and are an issue today as well.

The Torah is as relevant today as it was when Moshe received it for us atop Mt. Sinai. The knowledge bequeathed to us by God, to Moshe, and the direct lineage from our ancestors to us in the present is just as valuable, relevant, and important today as it was then; it will remain as important to our children and grandchildren in the future. The human condition is constant, and no amount of societal tinkering will alter what is constant in nature. The liberal Meliorists, while well-meaning, are misguided. We must always remember that the human condition is constant, and that the present is not better than the past. ☙

References

Blum, C. (1986). *Rousseau and the republic of Virtue: The language of politics in the French Revolution.* Ithaca, NY: Cornell University.

Burke, E. (1790). *Reflections on the revolution in France.* Retrieved from: https://www.bartleby.com/24/3/6.html.

- - -. (1796). *Letters on a regicide peace.* Retrieved from: https://people.ok.ubc.ca/ggrinnel/rom/Terror_htm_files/Letters%20on%20a%20Regicide%20Peace.pdf.

- - -. (1791). *A letter to a member of the National Assembly. Project Gutenberg.* Retrieved from: https://www.gutenberg.org/files/15700/15700-h/15700-h.htm#member_of_the_national_assembly.

- - -. (1770). *Thoughts on the cause of the present discontent.* Retrieved from: http://oll.libertyfund.org/titles/burke-select-works-of-edmund-burke-vol-1–5.

- - -. (1782). *Speech on the Reform of the Representation of the Commons in Parliament.* Retrieved from: https://oll.libertyfund.org/titles/burke-select-works-of-edmund-burke-vol-4/simple.

- - -. (1756). *The vindication of natural society.* Retrieved from: http://oll.libertyfund.org/titles/burke-a-vindication-of-natural-society.

Haidt, J. (2013). *The righteous mind: Why good people are divided by politics and religion.* New York, NY: Penguin Random House.

Haidt, J. & Lukianoff, G. (2018). *The coddling of the American mind.* New York, NY: Penguin Books.

Kessler, S. (2018). An 'ever better' constitution? Progressivism as ideology and the U.S. Constitution. *The VoegelinView.* Retrieved from: https://voegelinview.com/an-ever-better-constitution-progressivism-as-ideology-and-the-u-s-constitution/

- - -. (2018). When feelings became facts: Rousseau, Burke, and the origins of today's outrage culture. *The Imaginative Conservative.* Retrieved from: https://theimaginativeconservative.org/2018/07/feelings-facts-rousseau-burke-outrage-culture-steven-kessler.html.

Kirk, R. (1989). *The enemies of the permanent things.* Peru, IL: Sherwood, Sugden & Company.

Levin, Y. (2014). *The great debate: Edmund Burke, Thomas Paine, and the birth of right and left.* New York, NY: Basic Books.

Melzer, A. (1990). *The natural goodness of men: On the system of Rousseau's thought.* Chicago, IL: University of Chicago.

- - -. (1995). Rousseau and the modern cult of sincerity. *The Harvard Review of Philosophy*, Spring '95. Retrieved from: http://harvardphilosophy.com/issues/1995/Melzer.pdf

McIntosh, P. (1989). White privilege: unpacking the invisible knapsack. Retrieved from: https://www.racialequitytools.org/resourcefiles/mcintosh.pdf

Mischel, W. (2014). *The marshmallow test: mastering self-control.* San Francisco, CA: Back Bay Books.

Mora, G. F. de la (1987). *Egalitarian envy: The political foundations of social justice.* New York, NY: Paragon House

Mlotek, A. (2019, April 5). I'm an Orthodox rabbi who is going to start officiating LGBTQ weddings. Here's why. Jewish Telegraphic Agency. Retrieved from: https://www.jta.org/2019/04/05/opinion/im-an-orthodox-rabbi-who-is-going-to-start-officiating-lgbtq-weddings-heres-why.

Muller, J. (1997). Conservatism: An anthology of social and political thought from David Hume to the Present. Princeton, NJ: Princeton, New Jersey.

Nisbet, R. (1966). *The sociological tradition.* New Brunswick, NJ: Transaction Publishers.

Rousseau, J. (1753). *Discourse on the origins of inequality.* Indianapolis, IN: Hackett Publishing.

- - -. (1762B). *Emile, or education.* Retrieved from http://oll.libertyfund.org/titles/rousseau-emile-or-education.

- - -. (1750). *Discourse on the arts and sciences.* Retrieved from: https://www.stmarys-ca.edu/sites/default/files/attachments/files/arts.pdf.

- - -. (1762). *Letter to Beaumont.* Retrieved from: http://the-eye.eu/public/Books//4chan_pol_Archives/PDFs/Philosophy/Jean-Jacques%20Rousseau/Collected%20Writings%20of%20Rousseau%20%5Beds.%20Masters%20%26%20Kelly%5D%20%287%20vols.%29/Vol.%209%20-%20Letter%20to%20Beaumont%20%26%20Related%20Writings/Rousseau%2C%20Jean-Jacques%20-%20Collected%20Writings%2C%20Vol.%209%20%28UPNE%2C%202001%29.pdf.

- - -. (1762C). *The social contract.* Retrieved from https://www.earlymoderntexts.com/assets/pdfs/rousseau1762.pdf.

Ryn, C. (1978). *Democracy and the ethical life: A philosophy of politics and community.* Shreveport, LI: Louisiana State University.

Sacks, J. (2009, August 15). Re'eh (5769) – Judaism's Vision for Social Justice. *The office of Rabbi Sacks.* Retrieved from: http://rabbisacks.org/covenant-conversation-5769-reeh-greatness-and-humility/.

Schoeck, H. (1966). Envy: A theory of social behavior. Indianapolis, IN: The Liberty Fund.

Sowell, T. (1987). *A conflict of visions: Ideological origins of political struggles.* New York, NY: Basic Books.

Sylvester, G. (2012, July 1). Social Justice Lies at the Heart of the Jewish People. *Haaretz*. Retrieved from: https://www.haaretz.com/jewish/social-justice-lies-at-the-heart-of-the-jewish-people-1.5191080.

Tocqueville, A. (1836). Democracy in America. Chicago, IL: University of Chicago.

Torah.org. (2018). Pirkei Avot. Torah.org. Retrieved from: https://torah.org/learning/pirkei-avos-chapter4-1a/.

Siddur Avodat HaLev: *A New Siddur and Insights on the Old*

By: ATON HOLZER and ARIE FOLGER

A Siddur is many things at once. Primarily a devotional device, the Siddur orients our consciousness toward God, facilitating Divine service in the ideal manner. Its blessings attach to the gamut of human experiences, emotions and wonder. Mindfulness and interruptions to rote routine are portals to religious awareness. Praise of God, found in *Berakhot*, is expressed through such diverse experiences as the flavor of an apple, the startle of thunder, the genius of a scholar, the elation of a marriage ceremony, and even the searing pain of loss. In the sanctity of the commanded life, with all of its imperatives, the Siddur traces these channels back to their Source, and thus unites Man with his.

At the same time, the Siddur is also a teaching tool. Rav Joseph B. Soloveitchik writes, "Prayer tells the individual, as well as the community, what his, or its, genuine needs are, what he should or should not petition God about… In a word, man finds his need-awareness, himself, in prayer."[1] For Rabbi Lord Jonathan Sacks, "Scholars of Judaism, noting that it contains little systematic theology, have sometimes concluded that

---

1 Joseph B. Soloveitchik, "Redemption, Prayer, and Talmud Torah," *Tradition* 17:2, New York: Spring 1978, p. 62.

Rabbi Dr. Aton Holzer is Director of the Mohs Surgery Clinic in the Department of Dermatology, Tel Aviv Sourasky Medical Center, and was an assistant editor of the new Rabbinical Council of America (RCA) *Siddur Avodat HaLev.*

Rabbi Arie Folger is the rabbi of Beit Midrash Orchot Chajim in Vienna, Austria, the Rav haMachshir of Fidelity Kosher, a member of the Rabbinical Court of Austria, a member of the editorial team of the Conference of European Rabbis' rabbinic journal *Seridim* and was an assistant editor of the new RCA *Siddur Avodat HaLev.*

Cantor Bernard Beer, a coauthor of *Appendix A* to this article, is the Director Emeritus of the Philip and Sarah Belz School of Jewish Music, RIETS, YU, and the Executive Vice President of the Cantorial Council of America.

it is a religion of deeds not creeds, acts not beliefs. They were wrong because they were searching in the wrong place. They were looking for a library of works like Moses Maimonides' *Guide for the Perplexed.* They should have looked instead at the prayer book. The home of Jewish belief is the siddur."[2]

Indeed, the Siddur educates in several ways. The content of its petitions teaches us what we ought to want while the implied polemics and occasional catechism poems teach us what we ought to believe. But more than that, as Professor Joseph Tabory has noted,[3] the Siddur is an anthology par excellence—its materials span the full expanse of Jewish history, and three millennia of intellectual currents course through its passages. Every genre is represented, from Biblical battle songs to Mishnaic legal treatises to Kaliric aggadic tapestries to hasidic ecstatic paeans to *Shabbat*; only in the Siddur can a catalogue of Maimonidean principles share a binding with Zoharic mystical declarations, and Aramaic halakhic formulae with contemporary poetry reviewed by Shai Agnon.[4] The Siddur tells a story, our story. The mingling of Eretz Yisraeli *piyutim* and occasional prayer formulae within the otherwise Babylonian-dominated common *Nusaḥ*[5] may offer clues to the manner of development of Ash-

---

2 Jonathan Sacks, *The Koren Sacks Siddur* (Jerusalem: Koren Publishers, 2009) p. xxxv.

3 Joseph Tabory, "The Prayerbook (Siddur) as an Anthology of Judaism." *Prooftexts* 17: 2, Bloomington: May 1997, pp. 115-132.

4 After years of speculation, evidence has been discovered that conclusively shows that the Prayer for the Welfare of the State of Israel was authored by Chief Rabbi Isaac Halevi Herzog, and not by Shai Agnon. Herzog had merely sent it to Agnon for review, and the latter made only the most minor edits (reportedly just five words). See Joel Rappel, *Between Prayer and Politics (Heb.).* Hevel Modiin: Kinneret, Zmora-Bitan, Dvir, 2018.

5 The prayer versions of Ashkenaz, Edot ha-Mizrach, Spanish-Portuguese, Romaniote and earlier, defunct variants from the High Middle Ages like Tzarfat and Provence all are rooted in the *Nusaḥ* of early medieval Bavel; Ashkenaz retains the greatest degree of influences from the *Nusaḥ* of early medieval Eretz Israel, which has been reconstructed from documents recovered from the genizah of the Ben Ezra Synagogue of Fustat, among the last outposts of *Nusaḥ Eretz Yisrael* until the tradition was extinguished in the thirteenth century. See Mordekhai Akiva Friedman, "New Evidence of the Abolition of the Eretz-Israel Prayers and Prayer Rituals in Egypt in Abraham Maimonides' Times" (Heb.) in Uri Ehrlich, ed., *Jewish Prayer: New Perspectives* (Heb.). Jerusalem: Mosad Bialik, 2016, pp. 315-325; for the reconstructions of the prayer version(s) see Uri Ehrlich, *The Weekday Amidah in Cairo Genizah Prayerbooks: Roots and Transmissions.* (Jerusalem: Yad Ben-Zvi Press, 2013). Ironically, many of these traces, such as alternate endings to *Amidah* blessings of

kenaz/Germany as a major center of medieval Jewish life,[6] an abiding mystery of Jewish history. Its polemics cover our struggles with enemies inside and out, from Sadducees to early Christians and Gnostics to Karaites, and its texts bear the scars of despots as varied as the Assyrian Sennacherib, the Babylonian Nebuchadnezzar, the Sassanid Persian Yazdegerd II, the Byzantine Heraclius and Holy Roman Emperor Frederick I Barbarossa. Events such as the First Crusade, the Spanish Expulsion and the Khmelnytsky massacres (and in the RCA Siddur, the Shoah and, happily, the founding of the Jewish State) all have left their mark on the Siddur.

And so the Siddur takes us on a grand tour of the history of our people and its ideas; it situates ourselves in relation to the generations that precede us and contextualizes us within the eternal covenantal community—if we are paying attention.

The new RCA Siddur *Avodat HaLev: Nusaḥ Ashkenaz*, under the exceptional stewardship of Rabbi Basil Herring, is intended to potentiate both aspects. The Siddur leads with a newly translated essay by Rav Soloveitchik that is perhaps his clearest, yet most beautiful, expression of the principle of *ein od milvado* which animates the prayer context. The Siddur's commentary is studded with inspirational notes that are meant to uplift and direct the heart to the Source of Blessing, and its backmatter essays treating the meaning of prayer and *kavanah* range from the practical to the poetic. One reviewer objects: "While the siddur does a fine job in examining the nature of *kavanah*, it sheepishly avoids dealing with most perplexing questions of our age: What is the nature of a personal relationship with God? Is God 'responsive' to our prayers? Does prayer truly have or evoke healing power?"[7] but he seems to have been distracted by the "*sha'ar ha-kavanah*" section header; the issues he mentions are precisely the questions addressed in essays by Rav Aharon Lichtenstein, Rav Yehuda Amital, Rabbanit Rookie Billet and Rabbi Dr. David Mescheloff. It is gratifying to know that the Siddur indeed ad-

---

Retzeh and *Sim Shalom*, as well as the *Krovot* of Rabbi Eliezer Ha-Kalir for *Tal* and *Geshem* and four *Parshiyot*, have been entirely eradicated under the influence of the Vilna Gaon from the Nusaḥ Ashkenaz used in most contemporary Israeli Ashkenazi synagogues; in the Diaspora, these remain in use in most Ashkenazi communities, including but not limited to the various *Yekke* rites.

6 Haym Soloveitchik, *Collected Essays II* (Oxford: Littman Library of Jewish Civilization, 2014) pp. 141-143.

7 Rabbi Michael Leo Samuels at https://www.sdjewishworld.com/2018/12/22/book-review-siddur-avodat-halev/, accessed May 15, 2019.

dresses the most perplexing questions of our age. To this we can add other burning questions like the employment of fixed texts for what is meant to be heartfelt devotion, and the place of *korbanot* vis-a-vis modern sensibilities—ably addressed by the *Seridei Eish* and Rabbi Shalom Carmy, respectively.

The essays also contextualize specific prayers that have their own distinct properties. Rabbi Heshie Billet aims to understand the *Amidah* via a philological analysis of the word *tefillah*. We reprint Rabbi Pinhas Peli's classic exposition on *berakhot*. Rabbi Basil Herring presents an examination of *Shema* and *kabbalat ol malkhut shamayim*—very different from prayer—through the lens of Rav Soloveitchik, and we compiled an essay on the special rhythm of *tefillot* of *Shabbat*. The theology of *Shabbat* is not treated by the Rav frontally in any other known composition; this is a particularly obvious lacuna for a thinker who put so much emphasis on *kiyum she-ba-lev* in *mitzvot*.[8] The manner in which he does so in the compiled work solves a longstanding mystery in his theology of *kedushah*[9]—namely, why can *Shabbat* be an exception to Rav Soloveitchik's insistence in numerous places[10] that *kedushah* is man-made? (Spoiler alert: The holiness of *Shabbat* is ontologically prior to, and represents the very telos of, man-made sanctity.)

Rabbi Saul Berman authored a marvelous preface for the previous RCA Siddur, which unfortunately could not be retained after the previous publishing house terminated its contract with the RCA. After the

---

8 See Jeffrey Saks, "The Rav Between Halakhic Men and Lachrymose Lubavitchers," *Kol HaMevaser* X:1, New York: 2016, pp. 22-23.

9 Raised, for example, by Rabbi Gil Student in http://hirhurim.blogspot.com/2008/03/rav-soloveitchiks-confrontation-with.html, accessed May 15, 2019; and Avraham Wein, "Of Perspective and Paradox: Rabbi Joseph B. Soloveitchik's Analysis of Holiness," *Kol Hamevaser* IX:3, New York: 2016, p. 25. See also Sherlow, Yuval. *Ve-hayu le-aḥadim be-einekha: Medialektikah le-harmoniah be-mishnato shel Ha-rav Yosef Dov Halevi Soloveitchik* (Alon Shevut: Tevunot, 2000) p. 7; Yoel Finkelman, "Theology With Fissures: Contradictions in Rabbi Joseph B. Soloveitchik's Theological Writings," *Journal of Modern Jewish Studies,* 13(3) (Abingdon-on-Thames: 2014) pp. 399-421.

10 E.g. in his *Halakhic Man*, trans. Lawrence Kaplan (Philadelphia: Jewish Publication Society, 1984) p. 47; *And From There You Shall Seek*, trans. Naomi Goldblum (NJ: Ktav, 2008) p. 115; *Family Redeemed.* (NJ: Ktav, 2000) p. 64; *The Emergence of Ethical Man* (NJ: Ktav 2005), p. 150; also see Aharon Lichtenstein, "Joseph Soloveitchik," in Simon Noveck, ed., *Great Jewish Thinkers of the Twentieth Century* (Washington, DC: Bnai B'rith Adult Jewish Education, 1963, pp. 293-4. Rav Lichtenstein himself takes an altogether different approach to *kedushah* in his recent (posthumously published) *Kedushat Aviv.*

new Siddur was announced, Rabbi Berman voiced skepticism that a Siddur would be able to close the "God gap"—the distance that Western civilization and technological advances have placed between man and God.[11] In the new Siddur, we picked up that gauntlet and curated material that is at once uplifting and at the same time conceptually rigorous, and (hopefully) presented it in a manner that is accessible.

Like many contemporary Siddurim, there are boxout halakhic guides to inform the worshipper. But unlike any other, there is a guide to *halakhot bein adam le-ḥaveiro* in prayer, so critical to creating the proper atmosphere in prayer, yet so overlooked.

At the same time as it works to focus devotion, the RCA Siddur spares no effort to unpack the Siddur's messages and contextualize its many treasures.

First, all of the text was carefully reviewed, and its final version reflects conscious choices, rather than overlooked defaults. Some (not all!) examples from the first fifty pages alone:

- We ought to present the morning prayers in the actual order that they are to be said, instead of the thematic grouping which is found in other Siddurim. (Rav Hershel Schachter ratified this approach.)
- Do we restore the lost passages of *adon olam*? (No, it will be confusing.)
- What is the original *Nusaḥ* of the fifth line of *yigdal*? (*V'chol notzar yoreh*; confirmed by Professor Marc Shapiro. This version also fits best with the fifth Maimonidean principle.)[12]
- In *birkhot ha-shaḥar*, the feminine variants of *goyah* (or *nokhrit*) and *shifkhah* were considered as women's alternatives, and both Rav J. David Bleich and Rav Aharon Lichtenstein were consulted (the latter, via Rabbi Dov Karoll); Rav Bleich opined that it was

11 Rabbi Saul Berman at https://forward.com/culture/112469/even-a-new-siddur-can-t-close-god-gap/, accessed May 15, 2019.

12 We were also cognizant of the recent scholarship questioning the degree to which the thirteen Maimonidean principles were seen as binding in subsequent generations; see e.g. Marc B. Shapiro, *The Limits of Orthodox Theology* (London: The Littman Library of Jewish Civilization, 2004); and more generally, Kellner, Menachem. *Must a Jew Believe Anything* (London: The Littman Library of Jewish Civilization, 1999); but see also J. David Bleich, *The Philosophical Quest: Of Philosophy, Ethics, Law and Halakhah* (Jerusalem: Maggid Press, 2013) especially pp. 9-32. As such, we solicited an essay by Professor David Shatz to contextualize the *Ikkarim* for the contemporary *mispallel*.

appropriate to use the grammatical construct that best fit the speaker, while Rav Lichtenstein argued that the blessing is about the status or type of person that we are thankful not to be, which is gender neutral (and thus the male default); we do not intend to peg our blessing on a particular person. In the end, in a *maḥloket* between those two giants, we opted for the most common *Nusaḥ* regarding the *berakhot*, but in *Modeh Ani* and similar formulae we incorporated the grammatically correct alternative *Modah Ani* for a female worshiper.

- Professor Richard Steiner was consulted as to whether *(uv')/[u've]shokhbekha* takes a *shva na* or *naḥ*,[13] as was Rav Hershel Schachter.
- A decision was taken regarding the correct *ḥasimah* for the blessing that follows, which ends the *l-olam yehei adam* passage (*tarum* and *shimkha* are better attested in Ashkenaz manuscripts, confirmed by Rabbi Schlomo Hofmeister, than *tarim* and *shemo*),[14] with the assistance of Rabbi Dr. David Berger. Emendations made to the Siddur text were identified, some based on halakhic *sevara* (e.g., rendering the *v-yehi ratzon* following *ha-ma'avir sheinah* in plural rather than the original singular) and some (e.g., *hameikhin* versus *asher heikhin*) by well-meaning Siddur grammarians, based on grammatical assumptions that have been rendered outdated by advances in diachronic linguistics. Generally, we left these in place unless the original had already been popularized in a widely used contemporary Siddur, so as to avoid confusion.
- Some detective work went into understanding why many Siddurim (such as the prior RCA Siddur) have one difference between the *ketoret* passage before daily *Shaḥarit* and after *Mussaf* on *Shabbat* (*b-mikdash* versus *ba-azarah*, because some popular Siddurim copy-pasted only the post-prayer passage from its daily recitation in *Nusaḥ Sepharad*); and
- We relied on the best manuscripts of Siddur and *Sifra* to resolve the proper situation of the words *eḥad* versus *aḥer* in the *Rabbi Yishmael Omer* passage (and raised the question, do we translit-

---

13 See discussion at https://www.ou.org/blog/oupress/saying_shema_better/, accessed May 15, 2019.

14 We were also assisted by Rabbi Binyamin Shlomo Hamburger with regard to textual issues. See his "*Hagahat Siddur Ha-Tefillah Lefi Siddurim Kedumim*," *Yerushateinu* 6. Bnei Brak: Machon Moreshet Ashkenaz, 2012, pp. 262-296.

erate *Rabbi* or the original *Ribbi*? The world is accustomed to the former, and replacement would be *tamu'ah la-rabim*).

And this is before we even got to *Barukh She-Amar!*

The new RCA Siddur has been criticized by some reviewers[15] for preserving texts which seem to offend modern sensibilities. In preparing the text of the Siddur, we saw ourselves as custodians whose mandate is to preserve, transmit and sometimes restore the words recited by the generations that preceded us, not to critique them; instead we endeavored to make them understood to the contemporary *mispallel.* While our thinking was certainly informed by a resistance to what C.S. Lewis called chronological snobbery,[16] this sensibility typically did not need to be invoked. Our experience in editing the Siddur convinced us that the proper approach to our liturgists is akin to the principle of charity or principle of rational accommodation articulated by Donald Davidson[17] and Willard Van Orman Quine,[18] widely employed in the historiography of philosophy by those who wish to productively engage the ideas of earlier thinkers. By this principle, we avoid attributing irrationality, logical fallacies or falsehoods to the others' statements when a coherent, rational interpretation of the statements is available,[19] or as Quine said, "your interlocutor's silliness is less likely than your bad interpretation."[20] The profundity, complexity and range displayed by the (mostly) anonymous rabbinic authors of our liturgy convinced us that they deserved the benefit of rational accommodation, and the words themselves typically lent themselves to an understanding that was entirely compatible with contemporary ideas of justice and human dignity.

And it turned out that on closer scrutiny, the most plausible understandings of ostensibly problematic prayers sidestep the contemporary objections. For example, the series of three blessings beginning with "*she-lo asani ishah*" seems nothing less than a clear response to the sub-

---

15 E.g., Rabbi Dan Margulies, at https://morethodoxy.org/2018/12/18/the-new-rca-siddur-the-ravs-legacy-and-feminist-innovation/, accessed May 15, 2019, and Rabbi Michael Leo Samuels, note 4 above.

16 C. S. Lewis, *Surprised by Joy: The Shape of My Early Life* (New York: Harcourt, Brace and World, 1955) p. 207.

17 Donald Davidson, "Truth and Meaning," *Synthese*, 17, 1967, pp. 304-323.

18 Willard Van Orman Quine, *Word and Object* (Cambridge MA: MIT Press, 1960).

19 Pithy summary from https://onlinephilosophyclub.com/the-principle-of-charity.php, accessed June 1, 2019.

20 Davidson op. cit., p. 59.

stance of an anti-Judaism polemic which appears in the Christian Bible, in Galatians 3:28: "There is neither Jew nor Gentile, neither slave nor free, nor is there male and female, for you are all one in Christ Jesus." In context, Paul's epistle polemicizes against Judaism's focus on works of the Law that, with the advent of Jesus, have been replaced by faith, which harbors no distinctions.[21] This is the most famous verse in an epistle that is a sweeping rejection of the Torah, the key document which decisively removes early Christianity from Judaism. Scholars further suggest that the verse itself is a fragment of early Christian baptismal liturgy;[22] these items would have been familiar to first-century Jewish leadership struggling against this movement, which had made significant inroads in the Jewish community. It is thus plausibly suggested that the three *she-lo asani* blessings—which preserve these same distinctions, in their precise order—are a polemical response against that Christian doctrine, providing the added benefit that a closet missionary serving as a *shaliaḥ tzibbur* could be uncovered right at the beginning of *Shaḥarit,* long before he refuses to recite *Ve-lamalshinim.*[23] This dovetails nicely

---

21 Indeed, the phrase bears affinity to a pre-Christian Hellenistic thanksgiving formula, described in Greek as follows: "There were three blessings for which he was grateful to fortune: First, that I was born a human being and not one of the brutes; next, that I was born a man and not a woman, and thirdly, a Greek and not a barbarian." This is explored by Yoel Kahn, *The Three Blessings: Boundaries, Censorship and Identity in Jewish Liturgy* (Oxford: Oxford University Press, 2011). However, the relatively late date at which these blessings were formulated, and the evidence of contemporaneous anti-Christian polemic (e.g., *Elokai Neshamah*, probably *birkat ha-minim*, swaths of the Haggadah, etc.), make it seem far likelier to these authors that *Ḥazal* in this instance were responding to the Gospels rather than directly borrowing from Socrates or Plato.

22 See discussion and sources cited in Ronald Y.K. Fung, *The Epistle to the Galatians* (Grand Rapids, MI: Eerdmans, 1988) p. 176.

23 A few *berakhot* and associated liturgy trace their formulations to the first and second centuries of the Common Era, when early Christianity and Gnosticism were the chief ideological and political competitors of the Jewish community in the Holy Land, and polemics against these ideologies are discernable in numerous blessing formulae. A "neighbor" of *she-lo asani ishah*, the blessing *Elokai Neshamah* is seen by Rabbi Samson Raphael Hirsch, Kaufmann Kohler, Rabbi Dr. J.H. Hertz and others as polemicizing against the Christian doctrine of original sin ("the soul… it is pure"), even as the text continues with a description of bodily resurrection, which runs counter to Gnostic doctrine. The most obviously polemical formulae have been subject to censorship over time. See, e.g., Ruth Langer, *Cursing the Christians? A History of Birkat HaMinim.* (Oxford: Oxford University Press, 2012); see also Israel J. Yuval, "Easter and Passover as Early Jewish-Christian Dialogue," in Paul F. Bradshaw and Lawrence A.

with the explanation provided by sources contemporaneous with the *berakhah's* authorship, the *Tosefta Berakhot* 6:18 and *Yerushalmi Berakhot* 9:1 (that *she-lo asani ishah* was thus formulated to reflect that women are not obligated in [all] *mitzvot*). This seemed to us more likely the correct explanation than that the classical Rabbis aped a Greek axiology of persons; indeed, scholars have noted that misogyny, while a defining feature of Hellenistic thought and early Zoroastrianism, is not representative of Jewish scripture and the dominant stream in rabbinic tradition.[24]

One of the aforementioned reviewers supposed that "the [RCA] Siddur is deeply influenced by the critiques that the Orthodox feminist movement has raised over the years," since the RCA Siddur "endorses women's participation in *tefillah*" and encourages or at least validates daughters saying *Kaddish*, women reciting *zimun*, and the matriarchs are included in some *Mi She-berakh* headers.

Feminism, when defined as the advocacy of women's rights on the grounds of equality of the sexes, has undoubtedly influenced all modern societies in a profoundly salutary manner. The very existence of a female laity across the Orthodox spectrum that is well-educated, that functions at the highest levels of academic and professional life, and is ambitious in *avodat Hashem*—across the Orthodox spectrum—is a testament to the success of the global movement for women's human rights, and coupled with the advances of technology, it has revolutionized the way that we live.[25] The inclusion of women's variants in a Shul Siddur follows naturally from the presence of a religiously literate, sophisticated, and above all, participatory, *ezrat nashim*. The inclusion of women as commentators and essayists likewise reflects the extraordinary efflorescence of first-rate

---

Hoffman, eds., *Passover and Easter: Origin and History to Modern Times* (Notre Dame: University of Notre Dame Press, 2000) pp. 98-124. After his survey of what he sees as thoroughgoing polemic in the Haggadah, Yuval goes so far as to say "…in its deepest meaning, the Oral Law should be seen as the Jewish response to the Christian New Testament." The purist *Tefillat Yeshurun* Siddur reinstated the uncensored version of the *birkat ha-minim*.

24 See Tikva Frymer-Kensky, *In the Wake of the Goddesses: Women, Culture and the Biblical Transformation of Pagan Myth* (New York: Fawcett Columbine, 1992). See also Yaakov Elman, "'He in His Cloak and She in Her Cloak:' Conflicting Images of Sexuality in Sasanian Mesopotamia," in Rivka Ulmer, ed. *Discussing Cultural Influences: Text, Context and Non-Text in Rabbinic Judaism*. Lanham, MA: University Press of America, 2007, pp. 129-164.

25 Rav Soloveitchik often expresses himself in his writings in a manner that is compatible with, and even anticipates, some concepts in feminist ethical and political theory. See Shira Wolosky, "The Lonely Woman of Faith," *Judaism* 52:1-2 (New York: American Jewish Congress, 2004) pp. 3-18.

female Torah scholars and thinkers in recent years. The relatively modest amount of material we were able to gather—from the meager amount of prayer-relevant published material, and new contributions solicited from overburdened and overextended *yeḥidot segulah* circa 2009—already seems incongruous given the remarkable advances in the decade since, and women's intellectual share in the Siddur will surely reach equilibrium with that of their male counterparts in future editions.

The Orthodox feminist movement has had a more checkered reception from Orthodox rabbinic leadership. The movement is heterogeneous, and some in the movement consider radical egalitarianism in ritual and other halakhically circumscribed matters as a desideratum, or at least seem willing to disregard halakhic and hashkafic stances hallowed by centuries or millennia of jurisprudential interpretative continuity.[26] To that end, some have sought to admit women to observances that *halakhah* classically proscribes for women—or at least considers significant only when performed by men, in the presence of a *minyan*—including all *devarim she-bi-k'dushah.* In the 1970's, the question of the halakhic permissibility of women's prayer groups crystallized the positions of many leading *poskim* of the times regarding the movement. The Frimer brothers catalog these views, including that of Rav Soloveitchik:

> The Rav was uncertain as to what precisely the women participating in these services were seeking: greater spirituality resulting from increased *kiyyum ha-mitzvot* (fulfillment of the commandments), or—consciously or not—something else, perhaps public peer ap-

---

26 We term "jurisprudential interpretative continuity" as such interpretations of *halakhah* and halakhically relevant sources that occur within jurisprudential contexts and—due to continuity of interpretation—do not allow for re-evaluation of that interpretation in the halakhic context. An extreme example regards the prohibition against homosexual intercourse. Some authors claiming to belong to the Orthodox community have tried to suggest interpretations of the severe prohibition on homosexual intercourse in a manner that would allow condoning homosexual relations. Such interpretations invariably are at odds with all interpretations considered by *halakhah* since the earliest iterations of the Oral Law, and there is not a single traditional source that is accorded any halakhic import that supports those reinterpretations. With regard to other issues, in which those seeking reinterpretations of *halakhah* can muster some obscure sources, those sources had never been part of the ongoing halakhic discourse. That is what we term *jurisprudential interpretive continuity*: the existence of an interpretive tradition that was adopted within legal discourse, which displays sufficient continuity so as to render certain other, incompatible readings inadmissible.

> probation, conspicuous religious performance, or a sense of equality with men. If the real motivating factor was any of the latter, it was likely that a women's *tefillah* group would not truly satisfy their religious needs; on the contrary, the women's services would merely foster increasingly unfulfillable expectations, resulting in a greater frustration and perhaps even a break with halakha.[27]

Since the two of us were the ones who did the preliminary research—one of us (AF) discussed the matter with our *poskim*, and we wrote the commentary to those pieces—we wish to set the record straight. The only one of those inclusions that may be said to have been influenced by the encouragement of the Orthodox feminist movement is the endorsement of women saying *Kaddish*, a *davar she-bi-k'dushah*, and that was only done because no less than Rav Ahron Soloveitchik felt that this was something that we ought to permit. It is his teachings that made us consider and finally decide in favor of this inclusion, while noting that "customs vary regarding whether she should recite it in an undertone or out loud and whether or not she may recite it if she is the only mourner present" (p. 52).

Neither the inclusion of women's *zimun*, nor of the *imahot* in the *Mi She-berakh* for the sick, nor of a *Zeved ha-Bat* ceremony (which was not noted in the review) was motivated by critiques posed by the Orthodox feminist movement. Women's *zimun* is an explicit *halakhah* in *Shulḥan Arukh* (*OḤ* 199:7), anchored in the Talmud, and though the *Shulḥan Arukh* rules that it is *reshut*, the *Gra* is rather insistent that it is an actual obligation. We included women's *zimun* after I (AF) consulted with Rav Hershel Schachter, who cited a number of contemporary *gedolim* who had endorsed the practice (with certain limitations, the most obvious of which is in the Talmudic proviso that we do not do a mixed *zimun*). Among those Rav Schachter cited as endorsing women's *zimun* was Rav Shlomo Zalman Auerbach (and indeed, such is cited as his view in *Ve-alehu Lo Yibol*), provided the men present are all family.

The inclusion of the *imahot* in the *Mi She-berakh* for the sick is nothing more or less than an ancient *Nusaḥ* still used in many communities.

---

27 Aryeh A. Frimer and Dov I. Frimer, "Women's Prayer Services—Theory and Practice," *Tradition* 32:2 (New York: Winter 1998) p. 41. For research that seems to bear out the latter concern, see Michelle Shain, "Whence Orthodox Jewish Feminism? Cognitive Dissonance and Religious Change in the United States," *Religions* 9, Basel: MDPI, 2018, article 332.

As the resident *Yekke*, I (AF)[28] continuously brought older *Nusahot,* and especially those that remained in use among *Yekkes*, to the attention of the team. That is also why in *E-l Malei Raḥamim*, we use the words *taḥat kanfei ha-Shekhinah* as the leading *Nusaḥ*, offering *al kanfei ha-Shekhinah* merely as an alternate *Nusaḥ*. *Al* is an emendation by the Shelah, based on a teaching that it is converts that are gathered *under* the wings of the *Shekhinah*, while born Jews are *over* the wings of the *Shekhinah*. *Taḥat kanfei ha-Shekhinah* is undisputedly the original *Nusaḥ*; the emendation of the Shelah only makes sense if we'll actually care to distinguish in the *Nusaḥ* between prayers for deceased converts and deceased born Jews. Since that isn't done anywhere, it makes sense to keep the original *Nusaḥ*, as still practiced in many communities, including but not limited to *Yekkish* communities. This reversion to the original *Nusaḥ* was accepted by our *poskim*.

The *Zeved ha-Bat* ceremony (p. 1076) was indeed considered because more and more people desire to celebrate more formally the birth of a girl, but only included because it is many hundreds of years old, a common celebration among Sepharadim, and duly attested by the *Ya'avetz*, whose text we utilized. However, we grant that we cannot refute a theory that would posit that we were more sensitive to including this ceremony on account of being the happy fathers of mostly girls.

Returning to prayers that were marked for omission by some reviewers, *Kapparot* likewise has quite a bit more to the story than meets the eye, as we report in the text, which a different reviewer noted approvingly.[29] We likewise don't flinch from including the *ribbono shel olam* text at bedtime that references reincarnation, nor the incantational verses at bedtime, *Havdalah* or *Kiddush Levanah* (indeed, the reversed "*k'even yidmu*" verse is likely not the result of a misreading of Soferim[30] but is found in magical works from the genizah, as Professor Shai Secunda enlightened us); we provide a basis to rationalize their use per the Arizal in the bedtime context. Professor Secunda also provides a historical insight that serves as a robust defense for the continued recitation of

---

28 A zealous convert, I should term myself, as I grew up in *Nusaḥ Sepharad* and "converted" upon becoming the *rov* of the *Yekke* community of Basel, Switzerland, since it is a place with a real *minhag ha-makom*. (AF)

29 R. Israel Drazin, "The New Rabbinical Council of America Siddur," https://blogs.timesofisrael.com/the-new-rabbinical-council-of-america-siddur/, accessed May 31, 2019.

30 David S. Farkas, "Backward and Forward: An Unusual Feature of Kiddush Levanah," *Hakirah* vol. 7. New York: 2009, pp. 229-242.

Yekum Purkan, the passage which wrongly became early Reform's symbol for Orthodox liturgical ossification.[31]

In light of the principle of charity, a similarly satisfactory understanding can be found for the *Mi She-berakh* before *Mussaf* that excludes women from "*Ha-kahal ha-kadosh ha-zeh*"; one that immediately comes to mind is that "*hazeh*" is always understood in rabbinic literature as a deictic pronoun, evidenced in various aggadic and halakhic sources;[32] on the men's side of the *meḥitzah*, and for those families in which mothers are home with small children and unable to attend Shul at all, there are no women to "point" to; perhaps it was felt best for the blessing to be bestowed on those immediately adjacent[33] and proceed through them to women and children associated with them, since formal blessings are bestowed upon people (in *birkat kohanim*) or items (in *birkhot ha-nehenin*) that are immediately proximate and visible to the *mevarekh*. *V-ein kan makom le-ha'arikh*.

Whereas some reviewers suspected innovation, in point of fact we took great pains to make sure that any adaptation would first and foremost be solidly anchored in ancient *Nusaḥ*, traditional *hashkafah*, unassailable *halakhah,* and also be vetted by our *poskim*. Thus, we considered not only the need to have a Shoah remembrance ceremony, but were cognizant of (some on the team even adamant about) the critique of *Yom ha-Shoah*, which was instituted by the Knesset, as a result of a tug of war between right and left wing parties in which the concerns of the secular left ended up gaining the upper hand. The broad consensus of the religious public was to follow the lead of the Chief Rabbinate of Israel and enshrine the 9th of *Av* for mourning and the 10th of *Tevet* as *Yom ha-Kaddish ha-Klali*, thus ensuring that the martyrs would be mourned in a most traditional manner. The secular, left wing parties, however, wanted to remember first and foremost the Warsaw Ghetto uprising, and appended the memory of other victims of the Holocaust to that act of de-

---

31 See Jacob J. Petuchowski, *Prayerbook Reform in Europe: The Liturgy of European Liberal and Reform Judaism* (New York: World Union for Progressive Judaism, 1968) especially pp. 116, 122. See also the joke cited here, http://onthemainline.blogspot.com/2010/01/minhag-jokes-and-their-historical.html (item 2).

32 See *Menaḥot* 29b; *Yerushalmi, Shekalim* 1:4, Rambam, *Hilkhot Ḥametz U-Matzah* 8:4, et al.

33 The necessity of visual contact between the one who blesses and the recipient is noted in several places in the Torah commentary of Rabbi Ovadiah Seforno, most prominently in his comment on *Bereshit* 48:10. See discussion in Elhanan Samet, *Studies in the Weekly Parasha* (Series 3) vol. 1 (Heb.) p. 245.

fiance as almost an afterthought.[34] As a result, though all Jewish communities do commemorate the victims of the Shoah, not all celebrate *Yom ha-Shoah*. Even among those that do, many desire a more traditional mode to commemorate the victims.

Therefore, we have crafted a service centered around the study of *Mishnayot*, which serves to bring about an *iluy neshamah* in the manner that classical sources recommend. Because it centers around the study of Torah, it may be used on any day of the year—except for Tisha be-Av—and may thus also be used in *Nissan*. Upon considering the *Nusaḥ* of the *E-l Malei Raḥamim* to use for the martyrs of the Holocaust and of Israel's wars, we have taken into consideration Rav Soloveitchik's insistence to not ever use the phrase "*ba'avur she-anu mispallelim ba'avuram*," as that would be an unseemly attempt to condition our prayers on a particular result, a practice frowned upon as a form of *iyun tefillah* (cf. *Berakhot* 55a).[35]

In recent years, a new Shoah Remembrance Day has come about: *Yom ha-Shiḥrur ve-ha-Hatzalah*. This remembrance day was the result of a partnership between Russian Jews, who are much more secular, the Conference of European Rabbis, which includes rabbis from the full spectrum of Orthodoxy but leans more ḥareidi, the Chief Rabbinate of Israel, and Jewish organizations all over the communal spectrum. This day has been established with the blessings of many ḥareidi *gedolim,* with the result that ḥareidim eagerly take part in these commemorations. Even though hareidim do still participate in official *Yom ha-Shoah* ceremonies too, it is with much more reluctance. In 2018, the Knesset enshrined in law *Yom ha-Shiḥrur ve-ha-Hatzalah* through the *Ḥok Yom ha-Shiḥrur ve-ha-Hatzalah mi-Germaniah ha-Natzit*. Though it is too early to tell, the rising rates of participation across the religious spectrum raises the real possibility that this will become a fixed part of the Jewish calendar. Our liturgy for Shoah remembrance fits every bit as well for this remembrance day as for *Yom ha-Shoah*.

For the prayers of *Yom ha-Atzma'ut*, we consulted with Rav Aharon Lichtenstein. One of us (AF) made the phone calls and had repeated conversations with him on this and other topics relating to the Siddur. Rav Aharon Lichtenstein was negatively disposed toward the official Rabbanut-sponsored *Yom ha-Atzma'ut* liturgy; for him, we ought to say

---

34 See Roni Stauber, הויכוח בשנות החמישים בין הציונות הדתית לבין השמאל הציוני, in מדינה בדרך : החברה הישראלית בעשורים הראשונים, עלמועד יום הזיכרון לשואה (Zalman Shazar Center for the History of the Jewish People, 2001).

35 See, e.g., *Nefesh Ha-Rav*, p. 143.

Hallel, each one according to his *poskim*, either with or without a *berakhah*, or thank God in a different way, but he didn't appreciate the special liturgy. However, he nonetheless instructed us to include that liturgy in the Siddur, out of respect for the Chief Rabbinate of Israel. Even so, he expressed a stronger disapproval of the inclusion of the few lines from *Lekhah Dodi*. In line with his recommendation, we included the full *Yom ha-Atzma'ut* liturgy in the Siddur, while noting that actual practices may differ.

Regarding *Yom ha-Atzma'ut*, we also consulted with Rav Hershel Schachter who reported that the Rav, who was an ardent supporter of Zionism and outlined in one of his most famous essays (*Kol Dodi Dofek*) how he understood the modern State of Israel religiously, was not fond of reciting *Hallel* on *Yom ha-Atzma'ut*. When the MTA high school turned to him with a request to find a way to integrate *Hallel* into *Shaḥarit* of *Yom ha-Atzma'ut*, he responded that they should recite it without a *berakhah* after *Kaddish Titkabel*. During a lengthy conversation that spanned many aspects of *Yom ha-Atzma'ut*, other modern observances, and other aspects of the Siddur, Rav Schachter expressed his approval for reciting *Hallel* (without a *berakhah*), but in the process also made an intriguing theoretical suggestion: shouldn't we consider the possibility of saying both *Hallel* and *Taḥanun*? He suggested that because (a) the Tur records a minority view of saying *Taḥanun* on Purim, and (b) we owe tremendous gratitude to God for having been given the opportunity to live through the establishment and continuing development of the State of Israel; yet on *Yom Ha-Atzma'ut* the state was proclaimed and war also broke out, and it is thus both a very happy day and a day on which great sacrifices were demanded of the People of Israel. He did not make that suggestion in the expectation that it would be adopted practically, but the suggestion is nonetheless very thought-provoking. In that, he—possibly unwittingly—echoed the Rav, who, in a private conversation told Rabbi David Holzer, "For my part you could say *Tahanun*. But *Tahanun* and *Hallel* are not mutually exclusive."[36] It should also be clear that there is no inkling of a doubt that we owe God tremendous gratitude for this incredible miracle that is the return to Zion and the establishment of the independent, sovereign State of Israel.

Both the Shoah Remembrance and *Yom ha-Atzma'ut/Yom Yerushalayim* services are bolstered by essays by leading thinkers with ex-

---

36 David Holzer, "*The Rav: Thinking Aloud, Transcripts of Personal Conversations with Rabbi Joseph B. Soloveitchik*," 2009, p. 210. See fn. 28 ibid. which limits the Rav's statement to a voluntary (*reshut*) *Hallel*.

pertise in Jewish history, Rabbi Jacob J. Schacter and Rabbi Dr. David Berger, to ensure that the *mispallel* understands not merely the content of the additional services, but also why the *gedolim* of our community considered it important that we specially mark these recent events.

As we stressed at the beginning of the present essay, the Siddur is filled with kabbalistic texts (all the *Lesheim Yiḥud* formulas, for starters) and texts whose meanings have been enriched by kabbalistic understandings. As a result, we sought the counsel of a great *talmid ḥakham* who is a notable kabbalist, Rav Yaakov Hillel. One of the issues we discussed with him was the *Seder Tu bi-Shvat*; his advice can also be seen as a general framework in these matters. The "official" *Seder Tu bi-Shvat* comes from a controversial *sefer* called *Ḥemdat Yamim*. Though the work is anonymous, some scholars believe that they have identified the author.[37] The *sefer* includes a poem by Nathan of Gaza, who was the "prophet" of Shabbetai Tzvi. The inclusion of such a poem obviously makes the whole *sefer* suspect. The question of the status of *Ḥemdat Yamim* has implications not just for *Seder Tu bi-Shvat*, since it is from there that the *Ḥayei Adam* had copied *Tefillah Zakah* (which one reviewer had suggested we include) and made it popular.[38] (Indeed, since making this discovery, I [AF] have switched to reciting on *erev* Yom Kippur the *Vidui* of Rabbenu Nissim, instead, and add a *Nusaḥ* that represents one of the passages that the *poskim* found particularly important in *Tefillah Zakah*, namely where the penitent proclaims that he forgives all those who wronged him for any wrong for which he doesn't plan to seek redress in *beit din*).

We asked Rav Yaakov Hillel what he thought of *Seder Tu bi-Shvat*. His response was that (a) it is quite popular, especially among Moroccan Sepharadim; (b) nonetheless, "הצנועים מושכים את ידיהם כי אומרים שמחברו היה מאותו הכת", those who are scrupulous abstain from using that text, since it is suspected that the author was a Sabbatean; (c) he was, howev-

---

37 See Alan Brill, "Tu bShvat Seder—with Text," 2010, accessed May 30 2019 at https://kavvanah.wordpress.com/2010/01/25/tu-bshevat-seder-with-text/.

38 See "Tefillah Zakah: History of a Controversial Prayer," 2007. Accessed May 30th, 2019 at https://seforimblog.com/2007/09/teffilah-zakah-history-of-controversia/. One could argue that the inclusion of *L-David Hashem Ori* (Psalm 27) from *Rosh Ḥodesh Elul* until Simhat Torah should be struck from the Siddur on similar grounds. However, this practice has gained widespread acceptance in Ashkenazi communities. Also, it seems that the practice predates *Ḥemdat Yamim* by several years, as it appears in *Sefer Shem Tov Katan* (1706), *Sefer Zekhirah* (1709) and *Sefer HaMussar* (1724), which predate *Hemdat Yamim* (1731). See discussion in *Pardes Eliezer*, Rosh Hashanah, pp. 104-107.

er, supportive of the notion of a *Seder Tu bi-Shvat*, which fits right in to the whole genre of *tikkunim* (of which only the *Tikkun Leil Shavuot* and to a lesser extent the *Tikkun* of Hoshanah Rabbah and for the evening before a *brit* enjoy any significant enduring popularity). Therefore, he suggested crafting our own text based primarily on the Ramḥal's *Ma'amar Eitz ha-Sadeh*. The conclusion is obvious: the idea is good, but when a text is problematic, exchange it for a text with a better pedigree, for instance a text by Ramḥal. Such a text was to have appeared on the Siddur's supplemental website and may instead feature in an upcoming companion volume.

Texts that have "fallen out" of the Siddur are restored. Where recent Siddurim have purged the text of "extra" personal supplications to streamline the prayer experience, we return them so as to facilitate personal investment in prayer. *Gott fun Avrohom,* the most famous of all Yiddish *Teḥinot*—recited ubiquitously by our grandmothers in Eastern Europe but absent from other Koren Siddurim—is reinstated; and a section of *Teḥinot* for women is provided in translation to Hebrew, fittingly restoring to contemporary women a genre of self-expression in prayer that was innovated for them and by them centuries ago. While we were at it, we provided a Siddur in which women could find themselves as much at home as men, by supplying in-text female variants when appropriate, accounting for realities such as female heads of household, and providing for such halakhic options as women's *zimun* and *birkat ha-gomel*, all with the encouragement and assent of our *poskim*.

In the commentary and essays, we turned to Rav Soloveitchik more than any other contemporary figure not merely because of the Siddur's RCA pedigree—indeed, he was intimately involved behind the scenes in every aspect of that organization's endeavors,[39] and was the *rebbi* or grand-*rebbi* of the lion's share of its members—but because, as Lawrence Kaplan writes:

> Soloveitchik's writings on the nature of halakhah and the personality of halakhic man are endowed with a special, almost unique, authority, not shared by any other of the works in the modern era on these subjects. For Soloveitchik, alone among the leading Jewish thinkers in the modern era to have written on the philosophy of halakhah, was both a rabbinic figure of the first rank… and a creative theologian and philosopher who mastered the Western tradition of philosophical and scientific thought and was thus able to

39 See Louis Bernstein, "Challenge *and Mission: The Emergence of the English-Speaking Orthodox Rabbinate,"* (New York: Shengold Publishers, 1982).

write about the halakhah in universal philosophical and phenomenological categories.[40]

Since the target audience of this Siddur is one that is intellectually sophisticated and versed in the Western tradition of philosophical and scientific thought, and Rav Soloveitchik has left a significant corpus, and had a particular interest in, and devoted several major works to, *tefillah*, it was natural that his thought be overrepresented in our Siddur. Arguably, there are others who wore both hats of rabbinic leadership and mastery of the Western tradition whose oeuvre has grown quite a bit since the Siddur commentary was completed circa 2010, and future Siddurim would likely incorporate more thinkers such as Rav Aharon Lichtenstein and Rav Shimon Gershon Rosenberg (Shagar). As for halakhic instructions, some of the practices of Rav Soloveitchik have taken root in Yeshiva University and a plurality of Modern and Centrist Orthodox congregations, and it was felt appropriate to validate the diversity of practice in our target congregations.

On the theme of diversity, aside from Rav Soloveitchik, Rav Kook, Rav Lichtenstein, *ybl"ḥ* Rav Nachum Rabinovitch, and other luminaries of the centrist Orthodox/religious Zionist community, the commentary provides space for *gedolim* of the modern period who are typically assigned to other religious communities and are not often in the consciousness of the Siddur's target audience—Rav Chaim Kanievsky *ybl"ḥ*, as well as Rabbi Shmuel HaLevi Wosner, Rabbi Ovadia Yosef, Rabbi Ḥayim David HaLevi, and the Lubavitcher Rebbe. This is a marked departure from the prior edition of the RCA Siddur, which in the main presented insights from greats associated with the religious community of its editors.

Apart from inspiration, the commentary finds meaning that is often overlooked. Knowledge of Tanakh alerts us to prayer passages that incorporate snippets of *pesukim* as shorthand for profound ideas. In the very first passage, the presence of *rabbah emunatekha* in *Modeh Ani* calls attention to its source in *Eikhah*, the turning point at which the lamenting *gever* recognizes that despite the horrors he has endured, God's mercies are still in place—because Jews continue to wake up in the morning. We were fortunate to have access to the foremost minds in what may be

---

40 Lawrence Kaplan, "Joseph Soloveitchik and Halakhic Man," in Michael L Morgan, and Peter Eli Gordon, eds. *The Cambridge Companion to Modern Jewish Philosophy* (Cambridge: Cambridge University Press, 2007) p. 210.

termed the Literary School of Orthodox Jewish Tanakh study[41] as well as a direct line to religiously committed academic scholars with expertise in Jewish history, grammar and philosophy. The historical backdrops for various prayers and the concealed polemical messages are brought into full relief. Texts outside the canon like Ben Sira and archaeological findings that shed light on or appear to challenge our texts are discussed—Ancient Near East literature is mustered to help understand words like *totefes*, *ahavah* and *emunah*, and the special significance of the *brit* meal; the makeup of *ketoret* and *tekheilet* is helped by archaeology, and conversely, the mystery of the Dead Sea scroll "nun" verse for *Ashrei* is explained, and the most likely explanation reasonably vindicates our *Mesorah*. Scientific matters and identification of flora and fauna were assisted by Rabbi Dr. Natan Slifkin, who has special expertise in, and curates a museum for, Biblical Natural History. At the very same time, the broad tent of the RCA afforded us access to ḥasidic scholars and even *mekubalim* who helped us fully explicate kabbalistic prayers and avoid any obscurantism in our commentaries. The motto of the commentary was *karov Hashem lekhol kor'av, l-khol asher yikra'uhu b-emet.*

The astute reader would do well to compare the new Siddur's commentary with that of the previous RCA Siddur. Since much of the commentary was initially prepared when the Siddur was set to appear under its previous publisher, many of the "*diburei ha-maskhil*" (*sub verbis*) were retained, but the understandings are sometimes completely at variance, based on new (or newly considered) evidence. Matters of concordance had been retained in the first iteration of the new Siddur's commentary, and after change of publisher, were removed and replaced for copyright purposes.

Aside from restored prayers, the Siddur serves as a *mekitz nirdamim* in another aspect—the basis of the (heavily updated) translation is the elegant masterpiece by David de Sola Pool, perhaps the leading twentieth-century Sepharadic Rav in the United States, a true *gavra rabbah* described in the following terms by his successor: "If ever the American Jewish community could boast of an extraordinary rabbi who combined the talents of a congregational rabbi, the social activism of a genuine idealist, the eloquent advocacy of a Zionist partisan and the calm, deep writings of a fine scholar—that rabbi was David de Sola Pool. That this rabbi was Orthodox made him more unique. That this rabbi was Se-

41 See Yaakov Beasley, "Review Essay: Return of the Pashtanim," *Tradition* 42:1. (New York: Spring 2009) pp. 67-83.

phardic made him absolutely unique for his time and place."[42] Unfortunately, delays in publication meant that his work was superseded by Philip Birnbaum's, and the Siddur never saw the success it deserved.[43] Along with de Sola Pool's prose were brilliant poetic "free-form" translations of hymns by himself and his great-grandfather David Aaron de Sola and Rabbi Yosef Marcus, along with those of literary luminaries such as Israel Zangwill, Nina Salaman and Elsie Davis, which had previously appeared a few decades prior (in a series of British translated Maḥzorim co-edited by Chief Rabbi Hermann Adler's nephew).

Our greatest frustration in the Siddur's publication has been the hundreds of pages of quality material—essays, commentary, *yotzerot*—that had to be cut so that the Siddur could remain one portable volume. With the gracious consent of *Hakirah*, we present two essays that we wish could have been included—one on the kabbalistic schema of prayer which informs many passages in the Siddur, subject matter which is treated in a more general (and lyrical) manner in Rabbi Lamm's essay on ḥasidic perspectives on prayer; and one on *Nusaḥ ha-Tefilah*, in collaboration with an expert ḥazzan, which needed to be removed when one of our community's foremost *gedolim* asked to address the same topic, albeit, again, in a more general (and halakhically rigorous) way. We present them here for the readership of *Ḥakirah*. ☙

---

42 Rabbi Marc Angel at https://www.jewishideas.org/article/rabbi-dr-david-de-sola-pool-sephardic-visionary-and-activist, accessed May 15, 2019.

43 The Siddur's erstwhile competitor's review unfairly accusing Rabbi de Sola Pool of Christological influence did not help much, either. See Paltiel Birnbaum, "Siddur Ḥadash Ba La-Medinah," *Hadoar*, 2 Kislev, 5721, p. 85 and rebuttal by Chaim Dov Chavel, "Teshuvat Histadrut Ha-Rabanim De'Amerika," *Hadoar,* 2 Kislev, 5721, pp. 87–89. See the comprehensive treatment in Jonathan Krasner, "American Jews in Text and Context: Jacob Behrman and the Rise of a Publishing Dynasty," *Images* 7 (Leiden: 2015) especially pp. 74-77.

Appendix A

Nusah ha-Tefilah as Commentary: The Ashkenazic Liturgical music-Tradition as a Key to Unlocking Meaning in the Siddur

By: ATON M. HOLZER, ARIE FOLGER and BERNARD BEER

> Our Rabbis taught: When a man prays, he should direct his heart to heaven. Abba Shaul says: This is hinted in the verse (Psalms 10:17), "You will direct their heart, You will cause Your ear to attend." (*Berakhot* 31a)

Based on this Talmudic dictum, *halakhah* codifies the requirement to pray with *kavanah*, intent for and awareness of prayer. Rabbi Ḥayyim Soloveitchik of Brisk identifies several strata regarding the *kavanah* desideratum; the worshiper should understand the words of prayer, but the worshiper also has a more basic obligation—to be aware, in prayer, that he or she is standing before God (*Novellae on Maimonides' Mishneh Torah*, 4:1).

Nusaḥ ha-Tefilah, the liturgical music-tradition, masterfully uses melody to conjure up both sorts of *kavanah* in at least three ways.

First, its musical "modes" augment the content of the prayer. The modes evoke the diverse manners in which the Divine is encountered in different parts of prayer.

Second, its special melodies evoke a mood congruent with the particular day which is observed, evincing past experiences of standing before God on these special days.

Third, *Nusaḥ* highlights parallel content and themes between different prayers—drawing attention and imparting meaning to the words recited—by importing musical cues and moods to other contexts.

Musical Modes

The first goal is accomplished by use of modes[44]—musical scales in which the particular prayer is rendered. Some of these derive from already familiar contexts. For example:

---

44 For a survey of the history of, and literature on, the modes, or *shtaygers*, see Max Wohlberg, "The History of the Musical Modes of the Ashkenazic Synagogue and Their Usage," *Journal of Synagogue Music* 4 (1972) 1-2, 46-61.

- The *Shabbat* and Festival *Pesukei De-Zimrah*. This service includes the regular, weekday *Pesukei De-Zimrah*, supplemented with additional texts, to exalt God in song and praise on these days of heightened spiritual perception. This longer *Pesukei De-Zimrah* is rendered in a mode derived very closely from the traditional cantillation of the *Song of the Sea*—the Biblical epitome of a song of triumphant exaltation.
- *Minḥah* on *Shabbat* afternoon—whose *Amidah* text, *Atah Eḥad*, evokes the Messianic era, the ultimate fulfillment of Divine prophecies—appropriately uses a melody crafted from the traditional chant of the *Haftarah*, selections from the Prophets in which the descriptions of this glorious future appear.
- The traditional chant used for Jewish Torah study—recognizable to any contemporary visitor to a *Beit Midrash*—is applied to the familiar parent-child question-answer "study session" on Seder night, namely *Mah Nishtanah*, and also to the daily morning blessings, which contain the blessings over Torah study and Torah passages, and the *Korbanot* section that follows, as well. This melody emphasizes the "Torah study" theme, under whose rubric all of these practices are subsumed.

Other prayers are rendered in one of six original modes, chosen to reflect the tenor of their content. Some examples:

- *Kabalat Shabbat*, the "welcoming" of *Shabbat*, and the Friday evening *Kiddush* both celebrate the manifestation of Divine Sovereignty. They are therefore sung according to a majestic mode, borrowed from the coronation-like ceremony declaring God's majesty (*"Adoshem Malakh"*) at the removal of the Torahs from the ark.
- The *Ahavah Rabah* blessing, which includes a plea that God enlighten us in His Torah and also return us to our land, is appropriately rendered in a deeply emotive mode that is shared with the *Avinu Malkenu* supplications of the High Holidays.
- In the *Lekhah Dodi* hymn, there is no set melody,[45] but the chosen tune is tightly bound to content. As such, it is actually altered in the middle of the poem—from a more plaintive melody

45 Indeed, foremost Jewish musicologist Abraham Zvi Idelsohn estimated, in 1929 (!), that *two thousand* melodies have been composed for the *Lekha Dodi* text. See Abraham Z. Idelsohn, "Jewish *Music in Its Historical* Development" (New York: Schocken, 1929), p. 116.

reflecting the text's description of yearning from the depths of exile, to a joyous melody celebrating the arrival of redemption, as described in the stanzas that begin with *Lo Tevoshi* and continue through the end of the passage.[46]

Melodic Moods

The second goal of *Nusaḥ*—to use special melodies to coax the worshiper into a mood appropriate for the particular setting—is accomplished by the use of fixed melodies for particular times of year. The High Holidays, the three Festivals, *Shabbat* and weekdays each have unique musical signatures immediately recognizable to the regular synagogue visitor. These tunes evoke past spiritual experiences for the worshiper, and serve the purpose of the second form of *kavanah* mentioned above—the awareness of standing before God, in the particular manner in which He manifests to us in different times of year.

- The tone is set by *Barekhu*, the formal call to prayer, which is rendered in a different melody for each prayer service and time of year. Both in *Shaḥarit* and *Ma'ariv*, the tune of *Barekhu* defines the "flavor" of the coming passage.
- Similarly, there are no less than fourteen different widely used settings for the *Kaddish*, and each is used for a different occasion—to provide a moment for the worshiper to meditate prior to the coming section in a manner congruent with the mood of the moment.

Among these melodies, there are some which are invariant among most Ashkenazi communities. These melodies are known as "*Skarbove*" (Polish for "treasure") or "*Mi-sinai*"[47] *Nigunim*, which embody a corpus

---

46 The practice described appears to be of ḥasidic origin. Ḥazzan Bernard Beer suggests that the choice of *Lo Tevoshi* for this transition derives from the verse *ve-nivneta ir al tila*, "and the city will be built upon its mound," the rebuilding of Jerusalem, the anticipated climax of the (non-mystical read of) the poem. The Frankfurt Am-Main community and its descendants change the tune at the prior stanza of *Hit'oreri*, the numerical and thematic pivot of the poem, and would return to the prior tune for the final stanza of *Bo'i be-Shalom*. There is considerable mystery surrounding the origins of these practices.
See a discussion by Rabbi Ari Enkin at http://hirhurim.blogspot.com/2010/01/lecha-dodichanging-tune.html, accessed March 26, 2019.

47 This term has its origins in the context of Biblical cantillation, in Rabbi Judah He-Ḥasid's *Sefer Ḥasidim*, ch. 302.

of "holy tunes" that set specific atmosphere and solemnity of the holiday or occasion. Rabbi Jacob Mölin, a key figure in the preservation of Ashkenazic rites in the 15th century, argued that these tunes have particular halakhic significance and they must not be changed.[48] Most of these are among the universally familiar High Holiday melodies, but they also encompass a few others.

Meaningful Motifs

These two musical features create a musical landscape of Jewish prayer: the modes define the terrain while fixed melodies comprise its unique features. This scenery lays the groundwork for the third aspect of *Nusah*: subtle "cross-references" within the fabric of prayer. Motifs, "musical quotes," are borrowed from one context, sometimes in mid-prayer, to beautifully evoke the emotion within a particular phrase.

Sometimes **melodies** are borrowed. For example: the plaintive cry in the Festival *Musaf Amidah* that God restore the Temple, *Bnei Veitkha ke-vateḥila*, is rendered in the tune of *Eli Tziyon*, a major elegy of Tisha be-Av, the day of great mourning for the destroyed Temple. The borrowed tune stirs up a nostalgic longing even in the midst of the Festival celebration.

Other times, entire **themes** are transposed. The prayers for dew on Pesaḥ and rain on Sukkot evoke Divine judgment in the midst of Festivals; will water be plentiful in the coming agricultural season? Hence, these prayers are rendered in a melody derived closely from that of the High Holidays, which are the Days of Judgment.

Shared melodies and modes also draw our attention to parallel prayer sections: the weekday *Amidah* and the blessings after the *Haftarah*, for example, whose blessings resemble each other. The opening three blessings in the *Amidah* and the first blessing following the *Haftarah* embody fundamental belief in God. The fourteenth and fifteenth blessings in the *Amidah*, like the second and third blessings of the *Haftarah*, speak of God as Builder of Jerusalem, Who will restore Zion and the House of David (*Bone Yerushalayim* and *Matzmiaḥ Keren Yeshu'av*). The eighteenth blessing (*Modim Anakhnu Lakh*), and traditionally (*Berakhot* 34a), the latter three benedictions of the *Amidah*, like the last of the *Haftarah* blessings, are organized around the theme of thanksgiving.

---

48 *Sefer Maharil, Hilkhot Yom Kipur*, paragraph s.v. *yotzer.*

At times, the melodies may point to a forgotten aspect regarding the origin of a particular prayer, such as the hint of the Festival theme at the end of the Friday night *Va-yekhulu* service (cf. *Tosafot Pesaḥim* 106a).

Borrowed melodies also provide cues to the worshiper. For example, the end of *Kaddish* before *Musaf* on *Rosh Ḥodesh* or *Ḥol ha-Mo'ed* is rendered in the melody of the *Rosh Ḥodesh* and Festival *Musaf Amidah* prayer, to cue the worshiper regarding the upcoming prayer text.

The Place of Congregational Singing

While the musical *Nusaḥ* tradition dictates the use of certain tunes and puts constraints on what kind of other tunes may or may not be used in the synagogue services, it does not prohibit all innovation. Indeed, where appropriate, many new tunes have been incorporated within the corpus of this musical tradition. The Young Israel movement in particular has been noted for its introduction of congregational melodies, nineteenth-century European compositions by Louis Lewandowsky, Solomon Sulzer and others that are usually derivatives of motifs of the original *Nusaḥ*, or that fits prayers that did not previously have a set *Nusaḥ*. More recently, *Nusaḥ*-congruent *Nigunim* of Rabbi Shlomo Carlebach have become a fixture in American synagogues. The litmus test on whether new melodies are fit for the synagogue is whether or not they fulfill the above objectives—the goals of the musical *Nusaḥ* tradition.

Appendix B

Basic Notions in Kabbalah Which Undergird Aspects of the Siddur[49]

By: ARIE FOLGER and ATON HOLZER

Prayer is, by its very nature, a mysterious practice. How else can one explain how the infinite God has given us permission to address Him and to be heard by Him? In prayer, we break out of our finite, limited material existence; we rise above our bodily limitations to reach for the Infinite, to be touched by the Eternal. As such, the Siddur is filled with mystical secrets of generations of our sages.

Despite the Siddur's inherently mystical core, it has always been intended for a broad audience, for the entire people of Israel. Therefore, its mystical allusions are for the most part hidden, to be uncovered only by the most dedicated student. This is however—exceptionally—not true of the prayers authored by the kabbalists of 16th-century Safed, particularly *Arizal* (Rabbi Isaac Luria Ashkenazi, 1534-1572) and their successors. As a group, they have left their mark on the Siddur not merely through the incorporation of kabbalistic prayers,[50] but also by coloring the way in which other prayers, and indeed, the act of prayer as a whole, is understood. Through their teachings, ideas that had previously been restricted to Torah scholars immersing themselves in the study of *Zohar* and other esoteric teachings suddenly became broadly known, systematically explained, and disseminated throughout the Jewish world.

To fully understand and appreciate these prayers, as well as the many kabbalistically-oriented commentaries on the Siddur, it is necessary to be acquainted with certain major concepts promulgated by the *Arizal* regarding prayer.

---

49 We are indebted to Rabbi Yaakov Leib Altein and the scholars of *Ḥassidut Mevueret* for the Hebrew commentary piece upon which this essay is based. We thank Rabbi Ephraim Goldstein for reviewing several drafts of this essay, and Rabbi Yaakov Hillel for his input regarding some of the topics covered here.

50 Most notably *Lesheim Yiḥud*, *Berikh Shemei* and *Ana Be-Khoah*. It should be noted that despite their inclusion in most siddurim, the recitation of such prayers is not without controversy. Indeed, some communities, particularly those with origins in Western Europe, continue to abstain from the recitation of most of these texts. Of all kabbalistic prayers, only *Lekha Dodi* was accepted for popular use by virtually all communities.

In lieu of a comprehensive presentation of the subject, we present mainly a view of the kabbalistic understanding of *tefillah* through the lens of Rabbi Schneur Zalman of Liadi (1745-1812), the founder of the Habad hasidic dynasty. He was also an important influence on the kabbalistic thought of Rabbi Abraham Isaac Hakohen Kook and Rabbi Joseph B. Soloveitchik. What follows is based upon the recently published, outstanding multi-volume *Ḥassidut Mevueret* commentary on selections from Rabbi Schneur Zalman's hasidic discourses on the Torah portion, primarily *Torah Or* and *Likutei Torah*.[51] The explorations of the *Lekhah Dodi* hymn, however, draw upon additional sources, as indicated, though those explorations do fit within the kabbalistic understanding of Rabbi Schneur Zalman who writes:

> Prayer may be conceptualized as a ladder—more specifically, the ladder visualized in Jacob's dream (cf. Genesis 28:12), which was set on the ground, but reached into the heavens. Just like an ordinary ladder, this ladder, too, serves both to ascend and descend upon it (*Zohar I Vayetse*). Prayer serves the same purpose; through prayer, the soul ascends step by step from the ground to the highest heights... The notion of descending a ladder, too, manifests itself in prayer. After the soul has ascended the pinnacle, the most elevated levels, and reached what may be called the Divine Will, the soul will then be clothed in this Divine Will and thereby bring down blessing. This is the meaning of "And behold, the angels of the Almighty ascend and descend on Jacob's ladder," for on the ladder one both ascends and descends.[52]

I. Four Worlds

Rabbi Shneur Zalman's description of the ascent and descent of the soul is based upon *Arizal*'s understanding of the prayer service. Jacob's ladder is said to have had four rungs, which, in the *Zohar*, corresponds to four overlapping and interlocking spiritual realms to which the human soul can ascend. These are:

---

51 Our treatment of the subject matter is based on an unpublished essay made privately available by the team of *Ḥassidut Mevueret* to the present authors, which was mostly culled from throughout their work, in particular volume 3 (*Shabbat*), (Boro Park: Heichel Menachem, 2006) pp. 186-188, and volume 1 (*Mo'adim* vol. 1), pp. 399-402. A separate volume also exists on prayer (vol. 4).

52 *Torah Or*, *Va-yaqhel*, s.v. *Va-yaqhel Moshe*, p. 88.

- *asiyah* ("completion"), the spiritual within the ordinary physical world we inhabit and the lowest realm of Divine emanation;
- *yetzirah* ("formation"), the angelic realm;
- *beriyah* ("creation"), the realm of the souls and the Divine throne;
- and finally, *atzilut* ("emanation"), the realm where Divine Unity becomes apparent. Elsewhere, we can only sense traces of God's presence, but *atzilut* is the realm of encounter between God and man.[53]

The four realms are reflected in the following typology of the human soul: (1) The *nefesh* is the lowest element of the soul and is symbolized by the digestive organs. It exists in both man and beast and controls instinctive behavior. (2) The *ruaḥ*, or "spirit," is symbolized by the heart and lungs, and is the seat of our emotions. (3) The *neshamah*, or "breath," is symbolized by the brain, and it is the source of our intellectual and spiritual activity. Finally, (4) the *ḥayah*, or "life-force," represents our potential, what our soul can become. Likewise, when we reach for the realm of *atzilut* in prayer, we tap into limitless potentiality.

To ascend this ladder, we must sanctify ourselves. More specifically, we must sanctify our speech and our actions by engaging in both prayer and holy deeds. *Arizal* (*P'ri Etz Ḥayyim, Sha'ar Ha-Tefillah,* ch. 1) identifies certain prayers that should elevate our speech, and corresponding sacred actions that should sanctify our deeds. Thus, when we awaken there are four actions (relieving oneself/washing one's hands, putting on *tzitzit*—both small and the large *tallit,* wearing the arm-*tefillin,* and wearing the head-*tefillin*)[54] that respectively correspond to four rungs of the ladder. Likewise, the *Shaḥarit* service itself consists of four ascending sections (*Korbanot, Pesukei De-Zimrah*, the *Shema* with its blessings, and the *Amidah*) followed by descending sections that bring one back down to the world of *asiyah* at the end of the service. Through this system,

---

53 In Lurianic Kabbalah, an infinite number of further realms are said to exist, which lie (mostly) beyond human comprehension. The realm that is most immediately above *atzilut* is known as *adam qadmon*, "primordial homunculus." This fifth realm corresponds to the fifth aspect of the human soul, the *yeḥidah*, or "singularity," the unitive spirit of existence that lies beyond the reaches of our potential. The *mezuzah* is said to adorn the *yeḥidah*. Realms below *asiyah* also exist, known as *qelipot*, to which we should take care not to descend.

54 Or, among those who have the custom of donning the two types of *tefillin*, "*Rashi*" and "*Rabbenu Tam*" *tefillin*, the third and fourth actions are donning the *Rashi* and the *Rabbenu Tam* pair, respectively.

kabbalists made sense out of the prayer service as it has crystallized over the ages.

In addition, a number of prayers and practices were especially incorporated in the Siddur as an aid for meditatively transitioning between these realms. Examples include:

- *Ana Be-Khoaḥ* initiates the transition out of the lowest spiritual realm of *asiyah*, during the morning service.
- There is a custom to hold on to fringes of the *tallit* or *tzitzit* while reciting *Barukh She-Amar*, as we enter the second realm, of *beriyah*, which is also symbolized by the *tzitzit*.
- The kabbalists see most *kaddeishim* as special prayers for completing the transition between realms, such as, for example, a *Kaddish* recited between *korbanot* and the *Pesukei De-Zimrah*. However, in the Sepharadic tradition, as well as in the hasidic *Nusaḥ Sepharad*, *Hodu* is recited before *Barukh She-Amar*, and seen as a continuation of *korbanot*. As there is no *Kaddish* after *Hodu*, for them, Psalm 30 assumes the role of transition prayer. In the Ashkenazic rite, on the other hand, Psalm 30 does not need to fill this role.

Prayer enables man to cleave to God; its purpose is to allow man to "ascend" to God. Through the four stages of prayer, which are the rungs on the "ladder of prayer," the worshiper ascends from one spiritual level to the next. By the time the worshiper has progressed in his prayer to the recitation of the *Amidah*, he or she should feel that he is standing before his or her Master (*Shabbat* 10a). Indeed, the particular laws as to how one should present oneself during the *Amidah* follow from the expectation that the worshiper experiences the sense of standing before the Supreme King (*Shulḥan Arukh OḤ* 95, 98, 104).

II. Ten *Sefirot*

The early kabbalistic notion of ten *Sefirot*[55] represents the faculties through which God acts and thus reveals Himself in the world. Divine blessing comes about and is transmitted by way of the *Sefirot*. The ten *Sefirot* divide into three upper *Sefirot*—*Keter* ("crown," the Divine will),

---

55 The word *Sefirot* is commonly either translated as spheres or as enumerations. The latter is championed, for example, by the Gaon of Vilna. See *Orot ha-Gra*, (Benei Beraq 5746) p. 208. In its origin in *Sefer Yetzirah*, the term refers to the digits in the base-ten (decimal) system (see *Sefer Yetzirah* ch. 1).

Ḥokhmah ("wisdom") and *Binah* ("insight")—and seven lower *Sefirot,* which are attributes of action, respectively.

The individual *Sefirot* are rarely mentioned explicitly in the Siddur. They figure most prominently in the kabbalistic *Ribono Shel Olam* prayer printed at the conclusion of the Counting of the *Omer*, and in the kabbalistic *Ushpizin* prayer recited when entering the *Sukkah.* They are also quite clearly alluded to in the *Lekhah Dodi* and *Arizal*'s *zemirot* for each of the *Shabbat* meals: *Askinu Seudata* in its four versions for the three *Shabbat* meals plus *Melava de-Malka,* as well as *Azamer Bi-Shvaḥin, Asader Li-Se'udata* and *Benei Heikhalah.* In the latter, they appear in the context of five or six *Partsufim* ("faces")—overlapping arrays of Sefirotic configurations that roughly correspond to the Worlds—which figure prominently in the *Zohar.*

Most often, the *Sefirot* are mentioned in prayers through the lens of *dekhar ve-nukvah,* the masculine and feminine metaphor.

III. Masculine and Feminine

Spiritual awakening in the service of God results from human initiative on the one hand, and from Divine inspiration on the other. The human initiative to draw oneself toward God, particularly in prayer, is termed by *Arizal* as *the raising up of the female waters* (*ha'alat mayin nuqvin*), while the corresponding awakening initiated by Divine inspiration is called *the drawing down of the male waters* (*hamshakhat mayin dukhrin*). In this context, "male" and "female" are metaphors for the Giver of Divine bounty and its recipient, respectively. The metaphor employed draws, specifically, on the biology of the male and female roles in human reproduction. While some might prefer to avoid such gender associations, kabbalistic prayers cannot be understood without exploring this ancient paradigm.

Every "male" Divine initiative is commensurate with the human "female" awakening: while God desires to fill us with His blessing, we can only receive it to the extent that we have made ourselves into receptacles for Divine bounty. We become such receptacles by overcoming our ego and self-centeredness, to the point where we desire nothing but the fulfillment of God's will. This is the meditative backdrop of the prayer service.

While generally the "male" represents God and the "female" the Congregation of Israel or the individual Jew, the same imagery is used to describe the various stations of Divine bounty as it is "handled" by the *Sefirot* (see above) and as it traverses the four spiritual worlds. This "male" and "female" imagery may represent any two consecutive *Sefirot,* any two-way stations in the spiritual worlds or relate to several such relationships at once. The use of bride and groom imagery in *Lekhah Dodi* is to be understood in the same way: bride and groom, or male and female, represent multiple relationships by which Israel benefits from God's blessing.[56]

Lekhah Dodi also distinguishes itself through other remarkable features. It is almost entirely composed of scriptural, Midrashic, and Talmudic phrases. At first sight, those phrases seem to convey a simple, literal meaning. Upon investigation, however, the stanzas, which are each formed by several such phrases, are difficult to read literally.[57] Furthermore, they have often been significantly altered from their original forms, beyond that which is needed to fit the rhyme scheme. In reality, the stanzas only make sense—and the author's intent only becomes apparent—upon uncovering the multiple kabbalistic teachings he packed into the brief stanzas. The literal understanding of those phrases merely forms a thin non-mystical veneer, whereas the author only intended the song to be understood in its manifold kabbalistic dimensions.[58]

For instance, in its second stanza, the words *shamor ve-zakhor be-dibbur eḥad—"safeguard and remember"*—in a single utterance is a paraphrase of a rabbinic commentary in the Talmud (*Shavu'ot* 20b), but with a twist. There are two accounts of the Ten Commandments in the Torah (Exodus 20 and Deuteronomy 5), with slight differences between them. For example, in Exodus, we are enjoined to *remember the Sabbath day* (*zakhor*), while in Deuteronomy, we are to *safeguard it* (*shamor*). The Sages explain that both versions are correct, for God caused Israel to simultaneously hear the two complementary aspects of the *Shabbat* commandment, which the Talmud captures in the brief phrase, *Remember and safeguard were said in a single utterance.* In the present stanza, however, the order of the terms is reversed, with *safeguard* ahead of *remember.* Rabbi Shlomo Alkavetz, the author of *Lekhah Dodi*, did so not only to spell his name with the acrostic formed by the first eight stanzas, but primarily in order to allude to the following kabbalistic teaching.

The onset of *Shabbat* distinguishes itself from other times during the week, for usually, we must first reach up (*ha'alat mayin nuqvin*), before triggering a commensurate awakening of the Divine bounty. On Friday evening, however, God initiates the spiritual "love" relationship and

56 For more on this, see Rabbi Norman Lamm, "The Unity Theme and Its Implication for Moderns," *Tradition* vol. 4:1, Fall 1961, especially pp. 51-54.

57 For an extensive analysis of *Lekha Dodi,* particularly its mystical nature, see Reuven Kimmelman's monograph, *Lekha Dodi ve-Kabbalat Shabbat, Ha-Mashma'ut Ha-Mistit,* (Jerusalem: Magnes Press, 2003).

58 Ibid. p. 33.

spontaneously bestows His blessing upon the earth (*hamshakhat mayin dukhrin*). This initial passivity on our part is conveyed by the verb *shamor*, *safeguard*, which connotes passive attention. On *Shabbat* morning, it is our duty to actively re-initiate this relationship, which is conveyed by the verb *remember*, which conveys a more active role. Hence, the stanza puts *safeguard*, the service of Friday evening, ahead of *remember*, the service of *Shabbat* morning (*Maor va-Shamesh,* Deuteronomy 5:12).[59]

A second example, which also perfectly demonstrates the presence of multiple mystical teachings packed into a single brief phrase, occurs in the middle of *Lekhah Dodi*, in the fifth stanza: *livshi bigdei tifarteikh, ami—Put on your splendid clothes, My people.* On the surface, the *splendid clothes* refer to the priestly garments, and indeed, the conjunction of *clothes* with *splendor* occurs in Exodus 28:2. The nation of Israel, *My people*, is called upon to dress in priestly garments. However, *Tiferet* ("Splendor") is also the name of one of the lower *Sefirot,* the "middle" *Sefirah* which often is used to represent the six intermediate *Sefirot.* Instead of referring only to the nation of Israel, *ami*, *My people,* also, and primarily, refers to another *Sefirah*: the ultimate *Sefirah*, *Malkhut* ("Majesty"), also known as the *Shekhinah*. *Tiferet* is the paradigmatic "male," benefactor *Sefirah*, while *Malkhut* is the paradigmatic "female," recipient *Sefirah*. Their union, called *yiḥud* or *zivug* (see below), represents the bridging of the final waystation as God bestows His bountiful blessing on earth, and symbolizes the palpable Divine presence in the world. Thus, in this stanza, the *Shekhinah* is urged to cloak itself with "garments of splendor," i.e., to unite with *Tiferet*, which has reached out to her on *Shabbat*. Likewise, the worshipers, who are dressed in their *Shabbat* finery, are drawn toward God as He bestows His blessing upon them. *My people* thus refers both to the Divine Presence and to the Congregation of Israel, at once.[60]

Alternatively, it is not *My people* that is being exhorted to dress in fineries. Rather, as in the original verse in Isaiah 52:1, so, too in its paraphrase in the present stanza, the exhortation addresses Jerusalem and the Temple, the subjects of the previous stanza.[61] In this understanding, *My people* is not the subject of dressing, but rather its object, for the People of Israel and the splendid clothes are one and the same; as the people return to Jerusalem, she "cloaks" herself in them. Likewise, in *Lek-*

---

59 Ibid. pp. 36-42.

60 Ibid. ch. 5.

61 *Siddur Otzar ha-Tefillot, Iyun Tefillah* ad loc. See also Rabbi Marc B. Shapiro's blog post, *Taliban Women and More*, accessible at http://seforim.blogspot.com/2012/06/taliban-women-and-more.html, where he cites additional sources that make the same point.

hah Dodi, Jerusalem, as the seat of Divine sovereignty on earth, symbolizes the *Sefirah* of *Malkhut*, which cloaks herself at once in *Tiferet*, which it draws down, and in the physical People of Israel, which it animates spiritually. Again, in this interpretation, too, we see how the author of *Lekhah Dodi* packed multiple mystical teachings within single brief phrases.

Lekhah Dodi incorporates kabbalistic symbolism not only through its words, but also through its structure, down to its number of stanzas, words and letters. Thus, it is made up of ten stanzas, three related directly to *Shabbat*—corresponding to the ten *Sefirot*, and the three upper *Sefirot* among them, respectively. The chorus contains seven words, corresponding to the seven lower *Sefirot*. The word count of the stanzas is structured around the number 65, the numerical equivalent of the Name א-ד-נ-י, which corresponds to the receptive, "feminine" Divine faculty, as above. The letter count of the chorus is 26, the numerical equivalent of the Tetragrammaton, the Name י-ה-ו-ה, which corresponds to the "masculine" Divine faculty, of paradigmatic giving, as above. In this manner, *yiḥud* or *zivug*—the union of the upper and lower *Sefirot*, of the Divine Giver and Presence, and God and the Congregation of Israel—is subtly reflected in the very structure of the prayer itself.[62]

When applied to the *Sefirot*, the "masculine" and "feminine" roles in conveying Divine bounty are also known as *Ḥasadim* (kindnesses) and *Gevurot* (strengths), or *Kudsha berikh Hu* (the Holy One, Blessed be He) and *Shekhinah* (Presence), respectively. These terms are commonly found in kabbalistic prayers, such as in the *Lesheim Yiḥud* texts.[63] These texts are commonly recited (by some) right before fulfilling a number of *mitzvot*, such as wearing the *tallit* and the *tefillin*, counting the *Omer* and shaking the *lulav*.

IV. *Yiḥud*

Ultimately, approaching God's presence requires transcending the boundaries of material existence. Only great, undying, overwhelming love of God can bring one to the point of removing from oneself all

62 Yaakov Bazak, "Lekha Dodi—Rabbi Shelomo Alkavets," *Sinai* vol. 102, 5748, pp. 183-175, ch. 3.

63 In some *Le-sheim Yiḥud* texts, *Kudsha berikh Hu* and *Shekhinah* are called upon to unite with *Dehilu* and *Reḥimu*, the feminine and masculine monikers for the immediately preceding two *Partzufim* or worlds—and thus all four accessible Divine worlds are being called into union.

material desires, to be left with the overwhelming desire to unite with the Infinite (*deveikut*, or *unio mystica*), to place as one's own desire to do only the will of God. The goal of our service, in prayer and otherwise, is *bittul ha-yesh*, negation of "substance"—purifying oneself of the desires and ego that prevent us from seeing ourselves as *eivarim de-Shekhinta*, "limbs of the Presence," or extensions of the Divine Will. The resulting unification of lower with upper realms, whether in the contexts of "worlds," the *Sefirot*, or male/female imagery, is known as *yiḥud*, unification.

During the first three blessings of the *Amidah*, the worshiper engages in increasing *bittul ha-yesh*. Having made him- or herself into a receptacle for Divine blessing, life-force fills the worshiper's soul, connecting him or her with his or her Divine Source across all spiritual realms, as he or she recites the petitionary middle blessings of the *Amidah*. After thus having ascended to the spiritual plane of the Divine Will, the worshiper draws that blessing down to our material world when reciting the final three blessings.

"David Melech Yisrael Chai VeKayam": Kiddush HaLevanah, Midrash, Archeology and Redemption

Kiddush HaLevanah, History, Archeology (and the Yiddish Expression חַזִיר פְּיסָ'ל), *R. Shimon b. Pazi, and the Religious and Political Significance of* דוד מלך ישראל חי וקיים.

By: NACHMAN LEVINE

Rema, in a gloss to *Orach Chaim* 426:2, notes an Ashkenazic custom not recorded anywhere before his time: that of saying דוד מלך ישראל חי וקיים after the *berachah* of *Kiddush HaLevanah:*

> And we have a custom to say [during *Kiddush HaLevanah*] דוד מלך ישראל חי וקיים, since his sovereignty was compared to the moon [in *Tehilim* 88:38] and is destined to be renewed in the future like it, and *Kneset Yisrael* will return to be united to her Husband, who is the Holy One, Blessed Be He, like the moon that renews itself with the sun… and therefore we do actions of joy and dancing in *Kiddush HaChodesh* [sic.] as the joy of a wedding. (R. Bachyei, *Parshat VaYeshev*)[1]

This practice is not recorded *anywhere* before this; it doesn't appear in *Masechet Soferim* or the *Tur,* in any other sources of our *Kiddush HaLevanah*, or even the *siddurim* printed in 1525 and 1527.[2] Rema is the only one to record it, and he records it as a prevailing custom[3] in his time among Ashkenazic Jews. Today it is universal in all Ashkenazic, Sephardic, and Yemenite *siddurim.* And while it didn't appear until the 16th-century, I would submit that it may be the theological heart of our *Kiddush/Birkat*

1 ונוהגין לומר: 'דוד מלך ישראל חי וקיים,' שמלכותו נמשל ללבנה ועתיד להתחדש כמותה וכנסת ישראל תחזור להתדבק בבעלה שהוא הקדוש ברוך הוא, דוגמת הלבנה המתחדשת עם החמה שנאמר: "שמש ומגן ה'" (תהילים פד, יב) ולכך עושין שמחות ורקודין בקידוש החדש דוגמת שמחת נשואין (בחיי פרשת וישב וד"ע).

2 Trino 1525; Prague 1527.

3 Here and in *Darchei Moshe* on the *Tur,* he cites R. Bachyei, *Bereishit* 38:29 on its connection to *Kiddush HaChodesh.*

Nachman Levine teaches in Detroit. His works on Tanakh and Midrash appear in various journals.

HaLevanah.[4] *Siddur HaMekubal HaRav Hertz Shaliach Tzibur,* 1560, in fact, calls it a prayer. In Sephardic Baghdadi s*iddurim* it is a prayer; its form is דוד מלך ישראל חי וקיים אמן נצח סלה ועד here and in the writings of the Chida. In *Siddur Ben Ish Hai,* the custom is to dance together while singing it.

But what is its meaning and connection to *Kiddush HaLevanah*? Several *Bavli*, *Yerushalmi* and midrashic sources, together with discoveries in archeology, iconographic realia, and Talmudic geography might clarify not only its historical significance but more importantly, its essential theological relevance to the meaning of our *Kiddush HaLevanah.* Putting the disparate sources together in the interface of *halachah, minhag,* midrash, history, and archeology reveals a remarkable picture with profound implications for the theological meaning of David Melech Yisrael Chai VeKayam and *Kiddush HaLevanah* itself.

David Melech Yisrael Chai VeKayam: The Source

The text's source in context is a story in *Bavli Rosh HaShanah* 25a:

> אמר ליה רבי לרבי חייא: "זיל לעין טב וקדשיה ושלח לי סימנא: 'דוד מלך ישראל חי וקים'."
>
> Rebbi[5] [R. Yehudah HaNasi] said to R. Chiyya, "Go to Ein Tab and sanctify the moon—and send me a sign *(simana)*: דוד מלך ישראל חי וקיים.

Why is this significant? And what is a *simana*?

In the face of Roman persecution, the sanctification of the New Moon, which should be done by the Nasi,[6] in this case Rebbi of the

---

4 In Sephardic Siddurim always: *Birkat HaLevanah.* In Ashkenazic ones always: *Kiddush HaLevanah*, a term that doesn't appear in the *Bavli*, *Yerushalmi*, or Rambam, but does in Ashkenazic tradition since the 12th-century *Sefer HaEshkol* (*Hilchot Roshei Chodashim*). In Maharil (the source of Ashkenazic *minhag*) in *Hilchot Rosh Chodesh*: ומקדש והולך ,מקדשין הלבנה, etc., as in Rema's glosses to *Shulchan Aruch* ("מקדשים הלבנה"), interpreted as possibly signifying *Kiddush HaLevanah* as a replication of Kiddush HaChodesh. In R. Yosef Karo's (Sephardic) *Shulchan Aruch* it's always: ברכת הלבנה, in Rema's *Darkei Moshe* on *Tur* and *Hagahot* to *Shulchan Aruch*, always קידוש לבנה as here: ורקודין בקידוש החדש.

5 Actually: "*Rabbi*": "רַבִּי", throughout the *Mishnah*, *Tosefta*, etc.

6 *Mishnah Eduyot* 7:7; *Bavli Rosh HaShanah*; *Bavli Sanhedrin* 11a; Rambam, *Kiddush HaChodesh* 4:9–12.

family of *Malchut Beit David,*[7] had to be reported using a secret password sign; a סימנא.[8] (Rashi ad loc.: שגזרו שמד במקומו שלא יקדשו את החדש.) In fact, the *Talmud Yerushalmi* always calls the sanctification of the month סימנא.

What was at stake was not simply that preventing *Kiddush HaChodesh* would deprive the Jewish people of their very first *mitzvah.* Without a calendar, they would be bereft of a fundamental and indispensable basis of Jewish practice—and the Romans knew it. The *simana's* political/theological significance may be reflected in how once in R. Abahu's time the sign was גאולתינו, "our redemption." (*Yerushalmi, Rosh HaShanah* 3:1). It was an attack on Jewish practice and in its way, on Jewish sovereignty.

Thus, at the simplest level, the David Melech Yisrael *siman* would allude, as Rema noted, to the dynastic line of David's kingship which "like the moon will last forever" (כירח יכון עולם, Tehilim 88:38) [Rashi, *Bavli Rosh HaShanah* ad loc.].[9] It is also argued[10] that it could allude to the connection of David and the moon's diminution with *Kiddush HaChodesh* in the midrash of R. Shimon b. Pazi (Rebbi and R. Chiyya's relative and colleague[11]) in *Bavli, Chulin* 60a: "G-d told the moon '*Tzadikim* will be called by your name.' " This is to say, "the small luminary" which David was also called in Shmuel 17:14. R. Shimon b. Pazi's remarkable connection with Rebbi, R. Chiyya, and the Simana will be very significant.

Shaarei Efraim 10:36 cites *Berit Kehunat Olam* that דוד מלך ישראל חי וקיים is *gematria* of *Rosh Chodesh,* commenting: "This is amazing." *Iyun Tefilah* (*siddur* commentary by R. Yaakov Tzvi Mecklenburg, author of *HaKetav VeHaKabalah*) feels that was exactly what Rebbi intended. Historians go so far as to suggest that דוד מלך ישראל חי וקיים may well be a coded numerical equivalent (819) for (in earlier Palestinian Aramaic plural form), קדשנא ירחא בעינא טבא, "I/we sanctified the month at Ein Tab."[12]

---

7 *Tosefta Horayot* 2:2; *Bavli Ketubot* 62b*; Bavli Sanhedrin* 38a*; Bavli Shabbat* 56a*; Yerushalmi Ketubot* 12:3*; Yerushalmi Kelayim* 12:3. *Igeret* R. *Sherira Gaon,* B.M. Levin edition, 12.

8 *Korban HaEdah, Yerushalmi Sanhedrin* 1:1.

9 דָּוִד מֶלֶךְ יִשְׂרָאֵל appears in Mishlei 1:1, while חַיָּא וְקַיָּם in Daniel 6:26 describes God and becomes His idiomatic title חי וקים in *midrashim* and the liturgy. In a midrash in *Yerushalmi Shekalim* 2:5 R. Yaakov bar Idi, an Amora in the generation after Rebbi, says: וכי עלתה על דעתו של דוד שיהא חי וקים לעולמים.

10 *Sefer HaEshkol, Hilchot Roshei Chodashim*; Rabbeinu Bachyei, *Bereishit* 38:29.

11 Yerushalmi, *Shabbat* 12:13; Esther Rabah 4:4. See *Tosafot, Bava Kama* 149a s.v. *Mari.*

12 L. Ginzberg, *Commentary on the Palestinian Talmud*, III, 130.

In short, the sign meant: David, the moon, is alive and well (R. Bachyei, ibid).[13] There is probably even wordplay in the sign: Rebbi as *Nasi* of the line of David (דוד) told "[R.] *Chiyya*" (חי) to perform *Kiddush HaChodesh* for the *nesiut* (מלך ישׂראל) and report that he *fulfilled* [וְקַיָּם] the mission so he would know that: דוד | מלך ישראל | חי | וקים.[14]

Midrashim after Rebbi's time[15] equate the moon's thirty-day waxing and waning imagery with a thirty-generation cycle of Davidic sovereignty. *Etz Yosef, Shemot Rabah* 15:26, sees the textual subtext as "[החדש הזה] **לכם**" (Ex. 12:2) reversed to "**מלך**."

> "This month [moon] is for you." (Ex. 12:2). A sign for you, just as the moon has its fullness and decrease, David's reign, "like the moon will be forever. (Tehilim 89:38)
>
> If you merit, you will count to its fullness [fifteen generations from Avraham to David], and if not, to its decrease [fifteen to Tzidkiyahu, the *Beit HaMikdash's* destruction].[16]

In *Shmuel* I 20:18–29, David is specifically connected with the declaration of *Rosh Chodesh:*

> And Yonatan said to David: "Tomorrow is *Rosh Chodesh*, the New Moon. You will be missed because your seat will be empty… He said, "Let me go because our family is observing a sacrifice…"

---

13 R. Bachyei, Rema's source, also discusses its Kabbalistic significance.

14 The sign takes on a life of its own from here, from the text of the *LeShem Yichud* for *seudat Melaveh Malkah* in early Chassidic *siddurim* to a popular Israeli Zionistic folksong for its nationalistic undertones to the song on The Diaspora Yeshiva Band's *Live From King David's Tomb.*

15 *Pesikta Rabati, HaChodesh, Pesikta DeRav Kahanah* 12, collated in *Shemot Rabah* 15:26, *Tanhuma* (Buber) Bo 15.

16 In the *Kiddush HaLevanah 'Yehi Ratzon'* attributed to the *Ari Zal* (evidently based on *Siddur R. Hertz Shaliach Tzibur* and R. Todros Abulafia's *Otzar HaKavod, Rosh HaShanah* 25a) it is written: "May it be Your Will to fill the defect of the moon . . . and may it be fulfilled in us: 'They will seek their G-d and David their king' (Hoshea 3:5)." This startlingly combines *Bavli Sanhedrin* 42a/*Yerushalmi Berachot* 9:2's עד שתתמלא פגימתה—when the moon's crescent becomes full, the halachic deadline until when *Birkat HaLevanah* can be said—with *Pesikta Rabati's* waxing/waning Davidic reign metaphor אם זכיתם אתם מונין למליאתו ואם לאו אתם מונין לפגמו ("If you merit you will count to its fullness and if not, to its decrease")— and also with the moon's diminution in *Chulin* 60a. In this new metaphor, למלאות פגימת הלבנה now becomes a prayer for Davidic restoration to correct that cosmic defect.

So Rebbi sent R. Chiyya to sanctify the month and send back a sign—דוד מלך ישראל חי וקיים—from the *Beit HaVaad,* which was in Ein Tab.[17]

So Where Was Ein Tab and What Was its Significance?

Earlier sources and geographical historians[18] always placed Ein Tab in the Galil, east of Zippori (where Rebbi lived for some years[19]) and between Zippori and Tiberias. But that's not where it is. And where it is located makes it the heart of *Kiddush HaLevanah's* meaning.

After the Bar Kokhba wars and Hadrianic decrees, the Jewish population was largely forced to move to north Israel[20] (and the *Sanhedrin* and *nesiut* moved from Yavneh in Judah to the Galil in the north (*Bavli, Rosh HaShanah* 31a). They moved so far north that whenever *Talmud Yerushalmi* speaks of חכמי הדרום, the Sages of the south, it means the sages of Lod in the center of Israel where the Tel Aviv Lod airport is today.

Jews and Torah generally thrived in the Galil in the 2nd–4th centuries in a fruitful period that saw the creation of the *Mishnah, Tosefta* and the *Talmud Yerushalmi.* The *nesiut* thrived. But sanctifying the moon in Beit Din became a serious problem.

This is because both *Kiddush HaChodesh* and *Ibur HaShanah* (adjusting the lunar and solar years) should ideally be done in *Eretz Yehudah.* In a *Bavli Sanhedrin* 11b *Baraita:*[21] "We do not do *Ibur HaShanah* except in Yehudah and if they did it in the Galil it is *Me'uberet* [adjusted]". And in some opinions, if not done in *Yehudah,* it would still not be *me'uberet.*

This presented no problem in the *Beit HaMikdash* and in Yavneh after the *Churban* where the *nesiut* and *Beit HaVaad* were in the same place. But with the move of the *Sanhedrin* and the *nesiut* to the Galil, *Kiddush HaChodesh* in *Yehudah* presented a serious challenge, especially with the danger involved together with Rabban Yochanan b. Zakai's *Takanah* that witnesses of the New Moon should testify "only in the place of the *Vaad*" (*Mishnah, Rosh HaShanah* 4:4).

---

17 *Tosafot, ad loc.*, from *Pesikta Rabati* 21.

18 From R. Yehosef Schwartz, *Tevuot HaAretz* (1804) until contemporary times, Michael Avi-Yonah, גיאוגרפיה היסטורית של ארץ ישראל (1984), etc.

19 *Yerushalmi Kila'im* 9:3.

20 Dio Cassius, *Historia Romana*, 69, 1214: "Nearly all Judea was made desolate… many wolves and hyenas rushed howling into the cities."

21 Variant versions in *Tosefta Sanhedrin* 2:3, *Yerushalmi Sanhedrin* 1:2, *Nedarim* 6:40, etc.

After an attempt to do the *Ibur* in Lod in *Eretz Yehudah* met with fatally disastrous results, the Sanhedrin wished to move the sanctification of the year, and even of *Rosh Chodesh,* safely up to the Galil.

> Twenty-four carriages of the house of Rebbi went in to be *me'aber* the year in Lod and an *ayin hora* (evil eye) entered them and they all died at one time. From that hour on they removed [the *Ibur HaShanah*] from Yehudah and established it in the Galil. They wished to remove even the *simana* (*Kiddush HaChodesh*). R. Simon said to them, "We are not leaving in Yehudah even a remembrance." (*Yerushalmi, Sanhedrin* 1:2)

R. Simon protested that if it were moved, no remembrance of the *simana* would remain in *Yehudah.* R. Simon's name and his statement about the *simana* make for nice wordplay.[22] In a similar wordplay, the *Yerushalmi* continues with *Tosefta, Sanhedrin* 2:2: **על שלשה סימנין מעברין את השנה**.

R. Simon's protest was not theoretical. He was personally involved as a member of the Beit Din in the calculations and deliberations of both *Kiddush HaChodesh* and *Ibur HaShanah.* His participations and rulings in the *Kiddush HaChodesh* process were cited for generations as authoritative[23] and his detailed directives to *ibur* calculators (*Yerushalmi Sukah* 4:1) were later incorporated into Hillel II's calendar. In the midrashic context he taught

> Until Israel went out of Egypt, The Holy One Blessed be He sat and calculated and intercalculated the months and years and sanctified them, and when they went out of Egypt, He gave it over to them and said, 'From now on the *Roshei Chodashim* are given over to you', as it says **החדש הזה לכם**, even before they received the Torah. (*Pesikta Rabati, 'HaChodesh'*)

More importantly, he, like R. Chiyya in our *Bavli* source, was once sent by Rebbi to be *me'aber* the year and spent a Shabbat in Ono.

Moreover, R. Simon is in fact R. Shimon b. Pazi in the *Bavli,* author of the *Chulin* 60a midrash of the moon saying

> Master of the Universe, how can the sun and the moon share one crown? God therefore said to her: If so, go and diminish yourself.

---

22 Greek/Latin/Hebrew triple- wordplay on his name in *Bereishit Rabah* 93:4: "ויגש אליו יהודה": זו היא **השמת** עין? נהפך הדבר שאמרת **לסמיות** עינים: אמר רבי **סימון:** "**בנימוסות** שלנו כתיב ... ".

23 *Yerushalmi Rosh HaShanah* 3:1; *Yerushalmi Berachot* 4:1.

> She said: Master of the Universe, since I said a correct thing before You, I must diminish myself?... He said to her [to placate her]: Go; let the Jewish people count the days and years with you.[24]

After the Sanhedrin was forced to leave Yavneh, the locus of the Beit Din for *Kiddush HaChodesh* was moved, probably to Lod, and from there to Ein Tab. In fact, R. Simon's son R. Yehudah testified to his father's ruling there that the *Rosh Chodesh* Torah reading could replace the reading of a fast day for rain only at Ein Tab, since only there was it known clearly to be *Rosh Chodesh* (*Yerushalmi Berachot* 4:1).

But where is Ein Tab?

Ein Tab was previously assumed to have been between Zippori and Tiberias. It was thought that the *Beit HaVaad* had moved there so that *Kiddush HaChodesh* could be done safely, using a secret password.

However, as it turns out, Ein Tab was *not* there. It is now conclusively identified[25] as the ancient small village of Enteba, equidistant between Lod and Yavneh. Ein Tab is actually and significantly in Eretz Yehudah.

The identification is based on the Madaba map, the oldest-known geographic floor-mosaic and oldest-surviving cartographic depiction of the Middle East, Israel, and Yerushalayim. The map is in the early Byzantine Church of St. George at Madaba, Jordan.[26] The floor-map dates from the 6th-century when the midrash *Vayikra Rabah* was created in Tiberias and the *Talmud Bavli* was completed.

---

24 Strangely, while R. Simon lived in Israel, his Palestinian *Bereishit Rabah* midrash version has none of the *Bavli's* details, but simply that God diminished it since it entered the sun's domain and can be seen by day.

25 Shmuel Klein: *Sefer HaYishuv* I, "Ein Tab"; *Eretz Yehudah*, 79; Shmuel Safrai, "המקומות לקידוש חודשים ולעיבור השנה בארץ לאחר החורבן", תרביץ לה (תשכ"ו), 27; M. Avi-Yonah, אטלס כרטא לתקופת המשנה והתלמוד, Yehoshua Schwartz, היישוב היהודי ביהודה אחרי מלחמת בר-כוכבא עד הכיבוש הערבי.

26 מֵידְבָא: Bamidbar 21:30; Yehoshua 13:9,16; Yeshayahu 15:2; Divrei HaYamim I 19:7 and *Mishnah Mikva'ot* 7:1 about a Jewish community there in the times of R. Akiva.

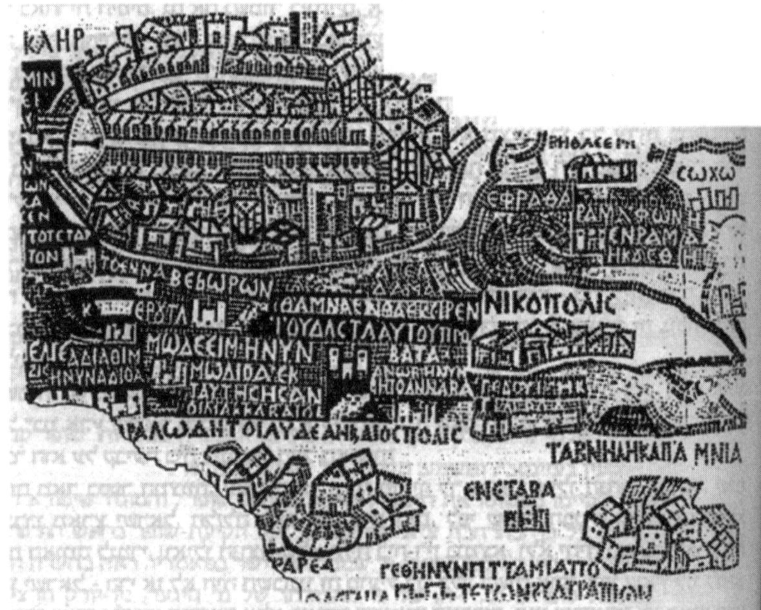

On the map, Ein Tab, Ευεταβα (ENETABA), appears clearly at the bottom, between Lod on the left and Yavneh on the right.[27] Z. Safrai[28] further identified Ein Tab more precisely as a satellite village of today's Kiryat Ono near Tel Aviv on the basis of a 16th-century Arabic administrative document[29] in which a village called EinTab in the Ono area was awarded by the Ottoman rulers to one of its administrators.

The Ono connection is very significant. In a *Bavli Sanhedrin* 11b *Baraita*: "We do not do *Ibur HaShanah* except in *Yehudah* and if they did it in the *Galil,* it is *me'uberet.* Chananiah Ish Ono testified: if they did it in the *Galil*—it is not *me'uberet.*"[30] *Bavli* continues:

> Rabbi Shimon b. Pazi [that is—R. Simon in the *Yerushalmi*!] said: "What is Chananiah Ish Ono's reasoning?" The Torah says, לשכנו תדרשו ובאת שמה. "[Only to the place HaShem your G-d shall choose amidst all your tribes to set His Name there] shall you

27 Yerushalayim is above it to the left with its Roman Cardo, the wide north-south thoroughfare with a columned portico on either side through the Old City which enabled Nachman Avigad, using the map, to excavate it in 1976. The depiction has even been used for studying *Hilchot Eruvin* (though post-Destruction Jerusalem/Alia Capitolina was probably laid out by Hadrian).

28 Etzion, כזה ראה וחדש.

29 H.S.T Stephan, *Quarterly of the Department of Antiquities in Palestine* 10 (1944).

30 Variant versions in *Tosefta, Sanhedrin* 2:3, *Yerushalmi Sanhedrin* 1:2, *Nedarim* 6:40, etc.

search after His dwelling" (Devarim 12:5): "Every searching you search, should only be in the place of His Dwelling."

So Chananiah of Ono, the town adjacent to the *Beit HaVaad* in Ein Tab, declares *Ibur* to be valid only if done in the place of the *shechinah* in Yehudah, and the one who explains that reasoning is R. Shimon b. Pazi—R. Simon in the Yerushalmi, himself a resident of Lod[31] in Yehudah, who had protested the *simana*'s removal from there.

So where Ein Tab is matters, and that was the *siman*. With *Kiddush HaChodesh's* return to Judah, David's sovereignty, like the moon, reemerged after diminution. It re-established halachic dominion of the *nesiut* as *Malchut Beit David* in the place *of David HaMelech*, in the "dwelling-place of the *Shechinah*" where *Kiddush HaChodesh should* be done. Thus לֹא יָסוּר שֵׁבֶט מִיהוּדָה, "The scepter shall not depart from Yehudah" (*Bereishit* 49:10) in both senses, the kingdom of Yehudah in Eretz Yehudah.[32] The *mitzvah* in reinstated place and format was alive and well: דוד מלך ישראל חי וקיים.

Historians connect the desire to return *Kiddush HaChodesh* to Judah with the stabilizing of R. Yehudah HaNasi's *nesiut,*[33] with control over the Jewish calendar as its most important manifestation. It is noted that while Rebbi does not mention any of the Sanhedrin's disputes with the *nesiut* after the *churban*, he does cite the two cases in which it deferred to the *Nasi*, both in regard to *Kiddush HaChodesh,* in *Mishnah, Eduyot* 7:7 and *Rosh HaShanah* 2:9.[34]

Tosafot (*Rosh HaShanah* 25a) concludes on the basis of *Pesikata Rabati* 21 that Ein Tab had a set *Beit Din* with the status of Yavneh.

> Why do they sanctify the moon at Ein Tab? Because it is the *Beit Vaad. HaKadosh Baruch Hu* said: "It is the *Beit Moed* for the entire world as it says, כי מציון תצא תורה (Yeshayahu 2:3) and the *Yerushalmi* [*Rosh HaShanah* 3:6] says, 'Just as they blow the *Shofar* in Yavneh [on *Rosh Chodesh,* even on *Rosh HaShanah* that falls on *Shabbat*], so they blow it in Ein Tab'.

---

31 *Yerushalmi Betzah* 1:7.

32 Ginzberg, *Commentary on the Palestinian Talmud*, II, 130.

33 Ginzberg, ibid. R. Yitzchak HaLevi, *Dorot HaRishonim*, II, 66; Urbach, ההלכה-מקורותיה והתפתחותה (1984), 346; Y. Tabori מועדי ישראל בתקופת המשנה והתלמוד.

34 Y. Levin, "*Tekufat Rabbi Yehudah HaNasi,*" in ארץ-ישראל מחורבן בית שני ועד הכיבוש המוסלמי, 108.

It is suggested[35] Ein Tab was chosen for *Kiddush HaChodesh* as the closest place to Yerushalayim that could still serve as a Beit Din where it was possible to convene on a monthly basis. R. Simon's protest succeeded and though *Ibur HaShanah* was moved to the Galil, Ein Tab continued to be the place of *Kiddush HaChodesh* throughout the time the calendar was based on testimony and possibly long after that. Several *Yerushalmi* sources describe this.[36] And R. Simon's son R. Yehudah reported his father's policies on that testimony (*Yerushalmi, Rosh HaShanah* 3:1) and how it was clearly known to be *Rosh Chodesh* there (*Yerushalmi Berachot* 4:1).

Maharsha, Sanhedrin 42b interprets the *Kiddush HaLevanah berachah* [37] as equating the returned crown of Israel and the moon and signaling the return of *Malchut Beit David's* kingship. He notes: "And therefore we say in the moon's renewal: דוד מלך ישראל חי וקים.[38]

Re-contextualized in *Kiddush HaLevanah,* דוד מלך ישראל חי וקיים now becomes a prayer[39] for that which we pray in the *berachah*: the Sanhedrin

35 Yehudah Etzion, "כזה ראה וחדש" Jerusalem: 1995 And see R. Y. HaLevi, *Dorot HaRishonim*, II, 66.

36 *Berachot* 4:1, *Rosh HaShanah* 2:4 and 3:6; *Sukah* 2:8; *Ta'anit* 2:14; *Nedarim* 6:5; *Sanhedrin* 1:2; etc.

37 The *berachah* is by R. Yehudah (bar Yechezkel), *Bavli Sanhedrin* 42a: R. Ashi said, "We [in Bavel] say as… R. Yehudah said, "אשר במאמרו ברא שחקים" etc." Since R. Yehudah passed away in 299 and Rav Ashi was born in 352, the *berachah* had been said in Bavel for well over half a century. R. Yehudah authored prayers as *Birkat HaIlanot* (*Bavli, Berachot* 43b) and arguably perhaps even our *Sheva Berachot* in *Bavli Ketubot* 8a, mentioned nowhere else.

38 The *berachah* doesn't explicitly equate David and the moon but alludes to verses that do. אשר במאמרו ברא שחקים וברוח פיו כל צבאם references *Tehilim* 33:6: בִּדְבַר ה' שָׁמַיִם נַעֲשׂוּ וּבְרוּחַ פִּיו כָּל צְבָאָם yet changes שָׁמַיִם to שחקים as *Tehilim* 89:21–38: "כְּיָרֵחַ יִכּוֹן עוֹלָם וְעֵד בַּשַּׁחַק נֶאֱמָן סֶלָה", the equation of David's kingship with the moon: "I found David My servant… his throne… like the moon will be established forever and as an enduring witness in the sky ["בַּשַּׁחַק"]." Avudraham, *Birchot HaReiyah*, notes "חוק וזמן נתן להם שלא ישנו את תפקידם", "A law and schedule He gave them that they not alter their task" references Yirmiyahu 31:34–35- through 3:20–26 equating David's kingship with their unchanging function: "Thus said God Who gave the sun for light by day, the laws of moon and stars… If these laws were annulled… only then could My covenant with My servant David be broken."

39 The Kabbalist R. Todros Abulafia, *Otzar HaKavod, Rosh HaShanah* 25a, writes that Rebbi's *simana* was a prayer.

receiving the *Shechinah*[40] in the place of the *Shechinah,* as *Siddur HaMekubal HaRav Hertz Shliach Tzibur* calls it: a prayer for Redemption.

Ein Tab: The Good Eye, The (Very) Bad Eye, the Wild Boar, and the Tenth Legion

But there's more. And here's where it gets very interesting. A very well-known series of midrashim—all of them from Rabbi Simon himself—identifies the Jewish people's archetypal enemy, Esav/Edom, and by extension, Rome,[41] as a hypocritical swine showing off its 'kosher' hooves (as the only animal with the outward kosher sign of split hooves).[42]

> *Midrash Bereishit Rabah* 65:1
> "The swine out of the wood ravages it [the vine [Israel] that G-d took out of Egypt]," (Tehilim 80:14). R. Pinchas and R. Chelkiah in the name of R. Simon said: 'Of all the prophets, only two, Moshe and Asaph, publicized it: Asaph said: "The swine out of the wood ravages it" while Moshe said: "And the pig, because it parts the hoof" (Devarim 14:8). Why does he compare [the Roman State] to a swine? When the swine lays down it puts out its hoofs, as if to say, 'I am clean'; so this wicked State robs and oppresses and pretends to be executing justice. In this same way, for forty years Esau would ensnare married women and violate them, yet when he attained forty years, he compared himself to his father, 'As my father was forty years old when he married, so I will marry at the age of forty.'

> *Midrash Vayikra Rabah* 13:5
> R. Pinchas and R. Chelkiah in the name of R. Simon said: Of all the prophets, only two, Moshe and Asaph, publicized it: Asaph said: 'The swine out of the wood ravages it,' while Moshe said: 'And the pig, because it parts the hoof' (Devarim 14:8). Why is it compared to a swine? Just as the swine when reclining, puts forth its hooves as if to say, 'See I am clean,' so does the empire of Edom [Rome] boast under the guise of establishing a judicial tribunal as it commits violence and robbery.' It happened that a governor in Caesa-

---

40 *Bavli Sanhedrin* 42a.

41 *Bavli Avodah Zarah* 10b; *Berachot* 62b; *Gitin* 57b; *Yerushalmi Shabbat* 10:9; *Taanit* 4:8; *Bereishit Rabah* 63:7,67:1; *Vayikra Rabah* 13:45; 15:9; 22:4; *Tanhuma,* Bereishit 7; *Eichah Rabah* 22:1; *Targum,* Yeshayahu 34:9. M. Hadas-Lebel, Jérusalem contre Rome (Paris, 1990), 46–82.

42 *Bavli Chulin* 59a.

rea put to death the thieves, adulterers, and sorcerers. He said to his counselor: 'I myself did these things in one night'.'

R. Simon's midrashim here are quite complex and beautifully constructed in several layers of biblical and midrashic intertextuality.[43] They are all built on the list of Four Animals/Four Exiles in Daniel 7:2–8. Three are "like a lion", "like a bear", "like a leopard", while the final, most frightening, fourth animal ("fearsome, dreadful, and very powerful… different from all the other beasts before it") is not identified. That connection is even spelled out in a later version of this midrash in *Midrash Tehilim* 80:

> ר' פנחס ור' חלקיה בשם ר' סימון אמרו למה לא פירש הנביא בשביל מלכות הרביעית, אלא משה ואסף.
>
> [… in the name of R. Simon said] "Why did no prophet but Moshe and Asaf explicate the Fourth Kingdom?

The "Ancient of Days" there in *Daniel* 7:2–27 explains it to Daniel as:

> The fourth beast [means]—there will be a fourth kingdom upon the earth which will be different from all the kingdoms; it will devour the whole earth, tread it down, and crush it . . . Then the court will sit and his dominion will be taken away, to be destroyed and abolished for all time.

Tannaim identify the fourth animal with Edom/Rome (*Mechilta Bo, Mesichta DePeschah* 14; *Sifrei* Bamidbar 84 and 161), based on references to the Exile of Edom in Ovadiah 1 and Yeshayahu 63, and because of Rome's harsh decrees at that time.[44] By one hundred years after that identification, *Amoraim*, among them R. Simon's teacher R. Yohanan, now characterize the Fourth Animal/Exile (Edom) midrashically as a pig, by lining up the list with that of the four unkosher animals in Vayikra 11:4–7 and Devarim 14:6–8, as the four oppressive Exiles. (*Vayikra Rabah* 13:50: "Moshe foresaw the empires in their activities. "The camel, the rabbit, the hare, and the pig" (Devarim 14:7.) "The camel is Bavel . . . The rabbit is Media . . . The rabbit is Greece . . . The pig is Edom.") This earliest equation becomes a salient motif in midrashim and *piyyutim*[45] from that period on.[46] Since only the fourth unko-

---

43 Yonah Frankel, *Darchei HaAgadah VeHaMidrash* I, 616, cites Zunz, *Gesammelte Schriften* III, p. 221 and the studies by Bacher, Krause, and Ginzberg.

44 Similarly, the later *Shemot Rabah,* 15:6.

45 Zunz, *Syn. Poesie,* 458–459.

46 See Bacher, *Amoraei Eretz Yisrael,* II, 45.

sher animal, the pig, is described with its (outward) kosher sign of split hooves,[47] R. Simon now lines it up with Tehilim 80:9–18's describing Israel as a vine that God moved from Egypt and planted, which a wild pig from the forest ravages:

> גֶּפֶן מִמִּצְרַיִם תַּסִּיעַ ... יְכַרְסְמֶנָּה חֲזִיר מִיָּעַר... שׁוּב נָא הַבֵּט מִשָּׁמַיִם וּרְאֵה וּפְקֹד גֶּפֶן זֹאת.
>
> You moved a vine from Egypt… and planted it… a wild boar ravages it, God of Hosts, turn again, look down from heaven and see, take note of that vine.

Since the "vine" in its plain sense here is a metaphor for Israel, the "wild boar" is necessarily a specific nation that ravages it, now read as Edom. R. Simon uses this to construct a critique of the Roman State's hypocrisy it piously claims is a system of law and justice.[48] I get the impression that he even artistically uses alliterative opening wordplay to connect the *Vayikra* and *Devarim* verses with *Tehilim* 80 [and *Daniel* 7:2–8] in the sounds of: "פרסמוה\"מפריס פרסה"\"אסף אמר":

> "מכל הנביאים לא **פרסמוה** אלא שנים, אסף ומשה: **אסף אמר**: "יכרסמנה חזיר מיער", משה אמר "ואת החזיר כי **מפריס פרסה**."
>
> ['Of all of the prophets, no one publicized it but two, Moshe and Asaph: Asaph said: "The swine out of the wood ravages it;" Moshe said: "And the pig, because it parts the hoof" (*Devarim* 14:8).]

From here Rome/Edom's duplicity is easily read back onto the emblematic personified hypocrisy of Esav's taking Canaanite wives, marrying at forty as his righteous father Yitzchak did. All of this is very familiar to us from Rashi's commentary on the Torah to Bereishit 26:34,

---

47 וְאֶת הַחֲזִיר כִּי מַפְרִיס פַּרְסָה הוּא וְשֹׁסַע שֶׁסַע פַּרְסָה וְהוּא גֵּרָה לֹא יִגָּר טָמֵא הוּא לָכֶם "And the swine because it has hoofs and it does not chew the cud, it is unclean for you (*Vayikra* 11:7); וְאֶת הַחֲזִיר כִּי מַפְרִיס פַּרְסָה הוּא וְלֹא גֵרָה טָמֵא הוּא לָכֶם, "Also the swine, because it has hoofs, it does not chew the cud is unclean for you" (*Devarim* 14:8).

48 Rabbi Shimon b. Pazi was also well-aware of and critiqued other manifestations of Roman life in Israel, saying in *Bavli Avodah Zarah* 18b: "Blessed is the man that has not walked in the counsel of the wicked nor stood in the way of sinners" (*Tehilim* 1:1). This refers to the theaters and circuses of the idolaters, and the Kenigiyyon [Greek/Latin: stadium animal fights the Romans provided in Israel]. He was aware of Roman Imperial military iconography, using it in *Shemot Rabah* 21:9 to describe Moshe's staff at the Yam Suf as if a זמורה a magistrate's fasces, a bundle of rods with a projecting axe blade carried by lictors in Rome as a symbol of a magistrate's power in administrative ceremonies, processions, and triumphs.

which eventually becomes popularized in the Yiddish expression, חֲזִיר פִּיסָ'ל, pig's feet, to mean hypocrisy.

But while these midrashim—all from R. Simon—all build on verses in Vayikra, Devarim, and Tehilim, and the four animals list in Daniel 7:7, and stand entirely on their own as midrashim without any need for historical context, it just so happens that the Roman Tenth Legion Fretensis (Legio X Fretensis), garrisoned in Yerushalayim for more than a century and a half, which destroyed the *Beit HaMikdash* and always fought the Jews,[49] had as its emblem a wild boar, and everybody knew it.[50]

The Tenth Legion was nicknamed "the boar" and its emblem, a boar or pig, was ubiquitous throughout Jerusalem, its base. Many ar-

---

49 Starting from 67 under Vespasian when he was supreme commander of Roman forces in Judaea before becoming emperor during the civil war in 68. After mid-69, its commander may have been Terentius Rufus. It besieged Jerusalem in 70 and Masada in 73–74 and fought Bar-Kochba in one of the greatest disasters befalling the Roman empire. It then evacuated its Jerusalem fortress when Jewish rule was restored, and probably took part in the last stand, the siege of Beitar in 136.

50 See A. Epstein, *Beit HaTalmud,* IV, 173, Ginzburg, *Legends of the Jews*, "Yaakov," note 162. Isaac Heinemann, *(Darkhe HaAgadah)* (Jerusalem, 1949), 32 [Hebrew]. Samuel Krauss, *Persia and Rome in the Talmud and Midrashim* (Jerusalem: 1948), 100–105; 177–178 [Hebrew]. Irit Aminoff, *The Figure of Esau and the Kingdom of Edom in Palestinian Midrashic-Talmudic Literature in the Tannaic and Amoraic Periods.* (1981), 258–265. Louis H. Feldman, *Josephus's Interpretation of the Bible* (Berkeley, 1998), 323. Ibid., *Remember Amalek: Vengeance, Zealotry, and Group Destruction in the Bible According to Philo, Pseudo-Philo, and Josephus* (Cincinnati: 2004), 67. Daphne Barak-Erez, *Outlawed Pigs: Law, Religion, and Culture in Israel* (Madison: 2007), 20. Jordan D. Rosenblum, "Why Do You Refuse to Eat Pork?": Jews, Food, and Identity in Roman Palestine" *JQR*, 100:1 (2010) 95–110; Misgav Har-Peled, *The Dialogical Beast: The Identification Of Rome With The Pig In Early Rabbinic Literature*, 2013. Ernest Wiesenberg, "Related Prohibitions: Swine Breeding and the Study of Greek." *HUCA* 27 (1956): 213–233.

chaeological findings, bricks, tiles,[51] and coins[52] (still being found to-day[53]) with its name and emblem substantiate its presence there. It's even suggested the emblem was intended to humiliate and antagonize the Jewish population, for whom it was forbidden to even raise pigs.[54] Moreover, historians suggest the symbolization of Rome as a pig may have come into prominence at the time of Hadrian and the fall of Beitar (135 CE) when, to insult the Jews, the image of a pig was attached to the southern gate of Jerusalem then transformed into the Roman colony, Aelia Capitolina.[55]

There is no explicit mention of the iconographic connection in any Midrash. However, in a very late eleventh-century version of R. Simon's Midrash in *Midrash, Lekach Tov* we find:

> "And Esav was forty years old" (*Bereishit* 26:34). This is as it says "the Fourth Animal," that Daniel saw but did not mention its name. "And it was different from all the other beasts" (Daniel 7:7); it is the image of a pig and Daniel did not mention its name since it was so repulsive; it is the kingdom of Edom, meaning the kingdom of Rome that on its flag was engraved the image of a pig; it was compared to a pig, as it says, "A wild boar ravages it" (Tehilim 80:14) since it raises its hooves when it lies down, to say, 'See I am pure'...

We also find in a Midrash that R. Simon taught—a pig (or two pigs). "...the pig dug its hooves into [the wall] and all of *Eretz Yisrael* trembled." Since the context describes the war between Hyrcanus and Aris-

---

51 "The Kilnworks of the Tenth Legion Fretensis," in *The Roman and Byzantine Near East: Some Recent Archaeological Research,* ed. John H Humphrey (Ann Arbor: *Journal of Roman Archaeology*, 1995), 273. H. Goldfus, B. Arubas, "The Kilnworks of the Tenth Legion at the Jerusalem Convention Center," *Qadmoniot* 122, no. 2 (2002): 111–119 (Hebrew).

52 Dan Barag, "The Countermarks of the Legio Decima Fretensis (Preliminary Report)," The Patterns of Monetary development in Phoenicia and Palestine in Antiquity. Proceedings of the International Numismatic Convention, Jerusalem 27-31 December 1963, ed. A. Kindler (Tel Aviv: Schocken, 1967), 117–125, plates IX-XI. K. A. Linnqvist, "New Vistas on the Countermarked Coins of the Roman Prefects of Judaea," Israel Numismatic Journal 12 (1992): 56–70. Countermarks of the boar emblem also appear on a Palestinian Judaea Capta coin of Titus and of Vespasia.n Barag, "Countermarks," 120. A. Spijkerman, "Some Rare Jewish Coins," Liber Annuus 13 (1962/3): 315, fig. 56.

53 A *Legio X Fretensis* tile was recently discovered near Jerusalem's Binyanei HaUmah.

54 Mishnah Bava Kama 7:7.

55 S. Krauss, *Monumenta Talmudica*, V, (Wien: 1914), 15.

tobulus, Rome's first entry into Israel, the pig motif has been interpreted to reflect the Fretensis Legion iconography.[56] (In *Avot DeRabbi Natan* I:4: Vespasian catapulted a pig's head onto the sacrificial limbs on the altar and Jerusalem was captured.) It's noted[57] in *Targum Sheni* to Esther 1:3 about the siege of Jerusalem: עד דאתא פרנטוס ונכס חזירא וזרק מן דמיה על בית מקדשא: "The gates did not want to open until פרנטוס came and slaughtered a pig and sprinkled some of its blood upon the Temple and defiled it and it opened itself" and that the name פרנטוס might parallel Fronto Haterius whom Josephus names as commander of the troops besieging the Temple Mount (*Wars* VI 238, 242), or that it might play on *perna*, Latin for ham[58].

What does this have to do with Rebbi, Ein Tab, and *Kiddush HaChodesh*?

Everything. This is what connects R. Simon's *midrashim* with his protest about *Kiddush Chodesh* leaving Eretz Yehudah. As mentioned, Rebbi's attempt to sanctify the *Ibur* in Lod met with fatally disastrous results (*Yerushalmi Sanhedrin* 1:2):

> Twenty-four carriages of the house of Rebbi went in to be *me'aber* the year in Lod and an *ayin hoRa* ['evil eye'] entered them and they all died at one time. From that hour on, they removed it [the *Ibur HaShanah*] from Yehudah and established it in the Galil. They wished to remove even the *simana* (*Kiddush HaChodesh*). R. Simon said to them, "We are not leaving in *Yehudah* even a remembrance."

What was the 'evil eye'? It was really evil. They were apparently attacked by the forces of Pescennius Niger[59] in the war between his armies and those of Septimius Severus in 193 CE, the year of the five emperors, in which five claimants fought for the title of Roman Emperor.[60] Rebbi

---

56 Tal Ilan, "The Civil War of the Hasmonean Brothers" [Hebrew] in בין יוסיפוס וחז"ל (Vered Noam, ed.), 318; Menachem Kister, "ביאורים באגדות החורבן באבות דרבי נתן", *Tarbitz* 67, 1988, 484–529. Ginzberg, *Commentary on the Palestinian Talmud*, IV, 36-37.

57 J. Rosenblum, "Why Do You Refuse to Eat Pork?", 108.

58 T. Ilan, ibid, citing Beate Ego, Targum Sheni zu Esther. Übersetzung, Kommentar und theologische Deutung, Tübingen 1996, 179–80.

59 G. Alon, תולדות ישראל בתקופת המשנה והתלמוד, vol. II; 64; 94–103.

60 *Dio Cassius.*

and the Jews sided with Septimius[61] (and received important privileges when he was victorious[62]). Septimus and the House of Severus was generally positive in relations with Jews[63] while Pescennius once threatened to tax the air Jews breathed in Judea.[64]

And in Judea, Pescennius' forces were the Tenth Legion.[65]

The *Ibur HaShanah* at Lod was attacked by the Tenth Legion.[66] We may surmise that if R. Simon generally had reason to have hostility to the Tenth Legion, this would certainly add to the antipathy. His protest against moving the *Kiddush HaChodesh* because of the attack thus becomes even more significant.

This is particularly poignant as Maharsha reads R. Simon's Chulin 60a *midrash* of God telling the moon, "Go and diminish yourself" as an allegory about Israel's exilic diminution and renewed dominion. R. Simon's protest to retain *Kiddush HaChodesh* in Yehudah effectively stabilized and reinstated the *nesiut's* dominion there: David HaMelech was alive and well at Ein Tab.

A *Siman Tov* for Us

Maharsha (*Sanhedrin* 42a) and Maharatz Chayes (*Rosh HaShanah* 25a) connect סמן טוב ומזל טוב יהא לנו ולכל ישׂראל, that we say in *Kiddush HaLevanah* with the [good!] סימן of דוד מלך ישׂראל חי וקים sent from Ein Tab. While סמן טוב from the 8th-century *Masechet Soferim* considerably predates the sixteenth-century custom of saying דוד מלך ישׂראל, reading the סמן טוב in connection with the "*David HaMelech*" *simana* (and saying it) expresses a great truth.

---

61 M. Avi-Yonah, בימי רומא וביזנטיום, 48–51; G. Alon, תולדות ישראל בתקופת המשנה והתלמוד, vol. II; 94-103. Coins struck in Tzippori, Rebbi's city, testify to Jewish admiration of Septimus Severus: Y. Meshorer, "מטבעות ציפור כמקור היסטורי", *Tzion* 42, 1978, 185.

62 Scriptores Historiae Augustae, Severus, IX, 5.

63 Ibid. Alexander Severus' pro-Jewish attitude was so well-known that his detractors mocked him as "The Severan *Archisynagogus*" (*Scriptores Historiae Augustae,* Alexander, 28.7).

64 Scriptores Historiae Augustae, Pescennius Niger, VII, 9.

65 *Dio Cassius.*

66 In its way the Roman attack on *Ibur HaShanah* emblematically embodied the midrashic opposition (*Bereishit Rabah* 6:6; *Tanhuma* (Buber) Bo 9; *Pesikta Rabati* 15): "The big one [עֵשָׂו בְּנָהּ הַגָּדֹל: Rivkah's big son Esav (*Bereishit* 27:15)] counts to the big one [הַמָּאוֹר הַגָּדֹל: the sun:] and the small one [בְּנָהּ הַקָּטָן: her small son Yaakov] to the small one [הַמָּאוֹר הַקָּטֹן: the moon]."

It is our prayer for a redeemed world in which the workings of the universe might be validated and sanctified by the sovereignty of the Beit Din.[67] In articulating the core premise of our *Kiddush HaLevanah Berachah,* the hope and belief in redemption and renewal by Moshiach ben David,[68] the *"David Melech Yisrael Chai VeKayam" simana* certainly is and continues to be a *siman tov* for us, that *David HaMelech* is alive and well. ☙

67 In Etzion's formulation in כזה ראה וחדש: a world in which every month the entire world would see how time can be sanctified on the testimony of two Jewish witnesses.

68 For Rebbi himself as the potential Moshiach: *Bavli Sanhedrin* 98b, and as identified by his students (among them R. Chiyya) as the actual Moshiach: *Yerushalmi Shabbat* 16:1; *Vayikra Rabah* 15:4; *Eichah Rabah* 4.

A Positive Light on the Nations: R. Moshe Isserles' Revisionistic Views on Christianity

By: RABBI ASHER TURIN*

Edited by: Jonathan L. Milevsky+

Opinions of the Geonim and Rishonim on the question of whether the Christian belief system is permissible for non-Jews who adhere to the Noahide code[1] range from a clear prohibition, based on the view that

---

* Rabbi Asher Turin, of blessed memory, was a student in Ner Israel Rabbinical Seminary in Baltimore, MD, and later a lecturer at Ner Israel in Toronto, Canada. He was the co-director of the Machon Tzvi institute in Jerusalem, the spiritual leader of the Baycrest Terrace Congregation, and the Chaplain of the Miles Nadal Jewish Community Centre.
This paper is part of a larger, unpublished work, which was researched and written, some of it by hand, by the late Rabbi Asher Turin for the NISHMA foundation. While no date is given for the paper, based on the sources he cites, this most probably dates to the early 2000s. I thank Rabbi Benjamin Hecht for providing me with a PDF copy of the paper—the original document is unfortunately no longer available. I also thank Dr. Albert Friedberg for the generous sponsorship of this editing project. Ed.

\+ The arguments made in the body of the paper are entirely R. Turin's own. I have reworded most of the sentences and rearranged many of the paragraphs, so that the argumentation is continuous, and have also removed some of the tangential discussions. Nevertheless, I have left the substance and structure of the paper unchanged, and the only supplementary information, clarification, and sources are inserted into the footnotes, all of which are identified by 'ed.' Ed.

1 The Noahide code is seen by some as including more than one commandment pertaining to idolatry. On this view, Christianity would be encompassed by one of the following commandments: it can be a violation of the commandment against blasphemy, either directly or indirectly, inasmuch as some argue that the belief in God is a presupposition of the commandment against blasphemy.

Jonathan Milevsky is a graduate of Ner Israel Rabbinical College in Baltimore, MD and holds a PhD in Religious Studies from McMaster University. He is an Ontario Graduate Fellow and recipient of the Hershel and Michael Recht Award in Jewish Studies. He has published academic articles in the fields of rabbinic thought, medieval Jewish philosophy, and modern Jewish thought. His manuscript, about Prof. David Novak's Jewish natural law theory, is being reviewed for publication with Brill.

Christianity is considered idolatrous,[2] all the way to a positive acceptance of Christianity as non-idolatrous.[3] In this article, we focus primarily on the seminal ruling of Rabbi Moshe Isserles (Rema),[4] and its reception, but we will also analyze the position of Menaḥem Ha-Meiri, who was R. Isserles' intellectual predecessor in this regard, and Rabbi Yaakov Emden, who was his successor.

In discussing the permissibility of a Jew causing a non-Jew to swear in the name of his or her religion, R. Isserles wrote that, with respect to the Noahide code, Christianity is not seen as idolatrous, and it is therefore not forbidden for non-Jews. Accordingly, it poses no halakhic problem for a Jew to cause Jesus' name to be uttered in an oath.[5] Even from this summary of his words, it is clear that Isserles' opinion belongs on the more lenient end of the spectrum.

Alternatively, it can be a facet of idolatry, but without a death penalty. But see R. Nissim Gerondi (Ran) on *Alfasi*, *Avodah Zarah*, chap. 1, citing Naḥmanides, who considered the possibility that swearing in the name of an idol is not one of the prohibitions included in the Noahide code.

2 Besides the opinion of Maimonides, cited in the following footnote, R. Turin also mentions Rabbenu Ḥananel ben Hushiel's commentary on Tractate *Sanhedrin*. Although I have not found an explicit statement from him about Christianity or *shituf*—the pertinent sections are missing from the Almanzi Codex—in one volume that contains the commentary of several Rishonim on *Sanhedrin*, there is an extensive commentary on *Sanhedrin*, which is attributed to Rabbenu Ḥananel. Two significant points can be found in the comments to folios 58a-65b. The first is a reference to Jesus in the context of a person who considers himself a god; and the second is a categorical prohibition of forming business partnerships with a non-Jew, lest the non-Jew swear in his or her god's name. Both of these statements seem to take it for granted that Christianity amounts to idolatry. *Otzar Ha-Geonim Le-Masekhet Sanhedrin*, ed. H. Toibish (Jerusalem: Mossad Ha-Rav Kook, 1966), 553, 555. I thank Dr. Albert Friedberg for this reference. Ed.

3 For the former, see Maimonides, *Commentary to the Mishnah, Avodah Zarah*, *Sanhedrin*, chap. 10 (in uncensored editions); Maimonides, *Mishneh Torah, Hilkhot Melakhim*, chap. 12; Maimonides, Epistles of Maimonides: Crisis and Leadership, trans. Abraham Halkin (Philadelphia: Jewish Publication Society, 1985), 98. For the latter, see Menaḥem Ha-Meiri, *Ḥidushei Ha-Meiri* on *Bava Kamma* 37b, 38a, 113a-b, vol. 5 (Jerusalem: Institute for Publication of Books and Study of Manuscripts, 1977), 40, 107; Rabbi David Kimḥi, *Pirush Rabbenu David Kimḥi al Ha-Torah* on Genesis 22:1, ed. A. Ginzburg (Pressburg: Schmid, 1842), 55.

4 R. Isserles (1530–1572) lived in Poland. He is considered the bedrock of present day halakhah.

5 See R. Moshe Isserles' gloss on *Shulḥan Arukh: Oraḥ Ḥayyim* 156.

As I shall argue, however, the sources upon which he based his argument do not seem to bear out his view of Christianity. On the contrary, the authorities he cited subscribe to the view that Christianity is idolatrous. Once this point is established, this article will then consider the parameters of this new extra-halakhic position. Finally, we will attempt to reconcile the more positive view of Christianity found in the writings of Meiri, R. Isserles, and R. Emden with that of the Rishonim and Aḥaronim.

The View of Tosfot

We begin with the view of Tosafot, which serves as R. Isserles's main source.[6] It should be noted at the outset that, in the comments of Tosafot, and in R. Isserles' remarks, the non-Jews to which they referred are Christians. Tosafot deal with the question whether a Jew who suspects that his non-Jewish partner has misappropriated funds can have him swear an oath to prove his innocence. In rendering their decision, Tosafot considered whether, in doing so, a Jew would be violating one of the following three prohibitions.

The first prohibition in question is that of a Jew mentioning the name of idolatry, emerging from the biblical commandment, "ושם אלהים אחרים לא תזכירו".[7] And later in the verse, "לא ישמע על-פִּיךָ". According to the Talmud, the first part of the verse refers to the biblical prohibition for a Jew to utter the name of an idol. The second part of the verse, however, refers to the prohibition for a Jew to swear or take a vow in the name of an idol or to cause another, even a non-Jew, to do so. The latter prohibition, which pertains to another party, may be biblical in origin, or it may be a loose allusion (*asmakhta*) rather than a proper biblical source, for the Talmud considers an alternate interpretation of that

6 Tosafot to *Bekhorot* 2b, s.v. *shema*, repeated in Tosafot to *Sanhedrin* 63b, s.v. *asur,* and cited by Asher ben Yehiel, *Tosafot Ha-Rosh* on *Sanhedrin* 63b, ed. C.B. Ravitz (Jerusalem: Mossad Rav Kook, 2004), 353; *Rosh, Sanhedrin* 7.3. See also Tosafot to *Gittin* 50b, s.v. *yetomin*; *Talmid Ha-Ramban* on *Sanhedrin* 63b, in *Sanhedria Gedolah Le-Masekhet Sanhedrin,* vol. 5, ed. G. Lezevnik (Jerusalem: Makhon Harry Fischel, 1968), 84.
Isserles' sources were inserted by a later author, who based them on Isserles' book *Darkhei Moshe Ha-Arukh* (Sulzbach: M. Bloch, 1692). The sources quoted by Isserles in *Shulkhan Arukh, Oraḥ Ḥayyim* 156 are those discussed by him in *Darkhei Moshe.* Isserles' other sources are Rabbenu Yeruḥem and Rav Nissim Gaon. Rabbenu Yeruḥem, *Toldot Adam Ve-ḥava* 17:5 (Kapust, 1837), 127; Rabbenu Nissim (Ran) to *Alfasi, Avodah Zarah*, chap. 1.

7 Exodus 23:12.

part of the verse.[8] Be that as it may, on this basis, the rabbis of the Talmud prohibit a Jew from forming a business partnership with a non-Jew, as it may result in the Jew being forced to take the non-Jew to a gentile court and the non-Jew taking an oath in the name of an idol.[9] (In the subsequent section, these halakhic concerns will be indicated with an A.)

The second prohibition relates to oaths. There is a distinct commandment against joining (*shituf*) in the context of oaths. The prohibition pertains to mentioning anything in the created universe alongside God's name. There may be one or possibly two prohibitions included in this commandment. 1. The biblical prohibition of a Jew swearing with *shituf.*[10] 2. There may be a violation of לא ישמע, meaning the commandment against making someone else swear with *shituf.* The question is whether a Jew would be violating this second prohibition by making a non-Jew take an oath in this fashion. (In the subsequent section, this halakhic question will be indicated with a C.)

The third prohibition is of ולפני עור לא תתן מכשל.[11] These words are understood to be a commandment for Jews against causing other Jews to sin. If, and only if, non-Jews are prohibited against *shituf* in oaths, a Jew may be violating the prohibition of לפני עור—in addition to the other prohibitions we have mentioned—by causing a non-Jew to take an oath with *shituf.* An example would be swearing in the name of God and joining the name of a Christian saint.[12] (In the subsequent analysis, this halakhic question will be indicated with a B.)

The issue before the halakhic decisors was whether a Jew violates the second part of the לא ישמע clause if he or she takes a non-Jew to

---

8 *Sanhedrin* 63b; Tosafot, s.v. *she-lo.*

9 Rabbenu Asher states that if the Jew sees that a non-Jew is about to take such an oath, the Jew should ideally not proceed, the reason being that the non-Jew may still lie and swear falsely in his or her deity's name; and that would mean that the Jew is making the non-Jew take a gratuitous oath in the name of an idol. This outcome is something the Jew should avoid. The Rosh adds, however, that the Jew is allowed to proceed if there is the remote possibility that, in the last moment, the non-Jew will admit his or her guilt out of fear of taking the oath. The Rosh seems to be assuming that the non-Jew will call upon his or her idolatry and that Christianity is therefore idolatrous. Asher ben Yehiel, *She'elot U-Teshuvot Ha-Rosh,* no.18 (Venice: 1607), 33–35.

10 *Sukkah* 45a-b; b. *Sanhedrin* 63a.

11 Leviticus 19:14.

12 Cf. Rabbi Henkin, *B'nei Banim* 3:36 (Jerusalem: 1997), 128–136, where it appears that Rabbi Henkin understands Tosafot to be referring to a lesser form of idolatry.

court and thereby causes him or her to take an oath. Tosafot referred to a disagreement about this issue: According to Rabbi Shmuel ben Meir (Rashbam), it is a biblical prohibition that cannot be permitted under any circumstance, including the case under consideration. According to Rabbenu Tam, however, the prohibition coming from the second part of the verse is an *asmakhta*, and the source is thus rabbinic;[13] and the rabbis did not apply this law in cases where such an oath is necessary for a Jew to prevent a monetary loss.[14] While Rabbenu Tam conceded that it is prohibited to enter into a situation where an oath of an idolater might be required, he stated that, when one is in that situation, in order to protect Jewish financial interests, one can ask the non-Jew to take an oath on the basis of the talmudic dispensation of collecting defaulted loans on a non-Jewish holiday.[15]

Rabbenu Tam then goes on to say that, in his time (i.e., in the 12th century), there is no longer the possibility of violating the commandment, for the non-Jews in his day do not mention the name of an idol in their oaths. Tosafot in *Bekhorot* includes a lengthy statement on this matter in Rabbenu Tam's name.[16]

> בזמן הזה כולן נשבעים בקדשים ואין תופסים בהם אלהות. A. ואע"פ שמזכירין [עמהם] שם שמים וכוונתם [לד"א[17] מ"מ] , ,אין זה [שם] עבודת כוכבים,[18] כי דעתם לשם עושה שמים וארץ.ואע"ג שמשתתף[19] ש"ש ודבר אחר אין כאן לפני עור לא תתן מכשול דבני נח לא הוזהרו על כך. B. ולדידן לא אשכחן איסור בגרם שיתוף.C.

13 The term *asmakhta* means that the biblical verse upon which the prohibition is supposed to be based is merely suggestive of that law. The law is therefore rabbinic in nature.

14 The view of Naḥmanides is similar to Rabbenu Tam's, as can be seen in the commentary of Rabbenu Nissim (Ran) on *Alfasi*, *Avodah Zarah*, chap. 1, in which he cites Naḥmanides. Naḥmanides went further than Rabbenu Tam, however. The former wrote that he was tempted to say that, if the non-Jew initiates the oath and formulates it according to his own beliefs, there is no sin on the part of the Jew (or non-Jew).

15 This dispensation similarly involves lifting a rabbinic prohibition.

16 The three separate halakhic issues discussed thus far will be indicated by their corresponding letter. Ed.

17 I.e., Jesus.

18 R. Isserles' other source, namely, Rabbenu Nissim (Ran), cited Tosafot as saying, "they do not swear in the name of idolatry." Rabbenu Nissim (Ran) to *Alfasi*, *Avodah Zarah*, chap. 1.

19 Other versions read *meshatef*, i.e., combining God's name with that of another being.

> At this time, everyone swears by the Saints and does not include any theistic meaning. And even though they mention the name of heaven and they intend something else, in any case this is not idolatry, for they mean the Creator of heaven and earth. And even though they combine the name of heaven and something else, there is no [prohibition of] "placing a stumbling block," because Noahides were not commanded on this. And for us there is no prohibition in causing "joining."[20]

Thus, Tosafot proposed the following about the three issues:

A. Although non-Jews are idolaters,[21] the talmudic prohibition of forming business partnerships with them no longer applies; and that is because non-Jews are no longer swearing in the name of Jesus. Instead, they are now swearing in the name of the saints and/or on the four books of the evangelists.[22]

---

20 The translation here is my own. Rabbeinu Tam's ruling pertains to an oath made by a non-Jew in the name of "God omnipotent and his holy four evangelists." See Jacob Katz, *Halakah Ve-Kabbalah* (Jerusalem: Magnes, 1984), 279, fn. 60. There are several legal implications to Rabbeinu Tam's statement, and R. Turin explains each point in the section that follows. Broadly speaking, the two main points that emerge from this ruling is that, both with regard to the saints (*kedoshim*) that are mentioned and with respect to combining God's name with another being (*shituf*), Jews do not have to be concerned that non-Jews include those terms in their oaths. The former, because the saints are not gods; the latter, because joining (*shituf*) is not prohibited to non-Jews. Ed.

21 Tosafot make this point about Christians in full view of their acceptance of God as creator. This belief does not seem to change Tosafot's halakhic view of Christianity as *avodah zarah*.

22 I.e., the New Testament or the evangelists. This expression comes from Rabbi Solomon ben Aderet (Rashba), who writes, "they swear on the four," meaning the four gospels of Matthew, Mark, Luke, and John. R. Solomon ben Aderet, *Teshuvot Ha-Rashba* 7:302, ed. A. Zalzik (Jerusalem: Makhon Yerushalayim, 2000), 79. In his edition, Rabbenu Yeruḥem substitutes the word *evangelion* for "their holy ones" (*kaddeshim*, alternatively *kedoshim*). Rabbenu Yeruḥem, *Toldot Adam Ve-Ḥava* 17:5 (Kapust, 1837), 127. More evidence comes from Prof. Y. Baer, who posits that Christians used oaths with the Latin words "*per deum omnipotentum et per ista sacra quattour evangelica*" (meaning, to the omnipotent God and his holy four evangelists), cited by Jacob Katz, *Halakhah Ve-Kabbalah*, 279, fn. 60.

B. A Jew is not violating the prohibition of causing another to stumble in this situation, for the commandment against *shituf* is not included in the seven Noahide laws.[23]

C. There is no prohibition to cause a non-Jew to make an oath with *shituf*, which would parallel the prohibition of causing another to make an oath in the name of idolatry. The reasoning behind this ruling is that the Talmud makes no mention of this prohibition.[24]

It should be noted that this statement appears to amount to a new type of *shituf*: in the talmudic era, non-Jews did swear in the name of Jesus. Here, however, Tosafot are concerned with the medieval custom of swearing in God's name with the addition of Jesus' name; and this is where Tosafot are lenient. Nevertheless, such an oath must still be considered invoking idolatry, and so it would be prohibited for Jews, and possibly non-Jews as well. That is to say, a Jew would be guilty of לא ישמע if he or she were to cause—directly or even indirectly—a non-Jew to do this. It must therefore be the case that Tosafot are thus only discussing the mention of God's name with the name of saints, and stating that, although Jews are commanded against doing so, they are not prohibited to cause another to engage in this type of *shituf*. And further, this *shituf* is not included in the Noahide laws, for it is to be seen as separate from the commandment against idolatry. It also follows that a Jew is not guilty of לפני עור if he causes a non-Jew to engage in this new kind of *shituf*.

The View of R. Moshe Isserles

In using the aforementioned Tosafot as the source for his ruling, Rabbi Isserles revealed a seemingly divergent understanding of it. On R. Isserles' reading, Tosafot suggested that, although non-Jews call on Jesus, Jews can still enter into partnerships with them, for Christianity is not considered to be idolatry. R. Isserles wrote as follows:[25]

---

23 It should be noted that Tosafot did not suggest that there is no prohibition against *shituf*, as if it were treating the matter of a belief in the Trinity. Its concern here is only with the status of making an oath that joins the creator with another created being or form.

24 Still, one would be violating the commandment of causing a Jew to make an oath in that fashion (לפני עור).

25 The positions on the three halakhic issues are indicated with A, B, and C. Ed.

ויש מקילין בעשיות שותפות עם העכו"ם בזמן הזה משום שאין העכום בזמן הזה נשבעים בע"א. מכל מקום כוונתם לעושה שמים וארץ אלא שמשתתפים שם שמים ודבר אחר.[26] ואע"ג דמזכירין הע"א[27] ולא מצינו שיש בזה משום לפני עור לא תתן מכשול דהרי אינם מוזהרין על השתוף.

There are those who are lenient in forming partnerships with non-Jews at this time because non-Jews at this time do not swear in the name of idolatry. And even though they mention idols, their intention is to the creator of heaven but they just combine the name of heaven with something else. And we did not find that there is in this [the prohibition of] placing a stumbling block in front of the blind, because they are not commanded on "joining" (*shituf*).[28]

With regard to issue A, what R. Isserles appears to be saying is that non-Jews mention the name of Jesus in their oaths, but that act is not idolatrous for non-Jews, the reason being that the oath shows their respect for the supreme God; and Jesus is a subordinate deity. That belief is not idolatry for them. Therefore, a Jew who causes non-Jews to take these oaths is not in violation of the causative part of לא ישמע.[29] The basis for that statement is that, in adding the name of God to the name of Jesus, non-Jews remove any hint of idolatry. On issue B, R. Isserles posited that the Jew is not violating the prohibition of לפני עור, since, as we just explained, Christianity is not idolatry. On issue C, R. Isserles did not accept the view that causing a non-Jew to join the name of God with a created being or form runs parallel to the causative prohibition which stems from the second part of לא ישמע. It also follows that causing a non-Jew to express a Christian belief does not constitute a sin.

Thus, in a few short lines, R. Isserles expressed a novel view that extends beyond the decisions of his predecessors. That is to say none of the sources he cited write that contemporary non-Jews no longer mention the name of idolatry, but R. Isserles seems to understand his sources as saying so. More to the point, he read those sources as saying that Christianity is not idolatry [*avodah zarah*] for non-Jews.[30] Further, R.

26 I.e. Jesus.

27 Isserles' gloss on *Shulḥan Arukh: Oraḥ Ḥayyim* 156.

28 Translation is my own. The context is clearly the status of non-Jews, rather than simply the meaning of their oaths, which in this case is a reference to both God and Jesus, and the plain meaning seems to be that non-Jews are no longer idolaters. Ed.

29 It is possible that this concept does not exist, even for a Jew.

30 This view is slightly problematic in light of the talmudic prohibition against *shituf* for non-Jews. In one statement in the Talmud, it is said that that which is

Isserles considered this new view to be authoritative and widely applicable. For example, in his gloss on *Shulḥan Arukh, Yoreh De'ah* 151, he sided with the lenient opinion and allowed Jews to sell Christians items that might be used in religious services. R. Shabtai Ha-Kohen (*Shakh*) cited it in the following manner:

> לשון ד"מ מיהו בזמן הזה יש להקל מטעם דמקילין להשתתף עמהם.[31]
> This is the wording of *Darkhei Moshe*. However, at this time, there should be lenience on the basis that we are lenient to partner with them.

However, according to many scholars, the Talmud refers to Christianity as idolatry [*avodah zarah*], and this law pertains to both Jews and non-Jews.[32] The same view is found in post-talmudic literature.[33] R. Isserles is the first decisor to refer to Christianity as *shituf*; Tosafot would

---

considered to be idolatrous for a Jew, and therefore punishable by a Jewish court, is equally prohibited to a non-Jew. *Sanhedrin* 56b. According to all the opinions in the Talmud, *shituf*, which, as we have seen, is the belief in the sharing of powers between God and other entities, is prohibited for a Jew. *Sanhedrin* 63a. Thus, *shituf* must be prohibited for non-Jews. Indeed, according to the opinion of Rabbi Meir Ha-Levi Abulafia, *shituf* is even worse than idolatry! R. Meir Ha-Levi Abulafia, *Yad Rama: Masekhet Sanhedrin* (Salonika, 1798), 70.

31 See the Shakh's gloss on *Shulḥan Arukh: Yoreh De'ah* 151:1, wherein he goes on to cite *Shulḥan Arukh: Oraḥ Ḥayyim* 156.
It may be rebutted that R. Isserles still believed that Christianity was *avodah zarah*, but he ruled that way in order to protect Jews. The basis for the ruling would be *davar ha-domeh*, or the idea that the sages have the power to uproot a law, even in the form of a *kum ve-aseh*, when there is a strong basis for doing so, such as that the case is similar to another Torah law. This idea appears in a number of places in the Tosafot regarding edicts and laws advanced by the Talmud, most prominently in Tosafot to *Yevamot* 89b, s.v. *keivan*. Thus, R. Isserles may have been taking his sources, which appear to accept Christianity as non-idolatrous, out of context, in order to justify what is in reality an uprooting of a Torah law in the form of a *kum ve-aseh*, meaning a decree through which one violates a Torah law through action rather than inaction. However, it is less than reasonable to assume that R. Isserles and his disciple, Rabbi Mordechai Yaffe, made such a change to the halakhah without informing or consulting with the sages of their generation. Also, if the operating assumption would be that Christianity has the status of *avodah zarah*, the case would be comparable to a *hora'at sha'ah* which cannot be enacted in cases of *avodah zarah*, despite the injunction of listening to the prophet (Deuteronomy 18:15).

32 See David Berger's "Jewish-Christian Polemics" in *The Encyclopedia of Religion*, ed. Mircea Eliade (New York: Macmillan, 1986), 389–95.

33 That is, apart from polemic and apologetic material, but this is not an appropriate basis for halakhic decisions.

not have done so. In Tosafot's rishonic frame of reference, something either is, or is not, *avodah zarah*. But R. Isserles actually interprets Tosafot to be saying that the *shituf* of Christianity—that is, an affirmation of God as the supreme God, along with a subordinate deity, namely, Jesus—is not *avodah zarah* and is permissible for non-Jews.[34] But in fact, Tosafot did not say that.[35]

In the vocabulary of Tosafot, *shituf* does not mean the Trinity. Rather, it means joining something created, such as a saint, with God's name, specifically in an oath or when dealing with other matters that concern God. In the view of Tosafot, Christianity is not "non-pagan *avodah zarah* in a monotheistic mode," in the sense that Tosafot viewed it as something less than full idolatry, as David Berger contends.[36] Tosafot used the Christian belief in God as creator only as an argument against the claim that, since they also mean Jesus, the term Lord is contaminated and assumes the status of *avodah zarah*.

Explaining Rabbi Isserles' Ruling: Censorship

How is it possible, then, that R. Isserles arrived at this view—an apparent misinterpretation of Tosafot? Perhaps the reason can be found in Christian censorship of Tosafot. The censorship can be detected by comparing the Tosafot on *Bekhorot* 2b, which was R. Isserles's main

---

34 And this is in fact the way many Aḥaronim understand R. Isserles' comments, as we will go on to show.

35 The Tosafists have a variety of views on the status of Christianity, so their position may be somewhat oversimplified by R. Turin. See for example Tosafot to *Avodah Zarah* 2a, where the following is written: "Even if they [non-Jews] were regarded as idol worshippers...," suggesting that some Tosafists felt otherwise. See also Rabbi Meir Hakohen's statement, citing Shmuel ben Meir's tradition from his grandfather Rashi, namely, that non-Jews of his day were not idolaters and would not "go and thank" their gods during their holiday for their business transactions. R. Meir Ha-Kohen, *Hagahot Maimoniot*, in *Mishneh Torah, Hilkhot Avodah Zarah* 9:4, ed. Shabsai Frankel, vol. 1 (Jerusalem: Shabsai Frankel, 2000), 171. I thank Dr. Buchman for these two references. Ed.

36 David Berger, "Jews, Gentiles, and the Modern Egalitarian Ethos: Some Tentative Thoughts," in *Formulating Responses in an Egalitarian Age*, ed. Marc Stern (Lanham, MD: Rowman and Littlefield, 2005), 98. For a more extensive treatment of the Tosafot at issue, see the Appendix to Berger, *The Rebbe, the Messiah, and the Scandal of Orthodox Indifference* (Liverpool: The Littman Library of Jewish Civilization, 2008), 175–177. Ed.

source, with all the other versions, especially the Tosafot Sens version.[37] As we will see, the censorship completely changed the meaning of the Tosafot.

A key change is the substitution of the word גם, which appeared in the original version and can be found in Tosafot on *Sanhedrin*, with the word כי, as the result of which the sentence becomes "מ"מ אין זה [שם] עבודת כוכבים, גם דעתם לשם שמים עושה".[38] Other changes made by the censor are to substitute "לישו" with "דבר אחר," and then to remove this phrase altogether. The words מ"מ [*mikol makom*] and שם were also removed, rendering it... אין זה עבודת כוכבים, giving the impression that Christianity is not perceived as *avodah zarah* at all.[39] We can now understand how R. Isserles may have been misled by this censored version. The difficulty with this explanation, however, is that Rabbenu Yeruḥem's version of the Tosafot was not censored; and R. Isserles cites him as a source for his ruling.[40] So how do we understand R. Isserles' interpretation?

We can attempt to offer an explanation based on a responsum attributed to R. Meir of Rothenberg.[41] This responsum reads, in part,[42] "משום ד(ב)גוים דחוץ לארץ לאו עובדי ע"ז הם." It should be noted that this view would be even more lenient than permitting the oath only in cases of financial loss. This responsum, however, does not cite Rabbenu Tam's ruling in its entirety. In order to understand Rabbenu Tam's, and thus R. Rothenberg's, views, it is necessary for us to analyze R. Yitzḥak

37 See *Tosfot Sens al Masekhet Bekhorot*, ed. Yaakov David Ilan (Jerusalem: Makhon Kenset Ha-Rishonim, 1997), 7-8. The Tosafot passage on *Bekhorot* is the one that was censored.

38 In any case, this does not have the [status] of idolatry. Also, their intention is to the Creator of heaven and earth. Translation mine. Ed.

39 For emphasis, the author writes the uncensored words in bold. I italicize them. Ed.

40 That is to say, R. Isserles would have presumably seen the uncensored version of Tosafot, but that did not affect his ruling. Ed.

41 R. Meir ben Barukh of Rothenberg, *Tshuvot Maram Me-Rotenberg*, vol. 2, no. 57, ed. Y. Z. Kahana (Jerusalem: Mossad Ha-Rav Kook, 1960), 52. It is possible, however, that this responsum is attributed to him in error. So *Likutei Ha-Rishonim* (Jerusalem: Makhon Le-Hotza'at Sifrei Rishonim, 1984), 297. The mistaken attribution may be based on another ruling of R. Rothenberg, in which he accepts the decision of Rabbenu Tam to allow a gentile to mention the name of his idol, provided it is for the purpose of saving Jewish funds.

42 Because (in the case of) the non-Jews outside Israel, they are not idol worshippers. Translation Mine. Ed.

ben Moshe's *Ohr Zaru'a*, which is where Rabbenu Tam's full ruling is mentioned.[43]

At the end of the first chapter of *Avodah Zarah*, R. Yitzḥak says why Rabbenu Tam believed non-Jews do not practice idolatry:[44] "לאו עובדי ע"ז הם אלא מנהג אבותיהם בידיהם". This statement is a reference to the Talmud, where it is written that gentiles that live outside of Israel are not serving idols.[45] But this teaching does not mean that non-Jews living outside of Israel are not *idolaters*. Referring to the level of religious fervour among non-Jews at that time, the teaching informs us that the everyday thoughts of non-Jews are no longer filled with devotion to their idols.[46] Therefore, Rabbenu Tam can still be understood as saying that there is a leniency in forming partnerships with non-Jews, and not because they are not true idolaters. Rather, the reason is that it is no longer certain that non-Jews would be inclined to swear in the name of their idol when they come to court. We might even say that such oaths can now be seen as a formality, not an affirmation of their belief system. In other words, perhaps the only significance of these oaths is in order to establish perjury, as is the case in modern times.

Explaining R. Isserles's Ruling: Noda Be-Yehudah Tenina

Notwithstanding the difficulties in understanding R. Isserles' view, it has become the halakhah. As a result, some of his contemporaries and successors attempted to make peace with it. Rabbi Shmuel Landau, who was the son of Rabbi Yeḥezkel Landau (author of the *Nodah Be-Yehudah*), understood R. Isserles as saying that Christianity is idolatrous, but *shituf* of an idol's name along with God's name is permitted. The words used in such an oath, which is a sign of deference to their God, would be, "I swear in God and Jesus."[47] Doing so is not an idolatrous

---

43 This was written by Rabbi Yitzḥak ben Moshe of Vienna, who was R. Meir of Rothenberg's teacher. Yitzḥak ben Moshe, *Ohr Zaru'a* (Zhitomir, 1862), 40.

44 Ibid.

45 *Ḥulin* 13b.

46 On this passage, see R. Tzvi Hirsch Chajes, who interprets it to mean that Christianity is not idolatrous outside of Israel, although this conflates this teaching with one that appears in a different context. Maharatz Chajes subsequently uses the same statement as a basis for stating that it is acceptable for non-Jews to practice *shituf*. Maharatz Chajes, *Hagahot Ha-Gaon Tzvi Hirsch Chajes*, *Berakhot* 57b.

47 This oath is not to be understood as saying, "You, Jesus, are my God," for that would legally be an act of worship.

act, but it is permitted only if God's name is mentioned as well.[48] R. Shmuel seems to be suggesting something novel, namely, that the prohibition of לא ישמע is violated only when the name of the idol is mentioned alone—without the name of God. It is far from obvious, however, that the insertion of an idol's name does not amount to an acceptance of that idol's yoke. Further, is this truly what R. Isserles suggested? The other problem is that none of the original sources upon which R. Isserles based his ruling, which implies that Christian worship cannot be equated with idolatry, either permitted causing a non-Jew to mention the name of idolatry, or suggested that Christianity is anything other than *avodah zarah*.[49]

Explaining R. Isserles' Ruling: Other Aḥaronim

Rabbi Shmuel ben Yosef Orgler,[50] Rabbi Yaakov Emden,[51] Rabbi Tzvi Hirsch Chajes,[52] and Rabbi Yaakov Tzvi Mecklenburg[53] all rely, either

48 Based on Maimonides' statement concerning the ultimate decay brought about by Enosh's idea of worshipping the heavenly bodies, in the first and second chapters of *Hilkhot Avodah Zarah*, R. Turin suggests that mentioning the heavenly bodies is forbidden only in a declaration of worship. That is to say it is only in the context of taking oaths that referring to other created beings serves to diminish the divine image, and that explains why Maimonides' terminology changes between the first four, and fifth, category of heretic in his *Hilkhot Teshuva*, 7:3. This interpretation differs from that of R. Yeḥezkel Landau and R. Shmuel Landau. See Y. Landau and S. Landau, *Nodah Be-Yehudah: Mahadura Tenina* on *Yoreh De'ah* 148 (New York: Halakhah Berurah, 1960), 93. Ed.

49 It seems, therefore, that R. Isserles was consciously appropriating Tosafot's language, taking it out of context and using it as a loose reference. We should therefore make note of R. Isserles' midrashic style in all his writings, particularly his *Torat Ha-Olah*. R. Isserles contends that Maimonides himself often presents a scriptural basis while knowing that those verses were not valid talmudic sources used to derive those laws. R. Isserles' opinion is that those sources only hint to the halakhah. That seems to have been the justification for R. Isserles' midrashic approach. For a full treatment of R. Isserles' usage of *remez*, *dugma*, and other techniques, see ibid., 19–40.

50 R. Orgler's *Olat Tamid* is frequently cited by Rabbi Abraham Gumbiner's *Magen Avraham*.

51 Much has been written on R. Emden's view of Christianity. In a recent article, Jacob J. Schacter places R. Emden's attitude in the context of his anti-Sabbatian views and argues that his positive view of Christianity was fueled, in part, by his rejection of Sabbatianism. Schacter also argues that Emden's view of Christianity reflects an ideal of what Christians can be, rather than his view of the Christians of his time. Jacob J. Schacter, "Rabbi Jacob Emden, Sabbatianism, and Frankism: Attitudes Towards Christianity in the Eighteenth

directly or indirectly, on the view of Rabbenu Nissim and Naḥmanides in order to understand the position of R. Isserles. These aforementioned Aḥaronim posit that non-Jews are not forbidden to worship intercessors to God, or those who possess powers that he has delegated. However, as we will show, Rabbenu Nissim and Naḥmanides do not actually state that such worship is permitted for Jews or non-Jews. A further challenge to the commentators, and to R. Isserles himself, comes from a teaching in the Talmud that states that both Jews and non-Jews are forbidden to worship any entity alongside God.[54]

According to R. Orgler, there are two types of *shituf*. The first of those is an equal sharing of power between God and something else. That type of worship is idolatrous.[55] The second kind of *shituf* is a hierarchical division of power between a supreme God and lower forces. The latter kind of worship is permissible.[56] For R. Shmuel, Rabbi Isserles cannot possibly intend the first type of *shituf* in his ruling, and so he must mean its second type. Thus, R. Shmuel understood R. Isserles as saying that Christians conceive of Jesus, as son of God, to be an intercessor or possessor of delegated powers. According to this view, R. Isserles is suggesting that *shituf* is permissible for non-Jews and, more important, that Christianity is not *avodah zarah*.

The difference that emerges here between shared power and hierarchy can also be seen in the thought of R. Emden, who was a prominent rabbinic authority in the 1700s. Much of R. Emden's discussion can be

---

Century," in *New Perspectives on Jewish-Christian Relations* (Leiden: Brill, 2012), 359–396. See also Jacob J. Schacter, "Rabbi Jacob Emden: Life and Major Works" (Ph.D. Diss. Harvard University, 1988), 701. Much like R. Turin's argument with regard to Meiri, the primary concern here is whether the sources upon which he bases his ruling can sustain his interpretation. Ed.

52 His views on the matter can also be found in *Hagahot Ha-Gaon Tzvi Hirsch Chajes* on *Ḥulin* 13b, *Horiyot* 18b, and in his *Tiferet Yisrael*, in Chajes, *Tiferet Yisrael*, in *Kol Sifrei Maharatz Chajes*, vol. 1 (Tel Aviv: Divrei Ḥakhamim, 1958), 483–491.

53 In his *Ktav Ve-Hakabbalah* on Deuteronomy 4:19 (Berlin 1880), 247–249.

54 These and other sources will be listed in the footnotes of the subsequent section.

55 An example of this type of *shituf* would be dualism.

56 R. Shmuel ben Yosef Orgler, *Olat Tamid, Oraḥ Ḥayyim* (Amsterdam: D. di Castro, 1681), 156.

found in his *She'elat Yavetz*.[57] In support of his position, he cited sections in tractate *Menaḥot* and *Berakahot* of the Babylonian Talmud.[58] In the former it is said that "they [non-Jewish nations] call him God of gods." Meaning, non-Jews recognize that God is higher than their gods. Based on this teaching, R. Emden legitimizes the worship by non-Jews of intercessors to God or of those who possess powers that God delegates. In the latter tractate, it is said that "[while Jews pray that non-Jewish idolaters repent], Jews need not say that prayer outside of Israel." For R. Emden, this statement suggests that non-Jewish idolaters do not need to repent, for *shituf* is permitted to them.[59]

---

57 R. Emden, *She'elat Yavetz*, vol. 1, no. 41 (Lemberg, 1739), 36b; *She'elat Yavetz*, vol. 2, no. 133, 40b. See also R. Emden, *Mor U-Ketzia*, vol. 1, no. 224 (Altona, 1761), 97-98.

58 *Menaḥot* 110a; *Berakhot* 57b.

59 It should be noted that R. Emden was writing about Protestants, and that he expressed reservations about the views of Catholics. Be that as it may, his attitude towards Christians can be seen in his letter to the Rabbinical Council of the Four Lands (*Va'ad Arba 'Aratzot*), a powerful self-governing apparatus for Jews in Polish lands. The treatise, which was first published in 1756 as an appendix to *Seder Olam Rabbah Ve-Zutta* and expanded in his *Sefer Shimmush*, was intended to help rabbis appeal to Christian leaders to act against the Frankist Sabbatian sects in Poland. In his letter, R. Emden took the unprecedented step of analyzing the New Testament. See Rabbi Abraham Bick (Shauli), *Rabi Ya'akov Emden Ish U-Mishnato* (Jerusalem: Mossad Ha-Rav Kook, 1974), 138-139. R. Emden noted that in Matthew 5 and Luke 16, Jesus says that he wants Jews to continue keeping every detail of the law. See *Sefer Shimush* (Amsterdam: 1758), 29–41; *Sefer Seder Olam Rabbah Ve-Zuta U-Megilat Ta'anit* (Hamburg, 1757), 32b–35b. A partial translation is found in O. Fasman, "An Epistle on Tolerance by a Rabbinic Zealot," in *Judaism in a Changing World*, ed. L. Jung (New York, 1939), 128–136, cited by Jacob J. Schacter, "Rabbi Jacob Emden: Life and Major Works," 603, fn. 58. R. Emden also writes that Jesus' message was intended for the gentiles, whom Jesus wished to compel to follow the Noahide laws. Further, R. Emden suggests that Jesus' disciple Paul was a learned and upstanding pupil of Rabbi Gamliel. Paul thoroughly understood rabbinic law and correctly applied it. Therefore, concludes R. Emden, just as Jews should help Christians in keeping the Noahide laws, Christians should encourage Jews to remain Jewish, instead of trying to convert them. Along the same lines, he writes that Christianity falls under the category of "an argument for the sake of heaven" (*maḥloket le-Shem Shamayim*), which therefore continues to thrive. R. Emden, *Leḥem Shamayim* on *Pirqei Avot* 4:11 in R. Emden, *Etz Avot* (Amsterdam, 1741), 41a-42a. Rabbi Harvey Falk extends these ideas seemingly beyond their original intent. Rabbi Harvey Falk, *Jesus the Pharisee: A New Look at the Jewishness of Jesus* (Eugene, Oregon: Paulist Press, 1985), 4–8, 76–78. Be-

But then R. Emden had a change of heart and proposed that Tosafot must view Christianity as *avodah zarah* and permit the mention of idolatry only in oaths, provided God's name is mentioned as well. R. Emden's new point of view created a new set of problems. Based on this view, he wondered why Tosafot had to enter into a discussion in order to arrive at the conclusion that non-Jews are permitted to join the name of Jesus with God while making an oath, for there is actually no sin for a non-Jew to utter the name of his idol even on its own.[60]

---

sides other issues, Falk's distortion of talmudic texts is evident even from a plain reading of his book.

60 R. Emden supports this last point from a statement in *Sanhedrin* 56b, which implies that a non-Jew is responsible for *avodah zarah* only when a Jew would be put to death for the corresponding violation. Since a Jew who transgresses לא ישמע by uttering the name of *avodah zarah* only receives lashes, it stands to reason that there is no prohibition for the non-Jew. R. Emden's arguments suggest that he interpreted Tosafot as stating the following: that a non-Jew does not contravene the commandment against *avodah zarah* by mentioning the name of God along with the name of his deity; that a Jew does not violate the prohibition of לא ישמע if he leads the non-Jew to make such an oath; that it is obvious that there is no commandment against *shituf* in oaths made by non-Jews; and that a Jew does not contravene לפני עור by causing such an oath to be made. However, this does not appear to be the correct interpretation. The question with which Tosafot are dealing is whether a Jew would be in contravention of the commandment לא ישמע when the non-Jew takes an oath that combines the name of God with either thoughts of Jesus or the name of Christian saints. But what if a non-Jew has both ideas in mind? To this Tosafot respond that they are mentioning the name of saints, which they do not recognize as deities [unlike Jesus, who is viewed as a deity], and their intentions are directed to the creator of the world. Therefore, the name Jesus does not tarnish the word God/Lord. What Tosafot were saying, then, was that in causing a non-Jew to take such an oath, a Jew is not violating לא ישמע. It also emerges that we do not find a law against making oaths that combine a reference to the creator with the mention of created beings: that law is a uniquely Jewish one. It follows that R. Emden must have had a radical understanding of Tosafot. In R. Emden's view, what Tosafot were suggesting was that the reference to God/Lord ameliorates the oath and removes the idolatry. In this sense, R. Emden seems to agree with R. Shmuel Landau. But what Tosafot were actually suggesting is that non-Jews mention the name of God along with the names of saints. And although they are thinking of Jesus when making their oaths, they are not actually saying "Jesus." If they were to do so, it would mean that the Jew who caused this oath would contravene לא ישמע, since he or she caused another to utter the name of idolatry. R. Emden seems to have been influenced by the mishnah in *Sanhedrin* that states that it is only a *lo ta'aseh*, that is, a prohibition that does not call for the death penalty, for a Jew to swear in the

A slightly different approach was taken by Chajes and R. Mecklenburg. Based on a verse in Deuteronomy 4:19, and Naḥmanides' interpretation of it in particular, they argued that the Trinity is not idolatrous for non-Jews, provided they live outside of Israel. Chajes and R. Mecklenburg also wrote that Christians are simply following the hierarchical system that God has set up for them.[61] R. Shmuel ben Yosef went further and posited that, for Maimonides, the state at the time of Enosh, when humanity began having reverence for the celestial system, was not idolatrous.[62] The only problem was that this new development would lead to idolatry.[63]

Thus, these commentators explain R. Isserles' view by reference to the concept of a hierarchical system designed by God for human worship. In support of such a view, we can bring the opinion of Rabbenu Nissim in one of his sermons,[64] and a separate statement from

---

name of a foreign deity. Based on the ruling we cited, namely, that a non-Jew is held responsible in matters of idol worship only if a Jew who violates the same commandment would incur the death penalty, logic would dictate that there is no sin at all for a non-Jew to swear in the name of Jesus. R. Emden's confusion and the question with which he remains therefore seem to support our interpretation, namely, that this is not ultimately Tosafot's concern. It is still possible, however, that a Noahide is prohibited to swear in an idol's name because it is *avodah zarah*, or a commandment subsumed under cursing God's name. I say this with full knowledge of Naḥmanides' uncertainty about whether there is a Noahide prohibition of swearing in such a fashion. R. Emden ruled, somewhat surprisingly, that mentioning the name of Jesus exclusively in an oath is not a violation of לא ישמע. However, he does consider the possibility that, if Christians conceive of the Trinity as a triune God, it is idolatrous.

61 It should be noted here that Rashi's opinion—cited in a Rashbam that is mentioned by Rabbenu Yeruḥem—namely, that French non-Jews are not idolaters, should not be misconstrued. Rashi actually believes that the non-Jews of his time are idolatrous but are not religiously fervent. As a result, their devotion is not intense enough to have an impact on everyday business practices. Therefore, Jews are not likely to be abetting non-Jewish practice of *avodah zarah* if they conduct business together with non-Jews. Rabbenu Yeruchem, *Toldot Adam Ve-ḥava*, 127.

62 Maimonides, *Mishneh Torah, Hilkhot Avodah Zarah*, chaps. 1, 2.

63 Yaakov Tzvi Mecklenburg, *Ktav Ve-Hakabbalah*, 247–249.
It should be noted, however, that, shortly thereafter, Maimonides refers to the belief in intercessors to God, and to the view of those men of Enosh's era that worshipping stars is a form of respect to their maker, as true idolatry. Maimonides, loc cit. See also *Hilkhot Teshuva*, 3:7.

64 Rabbenu Nissim, *Derashot Ha-Ran*§ 9, ed. A. Feldman (Jerusalem: Makhon-Shalem, 1976), 143–161.

Naḥmanides. Rabbenu Nissim argues that the belief in the existence of, and control by, lesser deities was a more reasonable starting point for humans than the Jewish belief in the supreme God. For someone who believed in a Supreme Being, says Rabbenu Nissim, the notion that this being has an interest in mundane human affairs diminished from its stature. However, lesser powers and deities would not be tarnished by that characteristic. Therefore, it was natural for human beings to worship those lesser powers.[65]

According to Rabbenu Nissim, revelation at Sinai was therefore necessary in order to lead Jews to the belief that God has an interest in humankind. The "I" [*anokhi*] of that revelation says, "I, the God of creation, am also the God who took you out of Egypt—I care." Seen in this way, this statement is not a command but an expression of the relationship between God and human beings. And the main function of the commandment about not having other gods, in the view of Rabbenu Nissim, is to serve as proof that God does "lower himself" to command human beings. It should be noted, however, that this conception does not preclude the possibility that the worship of intercessors is forbidden, even to gentiles. That is to say the essential concept that there are lesser powers and channels, specifically for other nations, which operate through the heavenly bodies such as the stars, may be sustained. But that does not mean that Rabbenu Nissim is sanctioning their worship, even for non-Jews.

Another exponent of this "intermediary" model is Naḥmanides. In his commentary on Leviticus, he wrote that there are various channels and powers for each nation, with distinct angels put in charge. The exception to this hierarchical model is the Jewish nation, but only when it is living in Israel.[66] In this case as well, however, there is no indication that worshipping these powers is an acceptable practice for the nations in question.

It seems that this issue depends on the interpretation of Deuteronomy 4:19, which reads, "And lest thou lift up thine eyes unto heaven,

65 It was also natural that the ancients felt connected to celestial bodies, such as the sun, moon and stars. According to this idea, however, it is not clear how Rabbenu Nissim explains the pre-Sinaitic Noahic ban on all idolatry. Perhaps he could say that Adam had a revelation about such a prohibition but it was forgotten over time, or that the ban pertained only to idolatry that does not recognize God as the highest power.

66 Naḥmanides to Leviticus 18:25. Naḥmanides, *Pirushei Ha-Torah Le-Rabbenu Moshe ben Naḥman*, ed. C.B. Chavel, vol. 2 (Jerusalem: Mossad Ha-Rav Kook, 1989), 109–112.

and when thou seest the sun and the moon and the stars, even all the host of heaven, thou be drawn away and worship them, and serve them, which HaShem thy G-d hath allotted unto all the peoples under the whole heaven."[67] The Talmud itself has conflicting interpretations of this verse. In *Megillah*, the Talmud implies that this verse permits the nations to worship the celestial bodies, which is why the translators commissioned by Ptolemy found it necessary to change the words. But in *Avodah Zarah*, the celestial creations are described as a ruse in order to hold those that worship them to account.[68] It is reasonable to suggest that the former interpretation is closer to the plain reading, to which the translators were attuned.[69]

Thus, we must conclude that the positions of R. Shmuel Orgler, R. Yaakov Emden, Maharatz Chajes, and R. Yaakov Tzvi Mecklenburg are not well supported. Yet, their approach, namely, that Christianity is not idolatrous for non-Jews since it recognizes the one supreme God with Jesus as a subordinate deity, does seem to be the most logical way to understand R. Isserles' position.[70]

---

67 Following the JPS translation.

68 *Megillah* 9b. Along these lines, Maimonides rules that it is idolatrous for anyone to accept any power besides God, even as intercessors to him, let alone as independent objects of worship. Maimonides' explanation for this ruling is based on one of the talmudic explanations of the verse, namely, that the planets were given to serve mankind. More broadly, Maimonides describes idolatry as having originated in an error made by the generation of Enosh. The people of that time decided to honor God by worshipping his great heavenly creations. For Maimonides, this is idolatry in its original form. In its later form, the practice of idolatry left out the Almighty God altogether. And in subsequent generations, human beings believed only in those powers and worshipped them exclusively. In contrast to these developments, the people of the world originally espoused the logically necessary principle that God in his essence is the only true and necessary existence, and that he created everything else and acts providentially. In his epistle to the Jews of Marseilles, Maimonides writes that after reading every available book on the subject, which he did while he was younger, he became convinced that astrology is a false concept and that it is being used to lure people into idolatry. Maimonides, *Kovetz Teshuvot Ha-Rambam Ve-Igrotav* (Leipzig, 1859), 25.

69 See also Rashi to *Megillah* 9b, who states that the latter interpretation is a midrashic one. I thank Dr. Guttman for directing me to this source. Ed.

70 Similar positive attitudes to Christians can also be found in the writings of Rabbi Mordechai Yaffe, student of R. Isserles and author of the *Levush*. He writes, for instance, that Christians are not included in any of the negative laws directed towards idolaters. R. Yaffe, *Levush Ateret Zahav, Yoreh De'ah* 148:12 (Jerusalem: Zikhron Aaron, 1999), 334. Other comparable views can be found in

The Rejection of R. Isserles' View

Rabbi Avraham Yeshayahu Karelitz, known as *Ḥazon Ish*, similarly understood the Tosafot in Sanhedrin as positing that non-Jews are not punished for *shituf*. But his interpretation of this aspect of Tosafot differs from what we have so far seen from R. Isserles and the Aḥaronim that followed him. *Ḥazon Ish* believed that Tosafot are referring to "mental *shituf*," which is not a punishable offense, rather than "verbal *shituf*," which is punishable by law.

In his treatment of the topic, *Ḥazon Ish* avoided an explicit disagreement with R. Isserles by not naming him. Instead, he directed the reader to the *Pitḥei Teshuvah* where it is argued that R. Isserles did believe that *shituf* is permissible for non-Jews and that his ruling is incorrect.[71] *Ḥazon Ish* further critiqued R. Isserles, albeit indirectly, by showing that his ruling is contradicted by his own sources.[72] *Ḥazon Ish* interprets Tosafot as ruling that Christianity is idolatrous, and therefore, if a Jew would cause a non-Jew to mention the name of Jesus, that Jew would be violating the causative part of לא ישמע. The debate in Tosafot, according to *Ḥazon Ish*, relates to causing a non-Jew to contemplate the name of Jesus while mentioning God's name. Such an outcome would not be a violation of לא ישמע on the Jew's part.

Ḥazon Ish seems to believe that Tosafot in *Sanhedrin* 63b begin with the premise that the prohibition of *shituf* while making oaths is of no concern; and the *shituf* that Tosafot are discussing must be similar to what was worshipped during the sin of the Golden Calf. The pertinent question relates to saying the name of God while thinking of another power. Tosafot's conclusion, according to *Ḥazon Ish*, is that this is not a violation of any law; and that is for two reasons:

1. The Jew has not caused the non-Jew to mention the name of idolatry, and thus there is no violation of לא ישמע.
2. While the non-Jew is forbidden to engage in this type of worship, he or she cannot be punished for a "mental" sin, and a Jew

R. Yehezkel Landau, "Hitnatzlut ha-Meḥaber" in *Nodah Be-Yehudah, Mahadurah Kammah* (New York: Halakhah Berurah, 1960), 8; in Rabbi Elazar Fleklish, *Teshuvah Me-ahava* (Prague, 1915), 2b–4a; in Chajes, *Tiferet Yisrael*, 489, and in R. Eliyahu Henkin, *Bnei Banim*, no. 35 (Jerusalem, 1998), 116–127.

71 Avraham Tzvi Hirsch Eisenstadt, *Pitḥei Teshuvah* to *Shulḥan Arukh, Yoreh De'ah* 147:2, vol. 2, 142.

72 This point is primarily based on Tosafot to *Bekhorot* 2b.

is punished only if he caused someone else to commit a punishable crime.[73]

Ḥazon Ish also learned from Tosafot that a person violates the prohibition of making an oath with *shituf* only if he or she mentions the names of other gods along with God. This idea is based on *Ḥazon Ish*'s conception of the Tosafot in *Sanhedrin* 63a, which he takes to mean that there is no prohibition against saying the name of another entity together with God, even in an oath, provided that the other being is not another god.[74] This interpretation, however, is difficult in both the plain and conceptual sense. It is unreasonable to suggest that there is a commandment against causing a thought, and Tosafot would not have had to discuss that issue as it relates to לא ישמע.[75] Indeed, it seems that Tosafot's discussion in *Bekhorot* 2b and *Sanhedrin* 63a similarly presupposes this idea.[76]

---

73 This idea is problematic. Also, the language of Tosafot—"they were not warned"—sounds as if it is completely permissible to have a thought of *shituf.*

74 R. Avraham Y. Karelitz, *Ḥazon Ish, Yoreh De'ah* 62:19-20 (Jerusalem, 1994), 96. However, the Tosafot probably meant that it is not permitted to mention anything together with God in an oath, since, by definition, the entities mentioned in an oath are spoken of in a context of *midi de-elohot.* As evidence, we can bring the ruling of Maimonides in *Mishneh Torah: Hilkhot Shvu'ot* 11:2, namely, that making an oath is tantamount to declaring God's power, which is why nothing that has been created may be included in an oath in the same breath as the name of God.

75 As for the issue of *lifnei i'ver,* that remains an open question.

76 Rabbenu Asher ben Yeḥiel, *Tosafot Ha-Rosh* on *Sanhedrin* 63a, ed. S. Wilman (Brooklyn: Defus Ḥemed, 1995), 60. This edition is based on the Oxford MS. The *Tosafot Ha-Rosh* is Rabbenu Asher's version of Tosafot. Since this was not published at the time of Ḥazon Ish, he never saw it. Rabbenu Asher also added a question from *Sukkah* 45b, in relation to the practice of walking around the altar while holding willow branches and saying, "to the Lord, and to thee, oh altar." For the Talmud, it is problematic that Jews would do this, because this act would constitute *shituf.* The answer provided is that the Jews said this expression in two separate clauses. Rabbenu Asher explains that the reason this expression would have been an act of *shituf,* if said in one breath, is because the altar is in certain respects *midi de-elohot,* a form of theology. That is to say the altar functions as an extension of God, bringing about forgiveness through sacrifices. But with the view of *Ḥazon Ish,* there should be no problem. Given his interpretation of Tosafot's ruling, that is, that any entities can be mentioned with God, provided they are not gods, mentioning the altar together with God should not be a problem. Further, it is unclear, according to

We should also note that R. Ephraim ben Yaakov Ha-Kohen,[77] R. Yonah Landsuper,[78] R. Avraham ben Yitzhak Ayish,[79] and R. Yosef ben Meir Te'Omim[80] all considered Christianity and the notion of the Trinity to be *avodah zarah*. Thus, they believed R. Isserles' opinion to be untenable and argue that he misinterpreted his sources.[81]

Normative Halakhah: Christianity is not Idolatry

Even as we consider the challenges to his position, the fact remains that R. Isserles—who was dealing with Catholics—was willing to entertain the halakhic view that Christianity is not idolatry, although there is no shortage of Rishonim who disagree with that position.[82]

Ḥazon Ish, how Tosafot would understand the question and answer of the Talmud in *Sukkah*. It is therefore difficult to accept *Ḥazon Ish*'s interpretation.

77 Ephraim ben Yaakov Ha-Kohen, *Sha'ar Ephraim*, no. 24 (Lemberg: E. Margashish, 1887), 11.

78 Yehudah Landsuper, *Me'il Tzedakka*, no. 22 (Prague: Grossman, 1757), p. 28.

79 Avraham b. Yitzḥak Ayish, *Bet Yehudah*, no. 5 (Livorno: A. Meldola, 1746), 62.

80 R. Yosef ben Meir Te'omim, *Pri Megadim* on *Shulḥan Arukh: Yoreh De'ah* 65:11, vol. 1, 141b.

81 R. Isserles' view is also undermined by the context of the various Rishonic opinions he cites. Every such decision, cited in R. Moshe Isserles, *Darkhei Moshe Ha-Arukh* 151 (Sulzbach, 1692), 51b-52, is concerned with the question whether permission (*heter*) can be granted for Jews to sell objects of worship to Christians. The fear is that such objects will be used for idolatry. Those who rule that it is permissible to do so base their decision on the fact that "the priest could get it elsewhere anyway." These discussions inherently assume that Christianity is to be treated as *avodah zarah*. Further, there is, as we have seen, a lack of evidence for his ruling. In light of these questions, we are led towards a radical interpretation of R. Isserles' ruling, namely, that R. Isserles based his decision on sources that were taken out of context. For more on his style of writing, see J. Ben-Sasson, *The Philosophical System of R. Moses Isserles*, 19–40, esp. 42. This type of proof, which resembles an *asmakhta*, is not without precedent. In fact, it can be seen as far back as the mishnah. See for example M. Kritut 8; *yShabbat* 6:1 ("*matnita amar ken*"); *Berakhot* 52a, 63 a-b; *Shabbat* 115a; *Eruvin* 51a; b. *Pesaḥim* 27a, 112, and Rashi thereon; *Bava Metziah* 109b, and Tosafot thereon, s.v., *mitalkinin*; Rabbenu Gershom to *Bava Batra* 11a; *Niddah* 7b, *Teshuvot Ha-Geonim: Shaarei Tzeddek* 4:3, ed. N. Moda'i (Jerusalem: Kelal U-Prat, 1966), 102.

82 In *Darkhei Moshe* 151, as quoted by the *Shakh* on *Shulḥan Arukh: Yoreh De'ah* 151:7, R. Isserles cites *Oraḥ Ḥayyim*, 156 as a supplementary source to permit the sale of materials that can be used by Christians for religious purposes. It would not be possible for him to make this claim if his view in *Oraḥ Ḥayyim* 156 were restricted to oaths, as explained by the *Nodah Be-Yehudah* 148. But R. Isserles' argument would also be untenable if he interpreted his sources to al-

Despite the various critiques of R. Isserles' view, we therefore ought to acknowledge that, by openly stating that Christianity is not *avodah zarah*, he must have deemed that position to be compatible with his perception of the Torah's view.[83] In this respect, he had a predecessor.

Menaḥem Ha-Meiri, a 13th-century talmudist and halakhist from Provence, is the first source we have on record to have a similar position on Christians.

R. Isserles never read Meiri's work, for it had not been discovered at the time that the former was writing, and there are some differences in the way the two of them wrote about Christianity. For example, Meiri's position takes Christianity's origins into account, as we see in relation to "Yom ha-Notzri."[84] He also draws upon Jewish practice over many generations to indicate that Judaism accepted Christians as non-idolaters. R. Isserles, on the other hand, seems to have given an assessment of them based on his own time. One may even argue that R. Isserles was only stating that Christianity is an expression of "One supreme being in charge," as explained by *Olat Tamid* and others.[85] On that basis, he posited that it was acceptable for non-Jews to hold that belief even though it would be *avodah zarah* for Jews to accept it.

Along similar lines is the explanation provided by R. Isserles for the communities that are lenient about non-kosher wine.[86] In his book on

low partnerships with Christians and permit their oaths solely on the basis that they no longer refer to Jesus in their oaths. In other words, R. Isserles' position stands or falls on the question of whether Christian beliefs are idolatrous.

83 For the cultural and philosophical influences of the Renaissance on R. Isserles, see Ilia M. Rodov, *The Torah Ark in Renaissance Poland: A Jewish Revival of Classical Antiquity* (Leiden: Brill, 2013), 37–54. Ed.

84 Meiri, *Ḥidushei Ha-Meiri* on *Avodah Zarah*, 2a–4a, vol. 6, 278. R. Turin seems to be suggesting that the origins of Christianity may have been associated with the cult of Nebuchadnezzar, which is why it shares a name. I thank Dr. Guttman for his comments on R. Turin's assertion. Ed.

85 See *supra* p. 9.

86 R. Isserles, *She'elot U-Teshuvot Ha-Rema*, no. 124 (Jerusalem: Yerid Ha-Sefarim, 2004), 396–399. In that responsum, R. Isserles entertains the possibility that Christians are not idolaters, and that they are to be compared to innocent children who touch wine, which, according to some authorities, one may even drink. This may even be extended to non-Jewish wine. There remains the problem, however, that non-Jewish wine should still be prohibited by the rabbinic edict of *stam yeinam*, which is based on the fear that the conviviality that may emerge from drinking their wine might lead to fraternizing and then possibly to intermarriage. A propos of this issue, some communities may have a basis in a similar leniency towards bread from non-bakeries. But where the

theology, *Torat Ha-Olah*,[87] R. Isserles explains that our forefather Abraham was a true believer, and he ingrained those beliefs into his descendants. Thus, Esau and Ishmael received their faith from Abraham. That is to say, at their core they are monotheists, but they supplemented their religion with idolatry. Still, they are far superior to true idolaters, who worship the stars.

We therefore see that, regardless of the position of the Rishonim on the question of whether Christianity amounts to *avodah zarah*, the intention of R. Isserles, who took a lenient view, appeared to be the removal of the stigma of *avodah zarah* from Christianity.[88] A similar development can be seen in the case of R. Isserles' predecessor, Menaḥem Ha-Meiri. Meiri unapologetically pronounced Christians, and more specifically Catholics (and by logical extension Muslims as well[89]) to be observant *b'nei Noaḥ*.[90] He wrote, in his commentary on the Talmud, that non-

main drink of the region is wine, there can be a leniency. Therefore, those communities are not to be castigated, even though R. Isserles' own practice was not to allow *stam yeinam*. Out of this discussion, however, actual permission emerges. Gentile wine is certainly then permitted for a bedridden person, assuming it is beneficial for him to drink wine, even though there is no threat to his or her life by their not being allowed to drink it. For such cases, the rabbis did not prohibit *stam yeinam*. While this responsum does not explicitly rule Christians out as idolaters, the ideas expressed there are of a piece with his lenient approach towards Christians. I thank Dr. Guttman for his comments on this section.

87 R. Moshe Isserles, *Torat Ha-Olah* 1:16, 19, ed. I. Jaffe, vol. 1 (Königsberg, 1854), 50b–54b, 57a–59b.

88 So R. Isserles in *Torat Ha-Olah*, see supra, fn. 113. Further, as we have seen, Meiri posits that we disagree with Christianity only in the details of their belief.

89 See *supra* note 63.

90 Much of the scholarly debate about Meiri relates to the question of how extensive his tolerance for Chistians really was, and the closely related question of how innovative it was. For Jacob Katz, Meiri's notion of *ummot ha-gedurot*, and its opposite in particular, is grounded by a philosophical view on the social-political nature of human beings. Katz, "Religious Tolerance in the View of R. Menaḥem Ha-Meiri in Halakhah and Philosophy," *Zion* 18 (1953): 26; Katz, "More on the Religious Tolerance of R. Menaḥem Ha-Meiri" (Hebrew) *Zion* 46 (1981): 243–245; Katz, *Exclusiveness and Tolerance* (Springfield: Behrman House, 1961), 121. David Berger admits having reservations about Meiri's view but later being convinced that there is a link in his thought between religion and "an ordered, ethical society." David Berger, "Jews, Gentiles, and the Modern Egalitarian Ethos: Some Tentative Thoughts," 94. Other scholars disagree that Meiri's view was innovative or that it embodied a "kernel of religious tolerance." Ephraim Urbach denies that the tolerance in the writings of

Jewish people of talmudic times were not governed by the ways of religion, but that was not the case with contemporary gentiles.[91] The latter qualify as observant because they "recognize the existence, oneness, and omnipotence of God, even though we believe that they are mistaken in some details."[92] Crucially, Meiri notes in his commentary on *Gittin* that

---

Meiri is grounded in a philosophical view, for he sees no philosophical basis in those discussions. Urbach does, however, see the novelty in Meiri's view in his having brought his distinction between types of non-Jews into the halakhic sphere, but Urbach suggests that doing so did not "bear real fruit." J. David Bleich downplays the significance of *ummot ha-gedurot*, framing it as a legal definition for economic matters, but he makes more of Meiri's statements about the gentiles' belief in God's unity and power. Bleich also raises the possibility that some of Meiri's favorable statements were made with an eye to the censor and that his notion of Christian beliefs had some misconceptions. Urbach, "Rabbi Menaḥem Ha-Meiri's Theory of Tolerance: Its Source and Its Limits," in *Studies in the History of Jewish Society in the Middle Ages and in the Modern Period: Presented to Jacob Katz* (Hebrew), eds. Immanuel Etkes and Yosef Salmon and Jacob Katz (Jerusalem: Magnes, 1980), 33–44; Bleich, "Divine Unity in Maimonides, the Tosafists, and Meiri," in *Neoplatonism in Jewish Thought* (Albany: SUNY Press, 1992), 237–254. For a wonderful article on the influences behind Meiri's humanistic view, see Yaakov Elman, "Meiri and the non-Jew," in *New Perspectives on Jewish Christian Relations*, eds. Elisheva Carlebach and Jacob J. Schachter (Brill: Leiden, 2012), 265–296. R. Elman argues that Meiri makes favorable distinctions in matters that pertain to personal relations with Christians, and holds up the relationship that Meiri had with the Christian that inspired his *Ḥibur Ha-Teshuva* as a paradigm. Ibid., 275–291. As we will see, R. Turin seems to agree with R. Elman, but by arguing that there is no halakhic basis for Meiri's decision, other than Meiri's own inclination, R. Turin makes the point even more clearly. R. Elman thus differs from Moshe Halbertal, who argues that Meiri's favorable view of Christianity stems from a philosophical tradition in Provence, particularly as it relates to the need for faith to complement philosophical analysis. Moshe Halberal, "R. Menahem Ha-Meiri: Bein Torah Le-ḥokhmah," *Tarbiz* 63.1 (1995): 63–118. To the extent that R. Turin sees Meiri as having based his views on his experiences, rather than through philosophical reasoning, R. Turin agrees with David Novak, who posits that Meiri's opinion is not developed philosophically. Novak, *The Image of the non-Jew in Judaism,* ed. Matt LaGrone (Liverpool: Littman Library of Civilization, 2011), 195–199. Ed.

91 *Ḥidushei Ha-Meiri* on *Gittin* 61b, vol. 4, 279.

92 See for example Meiri, *Ḥidushei Ha-Meiri* on *Sanhedrin* 63b and on *Avodah Zarah* 6a, vol. 6, 62, 189; idem, on Bava Kama 113a-b, vol. 5, 107; idem, on Gittin 61b, vol. 4, 278; Meiri, *Bet Ha-beḥirah al Masekhet Horiyot* 11a, ed. A Schreiber (Jerusalem: Sinai, 1958), 274; *Bet Ha-beḥirah al Maseket Yevamot* 22a, ed. S. Dyckman 91 (Jerusalem: Makhon Ha-talmud Ha-Yisraeli, 1967), 91. Elsewhere, Meiri notes that Christians accept the authenticity of the revelation at

the Christians believe in the three components of religious belief.[93] The three elements that form the core of this idea are the belief in God's existence, oneness, and omnipotence.[94]

A key component of Meiri's view of Christians is the statement *ummot ha-gedurot be-darkhei ha-datot*. This is the criterion upon which he drew for his favourable view of the non-Jews among whom he lived and on the basis of which he excluded them from the talmudic statements against heathens. But what does Meiri mean by that oft-repeated statement? We posit that the word *datot* refers to religiously inspired laws.[95] Otherwise, Meiri would have said *dinim u-mishpatim yesharim*—that is, just laws. In this regard, he may have been following Maimonides with respect to his requirement to ground the Noahide laws in divine origin. We should note, however, that even followers of the Noahide code who do so solely on the basis of reason, i.e., without any reference to revelation, are still seen as wise, even if they are not deserving of the World to Come.[96] Be that as it may, since Meiri was of the opinion that Christianity went beyond the requirements of the Noahide code—he writes that such nations are not only bound by the strictures of *datot* but also "believe in his existence"[97]—he may have also believed that Christians met Maimonides' ideal criteria.[98]

Based on this interpretation, the position of Moshe Halbertal, namely, that Meiri identifies Christians with non-idolaters rather than monotheists, is called into question. Building on an analysis of Meiri's writings

---

Sinai (*Torah me-Sinai*). On the same basis, Maimonides, in a responsum, allows Jews to study the Bible with Christians. Maimonides, *Responsa Pe'er Ha-Dor*, no. 50 (Amsterdam, 1664), 14b.

93 Meiri, *Ḥidushei Ha-Meiri* on *Gittin* 61b, vol. 4, 278.

94 Along the same lines, see Halbertal, who posits that it is not philosophical knowledge, which is reserved for a narrow group, but faith itself that serves as the category of those bordered by the ways of faith. Halbertal, *Between Torah and Wisdom*, 102-103.

95 Along similar lines, Halbertal argues that Meiri's tolerance came from an understanding of "faith." Halbertal, "R. Menaḥem Ha-meiri: Bein Torah Le-ḥokhmah," 110–114. Ed.

96 This statement is true of some manuscripts. In others, it states that those who keep the Noahide code in this fashion "are not even among the wise ones." On this issue, see S. Schwarzschild, "Do Noachites Have to Believe in Revelation?" *The Jewish Quarterly Review* 53.1 (1962): 30–65. Ed.

97 *Ḥidushei Ha-Meiri* on *Gittin* 61b, vol. 4, 279.

98 However, there is still the matter of the usage of icons, but that was a subject of debate among Christians themselves. To at least some Christians, any divinity attributed to a physical form was rejected.

on Psalms and Ecclesiastes, as well as his *Ḥibur Ha-teshuva* and introductions to *Bet Ha-Beḥirah* and *Pirqei Avot*, Halbertal defines Meiri's notion of *avodah zarah* as the inability to see any spiritual being beyond material existence. For Halbertal, it is for this reason that Meiri did not place Christianity in the category of *avodah zarah*.[99] However, in light of Meiri's statements about the minor errors made by Christians, and the triune theological foundation to which they subscribe, Halbertal's view is difficult to accept. A more convincing interpretation of the former statement is that Christianity is monotheistic at its core, even if it is mistaken in certain regards.

In trying to understand Meiri's view, it is important to be cognizant that Meiri lived in a culture best described as laissez-faire in ideas and beliefs. He also dealt with enlightened Christians.[100] Therefore, as was later the case for R. Isserles, there was an impetus for Meiri to investigate the possibilities for coexistence and construct a theory of religion on the basis of which he could build mutual tolerance and respect.

In support of the comparison between Meiri and R. Isserles, we can point to the fact that R. Isserles, like Meiri, is cognizant that Christianity represented a development beyond the blatant idolatry of the times of the Talmud.[101] This idea seems to be what compels Meiri to define the *sugya* in *Yoma*, which relates to the saving of lives on the Sabbath in a case of a building that collapses on a group of people on the possibility that there is at least one Jew under the pile, as referring only to ancient pagans and idolaters.[102] The Christians, who have kept the Noahide laws and built upon them,[103] must be saved on their own merit, even if no

---

99 Ibid., 103–105.

100 See for instance, Elman, "Meiri and the non-Jew," 275. Ed.

101 Halbertal sees the progress in the philosophical development of the nations of the world in grasping something beyond the sensual, widely known, accepted, and what Halbertal calls transcendental, as a concept he gets from Ibn Tibon. Unlike R. Turin, Halbertal seems to see progress in Meiri's conception as an intellectual, rather than a normative development. Halbertal, *Between Torah and Wisdom* (Jerusalem: Magnes Press, 2000), 103–108. Ed.

102 Meiri, *Ḥidushei Ha-Meiri* on *Yoma* 84a–85a, vol. 3, 227.

103 Following the Jerusalem edition (1875), the wording is "People whose values do not consider the lives of others." However, in his 1964 edition, Ravitz posits that the earlier version is a forgery. But even in Ravitz's view, the original version can still be detected: "The ancient idolaters who worshipped the stars." It seems that Ravitz wanted his edition to be accepted by the yeshiva world, and he therefore denied Meiri's position.

Jewish lives are in danger.[104]

Conclusion

Meiri lived in Provence at a time when its cultural renaissance had been flourishing for 200 years. The government tolerated other religions, and as a result, there was a proliferation of Torah study and yeshivot and great rabbinic scholars emerged. At the same time, there were enlightened Jewish philosophers who came into contact with Christian scholars. These developments led Meiri to argue not only that Christianity had progressed, but that it was not *avodah zarah* from its inception. This idea is what led him to interpret the Talmud in *Yoma* as meaning something other than Christians when it states that one cannot violate the Sabbath to save an idolater's life. As we have seen, Meiri believes that we must save b'nei Noah *de jure*, rather than *de facto*, i.e., not because of a fear of repercussions against Jews.

In a similar way, R. Isserles studied the humanities and philosophy and lived in Cracow.[105] This was the site of one of the medieval world's greatest universities and home of many intelligent Christians. We can assume at the very least that he felt Christianity had progressed beyond *avodah zarah,* and he reshaped the halakhah accordingly. This was in spite of the opinions of the Rishonim with which he was familiar. R. Isserles also read the words of the Rishonim to mean that a *shituf*-oriented belief in the Trinity is not idolatrous, given Christian acceptance of God the Creator.[106] Finally, along the same lines, R. Emden, who lived among enlightened Protestants, expressed reservation about the Catholic acceptance of the cross, but in reality he conceded that Christians have the status of righteous gentiles. ☙

---

104 To strengthen R. Turin's point, it ought to be noted that R. Isserles subscribes to a similar idea. As Jonah Ben-Sasson argues, for R. Isserles, the normative foundation of the Noahide laws joins the nations together, and it is through the laws that the people resemble that which they are intended to be, and enable God's presence to dwell. See Ben-Sasson, *The Philosophical System of* R. *Moses Isserles* (Jerusalem: Menaḥem Press, 1984), 127–129. Ed.

105 On the ontological importance of human beings that stemmed from Christian thought during the Renaissance, see J. Ben-Sasson, *The Philosophical System of* R. *Moses Isserles,* 111-112. Ed.

106 This recognition of non-Jews does not stem solely from the necessity of living among them, but it is part of an essential recognition in the fundamentals of faith. This recognition serves as the basis for social and economic living but also a co-existence as it pertains to law and order. Ibid. 289.

The Code of Esther: A Counter-Investigation

By: EMMANUEL BLOCH

Does the *Book of Esther* contain a hidden prophetic allusion to the Nuremberg trial? Might the execution of ten Nazi high dignitaries curiously echo the hanging of the ten sons of the villain Haman in *Megillat Esther*, despite the twenty-four centuries separating these two events?

Such has been the claim repeated for many years in some religious circles. To provide a brief overview: at the end of the *Book of Esther*, the queen makes a surprising request that the sons of Haman be hanged "tomorrow" (9:12); but they had already been killed in previous fights (9:7-10), so why this strange hanging of enemies already dead? The mystery thickens with another curiosity of the biblical text: letters of unusual size in the *Megillah*, three smaller (*shin*, *tav* and *zayin*) and a larger one (*vav*); what could they mean?

All would finally be enlightened by a numerical reading of the unusual letters. Small letters refer to the year 707 and the large *vav* refers to the sixth millennium, thus 5707 since the creation of the world, or 1946 according to the Christian calendar. In other words, the year of the Nuremberg trial. The parallels between Purim's account and Nuremberg's trial seem disturbing: in both cases, the number of executions was the same—ten. In both cases, the mode of execution was the same—hanging.

Moreover, the day of execution, October 16, 1946, fell on the day of Hoshanah Rabbah, identified by Jewish tradition as a day of judgment. Lastly, one of the ten Nazis, Julius Streicher, exclaimed as he rose to the scaffold "Purimfest 1946!"[1] Strange, right?

---

1 For more elaborate (and sensationalist) presentations, see the videos accessible at https://www.youtube.com/watch?v=gzaJZ0bGe0s&t=23s and at https://www.youtube.com/watch?v=mMhqEiu1p4s; those who prefer written text may consult https://ohr.edu/holidays/purim/deeper_insights/3440. Many other presentations along the same argument are easily accessible, in all languages, via a Google search.

Emmanuel Bloch, an Attorney-at-Law, is pursuing a PhD in Jewish Philosophy at the Hebrew University of Jerusalem. He has written peer-reviewed articles on German Neo-Orthodoxy and on the philosophy of halakhah. He is also active on various French Jewish websites.

Esther's mysterious prophecy has recently been revived as a Jewish version of the *Da Vinci Code*, the worldwide bestseller by novelist Dan Brown. Thus, in 2012, the French book *Le Code d'Esther,*[2] presented as investigative journalism, reproduced the above argument and created a small event in the world of French publishing, with more than 26,000 copies sold in the first few weeks after publication.[3]

On this side of the Atlantic, in 2014, appeared *The Esther Code,*[4] a thriller in which an FBI agent deciphers Queen Esther's mysterious prophecy with the help of a brilliant rabbi and finally arrests a serial murderer. The publishing house promised a disturbing investigation, based on a real phenomenon, and of which no skeptic, even the most hardened, could leave indifferent.

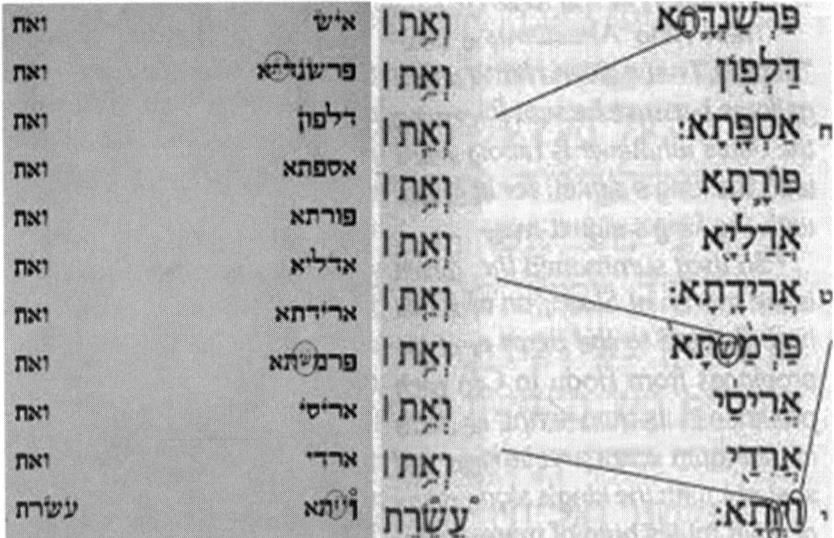

Unusually sized letters in Megillat Esther, chapter 9, verses 7-10

But is there really anything behind all the buzz? Is the "prophetic" phenomenon real or imaginary?

This article examines the code of Esther through the crucible of a critical and detailed analysis, a true counter-investigation in six separate acts. We will examine in succession the archeology of the biblical text, an ancient manner of punishing enemies, a little-known aspect of the anti-Jewish propaganda of the Nazi regime, and more.

---

2 Bernard Benyamin and Yohan Perez, *Le Code d'Esther* (Paris, FIRST, 2012).

3 That's the figure posted in *Times of Israel:* https://www.timesofisrael.com/french-best-seller-unravels-nazis-cryptic-last-words-about-purim/.

4 Michael Danneman and Sarah Holst, *The Esther Code* (Married to a Yid, 2014).

Act 1: In search of the original text

> *The claim: In the list of names of the sons of Haman (Esther 9: 7-10), three letters have since time immemorial been written in a smaller script: shin, tav and zayin.*
>
> *The reality: Ancient sources make no mention of these three smaller letters.*

Is it possible to verify whether the forms of certain letters in the *Book of Esther* differed from the rest in ancient times?

Absolutely. Two main routes are open to the investigator: one may study the rabbinical sources that teach how to write the text of the *Megillah*; alternatively, one may examine the ancient manuscripts, which bear witness to the practice of previous generations. We will follow these two paths successively.

Rabbinic texts first. Two major sources depict how the Sages prescribe the *Megillah* be written.

Let's first examine the Talmud:[5]

> ואת פרשנדתא וגו' עשרת בני המן אמר רב אדא דמן יפו עשרת בני המן ועשרת צריך למימרינהו בנשימה אחת מאי טעמא כולהו בהדי הדדי נפקו נשמתייהו אמר רבי יוחנן ויו דויזתא צריך למימתחה בזקיפא כמורדיא דלברות מאי טעמא כולהו בחד זקיפא אזדקיפו.
>
> The verse says, "And Parshandata ... the ten sons of Haman (Esther 9: 6-10)." Rav Adda of Jaffa taught: when reading the *Megillah*, the names of Haman's ten sons and the word "ten" must be recited in one breath. Why? Because their souls all departed together. Rabbi Yoḥanan taught: the *vav* of the name Vayzata must be elongated as a pole, like the steering oar of a ship. Why? Because they were all hanged on one pole.

Thus, the Sages explicitly teach the proper way of writing and reading the ninth chapter of Esther: the letter *vav* must be elongated, and some nouns must be pronounced in a single breath. But anything about small letters? Absolute silence. They are not mentioned, because for the Talmud, these letters are no different from the others: *shin*, *tav* and *zayin* are to be written in a normal size.

---

5 *Bavli Megillah* 16b; see also the parallel passage in the *Yerushalmi Megillah* chapter 3, halakhah 7.

A second collection of the Sages' teachings is important for our research: Tractate *Soferim*, one of the minor tractates of the Talmud. This tractate was written in the eighth century with the purpose of teaching how to write, exactly and precisely, the various books of the Torah. The *Book of Esther* is discussed in detail, and the particularities already discussed within the Talmud are duly noted.[6] But diminutive letters in chapter 9? Not a trace.

To recap: all authoritative rabbinical texts were totally mute regarding any tradition of writing the letters from *Megillat Esther* in a small size.

But how was *Megillat Esther* written in practice? We now consider some ancient manuscripts from the *Book of Esther*, preserved in the collections of prestigious university libraries, to examine the scribal traditions of the unfolding generations.

The oldest complete manuscript of Tanakh dates from the year 1008 and is considered particularly reliable; it belongs to the National Library of Russia in St. Petersburg (EBP. I B 19a), from which it derives the name by which it is best known: the *Leningrad Codex*.[7] Here is a screenshot of the verses in question (Esther 9:7-10) as they appear in the scanned version of the *Leningrad Codex* available online.

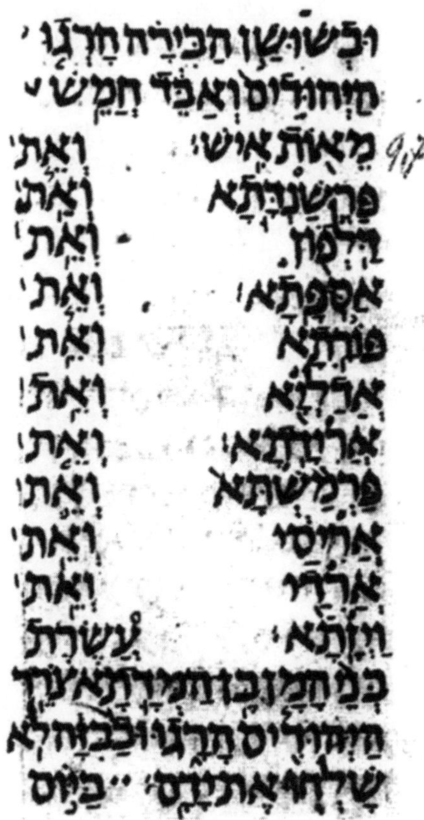
ובשושן הבירה הרגו
היהודים ואבד חמש
מאות איש
פרשנדתא ואת
דלפון ואת
אספתא ואת
פורתא ואת
אדליא ואת
ארידתא ואת
פרמשתא ואת
אריסי ואת
ארידי ואת
ויזתא עשרת
בני המן בן המדתא צרר
היהודים הרגו ובבזה לא
שלחו את ידם ביום

Leningrad Codex, screenshot

As can be seen, the *Leningrad Codex* coincides with the ancient rabbinical texts: it contains no small letters in the list of names of Haman's sons.

What about other manuscripts of the *Book of Esther*? As documented by Mordechai Breuer, the texts of two other ancient manuscripts, Add.

6 *Soferim* 13:4, and more broadly the whole beginning of chapter 13.

7 The *Aleppo Codex* (*Keter Aram Ẓova*) was several decades old by the time the *Leningrad Codex* was written. It is said that it is this manuscript that Maimonides consulted to verify the Masoretic text before codifying his laws of writing a *Sefer Torah*. Tragically, some parts of the *Aleppo Codex* have been lost, including the *Book of Esther* that interests us.

Ms. 5702 and Or. 2375, preserved at respectively Cambridge University and the British Museum, and perceived to be very reliable, are identical to the *Leningrad Codex*.[8]

Later manuscripts, too. Thanks to the efforts of the National Library of Israel to digitalize its collections of manuscripts, readers can now inspect this manuscript[9] from the thirteenth to fourteenth century and held by the Biblioteca Palatina of Parma in Italy; or the one,[10] which dates from 1494, from the collections of the National Library of France; or again, the fourteenth to fifteenth century manuscript Add. Ms 652,[11] preserved at Cambridge University. All these manuscripts follow the Talmudic tradition and contain no small letters in the *Book of Esther*.

Our conclusion seems clear as all the clues converge: for about 1,400 years, the *Megillat Esther* was written with no difference between the size of the letters *shin*, *tav* and *zayin* and the rest of the text.

Act 2: The canonization of confusion

> *The claim: The text of the Book of Esther has been transmitted identically, from generation to generation, from its original writing to the present day.*
>
> *The reality: The small letters of The Code of Esther are the result of errors eventually canonized during the transmission process.*

Is it possible to determine when the small form of letters first appeared? To a large degree, the answer is positive.

The very first occurrence I was able to detect lies in the *Midrash of Rabbi Akiva ben Yosef on small and large letters*. This ancient text deals with the particular form of certain biblical letters and may be consulted in two recent compilations of lost texts eventually rediscovered in medieval *genizot*.[12] Below follows the exact quote that concerns us:

---

8 מרדכי ברויאר, *נוסח המקרא בכתר ירושלים ומקורותיו במסורה ובכתבי יד*, הוצאת קרן המסורה, ירושלים 2003, עמ' 324.

9 https://web.nli.org.il/sites/NLI/Hebrew/digitallibrary/pages/viewer.aspx?presentorid=manuscripts&docid=pnx_manuscripts000070341-1#|FL32364330.

10 https://web.nli.org.il/sites/NLI/Hebrew/digitallibrary/pages/viewer.aspx?presentorid=manuscripts&docid=pnx_manuscripts000128751-1#|FL51792278.

11 https://cudl.lib.cam.ac.uk/view/MS-ADD-00652/607.

12 Judah David Eisenstein, *Ozar ha-Midrashim,* vol. 2 (NY: 1915), pp. 432-433; Shlomo Aaron Wertheimer, *Batei Midrashot,* vol. 2 (Mossad ha-Rav Kook: 1955), pp. 478-488. Both versions agree on the text.

(ז') זיי"ן, ויזתא ז' קטנה, לפי שהמן הלשין בשבעה דברים (...) רי"ש של פרשנדתא קטנה, שנתמעט ונתלה (...) שי"ן תי"ו של פרשנדתא קטנות, הסר פ' ור' וישאר שמתא.

The *zayin* of the name Vayzata is written small, because Haman slandered seven times the Jewish people (...). The *resh* of the name Parshandata is written small, because he was lowered and hanged (...) The *shin* and the *tav* of Parshandata are written small; remove the *peh* and the *resh*, and there remains the word "banishment."[13]

This text is difficult to understand, and its end definitely seems corrupted.[14] But finally we have the very first Jewish text indicating that *certain* letters of the *Megillah* must be written in smaller font: the *zayin* of Vayzata, as well as the *resh*, *shin* and *tav* of Parshandata. The list of small letters, however, does not correspond to that of *The Code of Esther*. Moreover, I did not find any subsequent rabbinic text quoting verbatim these teachings.[15]

Another important clue is offered by the Masorah, i.e., the system of notes devised by the scholar-scribes who worked between the sixth and the tenth centuries to preserve the textual integrity of the Torah. Thus, the Masoretic notes at the end of the *Leningrad Codex* (מסורה סופית) signal a small *shin* for Parshandata, a small *tav* for Parmashta, and no small letter for Vayzata.[16]

Not only does this not correspond to *The Code of Esther* either, but even more surprisingly, the Masorah on the *Leningrad Codex* does not reflect the actual text of the Codex itself! How can this discrepancy between manuscript and Masoretic notes be explained?

Menaḥem Cohen, in his superb introduction to the Keter edition of the *Mikraot Gedolot*,[17] notes that the phenomenon is much wider than *The Code of Esther*: the small and large letters noted by the Masorah are *never* reflected in the texts of the oldest manuscripts. He concludes that

---

13 According to my dictionary, the translation of the word *shamta* is "desolation" or "banishment." See also *Moed Katan* 17a, where Rav explains that the word is an indirect reference to death (*sham mita*).

14 See solutions proposed by Avraham Wertheimer in *Batei Midrashot*, p. 482, note 39.

15 The idea of Haman's slander against the Jewish people figures in *Bavli Megillah* 13b in the name of the sage Rava, but without association with the letter *zayin* or a sevenfold occurrence.

16 מרדכי ברויאר, *נוסח המקרא בכתר ירושלים ומקורותיו במסורה ובכתבי יד*, הוצאת קרן המסורה, ירושלים 2003, עמ' 324.

17 This introduction is actually to be found at the end of the sixth volume of the series (Joshua -Judges); see more specifically his remarks on the small and large letters on pp. 47*-49*.

the first lists of unusual letters, which initially appeared toward the end of the Masoretes' period, were for an extended period considered unauthoritative. Conflicts between different lists abounded, no scribe would take them into account in his work, and it is only centuries later that the first manuscripts with unusually sized letters are documented. In the case of Esther, the first recorded instance dates, to my knowledge, from the year 1312.[18]

Next, we turn to the Jewish communities of the eleventh to fourteenth centuries. A non-exhaustive review of the halakhic witnesses yielded no less than seven different versions of the small and large letters for the verses in question. All seven versions are mutually exclusive, and only one of them—the seventh and most recent—corresponds to the letters according to *The Code of Esther*. Summarized below are the seven versions, sorted in chronological order:

1. Maḥzor Vitry[19]:	ואת פרשנדתא ... ואת פרמשתא ... ואת ויזתא *Small zayin and large vav for Vayzata*
2. Raavia (Version 1):	ואת פרשנדתא ... ואת פרמשתא ... ואת ויזתא *Large alef for Parshandata and small alef for Parmashta*
3. Raavia (Version 2)[20]:	ואת פרשנדתא ... ואת פרמשתא ... ואת ויזתא *Large alef for Parmashta and small alef for Parshandata*
4. Sefer ha-Rokeaḥ[21]:	ואת פרשנדתא ... ואת פרמשתא ... ואת ויזתא *Small shin and tav for Parmashta, small zayin and large vav for Vayzata*
5. Hagahot Maimoniot[22]:	ואת פרשנדתא ... ואת פרמשתא ... ואת ויזתא *Small shin and tav, large alef for Parshandata; large vav and small zayin for Vayzata*

18 *Keter Shem Tov* by Shem Tov ben Abraham ibn Gaon, also known as *Sefer Tagey*, and formerly known as Ms. Sassoon 82 (small *shin* for Parshandata, small *shin* for Parmashta, small *zayin* for Vayzata).

19 *Maḥzor Vitry* (Simḥa ben Samuel, died in 1105, Vitry) *simanim* 247, 527, citing a tradition from R. Yehudai Gaon.

20 Raavia (= R. Eliezer ben Joel haLevi, 1140-1225, Germany), *ḥelek* 2, *Masekhet Megillah, siman* 548; see also *Ohr Zarua* (R. Isaac ben Moshe, 1200-1270 approx., Germany), *Hilkhot Megillah, siman* 373, who notes the same two alternatives.

21 Sefer ha-Rokeaḥ (R. Elazar ben Yehudah, 1160-1238, Germany), *Hilkhot Purim, siman* 235.

22 *Hagahot Maimoniot* (R. Meir ha-Cohen, late 13th century, Germany) on *Mishneh Torah, Hilkhot Megillah ve-Ḥanukah*, Chapter 2, Halakha 12, letter Ayin, which quotes the personal *Megillah* from Maharam of Rottenburg.

6. Sefer ha-Manhig[23]:	ואת פרשנדתא ... ואת פרמשתא ... ואת ויזתא *Small tav for Parshandata, small shin for Parmashta, large vav, large yud and small zayin for Vayzata*
7. Orḥot Ḥayyim[24]: (version used in *The* ***Code of Esther***)	ואת פרשנדתא ... ואת פרמשתא ... ואת ויזתא *Small tav for Parshandata, small shin for Parmashta, small zayin and large vav for Vayzata*

I found no comparable scribal irregularities in the writings of the Spanish sages of the same period.[25] So why this particular profusion in the German writings followed by the Provencal writings?[26]

Here we can only speculate. Prestigious researchers, including Haym Soloveitchik and Avraham Grossman, have long pointed out that the first communities in Northern Europe were the heirs of particular customs, probably stemming from ancient Babylonian traditions.[27] We may therefore suppose that these communities were the recipients of specific instructions regarding how to write the text of the *Megillah*; moreover, it is likely that they knew of the "Midrash of Rabbi Akiva ben Yosef"[28] and of the Masoretic notes examined above. The transmission, however, was clearly imperfect, and competing versions rapidly multiplied among German sages (versions 1-5). A few decades later, the Provencal sages, in contact with their colleagues in the Rhine valleys, inherited the tradition and added to the general confusion by "inventing" new possibilities (versions 6-7).

In all versions, a point of consensus remained constant: only the names of three sons of Haman (Parshandata, Parmashta and Vayzata)

---

23 *Sefer ha-Manhig* (Abraham ben Nathan, 12th - 13th century, Provence), *Hilkhot Megillah* p. 250, quoting from "scribes."

24 *Orḥot Ḥayyim* (Aaron ben Jacob ha-Cohen, early 14th century, Provence), *ḥelek* 1, *Hilkhot Megillah u-Purim*, number 17.

25 For example, see what Maimonides wrote in *Hilkhot Megillah* 2:12 (and in *Hilkhot Sefer Torah* 7:8). Not only are the small letters not mentioned, but even the large *vav* of Vayzata of Talmudic origin is not discussed. This last oversight surprised the commentators (*Magid Mishneh* and *Maasseh Rokeaḥ*). See the *ḥidushim* of R. Velvel Soloveitchik who proposes an innovative interpretation. Abudraham remains silent on this whole affair, as does Rabbeinu Yeruḥam. So too, earlier, did the literature of the Geonim (Seder of Rav Amram Gaon, Behag, etc.).

26 Some German books, however, remain curiously silent, as the *Siddur Rashi* (*siman* 341).

27 See Soloveitchik, *Collected Essays*, vol. 2, pp. 150-201 (The Third Yeshiva of Bavel and the Cultural Origins of Ashkenaz).

28 This is confirmed by Wertheimer's introductory remarks, *Batei Midrashot*, p. 467.

are spelled differently. It is within the precise details that various traditions arose.

In any case, the next question to consider is why the latest version, *Orḥot Ḥayyim*, eventually prevailed over all its competitors. In my mind, the reason is almost certainly the invention of printing.

Following the invention of printing by Guttenberg in the mid-fifteenth century, the first Hebrew Bibles appeared fairly quickly. In Venice, on the press of Daniel Bomberg, the first edition of *Mikraot Gedolot* appeared in 1516-1517. But it was the second edition of *Mikraot Gedolot*, printed on the same press in the years 1524-1526, which had a colossal influence on the diffusion of the biblical text.

The publisher, Jacob ben Ḥayyim ibn Adonijah (1470-1538), devoted immense efforts to clarify the biblical text, based on the manuscripts in his possession, in order to make it available to his readers. The importance of the work provided was widely recognized by the scholarly world of the time, with the result that this second edition of the *Mikraot Gedolot* served as a model for many editions of the Tanakh, even up to our own time.[29]

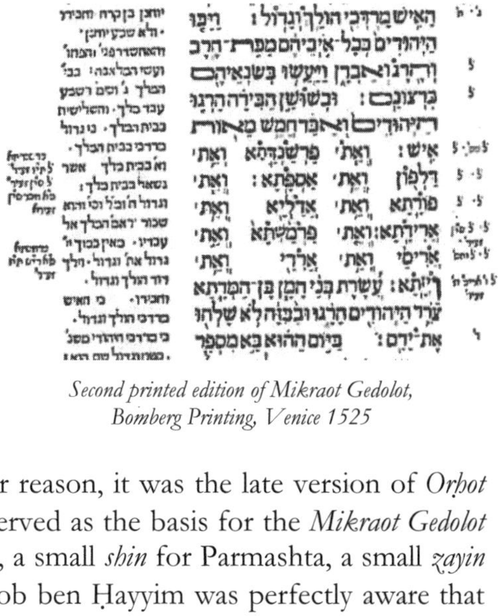
האיש מרדכי הולך וגדול: ויכו
היהודים בכל איביהם מכת חרב
והרג ואבדן ויעשו בשנאיהם
כרצונם: ובשושן הבירה הרגו
היהודים ואבד חמש מאות
איש: ואת פרשנדתא ואת
דלפון ואת אספתא: ואת
פורתא ואת אדליא ואת
ארידתא: ואת פרמשתא ואת
אריסי ואת ארדי ואת
ויזתא: עשרת בני המן בן המדתא
צרר היהודים הרגו ובבזה לא שלחו
את ידם: ביום ההוא בא מספר

Second printed edition of Mikraot Gedolot, Bomberg Printing, Venice 1525

And what was the solution adopted by Jacob ben Ḥayyim? To be absolutely clear, I went to investigate:

Jacob ben Ḥayyim had to choose a solution. For whatever reason, it was the late version of *Orḥot Ḥayyim* (version 7 above) that served as the basis for the *Mikraot Gedolot* text: a small *tav* for Parshandata, a small *shin* for Parmashta, a small *zayin* and a large *vav* for Vayzata. Jacob ben Ḥayyim was perfectly aware that several traditions existed for these verses; he pointed out their existence

29 Ironically, even Jacob ben Ḥayyim's text was flawed. As Moshe Goshen-Gottstein notes in an introduction to the reprint of the *Mikraot Gedolot* (Venice 1525) published in 1972, residual errors were not uncommon. The reference scientific edition today is the *Mikraot Gedolot ha-Keter*, prepared under the supervision of Menaḥem Cohen (Bar-Ilan University) and based on the text of the *Leningrad Codex*.

It is surprising that Mordekhai Breuer used ben Ḥayyim's version, instead of the more reliable text of the *Leningrad Codex*, in his *Keter Yerushalayim*.

in the margins left and right of the main text with the aid of a critical apparatus (also reproduced in the image above).

But what happened when the later editions of the Hebrew Bible, based on the text superbly compiled by Jacob ben Ḥayim, omitted the critical apparatus (which, certainly, could only be deciphered by the learned philologists)? Nothing less than the canonization of one unique version, the text of *Orḥot Ḥayyim*, now rid of all its rivals. And so, it comes full circle: the text of *Megillat Esther* becomes a detective story, the famous *Code of Esther*.

Three important remarks before concluding this part: first, the halakhic texts of the past 500 years absolutely do NOT reflect the printed, henceforth triumphant, version of the *Book of Esther*; in other words, Jacob ben Ḥayyim's work impacted only the scribes, not the rabbis. All legal works continue to faithfully perpetuate the Talmudic tradition: a large *vav*, no small letters.[30] Thus, there exists a discrepancy between the halakhic text and the printed text.

Secondly, other versions of the text continue to circulate, even if they are now in the minority.[31] Thirdly, the harmonizing effect had by printing the biblical text is a general phenomenon that affected all the books of the Tanakh, including (and most especially) the Pentateuch; I invite interested readers to read the article.[32]

To conclude: the average reader who opens his printed Bible to read *Megillat Esther* naturally assumes to have the "authentic" text. He has no awareness that this text has a long and tumultuous history. He does not realize that small and large letters are the result of the long historical process that we have just reconstructed. Can we really blame him? Certainly not. But the reality is that the little letters necessary to the claims made in *The Code of Esther* did not initially exist. They appear in our books only because of confusions and errors of transmission, finally canonized under the standardizing impetus of the printing of the Bible.

---

30 See *Tur, Bet Yosef, Shulḥan Arukh, Arukh ha-Shulḥan, Mishna Berura*, etc., all on *Oraḥ Ḥayyim* 691. *Eliyah Rabba* 691:9 explicitly notes the discrepancy between the "printed text" of the *Megillah* and the "halakhic text."

31 For example, the Soncino edition of the *Book of Esther* endorses a version halfway between versions 4 and 7 above, but I have never encountered such a version in any medieval work. I do not know if the editor worked from another version of the large and small letters, or if he deliberately chose to create a hybrid. The critical apparatus suggests that other traditions still existed (small *resh* for Parmashta).

32 https://users.cecs.anu.edu.au/~bdm/codes/CohenArt/.

Act 3: Which millennium exactly?

The claim: The large vav is a reference to the sixth millennium since the Creation.

The reality: Such a notation does not correspond to any Jewish dating system.

Throughout history, Jews have used many ways to note the passage of time. Thus, in the written Torah, an event in time was often located according to the accession to the throne of the king ("*during the year xyz of the reign of King David…*").[33] During Talmudic times, the passage of time was generally noted using the system called "*Minyan Shtarot.*" This method, which was employed mainly to date commercial documents, used the year 311 BCE as its point of departure.[34] Another method was to count the number of years since the destruction of the 2nd Temple.[35]

The dating system tracking the passage of time from Creation of the World did exist in Talmudic times.[36] But at that time, it was very seldom used. It is primarily since the tenth century that the calendar we know today began to take off, but the other dating systems remained in use for centuries (in Egypt, the calendar was kept according to the *Minyan Shtarot* until the sixteenth century, and in Yemen until into the nineteenth century).

These few facts are ample enough to demystify the "elongated" *vav* of the name Vayzata: first, according to certain rabbinical authorities, its size should be perfectly normal and not lengthened.[37] Second, a long *vav* has absolutely no meaning in the majority of dating systems used by Jews throughout history. Third, even when one counts the time since the moment of the Creation, the year 5,000 is systematically signified by a *heh* (whose numerical value is 5), and never by a *vav* (whose value is 6).

---

33 See many examples in the books of Samuel, Kings and Chronicles.

34 For an example, see *Avoda Zara* 10a. And see Rambam, *Mishneh Torah, Hilkhot Gerushin* 1:27.

35 This is often the case with inscriptions on the oldest tombstones we know.

36 See for example *Avoda Zara* 9b; the same dating system underpins the work *Seder Olam.*

37 Some authorities think that it is necessary to prolong the reading of the *vav* by singing it more slowly, but without changing its writing (Rabbeinu Yehonathan of Lunel, also mentioned by Meiri, Rosh and Ran); others think that the head of the *vav*, which is normally curved, must here be drawn straight (Ritva). The ancient manuscripts discussed above show that the practice was not uniform here (the *Leningrad Codex* does not have a long *vav*, but other manuscripts do). Here, too, I think that printing has had a unifying effect.

Linked here are a few examples among many, from Torah courses,[38] official Israeli documents,[39] or even Wikipedia.[40] I do not know of a *single* counterexample in which a *vav* would represent the sixth millennium. It would be illogical for a prophecy to rely on a dating system that has, in fact, never been practiced by any Jewish community in the world.

Act 4: Shushan, the city where they hang cold corpses ...

> *The claim: Esther's request to hang Haman's sons (9:13) makes no sense, since they had already been killed by the sword (9:6-10).*
>
> *The reality: There are many cases in the Torah in which the corpses of enemies are publicly exhibited.*

If there is a true mystery in *The Code of Esther*, it is this: the attentive reader of the Torah encounters many situations in which an enemy is killed and his body publicly exhibited. How, then, have so many scholars accepted as "incomprehensible" the request from Esther to hang the slain bodies of her enemies?

Some illustrations: when Joshua won a decisive battle against five Canaanite armies, he killed their kings and hanged them on trees until evening;[41] in another skirmish, he did the same to the city of Ai and its king.[42] King David, meanwhile, sometimes cut the hands and feet of his already dead enemies before publicly hanging their bodies.[43]

The Torah testifies that the other peoples of the time did the same: thus, when the Philistines found King Saul already dead, they cut off his head and tied his body on the wall of the city of Beth She'an.[44] Another community, the Gibeonites, was hardly more sympathetic to their enemies.[45] Beyond the Torah, the practice is also attested in other ancient codes of law.[46]

---

38 https://www.yeshiva.org.il/midrash/2337.

39 https://www.gov.il/he/departments/general/electronic_signature_law2.

40 https://he.wikipedia.org/wiki/%D7%94%27%D7%AA%D7%A9%D7%A1%22%D7%95.

41 Joshua 10:26.

42 Ibid. 8:29.

43 II Samuel 4:12.

44 I Samuel 31:10.

45 II Samuel 21:9.

46 *Code of Hammurabi* paragraph 21.

The practice is apparent through a literal reading (*pshat*) of one of the most famous verses of the entire Pentateuch, Joseph's interpretation of the dream of the Egyptian chief baker:[47]

> בְּעוֹד שְׁלֹשֶׁת יָמִים, יִשָּׂא פַרְעֹה אֶת-רֹאשְׁךָ מֵעָלֶיךָ ,וְתָלָה אוֹתְךָ, עַל-עֵץ; וְאָכַל הָעוֹף אֶת-בְּשָׂרְךָ, מֵעָלֶיךָ.
>
> In three days, Pharaoh will cut off your head and hang you on a tree, and the birds will eat the flesh of your body.

Moreover, a specific command of the Torah regulates the public display of corpses of those sentenced to death: it is only allowed until the evening, after which time the corpses must be buried.[48]

> וְכִי-יִהְיֶה בְאִישׁ, חֵטְא מִשְׁפַּט-מָוֶת--וְהוּמָת: וְתָלִיתָ אֹתוֹ, עַל-עֵץ. לֹא-תָלִין נִבְלָתוֹ עַל-הָעֵץ, כִּי-קָבוֹר תִּקְבְּרֶנּוּ בַּיּוֹם הַהוּא--כִּי-קִלְלַת אֱלֹהִים, תָּלוּי; וְלֹא תְטַמֵּא ,אֶת-אַדְמָתְךָ, אֲשֶׁר יְהוָה אֱלֹהֶיךָ, נֹתֵן לְךָ נַחֲלָה.
>
> When a man has committed a capital sin, he will have been put to death: you hang him on a tree; you will not leave his carcass on the tree, but you will bury him before the evening, because it is an offense against God to be suspended. And you shall not pollute the land which the Lord your God has given you for an inheritance.

The public display of corpses may seem odd to our modern eyes, but its reason is evident in the sociocultural context of the time. The bodies thus exhibited belonged to either enemies of the state or serious criminals. In both cases, society sought to prevent their emulation. The message of deterrence sent to observers was instantly understandable: "*See what happened to these enemies, to these criminals. Above all, do not do the same! Do not oppose us, do not commit these crimes.*"

Multiplying the examples brings to light another important point. The technique used to expose the body had little importance: to attach the body to a wall, to a tree, to impale it, or something else—whatever worked, so long as the objectives of publicity and deterrence were achieved. Further, this observation makes it possible to understand the internal logic of an argument from the New Testament: for Paul, the crucifixion of Jesus represents a "redemption" of the verses of Deuteronomy 21:22-23, that is to say, a way for Christians to no longer be

---

47 *Bereshit* 40:19 (personal translation).

48 *Devarim* 21:22-23 (personal translation). See the commentary of R. David Ẓvi Hoffmann, who insists that the "hanging" is not the cause of death, but its direct consequence; the verse in II Samuel 21:10 presents another more pragmatic reason—the fear of scavengers—to quickly bury the bodies.

bound by this commandment.[49] The body of Christ *on the cross* replaces the bodies *on the tree* of those sentenced to death.

Attention, therefore, to the errors of translation. It is quite possible, as some of the most authoritative English translations of the Bible suggest, that the sons of Haman were not really "hanged on a tree," but "exposed on gallows."[50]

In conclusion, Esther's request is not surprising in the context of her time, and there is no way to be certain that Haman's sons were hanged, like the Nazis much later, rather than exposed to the public in some other way.

Act 5: Purim, Jewish festival of violence

> *The claim: Julius Streicher, just before dying, exclaimed: "Purimfest 1946!" This sentence would have been incomprehensible in the context of the moment.*
>
> *The reality: The Jewish holiday of Purim was regularly quoted in the Nazi propaganda as an example of the violence exerted by the Jews against the nations who welcome them.*

In the years before World War II, Nazi propaganda regularly featured Purim as the quintessential expression of Jewish domination, greed, and violent oppression of non-Jews. Julius Streicher, founder and editor-in-chief of the newspaper *Der Stürmer*, was the great architect of the violent anti-Semitic propaganda of the Third Reich. He was perfectly familiar with the festival of Purim.

In March 1934, number 11 of *Der Stürmer* featured a lengthy report bearing the following title: "The Night of the Murder: The Secret of the Jewish Holiday of Purim is Unveiled" ("*die Mordnacht: Das Geheimnis des jüdischen Purimfestes ist enthüllt*"). Those with a strong stomach can read the original text in its entirety.[51]

Purim according to Streicher was a festival dedicated to the hatred and murder of non-Jews. Reinforced by Talmudic and rabbinical texts, Streicher sought to demonstrate to his readers that Jews celebrated, through the drunkenness of Purim, the mass murder of 75,000 innocent

---

49 *Epistle to the Galatians* 3:13. Targum Onkelos renders the verse of *Devarim* 21:22 "וְתִצְלוֹב יָתֵיהּ עַל צְלִיבָא," which I am hesitant to translate "crucify on a cross," especially since Bernard Grossfeld prefers to translate it "Impaled on the stake" (see Grossfeld, *The Aramaic Bible, Targum Onkelos to Deuteronomy*).

50 See Carey Moore, *Anchor Bible*, p. 85, on Esther 9:14. This is probably also the meaning of Esther 2:23—the conspirators of the plot foiled by Mordekhai were *exposed publicly after having been executed.*

51 http://www.humanist.de/kriminalmuseum/st-t3411.htm.

Persians, and that this murderous impulse is a historical constant in the relationships between Jews and the innocent people who generously welcome them into their lands.

The festival of Purim appeared regularly in Nazi propaganda. On November 10, 1938, the day after the terrorizing events of Kristallnacht, Streicher gave a speech to more than 100,000 people assembled to listen to him in Nuremberg; he justified the violence against the Jews, saying that the Jews had murdered 75,000 Persians in one night, and that the Germans would have the same fate if the Jews had been able to accomplish their plan to institute a new murderous "Purim" in Germany.[52]

In 1940, the best-known Nazi anti-Jewish propaganda film, *Der Ewige Jude* ("The Eternal Jew"), again took up the same theme. The whole movie can be viewed here,[53] with Purim appearing from minute 45:00.

In 1942, on Purim Day, the Nazis hanged ten Jews in the small Polish town of Zdunska Wola in order to "avenge" the murder of Haman's ten sons. In another incident a year later, during Purim 1943, the Nazis executed ten Jews from the Piotrkow ghetto. Similar incidents also occurred in Czestochowa, Radom and Szydlowiec.[54]

Adolf Hitler himself, in a speech on January 30, 1944, declared that if the Nazis were to be defeated by the allied forces, the Jews would celebrate "a second Purim."[55]

There can be no doubt on this point: Streicher was perfectly familiar with the Jewish holiday of Purim. His remarks on the scaffold are readily understandable: by doing violence to the Nazis, the Jews marked a new Purim in 1946.

In addition, the last words of Streicher—"*Purimfest 1946! [...] the Bolsheviks will hang you one day!*"—betray a certain fatalistic and mortiferous vision of history: the Jews now kill the Nazis who killed them before; the Russians will one day kill the American executioners who are triumphing for the moment. History is but an immense cycle of infinitely repeated violence, with death as the sole ultimate outcome.

---

52 Randall L. Bytwerk, *Landmark Speeches of National Socialism* (Texas: A&M University Press, 2008) p. 91.

53 https://www.youtube.com/watch?v=6MBjvQY6wD8 at 47:10.

54 Elliott Horowitz, *Reckless Rites: Purim and the Legacy of Jewish Violence* (Princeton: University Press 2006), p. 91.

55 Philip Goodman, *The Purim Anthology* (Philadelphia, 1949), p. 4.

Act 6: Imaginary coincidences and real cognitive biases

> *The claim: There are surprising coincidences between Megillat Esther and the Nuremberg trial.*
>
> *The reality: The human brain has a propensity to see connections even where they do not exist.*

The human brain, the result of a slow evolution over millions of years in which survival was the main objective and decision speed an essential asset, is a poor tool for getting to grips with the truth. We are programmed to jump straight to conclusions without bothering to check whether or not the reasoning is sound.

But, at least partially, it is possible to overcome these shortcomings. An awareness of the distortions of thought induced by our cognitive biases is an important factor in the development of critical reasoning. For example, we give more credit to information that confirms our pre-established beliefs (confirmation bias), or we establish pseudo-links between vague propositions and our real lives (Barnum effect) or between different yet distinct events.

These cognitive biases play fully in the perception of the "coincidences" of *The Code of Esther*: points of comparison seem instinctively much more convincing than points of divergence.

So, do Haman's ten sons correspond to the ten Nazi officials hanged in 1946? Not really, no. In reality, the number of defendants at the Nuremberg trial was twenty-four, more than double the ten sons of Haman. Not all of them were sentenced to death: eight were given prison sentences, and two Nazi dignitaries were even acquitted. The total number of death sentences was twelve: ten Nazis were executed, one committed suicide (Goering), and one had been tried *in absentia* (Bormann). None of these details of the Nuremberg trial have any parallel in the Purim account. Hitler, meanwhile, had committed suicide in his bunker more than a year earlier, unlike Haman, who was executed by hanging shortly before his sons (Esther 7:10).

Neither does the mode of execution of the Nuremberg trials match the Purim story. The sons of Haman died by the sword (Esther 9:5) before being publicly exposed on gallows; the Nazis, on the other hand, were killed by hanging, then immediately buried.

On the other hand, the day of Hoshanah Rabbah is indeed a day of judgment,[56] but only for those who are neither completely good nor

---

56 At least, according to medieval sources (*Sefer ha-Manhig, Hilkhot Sukkot*, pp. 402-403, *Zohar* 1: 220a, 2: 242a-b and 3: 31b-32a). The Talmud was not yet

completely bad. The perfectly righteous (*ẓadikim)*, as well as the thoroughly wicked (*reshaim)*, are judged on Rosh Hashanah.[57] In what category should we place the worst criminals of one of the deadliest regimes of all time?

Finally, note that death by hanging was not unusual. In fact, this specific point was controversial in 1946, when the Nazis asked to be shot, given their military status. The court eventually chose to administer a death by hanging, after having duly deliberated that the crimes of the Nazis were considered as going beyond categorically military crimes. They were guilty of crimes against humanity that could not be treated as merely military.[58] Death by hanging was in fact the most common form of death penalty during that period.

Conclusion

In the final analysis, the supposed prophecy of the book of Esther seems very ill-founded. Among its constituent elements, there is none that can long withstand a serious critical examination based on an in-depth study of facts and texts.

A humorous story claims that Adolf Hitler once went to consult a clairvoyant who would predict his future. "You will die on a Jewish holiday," the clairvoyant told him. "Which?" asked the dictator. "No matter," retorted the seer, "any day you die will be a holiday for the Jews."

Purim is an extraordinary celebration, in which we celebrate life, humor, children, and the ultimate victory of good over evil. All of these we continue to celebrate seventy-five years after the fall of another deadly enemy of the Jewish people.

So no, there is absolutely no relationship between Haman's sons and the Nazis convicted during the Nuremberg trial. *The Code of Esther* is more farce than prophecy, and the divine presence remains hidden behind the double screen of Nature and History. But, in the end, is it not precisely in this sober observation (and in a form of Jewish humor that—despite our frequent inability to perceive the Transcendent—reaffirms Life) that the true spirit of Purim resides? ☙

---

familiar with this idea. See *Halakhot Ketanot* 1:225 for an attempt at reconciliation.

57 Talmud, *Rosh Hashanah* 16b.

58 Telford Taylor, *The Anatomy of Nuremberg Trials: A Personal Memoir* (Skyhorse: 1992), pp. 601-607.

Loving the Convert Prior to a Completed Conversion: With a Test Case Application of Inviting Conversion Candidates to Pesach Seder and Yom Tov Meals

By: MICHAEL J. BROYDE and BENJAMIN J. SAMUELS

Introduction

The Torah enjoins us numerous times concerning the mitzvah of *Ahavat ha-Ger*,[1] which literally means the love of the stranger or sojourner, though is primarily understood in Jewish legal sources to refer more specifically to loving the convert to Judaism.[2] Furthermore, the Torah commands us that "you shall love your neighbor as yourself" (Leviticus 19:18), and also charges us to love God (Deuteronomy 6:4), creating multiple duties of love as halakhic obligations. This article will explore the question: When does the duty to love the convert commence and does it impact the conversion process? Does it apply only to a newly converted Jew, or to a Noahide who is in the process of converting, or even to a Gentile who has expressed an interest in converting?

The process of conversion to Judaism can be divided into three fundamental stages: In the first stage, the person makes a personal decision

---

1 See Leviticus 19:34; Deuteronomy 10:18-19. The Torah also prohibits oppressing the convert, "*lo toneh*" and "*Lo tonu*"—see Exodus 22:20; Leviticus 19:33; *TB Bava Metzia* 58b, 59b, and Ben Zion Katz, "Don't Oppress the Ger," *Seforim Blog* <https://seforimblog.com/2019/07/dont-oppress-the-ger/>.
However, this article will not investigate the question of when the prohibition against oppressing a convert begins, which may or may not track in parallel with the mitzvah of *Ahavat ha-Ger*.

2 See Yehuda Rock, "*Parshat Ekev – Mihu 'ha-Ger'?*" <https://etzion.org.il/he/פרשת-עקב-מיהו-הגר>.

Rabbi Michael J. Broyde served in a variety of rabbinic roles over the past 30 years and is a law professor at Emory University. He completed this article while a Visiting Professor of Law at Stanford University Law School (Fall 2019).
Rabbi Benjamin J. Samuels, PhD, has served as rabbi of Congregation Shaarei Tefillah in Newton, Massachusetts since 1995, and teaches widely in the Greater Boston Jewish community.

to join the Jewish people; in the second, that person undergoes the educational and experiential process of Judaization toward conversion; and in the final stage, the person undertakes the ritual completion of conversion, standardly defined by circumcision for a man, immersion in a *mikveh* and verbal acceptance of the yoke of commandments for a man or woman—all under the supervision of a rabbinical court.[3] At which stage does the mitzvah to love the convert begin? And if the mitzvah of *Ahavat ha-Ger* only attaches after a completed conversion, then what is added by this mitzvah when there is already an obligation of *Ahavat Yisrael*—to love our fellow Jews?[4]

This question has considerable practical ramifications. If the obligation of *Ahavat ha-Ger* starts before a conversion is halakhically completed, how does the duty to love the convert-to-be texture and shape the conversion process? What impacts would it have upon the attitudes and behaviors of rabbinical courts, supervising rabbis, host communities, and individual Jews in their interactions with prospective converts? What is the personal halakhic status of a convert-to-be within the Jewish community, and what rights and responsibilities attend such standing? Might this question have even larger implications for our halakhic obligations and emotional attitudes toward self-identifying members of the greater Jewish community who may not have halakhic status as Jews? To explore this question, we focus on a test case of inviting a person in the process of conversion for a Pesach Seder or a Yom Tov meal.

This essay is divided into two parts, besides this Introduction and the Conclusion. Part I presents, in three sections, the general schools of thought as to when the mitzvah of *Ahavat ha-Ger* commences. First, in Section One, we consider the view of Rambam that only a full convert—that is, post-conversion—must be loved. Additionally, we explore whether Rambam advances other reasons to love a convert-to-be. We also consider other halakhic authorities subsumed within this school of thought. Next, in Section Two, we analyze the more nuanced views of Rosh and Raavad who understand the mitzvah of *Ahavat ha-Ger* as attaching somewhere earlier along the conversionary process. Finally, in Section

---

3 See Benjamin J. Samuels, "The Contemporary Rabbinate and Conversion," in *Conversion, Intermarriage, and Jewish Identity,* edited by Adam Mintz and Marc D. Stern (Hoboken, NJ: Ktav, 2015) pp. 347-381.

4 The redundancy problem of *Ahavat Yisrael* combined with *Ahavat ha-Ger* is compounded by a certain paradox of praxis. As an extension of Mishnah *Bava Metzia* 58b, one is not supposed to identify nor treat a convert post-conversion as different from a born Jew, and yet the mitzvah of *Ahavat ha-Ger* demands specialized and preferential treatment. See Michael J. Broyde, *A Concise Code of Jewish Law for Converts* (New York: Urim, 2017) pp. 11-12.

Three, we examine the view of Rabbi Yitzchak of Barcelona who applies the mitzvah of *Ahavat ha-Ger* to a person professing a desire to convert to Judaism, and Rashba who similarly believes that a convert-to-be earns halakhic status as a *ger* even before conversion is fully completed.

The underlying issue of whether there is a duty to love the convert-to-be, or at least to help the conversion candidate progress in their process, has marked consequences regarding halakhic practice, educational inclusivity, and interpersonal relations. Thus, in Part II, we examine the practical test-case of inviting a convert-to-be for meals on Yom Tov, and to a Pesach Seder more specifically, in order to demonstrate the ramifications of each school's understanding of *Ahavat ha-Ger*. We note in this part that echoes of each of the three major views of the *rishonim* about the status of a convert-to-be can be found in the various views of *poskim* concerning inviting a convert-to-be for festival meals.

Part I: Loving the Convert: Before, As Part Of, or Only After Conversion?

Section One: The Duty to Love Applies Only After Conversion

The question of whether there is a formal duty to love the convert-to-be is implicitly discussed by the Rambam in his formulation of the obligation to love the convert. Rambam (*Mishneh Torah, Hilkhot De'ot* 6:4) formulates the obligation as follows:

> אהבת הגר שבא ונכנס תחת כנפי השכינה שתי מצות עשה, אחת מפני שהוא בכלל ריעים ואחת מפני שהוא גר והתורה אמרה ואהבתם את הגר, צוה על אהבת הגר כמו שצוה על אהבת עצמו שנאמר ואהבת את ה' אלהיך, הקדוש ברוך הוא עצמו אוהב גרים שנאמר ואוהב גר.
>
> Loving a convert who has come and entered under the protection of the Divine Presence fulfills two positive commandments: one, since the convert is included within [loving] "neighbors"; and two, because this person is a convert and the Torah states: "you shall love the convert" (Deuteronomy 10:19). God has commanded us to love a convert just as He has commanded us to love Him, as the Torah says: "you must love God, your Lord" (Deuteronomy 11:1). God loves converts as the Torah says: "and He loves converts" (Deuteronomy 10:18).[5]

---

5 In the preceding paragraph (*Hilkhot De'ot* 6:3), Rambam upholds the midrash-halakhic interpretation of Leviticus 19:18, "and you shall love your neighbor as yourself," as an obligation of *Ahavat Yisrael*—loving fellow Jews. See *Sifra, Kedoshim* 3:8:4, which also compares the duty to love one's Jewish "neighbor" to

In three different ways, it is clear from Rambam that this commandment is limited to people who have already become Jewish and does not apply to a person who has not yet completed the conversion process. First, Rambam notes that the convert is one who has already come forward and entered under the "wings" of conversion—i.e., Divine protection for Jews. Second, Rambam connects this obligation to the general duty to love all Jews, and thereby constrains the term "*ger*" to one who is also your Jewish neighbor. Third, by connecting the duty to love the convert to God's love of converts, Rambam arguably understands the mitzvah of loving the convert to be an extra obligation upon Jews to love *Jewish* converts.[6]

This is borne out as well by the formulation found in Rambam's *Sefer Ha-Mitzvot* (*Aseh* 207), which defines the parameters of the mitzvah as such:

> והמצוה הר"ז היא שצונו לאהוב את הגרים והוא אמרו יתברך (עקב י) ואהבתם את הגר, ואף על פי שהיה נכלל בזה עם ישראל באמרו ואהבת לרעך כמוך, לפי שזה הגר גר צדק, אבל בעבור שנכנס בתורתנו הוסיף לו האל אהבה וייחד לו מצוה נוספת ...
>
> The 207th *mitzvah* is that we are commanded to love converts, as God, may He be blessed, said: "You shall love the convert" (Deuteronomy 10:19). Even though [loving] the convert is also included

---

loving the *ger*. Indeed, the Torah's very language in Leviticus 19:34 regarding a convert, "and you shall love him as yourself," literarily parallels Leviticus 19:18, "and you shall love your neighbor as yourself." See also Jacob Jaffe, "Poetry, Conversion and the Memorial Prayer," <http://www.hakirah.org/Vol17Jaffe.pdf>.

6 See Rambam's "Letter to Ovadia *ha-Ger*," [*Responsa*, Freiman ed., no. 369] for a fuller articulation of this point. There is some uncertainty in the *aḥaronim* as to whether an *'eved kenani* is considered a convert regarding *Ahavat ha-Ger*. See *Minḥat Ḥinukh* 431, and *Pri Megadim*, *Eishel Avraham*, OḤ 156. Since a Canaanite slave is obligated in some mitzvot, the question arises as to whether such a person should be considered: a type of convert; a partial convert whose process will be completed after manumission; or a Gentile functionally obligated through subjugation to support the Jewishly-observant environment of his master. Although beyond the scope of this article, the question of whether a *ger toshav* is loved under the mitzvah of loving the convert or some other commandment requires further clarification. However, it should be noted that there exist halakhic indicators that a *ger toshav* enjoys special status. For example: one, he can validly slaughter kosher meat as a matter of Torah law (*Taz*, YD 2:1); two, the Talmud imposes upon him obligations of Sabbath observance (*TB Keritut* 9a); three, Jews have a duty to save the life of an endangered *ger toshav* (Ramban, *Commentary on Maimonides' Book of Commandments*, *Aseh* 16); and others.

> in [loving another] Jew, per "love your neighbor as yourself," since this *ger tzedek*—righteous convert—has now joined in our Torah, God increased love toward him, and assigned an extra commandment [to love him]...[7]

A similar formulation can be found in *Semag* (*Aseh* 10). Indeed, *Sefer Haḥinukh* (431) is even more explicit than the Rambam in this regard. He states:

> שנצטוינו לאהוב הגרים, כלומר שנזהר שלא לצער אותם בשום דבר, אבל נעשה להם טובה ונגמול אותם חסד כפי הראוי והיכולת. והגרים הם כל מי שנתחבר אלינו משאר האומות **שהניח דתו ונכנס בדתנו**, ועליהם נאמר (דברים י: יט) ואהבתם את הגר כי גרים הייתם.
>
> We are commanded to love converts, that is to say, we are warned not to distress them in any way, but we shall do good to them, and endow them with loving-kindness, as appropriate and possible. The converts are all those who join us from the other nations, **having abandoned their religion and joining ours**. About them it is said, "You shall love the convert since you were once strangers..." (Deuteronomy 10:19).[8]

---

7 Rabbi Joseph B. Soloveitchik interprets Rambam's careful formulation as further limiting the mitzvah of loving the convert to righteous converts, and not to less-than-fully sincere, albeit halakhically valid converts. The Rav states (*Reshimat Shiurim*, *Yevamot* 35b):

> ועוד נראה דמצות אהבת הגר וכדומה חלין רק בנוגע לגר צדק ולא בגר בעלמא.
>
> The duty to love the convert and other such mitzvot only applies to a righteous convert, and not a typical convert.

Rabbi Soloveitchik is proposing that the duty to love a convert does not apply, for example, to a person who converts for the sake of marriage, even though that conversion is valid. Per the Rav, there is still a duty to love the convert as a Jew, but without the additional "bonus" of *Ahavat ha-Ger*. See also Avraham Sherman, "Conversion: Mitzvah, Discretionarily Permitted, Forbidden," *Torah Sheba'al Peh,* vol. 19. Jerusalem: 5748 (1988), pp. 76-77. R. Sherman opines that Rambam's requirement of emotional love toward the convert stems from a *ger tzedek*'s framing spiritual commitments.

8 See R. Sherman, ibid., p. 77, who differentiates between *Sefer Haḥinukh*'s understanding of *Ahavat ha-Ger* as primarily superintending social interaction and kindness, and Rambam who focuses on emotional love, even as it is expressed behaviorally. R. Sherman also reconciles the aforementioned redundancy problem per this distinction. The mitzvah of loving one's neighbor legislates social acts of loving-kindness; see Rambam, *Mishneh Torah*, *Laws of Mourning* 14:1. The mitzvah of *Ahavat ha-Ger* requires an additional valence of emotional love toward a *ger tzedek* who stands as an exemplar of spiritual commitment. For the spiritual and social aspects of conversion, see also Aharon Lichtenstein, "On Conversion," *Tradition* 23:2, Winter 1988, pp. 1-18.

A considerable number of normative Jewish Law authorities adopt this view, whether explicitly or implicitly. For example, *Magen Avraham* (OC 156:2) when discussing the duty to love the convert inserts a single word to make this clear. He states:

> אהבת הגר שנתגייר.
>
> You should love the convert **who has already converted.**[9]

Maḥatzit Hashekel (156:2) quotes *Magen Avraham*'s formulation of "the convert who has already converted," as does *Mishnah Berurah* (156:4), directly limiting the duty to love the convert to one who has already converted.[10] *Arukh Ha-Shulḥan* (156:8) likewise limits the mitzvah to the already converted, although he adopts the longer formulation of Rambam

---

9 *Magen Avraham* OḤ 156, admittedly, is an unusual halakhic source. *Shulkhan Arukh* OḤ 156 in short form speaks to "The Laws of Commerce," and refers to a couple of halakhot that may arise in a workday. *Magen Avraham*, in a lengthy gloss, broadens the scope of the concerns of daily religious living and enumerates many other relevant mitzvot in what appears as a less legally formal writing-style. Nonetheless, we know of no reason not to consider *Magen Avraham*'s formulation of Loving the Convert as a normative halakhic interpretation. Subsequent commentators on *Shulḥan Arukh* follow *Magen Avraham*'s example of expansion, and often quote him verbatim. Cf. *Shulḥan Arukh HaRav* 156 who inexplicably omits *Ahavat ha-Ger*, while citing *Magen Avraham*'s other mitzvot of daily relevance.

10 *Mishnah Berurah*'s view here is consistent with his formulation in his *Sefer Mitzvot Hakatzar* 61, which parenthetically notes: "(the convert is also a member of the Jewish People)." The full text reads:

> מצות עשה לאהוב את הגר .שנאמר (דברים י׳:יט): "ואהבתם את הגר". וזוהי מצוה נוספת על "ואהבת לרעך כמוך," (שהרי הגר הוא גם כן בכלל ישראל). והקדוש ברוך הוא אוהב את הגר, דכתיב (שם י׳:יח): "ואוהב גר לתת לו לחם ושמלה", ונאמר (שמות כג:טו): "ואתם ידעתם את נפש הגר", ופירוש "גר" כאן, הוא: שבא מארץ אחרת ומעיר אחרת לגור אתנו, ומכל שכן גר שנתגייר .ונוהג בכל מקום ובכל זמן, בזכרים ובנקבות.
>
> A Positive Commandment to Love the Convert: As it states (Deuteronomy 10:19) "and you should love the convert." This is an additional mitzvah upon "love your neighbor as yourself" (since the convert is also part of the Jewish People). God loves the convert, as it states (Deuteronomy 10:18): "God loves the convert to give him bread and clothes," and it states (Exodus 23:15): "You know the life of the stranger/convert." And the explanation for the word "*ger*" here is: one who comes from another land or another city to reside with us, and even more so a convert who converts. This mitzvah applies in all places and times for men and women.

in *Hilkhot De'ot* (6:4), connecting the duty to love the convert to the obligation to love all Jews. He states:

> הגר שבא ונכנס תחת כנפי השכינה שתי מצות עשה אחת מפני שהוא בכלל ריעים ואחת מפני שהוא גר שנאמר (דברים י:יט) ואהבתם את הגר.
> The convert who has come and has entered under the wings of the Divine Presence [must be loved] per two commandments: one, since because he is included among [Jewish] "neighbors"; and two, because he is a convert, as it states, "You shall love the convert" (Deuteronomy 10:19).

What does this mean as a matter of halakhah? A practical, albeit premodern, example might help clarify this view. The Torah (Exodus 23:5; Deuteronomy 22:4) mandates that when one sees a Jew's animal struggling with the load it is carrying, one must stop and help the Jew unload and reload his animal. Consider a Jew who has only enough strength to help with a single instance of loading or unloading. This Jew encounters several people, including born Jews, converts, and non-Jews struggling with burdensome loads on their pack animals. Whom should this Jew help? Rabbi Joseph Teomim, in *Pri Megadim* (*Eishel Avraham* 156:2), his classical commentary on *Magen Avraham*, opines as follows:

> ומה שכתב אהבת הגר ב' מצות עשה, שם הלכה ד'. ונפקא מינה אי יש ישראל לפרוק וגר לטעון, עדיף לטעון לגר, שיש בו עשה יתירה ועדיף.
> Regarding that which he wrote, that "Loving the Convert" is two positive commandments ... A practical difference is that if a born Jew needs assistance unloading and a convert needs assistance loading (a case in which unloading usually takes precedence), it is better to help the convert load since by doing this one fulfils an additional commandment, which is better.

Rabbi Teomim proposes that we help the convert, who is now Jewish, before a born Jew, as this manifests the added love Jews are required to show to converts. By helping the convert, one fulfills two duties: loving

---

The author of the *Mishnah Berurah* seemingly follows Rambam here, yet also expands the definition of "*ger*" to "one who has come from another land or another city to dwell with us." Does this follow *Sefer Haḥinukh*'s (431) moralistic expansion of the mitzvah of *Ahavat ha-Ger* to include anyone dislocated from their homeland and family who may feel like a stranger among us? Does this refer to a Jew who relocates to a new community and may feel like a stranger? Or might this even refer to a non-Jew who is in the process of converting to Judaism? It is unclear. See *Encyclopedia Talmudit*, s.v. "*Ahavat ha-Ger*," 1:211, fn. 17.

the convert and loving the Jew—which is one more than one fulfills if one bypasses the convert and helps only the born Jew.

In short, this school of thought understands the mitzvah to love the convert as applying only to people who have already converted to Judaism. This appears to be the predominant halakhic viewpoint.[11] Rambam, and those Jewish law authorities who follow his view, therefore assert that there is no obligation to love the convert when dealing with a person who is not yet Jewish, even if they are on the path to conversion. Of course, this does not necessarily mean that there is no duty to convert a person who wishes to join the Jewish People, it means only that there is no formal duty to love the convert-to-be per the mitzvah of *Ahavat ha-Ger.*

Other Reasons Why for Rambam There Still May Be a Duty to Love, or at Least Help, the Convert-to-be

Even if the mitzvah of *Ahavat ha-Ger* does not apply, per Rambam, to a person prior to the completion of conversion, there still may be a general duty to facilitate conversion for people who wish to convert *and are ready for conversion*, and this might generate a duty to engage in conduct that is loving. The Talmud (*TB Yevamot* 47b) cites a *beraita* which asserts this:

> קיבל מלין אותו מיד: מ"ט שהויי מצוה לא משהינן
>
> If he (i.e., the conversion candidate) accepts upon himself [all of the aforementioned commitments], then they (i.e., the rabbinical court) should circumcise him immediately. [The Gemara asks:] What is the reason [to act immediately]? [Because] we do not delay the performance of a mitzvah.

Which mitzvah is being referenced? There apparently is a general obligation incumbent upon a rabbinical court to fulfill its duties, one of which is to convert a ready conversion candidate. Thus, the recently published encyclopedic work on conversion, *Mishnat Ha-Ger*, states: "It is a mitzvah incumbent on a *beit din* to accept converts after due examination of their fitness."[12] But, why there is such a duty remains unclear. Is this a mitzvah obligation incumbent on the People of Israel, who, in turn, are represented by the formal rabbinical leadership of the *beit din*? Or is there a category of mitzvot that apply solely to a *beit din*? Or do all Jews—both

---

11 See *Pri Megadim, Eishel Avraham* 156:2, discussed below. Similarly, *Mabit*, "Letter About the Ways of God," *Ne'ilat Shearim* 1:9, notes that this mitzvah, "adds more love to the love of all Jews." See also *Responsa Divrei Malkiel* 6:78; *Responsa Aseh Lekha Rav* 3:29; *Responsa Ateret Paz* EH 1:3; *Iggerot Moshe* EH 5:1; *Tzitz Eliezer* 18:65; *Teshuvot Vehanhagot* 2:691; *Lehorot Natan* 13:74; and others.

12 Moshe Klein, *Mishnat Ha-Ger* 3:14 (Machon Mishneh Torah, 2008).

learned leaders as well as simple Jews—have a personal obligation to assist serious aspirants to Jewish conversion?

There are two basic approaches to these questions, each of which deeply impacts upon the duty of how we treat and relate to the convert-to-be. The first approach can be found in Rambam's understanding of another halakhic obligation to love—namely, the mitzvah of *Ahavat Hashem,* loving God. The second approach is to posit that even though the mitzvah of *Ahavat ha-Ger* only applies post-conversion, there indeed is an independent mitzvah incumbent upon a *beit din* to convert ready candidates, which creates a duty to assist them to convert, and sometimes looks like "love."

Loving God Creates a Duty to Facilitate Conversion and Love the Person Seeking to Convert

In *Sefer Ha-Mitzvot*, Rambam's meticulous enumeration of the 613 mitzvot, Rambam intentionally first lists a Jew's fundamental obligations toward God: to believe in and demonstrate knowledge of God, affirm God's unity, love and fear God, pray and cleave to God, swear by God's name, emulate God, and sanctify the Divine name.[13] These mitzvot are theologically primary to the plentitude of the Torah's mitzvot, and foundational to the entirety of the halakhic system.[14] It is also worth noting that in Rambam's account of preparing a person for conversion, Rambam likewise emphasizes the candidate's embrace of primary Jewish theological doctrines prior to concerns of religious praxis and social affiliation.[15] In elucidating the mitzvah of *Ahavat Hashem* (loving God) in *Sefer Ha-Mitzvot* (*Aseh* 3), whose importance Rambam signifies by positioning it as positive commandment number three, Rambam states:

> They (i.e., our Sages) have already said that this mitzvah includes [facilitating] that all humanity seeks and are called to the service of God,

---

13 See *Sefer Ha-Mitzvot, Mitzvot Aseh* 1-9.

14 See Isadore Twersky, *Introduction to the Code of Maimonides (Mishneh Torah)* (New Haven: Yale University Press, 1980) pp. 356 ff.; "What Must a Jew Study—and Why?" in *Visions of Jewish Education*, ed. Seymour Fox, Israel Scheffler, and Daniel Marom (Cambridge: Cambridge University Press, 2003) pp. 46-76.

15 See *Mishneh Torah, Hilkhot Issurei Biah*, 13:2: "We make known to [a person who comes to convert] the principles of the religion, which are [belief in] the unity of God and the prohibition of idolatry, and we go to great lengths to expound this matter (i.e., doctrinal theological fundamentals)." *Shulhan Arukh* YD 268:2 includes Rambam's requirement to theologically orient and educate a conversion candidate as a necessary part of the conversion process, something which is perhaps assumed, but understated in earlier rabbinic sources.

> may He be exalted, and to believe in Him. This is because when you love a person, you place [the concerns] of your heart upon him, and praise him and desire for other people to love him. Applying this metaphorically, so too, if you truly love God per your understanding of God's truth, you will, without a doubt, demand of and call to heretics and fools the true knowledge [of God] that you know.
> [We learn that this *mitzvah* includes spreading love for God to others from] the language of Sifri: "'You shall love God (Deuteronomy 6:5)'—make God beloved among the creatures as your father Abraham did, as it is written, 'The souls that he made in Ḥaran' (Genesis 12:5)."
> That is to say, just as Abraham, who had loved God, as Scripture attests, "Abraham, who loved Me" (Isaiah 41:8), as a result of his great understanding of God, and strong love for God, sought to bring people to belief, so too, you shall love God to the extent that you draw others to Him.

Thus, we see that Rambam includes in the mitzvah to love God also a duty to bring others to the love of God, just as Abraham, per *Sifri*, created converts to monotheistic belief.[16] In *Mishneh Torah*, *Hilkhot Avodah Zarah* (1:3), Rambam retells:

> [There in Ḥaran,] he began to call in a loud voice to all people and inform them that there is one God in the entire world and it is proper to serve Him. He would go out and call to the people, gathering them in city after city and country after country, until he came to the land of Canaan—proclaiming [God's existence the entire time]—as it states: "And He called there in the name of the Lord, the eternal God" (Genesis 21:33).
> When the people would gather around Abraham and ask him about his statements, he would explain [them] to each one of them according to their understanding, until they turned to the path of truth. Ultimately, thousands and myriads gathered around him. These are the men of the house of Abraham.

A modest reading of Rambam's *Sefer Ha-Mitzvot* would suggest that as an extension of the mitzvah of *Ahavat Hashem* (loving God) there is a duty incumbent upon every Jew, per his or her capacity and competency, to emulate Abraham and bring others to monotheistic belief and love of

---

16 See also *Genesis Rabbah* 39:14, cited by Rashi on Genesis 12:5, which explains that Abraham proselytized the men, and Sarah the women.

God.[17] One might claim that one can dispatch this duty by creating Noahides, rather than Jewish converts. However, one may more strongly counterclaim that post-Sinai, a lover of God's unique and special relationship with the Jewish people naturally supports a process of enabling like-hearted people to convert and join the Jewish People.[18] Since God loves converts, "*v'oheiv ger*" (Deuteronomy 10:18), Jews manifest their own love of God, who loves converts, by helping people seeking conversion.[19] A maximalist reading of Rambam's *Sefer Ha-Mitzvot* would opine that an extension of our obligated love of God is a duty not only to help, but also even to love those who seek to convert.

For rabbinical judges comprising a *beit din*, this translates into a duty to facilitate conversion for those professing their belief in and love of God, and concomitant desire to accept upon themselves the yoke of commandments.

Part and parcel of Rambam's approach, however, defines the conversion candidate worthy of such help and love as a *ger tzedek*-to-be, one who is motivated by spiritual commitments as much as social affiliation. Rambam articulates readiness for conversion as follows (*Mishneh Torah*, *Issurei Biah* 13:4):

> וכן לדורות כשירצה העכו"ם להכנס לברית ולהסתופף תחת כנפי השכינה ויקבל עליו עול תורה צריך מילה וטבילה והרצאת קרבן, ואם נקבה היא טבילה וקרבן

---

17 See Yerucham Perlow, *Sefer Ha-Mitzvot of Rabbi Saadia Gaon*, *Aseh* 19, who understands this extension of love of God as an obligation incumbent upon each Jew.

18 See Azriel Ciment, *Mitzvat Ha-Melekh*, Chicago: Ot Chaim, 2005, p. 46, who clearly understands Rambam's expansion of *Ahavat Hashem* as referring to making converts.

19 See *Bamidbar Rabbah* 8:2 for a powerful parable describing why God loves converts:

> A king has many flocks of sheep… and one day a stag appears and joins the sheep. The stag grazes with the sheep and returns with them at night, as if he were a sheep. When the shepherds tell the king of the stag… the king takes great pride and interest in it and ensures that the shepherds treat the stag with special care. The shepherds question the king, asking "you have thousands of animals over which you take no personal interest… so why do you care so much about this one animal?" The king answers them, "My sheep have only this flock to join, and cannot leave, but this stag has the whole world to choose from, yet he chose my flock. He surely deserves my special attention and care."

The midrash concludes that we, as the Jewish people, should give tremendous credit to converts who have chosen to leave their family and their people to join our ranks. Our love of the king—God—ensconces our love of the convert.

שנאמר ככם כגר, מה אתם במילה וטבילה והרצאת קרבן אף הגר לדורות במילה וטבילה והרצאת קרבן.

And so, for all future generations, when a Gentile desires to enter into the covenant, take shelter under the wings of the Divine Presence, and accept the yoke of the Torah, he must undergo circumcision, immersion, and the offering of a sacrifice. And if (the Gentile) be a woman —immersion and a sacrifice, as it says (Numbers 15:15), "as it is for you, so too for the convert"—just as you (entered into the covenant) with circumcision, immersion, and the offering of a sacrifice, so too a convert throughout all the generations likewise (gains entry) through circumcision, immersion, and the offering of a sacrifice.

Per Rambam, a convert must desire to enter the covenant of Israel and seek spiritual closeness with God. The readiness of a convert is contingent upon his or her spiritual aspirations, and a *beit din* has a duty to bring a convert's desire to fruition. In the words of the Talmud (*TB Yevamot* 47b) cited above, this is not a mitzvah to be unnecessarily delayed. Which mitzvah? Per Rambam, the mitzvah of *Ahavat Hashem.*[20] Thus, although Rambam limits the mitzvah of *Ahavat ha-Ger* to a Jew post-conversion, Rambam's understanding of the mitzvah of *Ahavat Hashem* requires the proper, just, and kindly treatment of conversion candidates, including helping them to convert. We manifest our love of God by loving people who seek to join God's community.

Raavad, at first glance, seemingly concurs with Rambam, as he too points to the verse in Genesis 12:5, "and the people they (i.e., Abraham and Sarah) created in Ḥaran," as establishing a mitzvah to bring Gentiles to Jewish conversion. In *Ba'alei Hanefesh* (*Sha'ar Hatevillah*), Raavad asserts that when converting a minor, a *beit din*, per *TB Ketubot* 11a, recites the blessing formula of "*asher kideshanu be-mitzvotav*—who sanctified us with His commandments" immediately prior to the immersion of the child in a *mikveh*. He writes:

---

20 Chaim Jachter, "A Right to Convert? Developing an Idea of Rav Soloveitchik," <http://www.torahleadership.org/categories/a_right_to_convert_rcj.pdf>. R. Jachter writes: "Rambam clearly makes the conversion contingent only upon the desire of the non-Jew and his commitment to Hashem and His Torah, and not whether we believe it is in our best interest to accept him into our midst." Why isn't conversion likewise dependent on the wishes of the Jewish people, whose rabbinical representatives on a *beit din* may seek to reject a particular candidate for reasons unrelated to halakhic demands? The answer is that Jews bear a halakhic duty to convert those who wish to become converts. Cf. *Minḥat Asher* 1:51 who seems to posit that there is no such obligation.

כל המצוות כולן מברך עליהן עובר לעשייתן. ואם תאמר הא אמרינן עלה חוץ מטבילה ושופר, ההיא בטבילת גר דמקמי טבילה לא חזי לברכה דאכתי גוי ... ונ"ל דוקא בגר גדול, אבל בגר קטן שב"ד מטבילין אותו אי נמי בעבד קטן שרבו מטבילו בשלשה, שבית דין והאדון מברכין עליהם קודם הטבילה כדין כל שאר המצות. ואם תאמר היכן צוונו, מואת הנפש אשר עשו בחרן.

For all mitzvot one recites the blessing prior to their performance. And if you say that we say this for all matters other than immersion and blowing the shofar, since in [the case of] immersion of a convert it is inappropriate to recite a blessing [prior] since the person is still a Gentile … It appears to me that this is limited to an adult convert, but a minor who is immersed based on the determination of the rabbinical court, or [the case of] a minor slave whose master immerses him in front of three [judges], since the rabbinical court, or master, [are performing the mitzvah] then they make the blessing before immersion like the rule for all other commandments. And if you ask, "Where were we thus commanded?" [we answer], from the verse: "the people they created in Ḥaran" (Genesis 12:5).[21]

How, though, does Raavad construe an everlasting commandment from Abraham and Sarah's exemplary model of bringing people to monotheistic belief? The Torah never explicitly says that Abraham was thus commanded by God, as he had been regarding circumcision. Additionally, this occurred before the Revelation at Sinai when the commandments of the Torah were conferred upon the Children of Israel and their descendants.[22] Thus, it is possible that Raavad locates this commandment within the mitzvah of *Ahavat Hashem*, akin to Rambam.[23]

For the larger group of halakhic authorities cited above who concur with Rambam's conclusion and limit the mitzvah of *Ahavat ha-Ger* to a Jew post-conversion, the outstanding question is whether they also follow Rambam's view within his larger halakhic system that the mitzvah of *Ahavat Hashem* accommodates helping, and perhaps even requires loving, the convert-to-be.[24] If so, this nicely explains why it is a mitzvah for a *beit din* to convert a ready candidate.

If not, then we would still need to identify what obligation exists, if any, upon a *beit din* to convert a worthy aspirant. Tashbetz (*Zohar Haraki'a*,

---

21 Raavad, *Ba'alei Hanefesh, Sha'ar Hatevillah*, 3.

22 See R. Sherman, note 7 at pp. 77-78, who asks these questions in the name of Rabbi Menachem Mendel Kasher.

23 For an alternate interpretation of Raavad, see Section Two below.

24 See Sherman, Avraham. "Conversion: Mitzvah, Discretionarily Permitted, Forbidden," *Torah Sheba'al Peh* vol. 19, 5748 (1988), pp. 74-87.

Mitzvat Aseh 40) opines that since the Talmudic passage cited above (*TB Yevamot* 47b) calls conversion by a *beit din* a mitzvah, then there must be an independent mitzvah enumerated within the 613 mitzvot for a *beit din* to convert ready candidates.[25] Tashbetz, however, seemingly agrees with Rambam that the mitzvah of *Ahavat ha-Ger* only applies post-conversion.

Another way, however, to understand why a *beit din* has an obligation to convert a ready candidate is to see the mitzvah of *Ahavat ha-Ger* as attaching prior to full conversion, which brings us to the next school of thinking on this topic.

Section Two: The Duty to Love the Convert After Conversion Also Entails Loving the Convert-to-Be Prior to Conversion

The second school of thought on the question of "when does the mitzvah to love the convert begin?" posits that this obligation attaches during the conversion process, and is an outgrowth of loving the convert post-conversion. The logic for this view is as follows:

1. There is a clear and well-established mitzvah to love the convert post-conversion.
2. The most important way to love the convert is to ensure that the convert successfully integrates into the Jewish people after conversion.
3. To be successful, the conversion process must start far before completion, and involves prior to the conversion much preparation for life as a Jew after conversion.
4. Hence there is a duty to craft a successful conversion process, so that we can subsequently love the convert as a Jew.

The clearest exposition of this idea can be found in *Tosafot Harosh* (*Shabbat* 137b). Rosh addresses the question: Why should we make any sort of blessing over the circumcision of a convert-to-be? After all, circumcision, while necessary for conversion, does not complete the conversion process. Until verbal acceptance of the yoke of mitzvot and immersion in a mikveh have been completed, no conversion has taken place. After circumcision, a man who is *"mal velo taval*—circumcised but not immersed" is still a Gentile and not Jewish. Rosh answers:

> המל את הגרים אומר אשר קדשנו במצותיו וצונו למול את הגרים, **כי נצטוינו לאהוב את הגרים ואי אפשר להיות גר בלא מילה.**
>
> One who circumcises converts-to-be recites [the blessing], "who sanctified us with His commandments and directed us to circumcise

---

[25] See Tosafot, *Yevamot* 109b, s.v. *ra'ah achar ra'ah*, and Yerucham Perlow, *Sefer Ha-Mitzvot of Rabbi Saadia Gaon, Lo Ta'aseh* 363.

converts," **since we were commanded to love the converts, and it is impossible to be a convert without circumcision.**

Rosh asserts that the duty to love the convert is fulfilled by circumcision, even if it is only a preliminary, albeit necessary, condition, after which the convert-to-be is still a Gentile, and can even change his mind and choose not to convert. The duty to love the convert post-conversion, however, creates a mitzvah for people to help the person become a successful convert, which cannot be done without circumcision (for a man).

While Rosh contextualizes this application in the context of the penultimate stage of circumcision, the question remains as to how soon after the commencement of a conversion process does the mitzvah of *Ahavat ha-Ger* attach. Since a successful conversion process requires spiritual and theological reorientation, extensive Jewish literacy, Jewish communal and cultural socialization, and fluency in and comfort with halakhic praxis—in other words, a comprehensive conversion process, then crafting such a process would, per Rosh's logic, fulfill the mitzvah of *Ahavat ha-Ger*, even though the candidate is yet still a Gentile.[26] Superintending a process that creates converts who live faithfully and happily as Jews is a manifestation of love, and thus is entailed by God's commandment to love the convert, even prior to the actual conversion.[27]

Loving the convert-to-be at preliminary stages within the conversion process is therefore an exercise in anticipatory, strategic preparation. If converts are not loved, whether before or after their conversion, they might abandon Judaism after conversion to return to a Gentile community that better loves them. The concern of "*shema chozeir lesuro*—lest the convert return to their old faith" is thus commonly articulated in both

26 R. Joseph Rosen (the Rogatchover), *Tzofnat Pa'aneach*, Mahadurah Tinyana, *Hilkhot Yesodei HaTorah* 5:5, proposes that upon the completion of a successful conversion, Jewish status is retroactively conferred, at least to the stage of circumcision within a conversionary process. See J. David Bleich, "Observance of Shabbat by a Prospective Proselyte and by a *Ger She-Mal ve-lo Taval*," *Tradition* 25:3, Spring 1991, p. 59 fn. 9.

27 For another legal analogy, consider the "mitzvah" to marry, which, according to most authorities, is really only a prelude to the mitzvah of having children, and yet we recite blessings over its enactment. *Makhshirei mitzvah* are generally treated as mitzvot, as reflected in their rabbinicblessing formulations.

halakhic and midrashic sources.[28] At the same time, there is also something retrospective entailed in Rosh's understanding. Since we have to love the convert after conversion, then even prior to conversion we must support the candidate's mastery of the many aspects of Jewish life that need to be present after conversion, in order to assure a successful conversion and lasting commitment. Furthermore, at the time it is done, such support is a mitzvah of loving the convert, and, in the case of circumcision, per Rosh, a blessing can be recited. As another example, a person cannot start learning how to be an observant Jew only after their conversion is over. Therefore, to ensure a successful conversion, even at the most preliminary stages of the conversionary process, we put aside the prohibition of teaching Torah to a Gentile and teach Torah to the convert-to-be.[29] This holds true for training in most other commandments as well.

---

[28] See *Tosafot*, *Kiddushin* 70b; *Bamidbar Rabbah* 8:2, cited above in fn. 19. For the etymology of the Talmudic expression "*chozeir lesuro*," see Finkelstein, Menachem. *Conversion: Halakhah and Practice*, trans. Edward Levin. Ramat Gan, Israel: Bar Ilan University Press, 2006, p. 245, fn. 278.

[29] See *Maharsha*, *Chidushei Aggadot*, *Shabbat* 31a. Also see *Iggerot Moshe* YD 3:90, who powerfully notes:

> עוד כתב מהרש"א בח"א בשבת דף ל"א דעכו"ם הלומד תורה כדי להתגייר מותר משום דמפרש דלא גייריה הלל להנכרי שרצה להתגייר ע"מ שיעשוהו כ"ג עד שלמד שא"א לו להיות כ"ג ומה שלמדו תורה הוא משום דכיון דבא לגייר שרי ללמוד תורה ...ותמוה איך כתב בסוף שכיון שאזדא ראיית מהרש"א אין בכחי להתיר הא גמ' מפורשת שמותר ושכן צריכין לעשות אף שבדיעבד הוא גרות בלא זה כמפורש בשבת...
>
> Also Maharsha writes in *Ḥidushei Aggadot*, *Shabbat* 31, that a Gentile who learns Torah in order to convert is engaging in permitted activity since it is clear that Hillel did not convert the Gentile who wanted to [convert to] become a High Priest until he studied [Torah] and thereby learned that he could not possibly become a High Priest. And their teaching him Torah is permitted since he came to convert. … And it is astonishing that [Rabbi Akiva Eiger] [disputes] and dismisses Maharsha, concluding that he doesn't have the power to permit [teaching a conversion candidate] Torah, since a Talmudic source clearly permits, and thus we need to do so, even if a conversion [absent a preparatory Torah learning process] is valid after the fact.

Rabbi Moshe Feinstein posits that even those who do not agree with Maharsha and do not allow teaching Torah to a convert-to-be (like Rabbi Akiva Eiger) are only referring to a person who is far away from conversion. However, asserts Rabbi Feinstein, all agree that a person who is shortly going to convert has to be taught Torah, as otherwise he or she will be dysfunctional as a Jew. This aligns with the view of Rosh who applies post-conversion halakhic principles

Similarly, Raavad cited above in Section One, arguably aligns with Rosh's view that the mitzvah of *Ahavat ha-Ger* post-conversion by necessity applies pre-conversion in order to ensure a successful conversion and lasting commitment. Although Raavad cites the same proof text as Rambam—"And if you ask, 'Where were we thus commanded?' [we answer], from the verse: 'the people they (i.e., Abraham and Sarah) created in Ḥaran' (Genesis 12:5)"—there is no clear indication that Raavad understands the mitzvah to facilitate conversion as an extension of the mitzvah of loving God. Raavad just as easily may share in Rosh's reasoning and believe that in order to create converts, one must treat them in a loving fashion before conversion.[30]

In sum, Rosh, and possibly Raavad, minimally argue that while there is no duty to love a convert-to-be prior to conversion per se, since there is a duty to love the convert after conversion, we must also treat the conversion candidate lovingly prior to conversion. In other words, part of loving the convert after conversion, is loving the convert-to-be prior to conversion.[31]

Section Three: Loving the Convert Applies at the Time of Expressed Desire to Convert

The final school of thought proposes that the mitzvah of loving the convert applies to the convert-to-be at the time he or she expresses a desire to convert. Rabbi Yitzchak Barcelona (hereafter RI Barcelona) posits in his *Azharot*, a liturgical poetic summary of the mitzvot, that the mitzvah

---

and praxis earlier in the conversion process, and has applications as well to the test case (Part II below) concerning the permissibility of inviting conversion candidates to festival meals.

30 Raavad certainly doesn't align with Rashba cited in the next section below, i.e., that a blessing on circumcision is recited because quasi-Jewish status has been earned by the convert-to-be, otherwise Raavad would allow an adult conversion candidate to make his own blessing before circumcision and immersion.

31 By analogy, consider the love of a child by a parent prior to birth. Just like there is a mitzvah to invest in and raise one's children after they are born, sometimes one needs to invest in the mitzvah of raising one's children even before they are born, such as prenatal care. In the case of a convert, it is an open question of whether extending backward the mitzvah of *Ahavat ha-Ger* prior to conversion is a *deoraita or derabbanan* extension.

to love the convert applies to anyone who comes and expresses interest in converting.[32] He writes (in poetic meter):

Shelter in your shadow a convert who comes to convert	יחסה בצלכם גר הבא להתגייר
when he says, "In You, O God, I seek Shelter."	באומרו בך יי חסיתי
You shall accept him, and make known to him	יקבלוהו ויודיעוהו
some commandments, minor and major,	קצת מצות קלות וחמורות
lest he turn in his spirit and say, "What have I done!?	פן יחזור ברוחו ויאמר מה עשיתי
I cannot go with these, for I have not tried them."	*לֹא אוּכַל לָלֶכֶת בָּאֵלֶּה כִּי לֹא נִסִּיתִי*
(I Sam 17:39)	(שמואל א יז:לט)

It is clear from this formulation, that RI Barcelona is discussing a convert-to-be prior to conversion. Rabbi Yerucham Perlow, in his commentary on the *Book of Commandments of Rav Saadia Gaon* (*Aseh* 19), discusses this view:

> הן אמת שראיתי באזהרת הר"י אלברגלוני דנראה מדבריו ז"ל דס"ל דבכלל עשה דואהבתם את הגר נכללת ג"כ המצוה לקבל גרים להכניסם תחת כנפי השכינה. שכתב שם וז"ל יחסה בצלכם גר הבא להתגייר באומרו בך ה' חסיתי. יקבלוהו ויודיעוהו קצת מצות וכו' עכ"ל ... על כרחך צריך לומר **דאע"ג שעכשיו כשבא לפנינו אכתי לאו גר הוא, מ"מ כיון דבקבלה זו מתגייר קרינן ביה "ואהבתם את הגר."** ... ואין כאן מקום להאריך בזה. אבל הרי אנו רואים דהר"י אלברגלוני ז"ל מכניס אותה בכלל עשה דאהבת גרים.
>
> In truth, I saw in the *Azharot* of Rabbi Yitzchak of Barcelona of blessed memory that it appears from his words that he holds the view that included in positive commandment "and you shall love the

---

32 *Azharot* of Rabbi Yitzchak Barcelona (ברגלוני in some texts) is admittedly an unlikely halakhic source. *Azaharot* is part of a poetic tradition of the early medieval era in which mitzvot are summarized in short sentences to be recited liturgically at various times. We are more familiar with the similar liturgical form of *Akdamot* that we recite on Shavuot. For more on the RI Barcelona, see Israel M. Ta-Shma, *Talmudic Commentary in Europe and North Africa: Literary History*, vol. 1, Hebrew University Press, 1999:168-169. There is considerable evidence that RI Barcelona was a halakhic scholar of considerable stature, though his Talmudic works have primarily been lost to us and his ideas, for the most part, have not participated in the crucible of halakhic debate past the Sephardic Middle Ages. He may even be a direct ancestor of Ramban, as TaShma notes. Ramban quotes him six times in his commentary on the Talmud, and he is also cited by the Rashba, Rosh, Ran, *Nemukei Yosef*, and *Shita Mekubetzet*. *Beit Yosef* cites him as a halakhic source in *Ḥoshen Mishpat*. While he may be remembered generally by his surviving poetry, he was known in the Sephardic orbit as a thoughtful master halakhist, as well. For our purposes, since "rediscovered" by R. Yerucham Perlow in his commentary on *Sefer Ha-Mitzvot leRaSaG* (*Aseh* 19), his view of the duty to love the convert applying to the convert-to-be has been widely recounted and discussed in the halakhic literature on conversion.

> convert" (Deuteronomy 10:19) is also the mitzvah to receive converts and to bring them under the protection of the Divine Presence. He writes there: "Shelter in your shadow a convert who comes to convert/ When he says, 'In You, O God, I seek Shelter'. They should accept him and teach him some of the commandments…" It is necessary to say therefore that even though as of now when he comes before us he is not [yet] a convert, nonetheless since [his expressed desire to convert constitutes a halakhic commitment, i.e.,] "an acceptance" by which he is converting, we apply to him "and you shall love the convert"… This is not the place to expand upon this, but we see that Rabbi Yitzchak of Barcelona of blessed memory includes this as part of the commandment to love the convert.

Rabbi Moshe Klein in *Mishnat Ha-Ger* includes RI Barcelona's view in the central text of his contemporary summative compendium on the laws of conversion:

> There are those who write that the mitzvah of loving the convert attaches immediately from the time that [the person] reveals his mind and intention that he desires to take refuge under the sheltering wings of the Divine Presence, and not only after he completes his conversion process, therefore one should help him in all ways he needs from the time he begins the conversion process.[33]

The approach of RI Barcelona solves the important conceptual problem cited above in the introduction – namely, if the mitzvah of *Ahavat ha-Ger* attaches only after a completed conversion, what is added by this mitzvah when there is already an obligation of *Ahavat Yisrael*—to love our fellow Jews. For RI Barcelona, the mitzvah of *Ahavat ha-Ger* principally applies *during the conversion process,* rather than upon completion of conversion, when the mitzvah of loving your neighbor now protectively covers the newly fashioned Jew.

Not surprisingly, this approach is nicely consistent with the view of Saadia Gaon who believes that there is not a unique mitzvah at all to love a Jewish convert. Per Rav Saadia, the primary duty is to treat the convert

---

33 Klein, Moshe, *Mishnat Ha-Ger*, p. 193. See also Rabbi Eliezer Melamed, <https://www.yeshiva.org.il/midrash/7772>, who seemingly assumes that *Ahavat ha-Ger* applies to a conversion candidate, though he doesn't explicitly quote RI Barcelona. However, Rabbi Melamed told one of us (BJS, January 2019) that while the mitzvah of *Ahavat ha-Ger* influences his kindly approach to conversion candidates, he doesn't believe the mitzvah attaches until the conversion is completed.

identically to a born-Jew, with no favoritism in any direction.[34] If that is the case, then the mitzvah to love the convert is solely and exclusively focused on the convert prior to conversion, rather than on the convert post-conversion, when this person as a full and complete Jew is covered by the mitzvah of *Ahavat Yisrael.*

Without explicitly discussing the mitzvah of loving the convert-to-be, Rashba (*Yevamot* 71a) presents a similar idea regarding the recitation of a blessing on a conversionary circumcision:

> *אלא לאתויי גר שמל ולא טבל וקסבר אינו גר עד שימול ויטבול.* קשיא לי א"כ היינו גוי ואף על פי שמל הרי הוא כערל דהו"ל כערבי מהול, וליתא דשאני הכא דמילתו לשם יהדות **ואף על פי שלא נגמר גירותו מ"מ כבר התחיל ונכנס קצת בדת יהודית שאינו צריך אלא טבילה**
>
> This comes to include a convert who is circumcised but not immersed, and he holds the view that he is not considered a convert

---

34 See Commentary of R. Yerucham Perlow, *Sefer Ha-Mitzvot leRaSaG*, *Aseh* 82. It is worth adding here that Rav Saadia Gaon counts in his own *Azharot* listing of commandments, "כְּאֶזְרָח מִכֶּם יִהְיֶה לָכֶם הַגֵּר הַגָּר אִתְּכֶם"—"as a citizen among you shall be the convert who resides with you" (Leviticus 19:34) which emphasizes equivalence, and denies the special duty to love the convert uniquely. See for example, the *Azharot* as found in the *Siddur of Rav Saadia Gaon*, eds. Israel Dodson, Simcha Assaf, and Issachar Yoel, p. 159, line 22, as found at <http://www.daat.ac.il/daat/mitsvot/rasag-taryag.pdf>. We were recently shown a yet unpublished—but shortly forthcoming—manuscript of the newly rediscovered complete *Sefer Ha-Mitzvot of Rav Saadia Gaon*, which had been lost for centuries. This work, entitled ספר המצוות הוא כתאב אלשראיע לרס"ג (Jerusalem: Ben Zvi Institute & Keren Harav Rosen, 2019) was written in Judeo-Arabic, has been translated into Hebrew with annotations by Rabbis Chaim Sabato, Nissim Sabato and Eyal Fischer. Chapter 25, "Those Who Convert," makes it clear that Rav Saadia Gaon does not codify the duty to love the convert as a mitzvah at all, exactly in line with his *Azharot,* as noted above, and as recognized by Rabbi Yerucham Perlow. Instead, Rav Saadia Gaon believes that the duty is to treat a convert "כאזרח, like a born Jew," interpreting Leviticus 19:34 as: "The convert residing among you must be treated as your native-born."

The redundancy problem, a core tension within Rambam's view, is neatly solved by this approach. Only a person who is not yet Jewish, but is seeking to become Jewish, is loved under the rubric of loving the soon-to-be convert. For the already converted, this view mandates that one loves the convert as any other Jew, and further, one loves the convert precisely by ignoring the convert's pre-conversion history and treating the convert like every other Jew. However, Jewish law, as it developed, seems to have rejected this view based on Rambam's and others' incorporation of the duplicative duty to love the convert after conversion, requiring other resolutions to the redundancy problem.

> until [both] circumcision and immersion [are complete]. This is difficult for me, since this person is still a Gentile. And even though he is circumcised, he is [, Jewishly speaking,] like one who is uncircumcised, like a circumcised Muslim. But this is wrong. It is different because his circumcision is for the sake of Judaism, **and even though he has not finished converting, nonetheless he has already started [to convert], and has partially entered into the Jewish religion, since all he needs [to complete the process] is immersion.**

According to Rashba, a person attains the quasi-status of a convert even before he fully finishes the process, and halakhic Jewish identity is gained in stages.[35] Rashba clearly sees this as applying during the penultimate stages of a conversion process, at the very least immediately prior to circumcision. Where along the conversion process does a candidate attain this standing? For example, what marker along a conversionary process would endow such status upon a woman for whom circumcision isn't possible? And, if indeed, the Rashba believes it is possible to attain a quasi-status of a *ger* prior to full conversion, does the mitzvah of *Ahavat ha-Ger* obligate us to love the convert-to-be who has attained such standing?

There are a number of halakhic indications that a person who has made significant progress in a conversion process has attained partial Jewish status. Formally, this is discussed in the halakhic literature regarding one who has been circumcised but remains un-immersed in a *mikveh* – i.e., *ger she'mal velo taval*.[36] However, there is reason to believe that it is not circumcision per se that creates new standing, but the commitment to God and Judaism, i.e., *berit*—covenantal commitment, that leads to circumcision. Thus, such quasi-Jewish halakhic status is accessible to women

---

35 Joel Wolowelsky, "Two Aspects of Jewish Identity," *Shofar* 13:2, 1995, p. 22. Rabbi Wolowelsky highlights a distinction first introduced by Rabbi Aharon Lichtenstein between "*shem Yisrael*"—the name of, or affiliation with the People of Israel, which per Rosh and Rashba, is gained in stages, and "*kedushat Yisrael*"—the sanctity of Israel, which is achieved upon completion of conversion. See Lichtenstein, Aharon, "Brother Daniel and the Jewish Fraternity," *Judaism* 12:3, Summer 1963, pp. 260-280, and is reprinted in Aharon Lichtenstein, *Leaves of Faith; the World of Jewish Learning*, vol. II (Jersey City, NJ: Ktav, 2003-2004) pp. 57-83.

36 See R. Bleich, ibid., pp. 46-62. See also *Tosafot Yesheinim*, *Yevamot* 46b, who explains why a special midrashic derivation is required to exclude a person who is *mal velo taval* from participating in the *korban Pesach*: "[S]ince once they are circumcised they exit the status of being an *'arel* – an uncircumcised one who cannot eat the *korban* Pesach, even though they have not become "*yehudim gemurim*, complete Jews," until they immerse. See also *Tosafot Yesheinim, Yevamot* 48b.

for whom circumcision is not part of the conversation process, as well as to men.[37] As a result of gaining status as a *ger*, a fully committed conversion candidate may keep Shabbat and learn Torah, normally proscribed to Gentiles.[38] *Tzitz Eliezer* (10:28) permits medically treating a person who is *mal velo taval* on Shabbat without resorting to the halakhic justification of avoiding *eivah* (i.e., potentially mortally dangerous ill will). Likewise, the general duty of rescue of Jews in trouble also applies to such a person.[39] If a person fully committed to completing a conversion process dies before completing conversion, such a person may be eulogized as a Jew and be buried in a Jewish cemetery.[40] Such a person may possibly even be counted in a *zimmun*.[41]

Since, in this model, per RI Barcelona, once a Gentile expresses a serious interest in becoming Jewish, he or she develops the status of a *ger*, which is not one who has converted, but one who wants to convert. After they have converted, they are simply a Jew, and one must love them as one loves all Jews, no more and no less.

Allow us here to provide a more elaborate Talmudic and linguistic explanation of this view. In rabbinic literature, the word "*ger*," when standing alone, sometimes means a person who is pursuing conversion but has not yet converted, sometimes means a person who has already converted, and sometimes means a person who has taken some significant steps to convert, such as circumcision, but has not yet finished the process. When the Talmud wishes to make it clear that it is speaking about

---

37 Wolowelsky, ibid., pp. 22-23.

38 For a full discussion of these issues, see R. Bleich, ibid. To think about this conceptually, consider the case of a man who immersed, but is not yet circumcised, who upon circumcision then becomes Jewish (Rama YD 268:1), or a woman who verbally affirmed *kabbalat ha-mitzvot* in front of a *beit din* and is awaiting immersion in a *mikveh*. Each of these cases is arguably akin to a convert-to-be who was circumcised but not yet immersed. See *Sefer Haḥasidim* 690, who explicitly forbids feeding non-kosher food to a conversion candidate who has accepted upon himself mitzvah observance, yet still awaits circumcision.

39 See *Iggerot Moshe* EH 5:1.

40 See *Responsa Tzeror BaKesef* YD 18, quoted in R. Daniel Tirani, *Ikkarei Dinim* 1, OC 40; *Responsa Minḥat Elazar* 3:8; *Kol Bo Aveilut*, p. 190, fn. 21; *Wolowelsky*, ibid. pp. 24-25.

41 See Wolowelsky, op cit., p. 23, citing R. Yaakov Kamenetsky, *Emet leYaakov al haTorah,* New York: 5746/1986, commentary to Genesis 17:4, pp. 60-61. We are certainly of the view that if one invites a person for a Yom Tov meal while unaware of his status as a conversion candidate, one should rely on this view and not disinvite the person in order to avoid the generation of animosity or hurt feelings.

one who has already converted, it uses the phrase "*ger shenitgayer*" (גר שנתגייר) and not just the single term "*ger*." When the Talmud wants to make reference to one who is a Gentile but has had circumcision for the sake of conversion, it uses the phrase, "*ger she'mal velo taval*" (גר שמל ולא טבל). This helps explain the countless times (more than 50) that the two Talmuds use the longer phrase of "*ger shenitgayer*" to denote a person who has already converted. This also helps explain the frequent use in the rabbinic literature of the phrase "*ger haba lehitgayer*" (גר הבא להתגייר), which really should be "*goy haba lehitgayer*" (גוי הבא להתגייר), since this person is still a Gentile. Rather, RI Barcelona indicates that when the Torah mandates that one love the *ger* it is *not referring uniquely to one who has already converted, but instead to one who is in the process of converting.* One who has converted is simply a Jew and not a convert, and according to Rav Saadia Gaon is no longer entitled to the special love of a *ger*, but only the special love of every Jew.[42]

The RI Barcelona therefore tracks with Rashba by identifying this convert-to-be as developing an intermediate status, somewhat akin to a Canaanite slave: not yet a Jew, but no longer a Gentile. As Rambam (*Issurei Biah* 12:11) notes:

> העבדים שהטבילו אותם לשם עבדות וקבלו עליהם מצות שהעבדים חייבים בהם יצאו מכלל העכו"ם ולכלל ישראל לא באו.
>
> The Canaanite slaves who are immersed as slaves and accepted the commandments that slaves are obligated in, have left the status of Gentiles, but have not yet entered the status of Jews.

As cited above, the classic example of this is the status of a man who has been circumcised for the sake of conversion but has not yet immersed—*mal velo taval.* The fundamental conceptualization of this status is driven by different categories of people noted in rabbinic literature who are half-way in, but not yet converted, and are certainly not fully Jewish as a matter of law. Writing about such a case, *Binyan Tzion* (91) notes:

---

42 The view of RI Barcelona need not adopt the view of Rav Saadia Gaon that there is no special love needed for one who has already converted, although it does fit nicely. In truth, we find this view very persuasive textually, and but for the fact that most—and particularly Rambam—reject this view (as explained in Section One above), we might consider it normative. Let us note that the combined views of Rosh, Rashba, Raavad, and RI Barcelona strongly make a halakhic argument that the duty to love the convert applies to the convert-to-be, and together their views provide a counterweight to Rambam's view, both in logic and authority.

ולכן נלענ"ד דאף שעדיין לא נכנס לכלל ישראל גמור עד שטבל מכ"מ משעה שנכנס לברית מילה כבר נבדל מכלל בני נח.

Thus, it appears to me that even though this person has not become fully Jewish until immersion, nonetheless, once he is circumcised, he has separated from the Gentile population.

A similar sentiment can be found in a responsum of Radvaz (3:917) which also addresses the question of a man who is circumcised but not immersed. After concluding that wine he touches is not prohibited to drink, Radvaz writes:

ולענין להצטרף לכל דבר שבקדושה ולענין אי חיישינן לקידושיו הדבר ברור שאינו כישראל לשום דבר דקייל"ן מל ולא טבל כאלו לא מל. אלא שיצא מכלל עכו"ם שמצוה להחיותו ואין מגעו ביין טמא ולכלל ישראל לא בא עד שיטבול ודברים ברורים הם.

On the matter of counting him for sacred matters (e.g., a minyan), and whether we worry for the validity of his enacting Jewish marriage, the matter is clear that this person is not like a Jew for any such matters, since we hold that one who is circumcised but not immersed is like he is not circumcised [and thus is still not Jewish]. But this person has left the status of a Gentile and there is a duty to provide essential support for life (e.g., nourishment) and his touching wine does not prohibit it, but he is not Jewish until he immerses. This is clear.

A responsum of *Minḥat Elazar*[43] (3:8) goes even further in that it grants Jewish identity to someone who was not even in the process of converting but was identified as Jewish socially, and by the government. The facts of this case are simple and important. A Jewish man intermarried, and the woman never converted. They had a one-year-old son who died, and the man wanted to bury his infant son in a Jewish cemetery. The local secular law authorities identified the child as Jewish, as per the religion of his father, even though as a matter of halakhah such was not the case. After confirming that the child was certainly not Jewish as a matter of halakhah, and was not even on a path to conversion, and was not to be considered circumcised for conversion, the Munkacser Rav permitted the

[43] The author of *Minḥat Elazar* was the rabbi of the city of Munkacs, where he was also a Hasidic Admor and Rosh Yeshiva. In 2008, Rabbi Gedalia Dov Schwartz expressed to MJB that "if the Munkacser could be *meikil* (lenient) in this case, and he was a *kanai* (extremist), this is a reason for others to be *meikil* also in similar situations." We suspect that it explains the views of Rabbi Gedalia Dov Schwartz on inviting a convert for a Yom Tov meal as well, as will be explained in Part II. (We note our deepest prayers that God should grant Rabbi Schwartz a speedy recovery.)

child to be buried in the Jewish cemetery—albeit in a distant location in the Jewish cemetery, since he has a Jewish identity that attached to him as a matter of social reality. While the child never entered under the sheltering wings of the Divine Presence, the child did reside under the protection of the Jewish community, and thus is entitled to be buried in a Jewish cemetery. While not an example of *Ahavat ha-Ger*, this responsum is illustrative of the existence of a variety of "half-in" persons. The approach of *Minḥat Elazar* certainly recognizes that a convert-to-be who is already functionally a member of the Jewish community by identity is entitled to such a status.

Echoes of the basic approach of RI Barcelona are present in all of these cases: once one leaves the Gentile community and somewhat (socially or theologically or religiously) enters the Jewish community in fact, even if not as a matter of halakhah, then one becomes a *ger* halfway between a Gentile stranger and Jewish seeker and sojourner, and the community is called to treat that person with love and compassion. The mitzvah of *Ahavat ha-Ger* thus applies to a *ger haba lehitgayer*—literally, a convert who comes to convert.

Conclusion to Part I: There Are Many Reasons and Rationales to Act with Love to a Convert-to-Be

In summation:

1. Beginning with *Mishneh Torah*, halakhic codes and their commentaries primarily follow Rambam's view that the mitzvah of *Ahavat ha-Ger* attaches only post-conversion.
2. Rosh, and possibly Raavad, advance the application of *Ahavat ha-Ger* to earlier stages in a conversion process in order to enable *Ahavat ha-Ger* more fully after conversion.
3. Rabbi Yitzchak of Barcelona sees the mitzvah of *Ahavat Ha-Ger* as commencing when a Gentile expresses a desire to convert and thereby becomes a *ger haba lehitgayer*. Rashba likewise understands Jewish status to be achieved in stages. Many cases in the responsa literature support the view that different stages of spiritual commitment and communal affiliation create new halakhic statuses, with a variety of attendant practical halakhic outcomes, one of which may indeed be a pre-conversion obligation of the mitzvah of *Ahavat ha-Ger*.
4. Many Jewish law authorities recognize that there is a duty incumbent upon a *beit din* to convert one who is ready for conversion, and that there is a mitzvah to superintend a successful conversion process. This mitzvah to receive converts and treat them kindly, perhaps even lovingly, can be identified as: (1) *Ahavat Hashem,* per Rambam, and

those who adopt his view of *Ahavat ha-Ger*; (2) *Ahavat Ha-Ger*, per Rosh, possibly Raavad, Rabbi Yitzchak Barcelona, and possibly Rashba; (3) an independent mitzvah for a *beit din* to receive converts, per Tashbetz.

Functionally, for all the above-cited views other than the first, an attitude of loving-kindness (whether formally driven by *Ahavat Ha-Ger* or not) applies even prior to conversion, and even Rambam adopts this basic approach albeit for a different reason, i.e., the mitzvah of *Ahavat Hashem.*

Part II: A Test Case: Inviting the Convert-to-Be for a Pesach Seder or a Yom Tov Meal

The mitzvah of *Ahavat ha-Ger* functions both as a specific duty, and as an encompassing, orienting directive.[44] As mentioned above in the introduction, the question of when does the mitzvah of *Ahavat ha-Ger* commence thus has broad ramifications for both praxis and policy. If the obligation of loving the convert includes a conversion candidate, and not just a post-conversion newly fashioned Jew, then this mitzvah would assume orienting power even before a conversion is completed. It would consequently impact upon how conversion candidates are welcomed and supported through their conversion process by the varied members of the Jewish community, including *dayanim* (rabbinical court justices), rabbis, teachers, communal leaders, and Jewish members of the larger and more local Jewish community. Part of its encompassing directive and orienting influence would arguably even impact upon the adjudication of specific halakhic practices.

The halakhic scenario of whether and in what way it is permissible to invite a conversion candidate to a Pesach Seder or Yom Tov meal provides an excellent test case to gauge how the commencement-time of the mitzvah of *Ahavat ha-Ger* indeed influences *pesak halakhah*. The Talmud (*TB Beitzah* 21b) teaches that preparation of food on Yom Tov is permissible only for the sake of Jews and not for the sake of Gentiles.[45] Thus,

---

44 Rambam in his introduction to *Sefer Ha-Mitzvot* excludes Torah directives that are too generalized from his enumeration, see principle 4. However, mitzvot that have specific application, as well as broad-reaching, orienting force, are indeed counted. For example, *Mitzvat Aseh* 8, the duty to walk in God's ways and emulate God's noble attributes.

45 This is based on the Rabbi Akiva's midrash-halakhic reading of Exodus 12:16: "On the first day, a holy convocation…no work shall be done on them; only that alone which is eaten by everyone may be prepared for you"—"for you," i.e., Jews, "and not for Gentiles." See also *TB Beitzah* 20b, 28b.

the Sages did not permit a Jew to invite a non-Jew for a meal in his home on Yom Tov lest the food run out, and the Jewish host be tempted to avoid embarrassment and impermissibly prepare more food for the Gentile guest.[46] Rambam (*Hilkhot Yom Tov* 1:13) and *Shulḥan Arukh* (OC 512:1) record this prohibition as normative law. This proscription—at first glance—seems to be an insurmountable obstacle to inviting converts-to-be for a Yom Tov meal, since before conversion, a candidate is yet still a Gentile.[47]

At the same time, the factual predicate of inviting conversion candidates to a Seder or a Yom Tov meal is also important to state: It is almost universally agreed to by rabbis involved in training converts that participation in Yom Tov meals generally, and a Pesach Seder specifically, are important, perhaps even necessary, Jewish educational experiences for a conversion candidate. A proper and successful conversion depends on

---

46 See *TB Beitzah* 21b: "Rabbi Yehoshua ben Levi said: We invite a Gentile [to a meal] on Shabbat, and we do not invite a Gentile on Yom Tov, as a protective decree lest he increases on his behalf." *Rashba*, *Beitzah* 21b, s.v. "*Gezeira*," explains the concern as lest an additional, non-kosher dish be prepared exclusively for the Gentile, which has no license by virtue of the halakhic principle of "*hoe'il*—since guests might come" (*TB Pesachim* 46b), because it cannot even potentially be enjoyed by the Jewish hosts or unexpected Jewish guests. Cooking extra kosher food for a Gentile in the same pot as food prepared for Jews should be permitted for three reasons: first, per "*hoe'il*"; second, per the halakhic principle of "*mitokh*" (*TB Beitzah* 12a), i.e., once a labor is permitted for an allowable purpose, it is deemed generally permitted; and third, more ingredients in a pot makes for a better dish, see *TB Beitzah* 17a; *Shulḥan Arukh* OḤ 503:1. *Rosh*, *Beitzah* 2:4, and *Ran*, *Beitzah* 10b *bedapei haRif*, s.v. "*ve'ein mezamnin*," both define the concern here as lest additional separate dishes be cooked for the Gentile, which they understand as rabbinically proscribed by Rabbi Yehoshua ben Levi's decree. Others, like *Shitah Mekubetzet*, *Beitzah* 12a, s.v. "*lifligei*," understand the aforementioned midrash halakhah excluding Gentiles from the permit of cooking disallows cooking for them in all cases, even the same pot. Most later halakhic authorities generally follow Rosh and Ran, see *Shulḥan Arukh* and *Rama* 512:1, *Mishnah Berurah* 512:4, as well as *Arukh Ha-Shulḥan* 512:2.

47 Rabbinical scholarship addressing this question includes: Barilai, Mordechai. "The Status of the Conversion Candidate Prior to the Completion of his Conversion," *Hama'ayan* 3:4, Tammuz, 5764; Benayahu Broner. "Hosting Conversion Candidates for the Night of the Seder," *Tzohar Torah Journal* vol. 14, Spring 5763, pp. 133-137; Kraus, Gavriel. "Regarding Inviting a Gentile Intending to Convert for a Yom Tov Meal," *Kol HaTorah* 62, 5767, pp. 48-50; and Michael Zylberman, "Hosting Conversion Candidates for Yom Tov Meals," 2018, <https://www.yutorah.org/sidebar/lecture.cfm/918128/rabbi-michoel-zylberman/inviting-conversion-candidates-for-yom-tov-meals/>.

effective preparation. Beyond the direct lesson of how halakhically to observe the Jewish holidays, Yom Tov meals, and especially a Pesach Seder, demonstrate to a convert-to-be the central Jewish religious aspiration of rejoicing on holidays in spiritual connection to God; the foundational theological themes and master narratives of Jewish history; the importance of peoplehood, community, and family; the halakhic differences between Shabbat and Yom Tov, etc.

The question then is what to do about inviting the convert-to-be for a Pesach Seder or a Yom Tov meal? Surveying the extant halakhic approaches to this question, we suggest that there are three basic categorical approaches to this issue, each of them reflecting the above presented competing visions of the duty of loving the convert-to-be.

Section One: Practical Ramification if the Duty to Love Applies Only After Conversion

Most halakhic authorities seemingly follow Rambam's view that the mitzvah of *Ahavat ha-Ger* only applies to a complete convert. Furthermore, among these authorities, few explicitly indicate that they espouse Rambam's programmatic expansion of the mitzvah of *Ahavat Hashem* to include loving outreach to would-be converts. Correspondingly, it would stand to reason that this large group of Jewish law authorities do not advocate for leniencies regarding including Gentiles at Jewish holiday meals. Indeed, from the relative silence of contemporary halakhic texts regarding exceptions to the rule prohibiting inviting Gentiles for Yom Tov meals, and the paucity of discussion about inviting conversion candidates, we can infer that conversion candidates have not normatively been deemed exceptions to this prohibitory rule.[48]

---

48 Although this constitutes an admittedly tenuous argument from silence, one still cannot help but notice that many who have written on hilkhot Yom Tov and Pesach are primarily silent on the matter of inviting Gentiles who are conversion candidates. As Rabbi Asher Weiss notes, the silence of the *poskim* sometimes speaks volumes (see, for example, *Minḥat Asher* 3:66). In the *Eretz Yisrael* context, *Shemirat Shabbat Kehilkhatah*, vol. 2 (5749), makes no mention of inviting Gentiles who are conversion candidates to a meal in his discussion of the laws of Yom Tov, see Index, s.v. "נכרי," p. 460. While Rabbi Simchah Bunim Cohen's *The Laws of Yom Tov* (ArtScroll, 1997), pp. 36-43, in the American context, briefly discusses the prohibition of inviting Gentiles to a Yom Tov meal or Pesach Seder, and allows for an uninvited Gentile guest, or a Gentile business associate whose lack of an invitation may generate animosity, no mention is made of a conversion candidate. One might opine that the lack of discussion reflects a sociological reality of the scarcity of conversion candidates within the segments

There may also be a secondary motivation at play—namely, once they convert, converts to Judaism will similarly be expected not to include Gentiles at their own Yom Tov meals. The argument goes: part of the process of preparing conversion candidates well is to inculcate within them an appreciation of how finicky and strict they will need to be after they convert towards not cooking for the many Gentiles within their social orbit—biological family and loved ones, as well as other candidates for conversion—who will want to come for a holiday meal. Only by role-modeling for a convert a firm line regarding not cooking for Gentiles on Yom Tov, including converts-to-be who are still Gentiles, will we properly train the convert to do the same in their Jewish lives. Creating leniencies for any type of Gentile, therefore, should be neither normative, nor occasionally acceptable.[49]

Section Two: Practical Ramification if the Duty to Love Functionally Applies Before Conversion

A second school of thought, aligned with Rosh and Raavad's views of the mitzvah of *Ahavat ha-Ger*, and even Rambam's view of an expansive mitzvah of *Ahavat Hashem*, believes that part of loving a convert post-conversion requires us also to treat a conversion candidate lovingly. This school would therefore argue that the mitzvah of loving the convert directs us to

---

of the Orthodox community that tend to produce specialized halakhic treatises and contemporary codes. It is unclear if said sociological reality reflects a certain negative orientation toward conversion to Judaism and its aspirants, or at least a halakhic view that there is no binding Torah obligation to love the conversion candidate.

49 Both Rabbi Yosef Karo and Rama, *Shulḥan Arukh*, OḤ 512:1, uphold as normative law the Talmudic prohibition (*TB Beitzah* 21a) of inviting Gentiles to one's home for festival meals. *Mishnah Berurah* 512:6, notes, contra Rama, that even sending food as a gift to a Gentile's home on Yom Tov should be forbidden since it may entail cooking extra. However, *Mishnah Berurah*, ibid., in the name of "*aḥaronim*," rules leniently in cases of animosity or financial loss so long as one is cooking on Yom Tov for both Jews and Gentiles, even including food items, like blintzes, each of which requires individuated preparation. The question is whether concerns of animosity or financial loss should even permit including Gentiles at a Yom Tov meal? As mentioned, contemporary author Rabbi Simchah Bunim Cohen, ibid., p. 43, rules leniently. Might by extension such concerns likewise lead us to permit the inclusion of conversion candidates since their exclusion might also generate animosity or hurt feelings? However, even here there is no special exemption being suggested for conversion candidates, rather more general circumstantial exceptions for Gentiles of different types.

search hard to find valid halakhic license to allow a conversion candidate to participate in Yom Tov meals. This school of thought does not grant special essential status to a conversion candidate, but would argue that in practice, we must meet the educational needs of the convert-to-be and thoroughly ground their conversionary preparation in functional knowledge of Jewish living.[50]

Since this approach doesn't grant special status to the conversion candidate per se, but still categorizes an aspiring convert as a current Gentile, it must rely on at least one of the variety of creative leniencies that have been suggested to allow a Gentile to eat at the home of Jew on Yom Tov.[51] These leniencies are listed below in preferential order of halakhic viability, as we sense it, with 1 and 2 being indisputably proper:

1. Gentiles who drop in without an invitation may be fed, as they have no expectation of plentiful food, since they were not previously invited.[52]
2. One can invite any Gentile for a festival meal that coincides with Shabbat. Whenever Yom Tov falls out on Shabbat, the Talmudic decree proscribing inviting Gentiles to Yom Tov meals does not apply since further food preparation is prohibited in any event.[53]

---

50 See R. Kraus, ibid., for a clear articulation that a conversion candidate is yet still fully a Gentile. Also see R. Nissim Karelitz, *Ḥut Shani* OḤ 512:1, p. 64: "A Gentile intending to convert, and at present is learning the rules of the holy Torah, his status is as a Gentile regarding this matter"—i.e., the laws proscribing inviting Gentiles to a Yom Tov meal.

51 While many of these leniencies developed in the medieval and early modern periods, they have taken on new import in the past century with rising intermarriage rates, a preponderance of non-observant Jews who may have a halakhic status akin to a Gentile regarding cooking on Yom Tov, an increased appreciation for educational Jewish outreach, and rising interest in conversion to Judaism. See, for example, *Responsa Bemareh Habezek*, 3:56, p. 94; Lau, Yisrael-Meir. "Inviting a Secular Jew to a Festival Meal," *Techumin* vol. 31, 5771, pp. 175-180; Chaim Jachter, "Cooking for Non-Observant Jews on Yom Tov," <https://www.koltorah.org/halachah/cooking-for-non-observant-jews-on-yom-tov-by-rabbi-chaim-jachter>.

52 Rambam, *Mishneh Torah, Hilkhot Yom Tov* 1:13; See also *Maggid Mishneh*, ad loc.; *Beit Yosef* OḤ 512; *Shulḥan Arukh* 512:1; *Mishnah Berurah* 512:10-11; R. Simchah Bunim Cohen, ibid., p. 39. Cf., however, Tur OḤ 512 who further requires a verbal disclaimer that no more food will be prepared just in case the available servings prove insufficient.

53 See *TB Beitzah* 21b. The rabbinic decree was limited to a situation in which a Jew can cook for a Jew, but not for a Gentile. In a situation in which no additional cooking is allowed for anyone, one can invite a Gentile. When the food runs

3. In a hotel setting or any situation where a Gentile is actually doing the cooking, there is no prohibition for a Gentile to cook for other Gentiles on Yom Tov.[54]
4. One can say to Gentiles that one hopes or expects to see them without actually inviting them or one can tell a Gentile that Jewish law prohibits their invitation, but if they come over uninvited, they are welcome to eat.[55]
5. One can transfer the food to the possession of the non-Jew prior to Yom Tov, and thus the Gentile is eating his own food.[56]
6. If the person is a conversion candidate, one can assume that the candidate is anxious to make a good impression, and comes beseechingly without demands, so that there is no fear that the host will feel pressured to make extra dishes to make a good impression in the opposite direction.[57]

---

out, one tells all—Jew and Gentile alike—that no more food can be prepared. Therefore, only on Yom Tov were the Talmudic rabbis afraid that Jews would be embarrassed to tell a Gentile that it is prohibited to cook additionally for a Gentile, but permitted to cook for a Jew. For more on this, see R. Moshe Yehuda Leib Zilberberg, *Responsa Zayit Ra'anan* Volume 2:7 (paragraph 4), which discusses cases of overlap of Shabbat and Yom Tov, each of which do not have identical rules as the other. Thus, for example, in the matter of inviting Gentiles for a meal, the Shabbat rule is more lenient, even though, generally, Yom Tov rules regarding food are more lenient.

54 See, for example, *Minḥat Yitzchak* 2:118 and 4:47, as well as *Piskei Teshuvot* 512:1.

55 This leniency is based on *Beit Yosef*'s OC 512 understanding of Rambam, *Mishneh Torah*, *Hilkhot Yom Tov* 1:13, via the interpretation of *Maggid Mishneh*, ad loc., that the Talmudic decree forbids invitation, and not the feeding of Gentiles, per se. This and other *heterim* can be found in R. Mordechai Barilai, ibid., pp. 22-32, fn. 49-55, and R. Michoel Zylberman, ibid. See also R. Nissim Karelitz, ibid., p. 64, who writes that if one merely states, "I have food available for you," without any formal invitation that would be permissible. *Shulḥan Arukh HaRav* OḤ 512:1 limits the prohibition to an invitation to dine, leading later authorities to permit an invitation for conversation, see R. Yisrael Meir Lau, ibid., p. 178.

56 See for example R. Gavriel Krauss, ibid., who explains in detail how to do this. R. Yisrael Sklar (ed.), *Ḥiddushei HaRashba LeMasekhet Beitzah* (Jerusalem: Mossad HaRav Kook) p. 175, fn. 188, credits this approach to Rabbi Yosef Shalom Elyashiv.

57 See for example *Shulḥan Shlomo* OḤ 512:7 which notes:

> ונשאל מרן זללה"ה אודות ראש ישיבה ברוסיה שנהוג שם שהרב מארח בחורים לסעודות יו"ט, וחלק מהבחורים הם גויים גמורים החפצים להתגייר, כיצד ינהג? ואמר מרן זללה"ה שלדעתו אין צריך בנד"ד לזכות את מנותיהם מעי"ט, משום שכל הגזירה היתה שמא לכבודו ירבה עבורו, ובפרט להשיטות שריבוי בשיעורין הוא אסור רק מדרבנן החשש הוא שבישל במיוחד עבורו, וזה שייך רק באורח שהמארח

Rabbi Asher Weiss, as cited by his student Rabbi Akiva Dershowitz, generally allows one to invite non-Jews to Yom Tov meals in extenuating situations.[58] The following factors motivate his lenient view:

1. Today, most people pre-cook their festival food in advance of Yom Tov, and thus the reason for the original Talmudic proscription is less relevant.
2. Meiri allows one to invite a Gentile to a Yom Tov meal so long as one says to him upon his arrival, "I have invited you on condition that you are satisfied with what has been prepared for you as it is not possible for us to add more for you."[59] It is easy to say this in our day, since nothing new is cooked for anyone!

מתכבד בו (כמש"כ במ"ב ס"ק ג), אולם אורח המארח עושה טובה שהוא מארחו בביתו, אין חשש שיבשל בעבורו, וביותר נראה שבנד"ד כל מטרת האירוח היא לצורך התקרבות ליהדות, וא"כ אדרבא המארח יסביר לו את ההלכה שאסור לבשל במיוחד בשבילו ביו"ט...

Our master [Rabbi Shlomo Zalman Auerbach] *zt"l* was asked about a Rosh Yeshiva in Russia who was inviting many students for meals on Yom Tov. Several of the students were Gentiles who desired to convert. What should the Rosh Yeshiva do? Rabbi Auerbach replied that in his view there is no need in this situation to legally transfer to them their food on the eve of the Festival, since the whole rabbinic decree here was that maybe in honor of the guest the host will cook more, and particularly according to those opinions that hold that adding more is only prohibited rabbinically lest one cook a unique portion for that person [i.e., a Gentile]. This is limited to a guest whose presence honors the host (as *Mishnah Berurah* 512:3 notes). But this is not applicable to a guest whom the host benefits by his hospitality, [and thus,] there is no fear that the host will cook more for him. Indeed, it is more logical to conclude that, in this case, the entire purpose of hospitality here is to bring them closer to Judaism. If so, then the exact opposite is true, and the host will explain to the guest the halakhah that is prohibited to cook uniquely for him on Yom Tov…

58 Akiva Dershowitz, "Inviting Gentiles to Meals on Yom Tov in Present Times," *Ohr Yisroel* 75 (Tishrei 5778), pp. 137-142. The factual predicates of this *teshuvah* and novel *halakhic* approaches to this issue are changing social, cultural, and technological aspects of Jewish life in modern society. In short, for example, with the advent of refrigeration and easy reheating, people rarely cook on Yom Tov itself anymore, but tend to prepare cooked-food items in advance. This might hold less true, though, in the Diaspora for the observed second day of Yom Tov. It is certainly true, however, for the first-night Seder, for which (nearly) all cooking is done before Yom Tov.

59 *Meiri*, *Beitzah* 21b. We would like to add another rationale, also grounded in the Meiri. One who looks closely at the authentic text of the *Meiri* (*Beit Ha-Beḥirah*

3. The *Sefer HaTanya*'s view (quoted by *Magen Avraham*) is that if the food is already prepared before Yom Tov one may invite a Gentile.[60]
4. Rashba explains that the reason one may cook food for his non-Jewish servant on Yom Tov is that the householder will cook a copious amount for his needs and his servant will make do with whatever had been cooked, without likely concern of additional cooking for the servant. Since nowadays we cook all our food before Yom Tov, like in the case of the non-Jewish servant, there is little likelihood of additional cooking.[61]

With specific regard to a conversion candidate, let us add that if the absence of a Gentile would diminish the festive joy of the Jews present, many authorities permit inviting him or her so long as the food is already prepared.[62] Furthermore, *Tzitz Eliezer* argues that many *rishonim*, led by Rashba, limit the whole prohibition of inviting Gentiles to situations where the Jew might cook non-kosher food for his Gentile guest, which

---

Beitzah, ed. Y. S. Lange and K. Schlesinger (Jerusalem: 5729), pp. 117–118) sees that the Meiri does not apply this decree proscribing cooking for idolaters to monotheistic and civilized Gentiles. A convert-to-be certainly meets Meiri's standard for exemption.

60 *Magen Avraham* 512:2. Cf. *Mishnah Berurah* 512:3; *Sha'ar Hatzion* 512:3,4.

61 *Rashba, Beitzah* 21b. See, for example, *Kaf Hahaim* 512:7 who notes that one can make coffee for a Gentile guest, so long as a Jew drinks some also, even if one's "true" intent is to serve the Gentile, because being a good host, and manifesting *derekh eretz*, are also considered great needs of the festival. Of course, we acknowledge the sociological underpinnings of the statement, "Since nowadays we cook all our food before Yom Tov," and we suspect that this might not be true at all times and for all places. There may also be differences in practice between Israel and various diaspora communities.

62 See *Biur Halakhah* 512, s.v., "*assur le-hazmeno.*" Although *Biur Halakhah* emphasizes festive joy as the license, and not avoidance of animosity, others legitimate affirmatively inviting important Gentiles to a Pesach Seder if that reduces hatred of Jews. See for example, *Ma'adnei Shlomo*, p. 24:

> ...והוסיף מרן זללה"ה שבשנים קדמוניות היה נהוג שהיו מזמינים גויים נכבדים לליל הסדר כגון קונסולים, וכנראה שהיה ענין חשוב שלא ישנאו את היהודים וגם הדבר היה ידוע שליל פסח הוא זמן מיוחד שמזמינים אותם,
>
> Rabbi Shlomo Zalman Auerbach *zt"l* adds that in the days of old the custom was that eminent Gentiles were invited for Pesach Seder like diplomatic consuls. It appears that it was important that these people not hate the Jews and it was well known that Seder night was a special time to invite them.

See also R. Mordechai Barilai, ibid., p. 32, who notes that the practice of Rav Herzog, the late Ashkenazic Chief Rabbi of Israel, was to invite Gentile ambassadors for Seder.

is very unlikely for a convert-to-be who comes specifically for dining in a kosher home.[63]

Relying on these many and diverse halakhic leniencies allows for the crafting of a conversion process that enables the convert-to-be to participate in festival meals and learn what needs to be learned. The orientation of seeking leniency is inspired by either the mitzvah of *Ahavat ha-Ger* or *Ahavat Hashem*, but also needs to satisfy the halakhic rules that more normatively proscribe inviting Gentiles for festival meals.

It is also possible to argue that one should be more lenient here than in other situations of inviting a Gentile for a meal based on an *Ahavat ha-Ger* orientation. Let us explain how and why: Although Rabbi Moshe Feinstein follows the view of the first school which applies *Ahavat ha-Ger* only post-conversion, he understands the orienting mitzvah of *Ahavat ha-Ger* as mandating leniency in all halachic situations for which the mitzvah applies.[64] Rabbi Feinstein writes (*Iggerot Moshe* YD 4:26):

> אבל למעשה יש לידע, שהמצווה של ואהבתם את הגר (דברים עקב י:יט) מחייבת אותנו לקרבם ולהקל בכל עניינים אלו.
>
> But on a practical level, one needs to know that the commandment to love the convert obligates us to draw in the convert and be lenient on all these matters.

It is important not to under-read this responsum. Rabbi Feinstein avers that when there is more than one reasonable halakhic approach that impacts a person to whom the mitzvah of loving the convert applies, one should adopt the view that expresses love for converts, and brings them closer, and better integrates them, even if more halakhically lenient than one might otherwise be accustomed. One does this by seeking halakhic constructs that diminish the exclusion of converts. Of course, Rabbi Feinstein affirms that one cannot transgress halakhah to make a convert feel more comfortable, welcome, or integrated, but must develop legitimate halakhic solutions. To put it in a slightly different way, for Rabbi Feinstein, the mitzvah of *Ahavat ha-Ger* is fulfilled when given the choice between two legitimate halakhic outcomes, a *p'sak* is rendered and a pathway forward is set that is favorable to the convert.

If one thought that the mitzvah to love the convert requires loving treatment of the convert-to-be as well, then, per this approach, one would be prepared to rely on leniencies to invite a conversion candidate to a

---

63 *Rashba, Beitzah* 21b. *Tzitz Eliezer* 8:17.

64 See *Iggerot Moshe* EH 5:1 for why we think Rabbi Feinstein seems to rule that loving the convert does not apply prior to conversion.

Pesach Seder or Yom Tov meal, in ways one would not for a committed Gentile.[65]

Section Three: Practical Ramifications if the Duty to Love Essentially Applies Before Full Conversion

The school of thought associated with RI Barcelona, who maintains that the duty to love the convert-to-be commences with his or her expressed intent to convert, allows for a deeper structure of halakhic leniency for a conversion candidate. Likewise, per Rashba's aforementioned view, since Jewish status is gained in stages, somewhere further along the conversion process the convert-to-be stops being a complete Gentile, even if they have not as of yet become a full Jew.[66] In this model, the rabbinic decree

---

65 See for example, Rabbi Nissim Karelitz, who suggests in *Ḥut Shani, Yom Tov* 4:3 that he does not think that one can rely on the *heter* of transferring ownership of a festival meal to a Gentile prior to the onset of Yom Tov in order to justify inviting the Gentile to a Yom Tov meal. However, he is cited in *Leket Hilkhot Yom Tov* 3:4 as stating unambiguously that one can rely on this *heter* for a person who is a candidate for conversion. What justifies the difference in these contradictory rulings is that the duty to love the convert allows for leniency. See also *Mishnah Berurah*, Dirshu edition, on 512:1. While this is certainly true if one holds *Ahavat ha-Ger* begins prior to conversion, it also may be true for adherents of the first two schools represented in Part I of this article. For more on this, see Reiss, Yona, *Kanfei Yona*, 2018, pp. 128-132 (Chapter 10).

66 Allow us to present this view in a philosophical model. In *Kol Dodi Dofek: Listen—My Beloved Knocks* (ed. Jeffrey R. Woolf, trans. David Z. Gordon. Hoboken, NJ: KTAV, p. 65), Rabbi Soloveitchik observes that Jewish identity is a composite of two types of covenantal relationships with God: *Berit Avot* and *Berit Sinai*, the covenant of national belonging through Abraham and the other Patriarchs, and the covenant of Torah obligation through Moses and Sinai. Similarly, Rabbi Aharon Lichtenstein asserts in his aforementioned essay, "Brother Daniel and the Jewish Fraternity," that Jewish identity has two components: *Shem Yisrael*, halakhic Jewishness; and *Kedushat Yisrael*, membership in the Jewish people and their destiny. Per Rabbis Soloveitchik and Lichtenstein, one can claim that one can theoretically be part of the Jewish people without being Jewish as a matter of Jewish law, and conversely, that one can put oneself outside of Jewish destiny, even if one is halakhically Jewish, as, for example, in the case of an apostate who per most authorities is still Jewish as a matter of Jewish law. A convert-to-be who has religiously, socially, and culturally joined the Jewish people and is just awaiting a formal conversion—even if not yet circumcised—may have already entered the "Covenant of Abraham," thereby gaining *shem Yisrael*, and thus be entitled to the privileges thereof. As mentioned earlier, *Minḥat Elazar* 3:8 proposes that burial in a Jewish cemetery is one such outgrowth of this intermediate status. RI Barcelona posits that the mitzvah of loving the convert is another.

prohibiting inviting a Gentile does not apply to the convert-to-be at all. This convert-to-be is not the *nokhri* whom one is prohibited to feed, since this person is already connected to the Jewish community. Furthermore, as mentioned above, Rashba understands the prohibition to invite Gentiles to a Yom Tov meal to be based on a concern of cooking non-kosher for them, something not applicable to a person who has achieved partial Jewish status.[67] Among contemporary halakhic authorities, this approach is taken by Rabbi Gedalia Dov Schwartz of the Chicago Rabbinical Council and Beth Din of America, and Rabbi Shlomo Aviner.[68] This approach is hinted at by others as well,[69] and it has also been recorded as the position of former Israeli Chief Rabbi Avraham Shapiro.[70]

Conclusion of Part II:

In Part I of this article, we showed that there are three different basic halakhic ways to view the convert prior to conversion. Part II shows that these three views produce three different results practically in the "test case" of inviting a convert-to-be for a meal on Yom Tov. This tripartite method of analysis and application can be applied to other areas of halakhah impacting upon conversion candidates, and the aforementioned different schools correlate with different levels of halakhic stringency and leniency.[71]

---

67 See *Tzitz Eliezer* 8:17, who excludes non-observant Jews from the decree of not inviting Gentiles based on *Rashba, Beitzah* 21b. This is true as well for a convert-to-be who is also only interested in kosher food.

68 Rabbi Gedalia Dov Schwartz's rationale is based on *Binyan Tzion* 91, and *Minḥat Elazar* 3:8, and is cited by R. Zylberman, ibid. In 2008, one of us [MJB] heard this directly from Rabbi Schwartz, as well. For Rabbi Shlomo Aviner's view, see <http://www.ravaviner.com/2011/04/shut-sms-109-hilchot-pesach.html>.

69 See, for example, *Yavetz, Yevamot* 48b; *Mekor Ḥesed* commenting on *Sefer Haḥasidim* 690. See R. Mordechai Barlai, ibid., p. 31.

70 Such is noted by the editor (not the author) at R. Benayahu Broner, ibid., p. 137, fn. 12.

71 Consider for example how this might apply to the duty of loving people who have undergone a non-halakhic conversion, and who identify as fully Jewish, without actually being Jewish as a matter of Jewish law. The approach of RI Barcelona—and maybe the broad general approach of Rosh, Raavad, and Rashba that once a person undertakes significant steps to acquire Jewish identity, one has developed the status of a *ger* for the purpose of the mitzvah to love the *ger*, also impacts how we ought to view people who undergo such non-halakhic conversions. A close look at the language and formulation of the RI Barcelona and Rashba indicates that once one seeks to put oneself Jewishly under the wings of the Divine, one develops an interim status of both no longer being

IV: Conclusion

This exploration of the mitzvah to love the convert has revealed a fault line that is quite clear in the *rishonim.* On one side is Rambam who directly rules that the duty to love a convert applies only after conversion, though he upholds that the mitzvah of loving God entails a duty to lovingly convert people who wish to become Jewish. On the other side are many *rishonim* who rule in various ways that the duty to love converts applies before the actual conversion has been completed. Rosh, Raavad, and Rashba's view is that this applies only after concrete steps toward conversion have taken place. RI Barcelona avers that the duty applies upon expressed interest to convert.

While most post-medieval halakhic authorities follow the view of Rambam, there is a considerable number of weighty *rishonim* who have adopted the broader view, and more than a small number of *aḥaronim* who

---

a Gentile for some rules and being a *ger*—a convert-to-be—for other rules. This is particularly true according to the approach of Rosh who sees circumcision as achieving a new stage of identity. For a woman, one would have to posit a corresponding stage in her conversionary process. Logic would indicate that this is even more so true for someone who sincerely thinks that they have already successfully converted, even if as a matter of halakhah they are not yet Jewish, and if a man cannot count in a minyan, and if a woman cannot fulfill mitzvot for other women either. There is logic to the claim that such people should be considered akin to a "convert-to-be," somewhat like the category of *mal velo taval.* Rambam (*Mishneh Torah, Hilkhot Melakhim* 8:10) suggests that there may be a time limit of a year from professed desire to convert before a *beit din* to circumcision (for a man), and by implication until the completion of a conversion process. However, in that context, the delay indicates a change of heart, or a lack of identification, which is not the case for people who consider themselves Jewish. The duty to love them would then already apply in the model of all these *rishonim* other than the Rambam. Other mitzvot might apply to them as well, like the duty of rescue—see, for example, *Iggerot Moshe* EH 5:1, who requires the saving of Ethiopian Jews as Jews, even though Rabbi Feinstein rules that they are not to be considered halakhically Jewish, or the ruling of the Munkacser Rebbe (*Minḥat Elazar* 3:8) that such a person can be buried in a Jewish cemetery. See also R. Mordechai Barilai, ibid., 30, who cites Rabbi Shlomo Goren as explicitly permitting the burial of non-Orthodox converts in a Jewish cemetery, albeit at a distance of eight *amot,* since they lived as Jews in all ways. See also Goren, Shlomo. "Our Connection to Those Who Converted non-Halachically," *Teḥumin* vol. 23, 2003, p.209, and "Burial of a Soldier Who Was Not Jewish, but Had a Jewish Father," *Techumin* vol. 26, 2006, p. 217. This is even more so true, we note, for cases of people who have converted according to minority views within the halakhic community, whether normatively accepted *bedieved*, or *leḥumrah,* or not at all.

consider it as well, and factor this view into contemporary halakhah. In the prototypical example at hand—inviting a convert-to-be for a Pesach Seder or Yom Tov meal—we see how this approach is applied in fact, from those who prohibit any leniencies at all, to those who seek leniencies for the convert-to-be within the conventional halakhic framework, to those who are consistently lenient.

Further, while the mitzvah of *Ahavat ha-Ger* has specific halakhic applications, it also engenders an orienting influence toward those who are seeking to convert and conversion, more generally, and in the adjudication of halakhic issues, more particularly. The question of whether *Ahavat ha-Ger* applies to conversion candidates also has ramification for broader conversion policy.

May we be blessed to form a community that is lovingly welcoming to converts.[72] ☙

---

72 Finally, we wish to propose that upholding RI Barcelona's approach as more widely normative in the *rishonim* than generally understood solves a widely discussed problem in the *Sefer Haḥinukh*, *mitzvah* 431. After explaining in the opening discussion of the mitzvah to love the convert, and noting that the mitzvah is limited to converts who join the Jewish community, *Ḥinukh* then adds:

> ויש לנו ללמד מן המצוה היקרה הזאת לרחם על אדם שהוא בעיר שאינה ארץ מולדתו ומקום משפחות אבותיו, ולא נעביר עליו הדרך במוצאנו אותו יחידי ורחקו מעליו עוזריו, כמו שאנו רואים שהתורה תזהירנו לרחם על כל מי שצריך עזר, ועם המדות הללו נזכה להיות מרחמים מהשם יתברך, וברכות שמים ינוחו על ראשינו, והכתוב רמז טעם הצווי באמרו כי גרים הייתם בארץ מצרים, הזכיר לנו שכבר נכוינו בצער הגדול הזה שיש לכל איש הרואה את עצמו בתוך אנשים זרים ובארץ נכריה, ובזכרנו גדל דאגת הלב שיש בדבר, וכי כבר עבר עלינו, והשם בחסדיו הוציאנו משם יכמרו רחמינו על כל אדם שהוא כן.
>
> We should learn from this precious commandment to have mercy on a person who is in a city that is not the land of birth and the place of his ancestral family. And we should not pass this person by on the road when we find him alone and those who can help him are far away. Just as we see that the Torah warns us to have compassion on anyone who needs help. And with these traits, we will merit to receive mercy from Blessed God, and the blessings of Heaven will rest upon our heads. And Scripture hints to the reason of the command when it states, "since you were strangers in the Land of Egypt." It mentions to us that we were previously harmed by this great pain that there is to every person who sees themselves among foreign people and in a foreign land. And upon our remembering the great worry of the heart that there is in the matter, and that it already passed over us and that God, in His kindnesses, took us out of there, our mercies for any person like this will overwhelm [us].

These famous words, the *Minḥat Ḥinukh* suggests, was an attempt to introduce an additional valence of ethical and extra-legal insight to these legal rules. We wish to suggest a different approach: this insight of the *Ḥinukh* may seek to expand the legal approach of RI Barcelona that the mitzvah applies not only to people who are seeking to join the Jewish people, but to any stranger, Jew or not, who is lost and seeking shelter under the protective wings of the Jewish community. It is very much the style of the *Ḥinukh* to introduce the legal insights of the Ramban, Rashba, and the Spanish commentators (like RI Barcelona) into his essentially Maimonidean work, and these words accomplish that.

Idle Chatter or Vital Chat? A Janus-Faced Talmudic Dictum

By: DAVID NIMMER*

"Our complete Torah shall not be like your idle talk." In three separate places, this distinctive phrase caps a story from rabbinic literature in which Rabban Yoḥanan ben Zakkai dismisses a sectarian. The message in each instance is: Opponents of normative Judaism are such fools as to not even deserve the dignity of a response. Theirs is mere *idle chatter.* Thus have many distinguished rabbis across the ages deployed this dictum—for example, Rashba in the fourteenth century.

And yet, other rabbis, of no less distinction than Rashba, have used the phrase in essentially the opposite sense. In particular, Joseph Saul Nathanson used the phrase to engage with the wisdom of other traditions—indeed, in deciding how to apply Torah in 1860 Lemburg to copyright protection, he took the occasion to engage in a *vital chat* with the examples of Russian and Austrian laws. Thus arises a mystery.

I. The Three Tales

A. Fast Talk

All three stories[1] are found in the commentary to *Megilat Ta'anit*, the oldest extant rabbinic text.[2] Its cryptic language sets forth thirty-five calendrical commemorations of minor victories on which fasting is prohibited. Those events unfolded during the half-millennium from Ezra to Ca-

---

 I gratefully acknowledge our outstanding librarians at the UCLA School of Law, including Rachel Green, Gabe Juarez and Shang-ching Huitzacua. Profound gratitude again to Joel Zeff and further thanks for valuable comments from Ron Kleinman, Abraham Lieberman, Gary Linder, Neil Netanel, Marc Shapiro, David Stern, Yochanan Rivkin, and Avivah Zornberg. Unless otherwise noted, all English translations from the Hebrew are mine and all Biblical translations are quoted from the King James Version.

1 "Rabbinic texts have a fondness for multiple tellings of the same story." Barry Scott Wimpfheimer, *Narrating the Law: A Poetics of Talmudic Legal Stories* 75 (Pennsylvania 2011).

2 Vered Noam, "Megillat Ta'anit—The Fasting Scroll," in *The Literature of the Sages: Second Part* 339 (Shmuel Safrai et al., eds. Fortress 2006).

David Nimmer is the author of *Nimmer on Copyright* (11 volumes, LexisNexis).

ligula. Since ancient times, later elaborations of a piece with Talmudic material have accompanied the *Fasting-Scroll* called the scholion (from the Greek σχόλιον, "comment"). Since late medieval times, the two manuscript versions of that commentary have been mixed (sometimes giving rise to internal contradictions).

The three stories have in common an encounter between Rabban Yoḥanan ben Zakkai (RYBZ) and either the Sadducees or their close allies, the Boethusians. RYBZ occupies unique importance in the annals of Jewish history after being smuggled out of Jerusalem on the eve of the Temple's destruction to perpetuate Torah studies at Yavneh.[3] The Sadducees are noteworthy as the opponents of the Pharisees, antecedents to the later rabbis of the Talmud.[4] (For current purposes, we treat the Boethusians[5] as synonymous with their fellow sectaries.)[6]

Let's start with the most distinctive instance story (the only one lacking a parallel text in the Babylonian Talmud).

Story 1

[1] *On the 27th of Cheshvan, flour returned to be brought up upon the altar.* Because the Sadducees said to eat flour with meat. RYBZ said to them, "Whence do you derive that?" And no one knew how to bring a proof from the Torah, until one of them chattered against him, "Because Moses loved Aaron, so he said, 'Don't eat meat alone but rather have flour with the meat,' just as a person tells his friend, 'Here is some meat, and have some bread along with it.'"	מגילת תענית (ליכטנשטיין) הסכוליון // /עשרים ושבעה בחשון/ בעשרין ושבעה ביה תבת סלתא למסק על מדבחא. מפני שהיו הצדוקין אומרין אוכלין מנחת בהמה. אמר להם רבן יוחנן בן זכאי מנין לכם? ולא היו יודעין להביא ראיה מן התורה אלא אחד שהיה מפטפט כנגדו ואומר מפני שהיה משה אוהב את אהרן אמר אל יאכל בשר לבדו

3 Solomon Zeitlin, *The Takkanot of Rabban Jochanan Ben Zakkai,* 54 The Jewish Quarterly 288 (1964); Hayim Lapin, *Rabbis as Romans* (Oxford 2012).

4 Some scholars have questioned the rabbinic connection back to the Pharisees. Isaac Roszler, *Law as a Prism into National Identity: The Case of Mishpat Ivri,* 38 U. Pa. J. Int'l L. 715, 726 n.45 (2017). Indeed, in Mishnah Yadayim 4:6, our very own RYBZ, in discussion with the Sadducees, distances himself from the Pharisees! Binyamin Lau, *The Sages Vol I: The Second Temple Period* 342 (Maggid 2007).

5 One possibility is that their name represents "the house of (BYT) the Essenes," thus identifying them as the famous sect that lived by the Dead Sea. Seth Schwartz, *Imperialism and Jewish Society: 200 B.C.E. to 640 C.E.* (Princeton 2001) at 92.

6 "[R]abbinic portrayals of these two groups are sometimes indistinguishable." Richard Kalmin, *Jewish Babylonia between Persia and Roman Palestine* 168 (Oxford 2006).

RYBZ answered him with the verse, "Then they came to Elim, where there were twelve springs and seventy palm trees." [Ex. 15:27] He replied, "What does one have to do with the other?" Then [RYBZ] said, "Fool! Our complete Torah shall not be like your idle talk. We already have a verse, "You shall make a burnt offering to the Lord, along with its meat offering, and drink offerings, a sweet savour, a sacrifice made by fire unto the Lord."	אלא יאכל סלת ובשר כאדם שהוא אומר לחברו הילך בשר הילך רכיך. קרא לו רבן יוחנן בן זכאי ויבאו אילמה ושם שתים עשרה עינות מים ושבעים תמרים. אמר לו מה ענין זה אצל זה? אמר לו שוטה ולא תהא תורה שלמה שלנו כשיחה בטלה שלך. והלא כבר נאמר יהיה עולה ליי ומנחתם ונסכיהם לריח ניחח אשה לה'.

The essence of this tale is that the sage vanquished the Sadducean heresy—and to remember that happy day, we refrain from fasting on its anniversary. But the clipped story poses questions:

What is the context of eating meat with flour? Without delving into the minutiae of Temple sacrifices, some offerings are entirely consumed at the altar whereas others are partially eaten by the priests. Everyone admits that a meat sacrifice entirely consumed by the altar does not result in giving any bread to the *kohen*. Turning to animal sacrifices that priests may partially eat, the Sadducees maintained that the priests may likewise eat the accompanying meal offering, whereas Pharisaic law disallowed that approach. Although the challenge to the Sadducees was "to bring a proof from the Torah," their actual defense fell short of that mark. Grounded instead solely in "public policy," they offered the rationale that Moses would have wanted his brother Aaron to have the benefit of a sandwich, if you will, rather than eating unadorned cold cuts.

How does one episode from the forty years of wandering in the desert disprove the thesis at issue? Of what significance is it that, at one point, the Israelites "came to Elim, where there were twelve springs and seventy palm trees"? That verse appears to be a *non sequitur*, amply warranting the response, "What does one have to do with the other?" The midrash interprets a reference to the seventy palm trees as the seventy sages, which naturally suggests the giving of the Oral Torah.[7] The riposte that one must add insights from the Oral Torah might hit the mark in the context of the later stories, where the opponents support their view from the Written Torah. In the instant case, however, given that the Sadducee simply adduced public policy, it misses the mark to tell him that the Oral Torah must be added to the Written Torah to reach the correct result.

7 Rashi to Ex. 15:27, following *Mekhilta de-Rebbi Yishmael*. I have authored a whole article following that suggestion. David Nimmer, *Miriam's Oasis*, 34 Touro L. Rev. 983 (2018).

Accordingly, we need to posit a different interpretation of that verse. One source[8] suggests it be interpreted in light of a different verse that is close by: "And Moses said, This shall be, when the Lord shall give you in the evening flesh to eat, and in the morning bread to the full." [Ex. 16:8]. That verse teaches that separate times exist for consuming meat *versus* bread, thereby disfavoring the Sadducee's public policy goal of combining the two in a sandwich.

What does the final verse prove? The midrashic technique at issue in the quoted verse[9] is *hekesh*, which allows words in proximity to be interpreted to the same effect. Given that the reference to the flour offering (ומנחתם) is adjacent to the word for an offering that is entirely consumed by the altar (עולה), we can conclude that the priests do not eat of that flour, either.[10]

Story 2

[2] *On the 24th of Av, we returned to our rulings.* In the days of the Greek kingdom, they used to rule by Gentile law. And when the Hasmoneans prevailed over them and canceled their rulings, they reverted to judging by the Laws of Israel, and that day of cancellation they made into a holiday. For the Sadducees used to rule: "A daughter should inherit along with the daughter of a son." RYBZ said to them, "Whence do you derive that?" And no one knew how to bring a proof from the Torah, until one of them chattered against him, "If the daughter of a son can inherit, whose entitlement arises from her father, then a daughter of the testator himself should all the more inherit." RYBZ answered him with the verse, "These are the sons of Seir the Horite, who inhabited the land; Lotan, and Shobal, and Zibeon, and Anah." [Gen. 36:20] "And there is another verse, 'And these are the children of Zibeon; both Ajah, and Anah: this was that Anah that found the mules in the wilderness, as he fed the asses of Zibeon his father.' [Gen. 36:24] This teaches that Zibeon had sexual relations	מגילת תענית (ליכטנשטיין) הסכוליון // /עשרים וארבעה באב/ בעשרין וארבעה ביה תבנא לדיננא. בימי מלכות יון היו דנין בדיני הגוים וכשגברה ידם של בית חשמונאי בטלום חזרו לדון בדיני ישראל ואותו היום שבטלום עשאוהו יום טוב. שהיו הצדוקין דנין בדיניהם לאמר הבת יורשת עם בת הבן. אמר להם רבן יוחנן בן זכאי מנין לכם. ולא היו יודעים להביא ראיה מן התורה אלא אחד שהיה מפטפט כנגדו ואומר לו אם בת הבן הבאה מחמת אביה הבא מכחי יורשתני, בת הבאה מכחי לא כל שכן. קרא לו רבן יוחנן בן זכאי את המקרא הזה ואלה בני שעיר החרי יושבי הארץ לוטן שובל וצבעון וענה וכתוב אחד אומר הוא ענה אשר מצא את הימים במדבר ברעותו את

8 Avraham Eliyahu Bornstein, *Megillat Ta'anit* 54 (1908) (Hebrew).

9 The precise verse that RYBZ quotes does not exist. Over the course of millennia, corruption can afflict manuscript copying. In this case, Lev. 23:18 differs from the quoted text in only insignificant details. Vered Noam, *Megillat Ta'anit: Versions • Interpretation • History* 254 (Yad Ben-Zvi 2003) (Hebrew).

10 *Id.*

with his mother and begot Anah." He replied, "Behold, you are just playing around with us." He said, "Fool! The words of our complete Torah shall not be like your idle talk." He said, "With that you dismiss me!?" [RYBZ] replied, "If the daughter of a son possesses a right that is valid in the presence of brothers, can you say the same with respect to his daughter, whose ability is impaired in the presence of brothers?" The day that they were vanquished was made a festive day.	החמורים לצבעון אביו אלא מלמד שבא שבעון /צבעון/ על אמו והוליד ממנה ענה. אמר לו הרי אתה משחק בנו. אמר לו שוטה ולא יהו דברי תורה שלנו כשיחה בטלה שלכם. אמר לו בכך אתה מוציאני? אמר לו ומה בת בני שכן יפה כחה במקום האחים תאמר בבתי שכן הורע כחה במקום האחין דין הוא שלא תירשני. יום שנצחום עשאוהו יום טוב.

In this instance, the Sadducee argues for equity in inheritance.[11] Imagine a family constellation of Father, Daughter, Son, and Granddaughter (namely, Son's offspring). All disputants accept that Torah law gives primacy to sons—at the death of Father, as between living Daughter and Son, the latter inherits all. But what happens if Son predeceases Father? In that instance, the tradition holds that Granddaughter inherits the entire share of her dead father. Against that policy, the Sadducees argue that Daughter should share 50% of Father's estate with her. Their reasoning is *a fortiori*: "If the daughter of a son can inherit, whose entitlement arises from her father, then a daughter of the testator himself should all the more inherit."

Is the verse about Seir the Horite another non sequitur? Against their logic, RYBZ juxtaposes two verses from Genesis. One adduces Anah and Zibeon as two sons of Seir, but the other portrays Anah as the son of Zibeon. How could he be both? The answer is incest—Zibeon lay with his mother to produce Anah, who therefore qualifies as Seir's grandson as well as his son.[12] So why did the first verse list them both together? To teach that a grandson can inherit equally the share attributed to his deceased father.[13]

---

11 The story appears in slightly altered form in the Gemara as well. T.B. *Bava Batra* 115b. (Note the parallel in *Tosefta Yadayim* 2:20.) For instance, the version there commemorates 24 Tevet rather 24 Av.

12 A different explanation would be that there may have been two people named Anah. The parallel passage in the Gemara cited above posits just that possibility, and then diverges into a sizable interpolation about a certain King Shapor, who likewise discussed Anah.

13 Rabbi Yosaif Asher Weiss in *ArtScroll Talmud Bavli* 115b2 (1994).

The unconvinced Sadducee remonstrates, "With that you dismiss me!?" He reasonably objects to that outré invocation of incest by virtue of juxtaposition—although a possible reading, the incest hardly jumps out from the text (as regarding Lot's daughters). Indeed, the Gemara even entertains, as a serious possibility, that there may have been two people named Anah. Thus, to premise the entire edifice on Anah's bastard-status is hardly self-evident.

What point was RYBZ making about the presence of brothers? More particularly, the Genesis verses just quoted deal with the grand*son* of a deceased son, as opposed to the Sadducee's case of the grand*daughter* of a deceased son. So, it would seem that RYBZ's verses do not effectively refute the argument. Going further still, RYBZ's interpretation works only on the assumption that Zibeon was dead—which is nowhere stated.

Evidently aware that he has failed to prevail until now, RYBZ confronts the Sadducee on his own terms, namely through answering his logical proposition: "If the daughter of a son can inherit, whose entitlement arises from her father, then a daughter of the testator himself should all the more inherit." To reiterate, given that Granddaughter admittedly inherits the entire share of her dead father, the Sadducees argue that Daughter should share 50% of Father's estate with her.

To understand the refutation, it helps to expand the family constellation. Let us now add to Son1 brothers Son2 and Son3. Examining the status in light of the famous story of the daughters of Zelopheḥad [Num. 27], we can conclude, at the death of Father, that Son2 and Son3 have to share their inheritance with the progeny of predeceased Son1—even if that progeny contains only daughters. But Son2 and Son3 do not have to share with Daughter—even the Sadducees acknowledge that a living son dispossesses her interest.

To summarize, it was common to both Sadducees and Pharisees that Daughter does not inherit when Son2 and Son3 are alive—but the Sadducees wished to posit a special case when the only children of Father were deceased Son1 and Daughter. RYBZ capitalized on their concession that Daughter cannot inherit in the presence of brothers (namely Son2 and Son3) by deriving from it that the rights of Daughter are inferior to the rights of her brother, *i.e.* Son. Yet the rights of a Granddaughter are equivalent to the rights of her father, *i.e.* Son (thanks to the Zelopheḥad example). So we can now infer that Granddaughter's rights trump Daughter's rights. With that conclusion, he exploded the Sadducee's *a fortiori* argument.

Finally, we reach the last story, in which the adversarial role has switched from Sadducees to Boethusians.

Story 3

[3] *On the 8th of Nisan until the end of the festival, the holiday was fixed, not to make eulogies or to fast.* What holiday? The festival of Shavuot. For it was not necessary to list all the festival days in the scroll, but rather was set forth in opposition to the Boethusians, who said that Shavuot comes only after the Sabbath, as in the verse "And ye shall count unto you from the morrow after the Sabbath, from the day that ye brought the sheaf of the wave offering; seven Sabbaths shall be complete." [Lev. 23:15]

A certain Boethusian said to RYBZ, "Moses loved Israel, and he knew that Shavuot is only one day long, so he fixed the time for them to come after the Sabbath, so that they could rest two days, one after the other."

Rabban Yohanan ben Zakkai joined into discussion with him and said, "'There are eleven days' journey from Horeb by the way of Mount Seir unto Kadeshbarnea.' [Deut. 1:2] If Moses loved Israel so much, then why did he detain them for forty years in the desert!?"

He replied, "Behold, you are just playing with us."

He said, "World-class fool![14] Our complete Torah shall not be like your idle talk."

He said, "With that you dismiss me!?"

[RYBZ] replied, "Does not one verse say, 'It shall be seven complete weeks' [Lev. 23:15] and [the next] verse say 'You shall count fifty days'? How so? If the festival falls on the Sabbath we count seven weeks; if it falls after the Sabbath we count fifty days. So when you read 'You shall count from the morrow after the Sabbath,' it is from the morrow of the first festival day of Passover."[15]

מגילת תענית (ליכטנשטיין)

הסכוליון // /שמונה בניסן/ מן תמניא ביה ועד סוף מועדא אתותב חגא דילא למספד ודילא להתענאה. ואיזה חג זה יום טוב העצרת והלא לא נצרכו לכתב כל הימים הטובים שבמגלה אלא שהיו דנין כנגד בייתוסים שהיו אומרים אין עצרת אלא לאחר השבת שנאמר וספרתם לכם ממחרת השבת... אמר חד ביתוסא לרבן יוחנן בן זכאי: משה אוהב היה את ישראל והיה יודע שעצרת אינה אלא יום אחד וקבעה להם אחר השבת שיהיו נחים שני ימים זה אחר זה נטפל לו רבן יוחנן בן זכאי ואמר לו אחד עשר יום מחורב דרך הר שעיר עד קדש ברנע אם משה אוהבן היה מפני מה עכבן במדבר ארבעים שנה. אמר לו הרי אתה משחק בנו.

אמר לו שוטה שבעולם לא תהא תורה שלמה שלנו כשיחה בטלה שלכם. אמר לו בכך אתה מוציאני. אמר לו לאו כתוב אחד אומר שבע שבתות תמימות תהיינה וכתוב אחד אומר תספרו חמשים יום הא כיצד חל להיות יום טוב בשבת מונין שבע שבתות חל להיות אחר השבת מונין חמשים יום וכשאתה קורא וספרתם לכם ממחרת השבת ממחרת יום טוב הראשון של פסח... ורבי אליעזר אומר אינו צריך...

14 Or "worldly fool." Michal Bar-Asher Siegal, *Jewish-Christian Dialogues on Scripture in Late Antiquity* 67 (Cambridge 2019).

15 At this point, the text turns to four alternatives that prove the same proposition. Rabbi Eliezer posits that the proof offered by RYBZ is not needed because it is the Beit Din that determines the pertinent date; Rabbi Joshua reasons by analogy to parallel verses about counting; Rabbi Ishmael reasons by analogy to parallel verses about offering sacrifices; and Rabbi Judah ben Beteirah reasons by usage of the word "Sabbath" elsewhere in proximity to bread.

By this time, the pattern is clear. This particular dispute is well-known as an oft-discussed example of Jewish textualism versus oral law.[16] Strictly as a matter of approaching the verses, the Boethusian has the better argument—*Leviticus* begins the counting from "the morrow after the Sabbath." But Pharasaic tradition holds the contrary. In this instance, RYBZ was able to answer them effectively on their own level—he countered the supposed love that Moses had for Israel by giving them one long weekend every year with the observation that Moses detained them for forty years in the desert—on a journey that only required eleven days!

In addition, RYBZ was able to adduce textual support for his own position. By juxtaposing one verse that counted weeks with another that counted days, he was able to allocate the former to a situation when Passover ended on Saturday night and the latter when it ended later in the week. Thus did he blunt the Boethusian's "plain text" argument. So we are left with a final question.

How can the innovation in the law be ascribed to Moses, who simply took dictation from the true Author of the Torah? As in Story 1, one obvious defect with the opponent's initial logic is to attribute innovation to Moses—that Moses loved his brother Aaron and gave him a sandwich or loved all of Israel and gave them a long weekend. Both instances posit that Moses was composing the Torah originally rather than accepting divine dictation. The normative view could hardly accept that proposition! Yet RYBZ's riposte steers clear of that defect on both occasions.[17] It is strange that the text itself fails to raise that objection.[18]

---

16 In this instance, the parallel in the Gemara discusses Sadducees rather than Boethusians. T.B. Menaḥot 65a. It first rehearses the identical quartet noted above, namely Rabbi Eliezer, Rabbi Joshua, Rabbi Ishmael, and Rabbi Judah ben Beteirah. Then, it adduces a wholly different *baraita* containing additional arguments to defeat the interpretation that Shavuot always falls on Sunday. *Id.* 65b–66a. Finally, Rava pronounces that many of the foregoing positions can be refuted, so that only a few withstand challenge. *Id.* 66a. In particular, reverting to the first set, only the logic of Rabbi Ishmael and Rabbi Judah ben Beteirah holds up.

17 Maharsha explicitly makes this point in *Ḥidushei Agadot* to *Menaḥot* 65a (ascribing authorship to Moses labeled "close to *minut*").

18 A potential explanation may emerge from "the most extreme expression of disapproval of the Sadducees found in any ancient rabbinic text," namely a reference to "two disciples of the sages from among the disciples of Moses … to exclude Sadducees." Kalmin, *supra* n. 6, at 150–51, citing T.B. Yoma 4a. Stories 1 and 3 may have appreciated that the opponents in these instances ex-

Instead, both *Megilat Ta'anit* and *Bava Batra* discuss at length alternatives to RYBZ's points leading to the same outcome. But the Bavli's more complete discussion is telling—it concludes that only some of the alternatives hold water, leaving the balance to drown. It follows that RYBZ's logic is not airtight enough to end discussion; instead, further analysis is needed. When that analysis unfolds, the victorious viewpoints pointedly do not include RYBZ's. Clearly, then, we are not dealing with obvious truth versus rank idiocy. For that reason, the epithet "Fool!" hardly seems apropos. In turn, the antinomy between "our complete Torah" and "your idle talk" is not as pristine as RYBZ makes it out to be.

B. Composite Message

It is a truism that the victors write history. Our sources accordingly portray consistent defeat of the Sadducees and their allies.[19] The common feature of all the stories is that those groups propound a viewpoint against the mainstream, which they defend based on either the plain language of the Torah or on public policy. The sectarians are unable to offer a cogent response, until one of their number chatters[20] against RYBZ. The latter tosses off a bizarre verse in response, to which the response is incredulity. At that point, RYBZ calls him a fool and then issues what we will henceforward label as our *Dictum*: "The words of our complete Torah shall not be like your idle talk." He follows up by issuing a more pointed proof text that bolsters the Pharisaic position. His defeat of the sectarian position warrants the proclamation of a holiday.

The key components of the Dictum juxtapose "our complete Torah" against "your idle talk." Some take "complete Torah" to signal a composite of both Written Torah and Oral Torah, attributing to RYBZ the sensibility that his more panoramic perspective refutes the narrow fixation of his opponent (who are effectively cast as Karaites *avant la*

---

pressed their fealty to Moses, and therefore did not wish to single them out for criticism on that basis.

19 Charlotte Fonrobert, *When Women Walk in the Way of their Fathers: On Gendering the Rabbinic Claim for Authority*, 10 J. Hist. Sexuality 398 (2001) ("the rabbis depict both Samaritans and Sadducees as consulting with them regarding matters of law in order to bolster their own authority over and against the leaders of these other groups").

20 Various translations into English for מפטפט include *babble* (Kalmin), *mumble and stumble* (Neusner), and *taunt* (ArtScroll).

lettre).[21] That reading is pointed for Story 3, in which the Sadducee brought a specific verse for his point of view;[22] yet the other two stories lack that feature, so it is less than a full explanation. Turning to "your idle talk," the phrase arises against the previous usage of "chatter" but actually brings a more neutral word that means "talk." We will mine that aspect presently.

In any event, the bottom line is that RYBZ scolded his adversaries.[23] Far from treating them as equals or even trying to teach his inferiors, he altogether rejected any value from engaging with them, holding them up instead for ridicule.[24] A modern paraphrase of the Dictum could be, "You are so worthless that I won't even dignify your 'points' by engaging them."

C. The Wages of Lightning Fast Analysis

Before considering later reception of the Dictum, the final word about our three stories is to test how well RYBZ's criticism has withstood the test of time. In each of the stories, he is quick to dismiss his adversaries. So entrenched is he in the wisdom of his own approach that he cavalierly rejects any questioning as the product of "Fools." In that light, it is fascinating to reflect that Jewish tradition actually rejects his reasoning (albeit not his bottom-line ruling) in each and every instance.

Story 1. RYBZ explicitly marshaled two verses for his interpretation, Ex. 13:27 and Lev. 23:18. Yet, unlike his viewpoint, later sages explain the Mishnah(which justifies the priest not eating the flour brought along with a meat sacrifice) on a wholly different basis, with no reference to any verses.[25]

Story 2. The bulk of this story concerns RYBZ's explication of Anah's genealogy, with the aim of demonstrating that he was the prod-

---

21 Jacob Neusner, *A Life of Yohanan Ben Zakkai* 81 (1970); Kalmin, *supra* n.6, at 166–67 (attributing stance to Josephus' influence on Babylonian rabbis); Zeitlin, *supra* n. 3, at 300.

22 In Story 3, the Sadducee's viewpoint represents his understanding of the *peshat* of "And ye shall count unto you from the morrow after the Sabbath, from the day that ye brought the sheaf of the wave offering; seven Sabbaths shall be complete."

23 Noam, *supra* n. 9, at 176 (on Story 3).

24 *Id.* at 254 (on Story 1).

25 The subject matter here is M. Menaḥot 6:2 which, in typical mishnaic fashion, simply sets forth the rule without any explanation. But the standard commentator proceeds on the basis of a different scriptural justification: Num. 15 makes no mention of consumption by the *kohanim*, so this sacrifice is completely burnt upon the altar. Yad Avraham *ad loc.*

uct of incest. Yet the version in the Gemara posits the reasonable possibility that there may have been two people named Anah; although it ultimately rejects that point of view, the very fact that it is entertained dispels the notion that the Sadducee was an out-and-out fool for questioning the matter. Even more pointedly, Ramban accepts the proposition that there was another Anah![26] Accordingly, RYBZ's contempt for his adversary seems out of place.[27]

Story 3. This case contains the most extreme rejection of the view put forth by the erstwhile sage. Rabbi Eliezer posits that the proof offered by RYBZ is not needed. More remarkably still, the Gemara continues by citing a different *baraita* to defeat the Boethusian's interpretation that Shavuot always falls on Sunday, and then ends with Rava refuting much of what has gone before such that RYBZ's proof no longer remains operative. So, the full text again undermines the latter's arrogance towards his foes.

As if that set-back were not enough, consider RYBZ's final explanation—that the two verses of Lev. 23:15–16 exist to distinguish between Passovers that fall on Saturday and those that fall on other days. In contrast to that reading, the normative explanation for those two verses is that one commands the counting of days and the other mandates the separate counting of weeks.[28] So almost no aspect of the venerable sage's reasoning ultimately survives unscathed.

In sum, our stories show three instances of RYBZ's contempt and arrogance for any who would dare question his explanations[29]—but far from supporting those explanations, the subsequent rabbinic tradition[30]

---

26 Ramban on Gen. 36:24, makes the salient point that the text identifies him as the Anah who was tending to the donkeys in order to distinguish him from his uncle of the same name.

27 The Sadducee proposal itself has been described as "mature, moderate and equitable" Reuven Yaron, *Sadducees and Pharisees: Two Controversies*, 33 Isr. L. Rev. 743, 751 (1999).

28 T.B. *Ḥagiga* 17b.

29 That arrogance stands in contrast with RYBZ's depiction in Mishnah *Shabbat* 16:7 and 22:4, both of which times he limits his conclusion to the statement "I suspect that he is liable for a sin offering." That soft-pedaling "undermines the picture of R. Yohanan as an authoritative rabbi." Moshe Simon-Shoshan, *Stories of the Law: Narrative Discourse and the Construction of Authority in the Mishnah* 116 (Oxford 2012)

30 It should be recalled that RYBZ lived much earlier than the sages of the Talmud. His method of expositing scripture may have worked for people of his own generation, but was removed from later sensibilities. Neusner, *supra* n. 21, at 124.

has rejected his reasoning on each occasion.[31] When one adds that the contrary position in each instance was itself defensible, his extreme reaction stands out as difficult to justify. On the one hand, RYBZ is a foundational figure, so his viewpoint in the Dictum deserves deference. On the other hand, however, we have just seen problems with each enunciation of the Dictum. Future figures could therefore take it either at face value or with more nuance—which is exactly what later transpired, as we shall now see.

II. In the Hands of Later Generations

A. Holding Hard and Fast

Over the ensuing millennia, commentators have invoked our Dictum in the manner of RYBZ to deride the approach of their opponents,[32] sometimes in very harsh terms.

In a lengthy polemic against a Jerusalem butcher of the seventeenth century who relied on surgical manuals to make determinations about disqualifying blemishes, Rabbi Ḥayyim Benveniste, a Turkish rabbi who died in 1673, used our Dictum to heap scorn upon his adversaries. He then concluded by asking rhetorically, "Is there no G-d in Israel to expound Torah from sages and books, that he must go after delusions and nothingness!?"[33]

Another example is Solomon ben Abraham Adret (1235–1310). Rashba addressed the case of a father in Perpignan who claimed the right to inherit his deceased daughter's dowry.[34] The father claimed that he had priority over his late daughter's husband, citing two sources of entitlement under Jewish law:[35]

1) Custom—"everyone knows" that the Jews in that city "follow Gentile law," and since that is the local practice, everyone marrying

---

31 This situation reflects the inverse of "later Babylonian authorities eschew[ing] the radical midrashic techniques of past rabbis, even as they praised their interpretive pyrotechnics." Christine Hayes, *Rabbinic Contestations of Authority*, 28 Cardozo L. Rev. 123, 131 (2006). Although later authorities ruled to the same effect as RYBZ in each instance, they did not celebrate his interpretive pyrotechnics but instead grounded their rulings in different midrashic techniques.

32 Responsa of Maharit, part 2, *Yoreh De'ah* 9.

33 *Knesset Gedolah Hagha'ot Tur, Yoreh De'ah* 39.

34 Rashba responsum 6:254. See Ron S. Kleinman, *To what Extent Should Adjudication Be According to Civil Law?*, 37 Techumin 388 (2017) (Hebrew).

35 The case was actually brought in secular court, but the father wished to vindicate his rights under *halakhah* as well. A Beit Din can apply secular law and a secular court can apply Jewish law, under appropriate circumstances.

there is aware of this fact, thus in advance agreeing to Gentile law, and it is deemed as if he had stipulated so explicitly; and 2) this law was legislated by the king and "the law of the State is law."[36]

Those two categories correspond to two bases for bringing secular law into halakhic decision-making: *minhag ha-medinah* and *dina d-malkhuta dina.* It is instructive to review the great Spanish rabbi's response to each argument.

In terms of the argument rooted in *local custom*, Rashba rejects the father's claim that the pious residents of Perpignan, that "place of Torah and great wisdom"[37] would have agreed to adopt secular law, a practice "which our complete Torah has forbidden."[38] The upshot is that a recognized Torah giant has invoked our phrase for the purpose of rejecting the importation of general secular law as a governing *minhag* to which *halakhah* should yield.[39]

What about the other argument that the father advanced in Perpignan, rooted in *governing secular law*? On that score, Rashba was even more harsh: "*By saying so, you have abolished* the inheritance of the eldest son… and completely *uprooted all the laws of our complete Torah*."[40] He embroidered on that sentiment even further, "What is the purpose of all the holy books composed by Rabbi [Yehudah ha-Nasi if instead] they teach their children the laws of non-Jews… Heaven forbid. This cannot be allowed in Israel, lest the Torah wrap itself in the sackcloth of mourning."[41]

In sum, Rashba's deployment of the Dictum is fully congruent with RYBZ. The great Sephardic sage relied on elements of the Dictum from over a millennium earlier to deride any value at all to secular law, erecting a high barrier around Torah.

---

36 Ron S. Kleinman, *Civil Law as Custom: Jewish Law and Secular Law—Do They Diverge or Converge?*, Rev. Rabbinic Judaism 11, 19 (2011).

37 Given its roots in Provence, Perpignan was distinct from such northern French locales as Troyes, home to Rashi.

38 Kleinman, *supra* n. 36, at 20. Kleinman posits the further nuance that the problem in that particular case was that the intent was to renounce Jewish law—as noted above, the father filed the case before a civil court, albeit he asked that body to apply Jewish law. *Id.*

39 Not only is Rashba a well-respected halakhist on whom to place reliance, but this particular responsum is cited by Joseph Karo and many other decisors. *Id.* at 20.

40 *Id.* at 31 (emphases original).

41 *Id.* On Rashba's typology of heresy, see Adiel Schremer, *Brothers Estranged: Heresy, Christianity, and Jewish Identity in Late Antiquity* 25 (Oxford 2010).

B. Playing Fast and Loose

As reasonable as is the foregoing, some sages have applied the Dictum in the opposite sense. We thereupon enter into the realm of paradox.

1. Early Exemplars

Moses Maimonides quoted our Dictum in his *Guide to the Perplexed.* The particular invocation arises to justify the invocation of the authority of the Torah, rather than pure philosophic reasoning. As he reasoned there, if invoking the Sabians is good enough for Aristotle, then he has every right to invoke our complete Torah.[42]

Moses Sofer did the same many centuries later. The question arose whether Gentile contractors building a synagogue could continue their labors on the Sabbath—after all, it is not as if Jews would act as the construction workers, and the congregation did not yet occupy the building. Rabbi Mordechai Breisch (died 1976) explained that Gentiles do not labor on their own holy day, as that would be a desecration in their eyes.[43] He then proceeded to quote Ḥatam Sofer[44] asking, "Is there a greater desecration of G-d's name than this [Jews not honoring their own holy day by allowing Gentile contractors to build on it]? Woe to that embarrassment and shame; 'our complete Torah shall not' etc." At the end of the day, the ruling was that, even though *halakhah* allows a leniency, we dare not utilize it and thereby allow another nation to become more holy than we.

We have now relocated to an entirely new realm. Rather than dealing with worthless Sadducees, the point of comparison is pious Christians. They observe a Sabbath (albeit Sunday rather than Saturday), so the obligation falls on us to be even more scrupulous, lest we appear impious in comparison. What remains constant is that Torah represents the Best. But the comparison is no longer with the Worst—instead, it is with the Very Good. Matters have changed significantly over the course of the many centuries since RYBZ first formulated the Dictum.

2. Nathanson

Matters get even more extreme when we progress some decades forward from Ḥatam Sofer. Joseph Saul Nathanson, born in 1810, was elected in

---

42 *Guide to the Perplexed* part 2, chap. 23.

43 *Shu"t Ḥelkat Ya'akov, Ibn Ha-Ezer* 14.

44 In context, Sofer was commenting on *Magen Avraham*, a work by Avraham Gumbiner of Poland (d. 1682).

1857 to serve as rabbi for the chief town in his native Galicia. The modern Ukrainian city of Lviv is far removed from the center of world culture.[45] But, in 1860, the town known by its German name Lemberg could claim to be a metropolis in good standing located at the cradle of civilization[46]—the first city in Europe, for example, to feature street lights.[47] Its Jewish residents (almost a third of the population) considered it the "New Jerusalem,"[48] one of the "mother cities" of Judaism,[49] in competition with Prague or even Paris.[50]

Nathanson officiated in Lemberg until his death in 1875. By then, he had secured recognition as one of the most famous Torah scholars of the nineteenth century, "the outstanding *posek* and writer of responsa of his generation."[51] In fact, he is known by the name of his *magnum opus* in six volumes of *teshuvot*, the *Sho'el u-Meshiv*, namely *Questioner and Respondent.*

But he also has another moniker. Nathanson was so prolific in issuing *haskamot* (book approbations or commendations) that Solomon Buber said of him that "without exaggeration there are extant 300 commendations by him,"[52] which translates to "more approbations by him on rabbinic books than by any other rabbi."[53] Such profusion earned Nathanson the sobriquet *Sar ha-Maskim*,[54] *i.e.* "Chief Approver."

My own field is the law of copyright, so I first delved into the matter of approbations when collaborating with my friend and UCLA Law School colleague Neil Netanel to author a book about Jewish copyright responsa.[55] After writing up the divergent copyright approaches in the

---

45 Michael Stanislawski, *A Murder In Lemberg* 22 (Princeton 2007).

46 Galicia was "the demographic centre for Austrian Jewry throughout the nineteenth century." Robert S. Wistrick, *The Jews of Vienna in the Age of Franz Joseph* 41 (2006).

47 http://en.wikipedia.org/wiki/Lviv (visited June 11, 2012).

48 Jacob Weiss, *The Lemberg Mosaic* 7, 9 (2010).

49 Israel Bartal & Antony Polonsky, "Introduction," in *Polin: Studies in Polish Jewry, Volume 12 Focusing on Galicia* 3, 8 (Israel Bartal & Antony Polonsky, eds. 1999).

50 Stanislawski, *supra* n. 45, at 22; Weiss, *supra* n. 48, at 7, 9.

51 Shillem Warhaftig, "Nathanson, Joseph Saul," 15 *Encyclopedia Judaica* 18, 18 (2007). "Problems reached him from all parts of the world and he corresponded with all the great contemporary scholars." *Id.*

52 Shillem Warhaftig, "Nathanson, Joseph Saul," 12 *Encyclopedia Judaica* 866, 868 (1972).

53 Solomon B. Freehof, *A Treasury of Responsa* 270 (1962).

54 Warhaftig, *supra* n. 52, at 868. That title represents a transposition of the reference to Pharaoh's chief butler, *Sar ha-Mashkim.* Gen. 40:9.

55 After my initial efforts, Prof. Netanel masterfully brought the whole project to fruition. With characteristic grace, he styled the title page: *From Maimonides to*

early nineteenth century between Moses Sofer and Mordechai Banet,[56] I turned to the dispute later in that century between Nathanson and his student, Isaac Judah Schmelkes (1827–1905), known as *Beit Yitzhak*. It was then that I had my first exposure to our Dictum, as part of Nathanson's famous copyright responsum regarding *Ashlei Ravrabi*, a work first published in 1836 [57]

Let us turn to its particulars. In his responsum dated November 25, 1860,[58] Nathanson at the outset expressed himself in opposition to "the incisive rabbi, our teacher, the *Av Beit Din* of Zolkiew,"[59] who had effectively denied copyright protection to the claimant. He continued that the latter's words

> are puzzling because this is certain, that if an author prints a new book and he merits that his words are received all around the world, he obviously has an eternal right [to his work], because in any case if one prints or invents some type of craft, another person is not allowed to do so without his consent. And it is known that Rabbi Abraham Jacob of Harobshob, who invented a machine to do arithmetic, received throughout his life payment from the government in Warsaw; and "our complete Torah shall not be like their idle talk." This is something that common sense rejects, and it is a daily occurrence that one who prints a work, he and those empowered by him retain the rights.

The reversal threatens whiplash! When RYBZ formulated the Dictum that "our complete Torah shall not be like your idle talk," we have seen that its meaning was essentially, "You are so worthless that I won't even dignify your 'points' by engaging them." By contrast, the opening words from Nathanson's *teshuvah* move in the opposite direction. Given the fact that Reb Abraham Jacob[60] received lifetime patent royalties

---

Microsoft: The Jewish Law of Copyright since the Birth of Print, by Neil Weinstock Netanel with contributions by David Nimmer (Oxford 2016).

56 David Nimmer, "In the Shadow of the Emperor: The Ḥatam Sofer's Copyright Rulings," 15 *Torah U-Madda* J. 24 (2010); David Nimmer, "Rabbi Banet's Charming Snake," 8 *Ḥakirah* 69 (2009).

57 Netanel, *supra* n. 55, at 217-21. The work setting forth *Yoreh De'ah* bore the Aramaic title for "great tamarisk trees," a poetic connotation of "the seminal sources of *halakhic* interpretation upon which one should rely." *Id.* at 217.

58 *Sho'el u-Meshiv*, part 1, # 44.

59 The reference is to Rabbi Samuel Valdberg (1829–1907). Netanel, *supra* n. 55, at 217-18.

60 The individual in question was Abraham Jacob Stern (1762–1842). When presented with the machine, Tsar Alexander I decreed that Stern would receive

from the Russian government for his proto-computer, and with a further nod that Austrian law directly grants copyright protection,[61] it would be a dishonor to the Torah, and something that common sense rejects, for the Jewish legal system to be less solicitous. After all, "our complete Torah shall not be less than their idle talk." An expansion of his logic thus runs, "These other legal systems are so worthwhile that I will consider their points as vital stepping stones on which to build my Torah edifice."[62]

In this manner, we see a fascinating progression. Nathanson invoked a familiar phrase to signal his own vector about proper grounds for interpretation. What is novel is the direction in which it pointed: Nathanson totally inverted RYBZ's methodology. Whereas the originator of the saying meant that he cared not a fig to align *halakhah* with norms drawn from outside the tradition, Rabbi Nathanson signals at the outset that he intends to engage in a halakhic journey to vindicate the application of Jewish law with a weather eye on surrounding legal regimes. Indeed, as he continued, "common sense rejects" any other disposition.

It is not only Nathanson who looked at legal frameworks beyond the Jewish realm. Galician Jewry was part and parcel of the German-speaking world[63] so it is not out of character to find a reference to Austrian[64] copyright law.[65] Nathanson's biographer emphasizes that his rul-

---

yearly treasury payments for life. Naḥum Rakover, *Copyright in Jewish Sources* 251 n.6 (Sifri'at Ha-mishpat Ha-'ivry 1991) (Hebrew); Ira Robinson, "Hayim Selig Slonimski and the Diffusion of Science Among Russian Jewry in the Nineteenth Century," in *The Interaction of Scientific and Jewish Cultures in Modern Times* 49, 55 (Yakov Rabkin & Ira Robinson, eds., Mellen 1995).

61 The *teshuvah* notes that, "in our own country," civil law itself forbids republication.

62 In Story 2, the Dictum denoted the utter rejection of giving any consideration to Greek inheritance law. By 1860, the Dictum denoted consideration of Russian and Austrian copyright law, and reaching Torah results accordingly.

63 Robinson, *supra* n. 60, at 58 ("Without German there can be no cultural educated Jew"). It is said that Jewish schoolboys of the 1860s "secretly read Schiller and Lessing hidden inside volumes of the Talmud." Jerzy Holzer, *Enlightenment, Assimilation, and Modern Identity: The Jewish Élite in Galicia*, in Polin, *supra* n. 49.

64 The enactment in question is the Austrian Law for the Protection of Literary and Artistic Property of 1846. Regarding Nathanson's reliance on that law, in the context of its antecedents within Prussian, Russian, and French copyright laws, see Netanel, *supra* n. 55, at 225–26.

65 Decades earlier, a rabbi in Lemberg was caught "reading Montesquieu's *Spirit of the Laws* while still clad in *tallit* and *tefillin*." Stanislawski, *supra* n. 45, at 42.

ings took contemporary circumstances into consideration[66]—such as his most famous responsum validating machine-made matzah[67]—at times evincing surprising flexibility in the process.[68]

We have now seen that RYBZ invoked our Dictum to compare the Best to the Worst, whereas *Sho'el u-Meshiv* quotes the same language to compare the Best to the Very Good. In the former context, *siḥa beteilah* is mere *idle chatter.* In the latter, though, it has become a *vital chat* to allow Torah to extend to the full extent of its destined glory.[69]

Given that disparity from the original meaning, it is not surprising to find Schmelkes not only disagreeing with his teacher's bottom-line result but also citing the exact same Dictum in the course of reaching his own diametrically opposed conclusion.[70] But that usage lays bare the inquiry: Is it really possible for our Dictum to mean the opposite of itself? To answer that question, we need to catalogue the Dictum into its proper channel.

III. Typology of Talmudic Dialogues

A. Excursion into History

Story 2 celebrates a return to Jewish law. It tells the tale of the Hasmoneans chasing out the Greeks and thereupon discarding Hellenistic inheritance law. The sensibility corresponds to both 2 *Maccabees* and Josephus, restoring ancestral Torah law in place of that foreign implant.[71] In the ancient struggle between Athens and Jerusalem,[72] it cele-

---

66 Warhaftig, *supra* n. 51, at 18. Another example was when he validated the death certificate of a Jewish soldier listing his name incorrectly, allowing his widow to remarry, given that rank, branch of service, and other details matched the deceased. Leo Landman, *Jewish Law in the Diaspora: Confrontation and Accommodation* 211 n. 37 (1968).

67 Solomon B. Freehof, *The Responsa Literature* 184–88 (1955).

68 Nathanson once publicly endorsed heterodox candidates, including the preacher of the Lemberg Temple. Rachel Manekin, *Politics, Religion, and National Identity: The Galician Jewish Vote in the 1873 Parliamentary Elections*, in Polin, *supra* n. 49.

69 Cf. Tamar Ross *Expanding the Palace of Torah* (Brandeis 2004).

70 "And regarding what the *Sho'el u-Meshiv* wrote that if one innovates a new craft, then another person is not allowed to do so in the same format without the former's consent, because 'our complete Torah shall not be like their idle chatter,' this is not in accordance with what we learned about the Torah: 'Just as I give it freely, so you shall give it freely.' The Torah is not an axe to cut with." *Shu"t Beit Yitzḥak, Yoreh De'ah*, part 5, # 75 (1899).

71 Brent Nongbri, "The Motivations of the Maccabees and Judean Rhetoric of Ancestral Tradition," 85, 93–94 & n.29, in Carol Bakhos, ed., *Ancient Judaism in Its Hellenistic Context* (Brill 2005).

brates the latter's victory (regardless of its historical verisimilitude)[73] that Greek inheritance law was banished from Israel.[74]

Nonetheless, one aspect of the tale stands out as a glaring anachronism. The Hasmoneans victory occurred around the second century BCE, long before the birth of RYBZ. One need not resort to exotic gymnastics to resolve the discrepancy—it results from the two different versions of the scholion,[75] one of which recounts the Greek judgments abrogated by the Hasmoneans without mentioning names,[76] and the other of which pits RYBZ against the Sadducees without mentioning Gentile law.[77] The two were artificially combined in the Middle Ages and have been printed in that fashion since.[78]

The rabbis of the Talmudic period may have known the contours of laws imposed by the systems of their Greek and Roman rulers, but the point here is not to explicate that facet.[79] For our present concern is not

---

72 In classical times, Greeks did not register the existence of Jews. "Herodotus did not happen to visit Jerusalem. A page of Herodotus would have been sufficient to put a battalion of biblical scholars out of action." Arnaldo Momigliano, *Alien Wisdom* 81–82 (Cambridge 1975).

73 The stories' "highly stylized form, … together with the dubiety of commemorating Yohanan's victories with festival celebrations, casts doubt on the historicity of the account." Neusner, *supra* n. 21, at 81.

74 Even in RYBZ's own sanctuary at Yavneh in the 1st century CE, two documents have been found that "invoke 'Greek law' or 'custom' to guarantee maintenance of wife and children," indicating that the victory was not as great as advertised. Lapin, *supra* n. 3, at 50.

75 Prof. Noam identifies them from their manuscript locations, one at Parma and the other at Oxford. Noam, *supra* n. 2, at 341, 351. Others maintain, to the contrary, "that in fact we have a sequential reworking on the Babylonian Talmud," thereby "clearly dating the commentary later than Noam's conclusions." Isaiah Gafni, "The Modern Study of Rabbinics and Historical Questions: The Tale of the Text," in *The New Testament and Rabbinic Literature* 43, 56 (Reimund Bieringer et al., eds., Brill 2010).

76 Noam, *supra* n. 2, at 351 (quoting Oxford version).

77 *Id.* (quoting Parma version). Note that the Parma version focuses on the Sadducees and never mentions Boethusians, whereas the Oxford version mentions them twice. *Id.* at 352.

78 *Id.* at 355. The conflation may trace back as early as the ninth century. *Id.* at 355–56. It led to a printed version in Mantua in 1514. *Id.* at 359.

79 "Rabbinic sources show familiarity with the terminology and practices of Roman legal institutions consistent with the rabbis' status as elite members of a provincial minority. Christine Hayes, *What's Divine About Divine Law?* 325, 306 n. 25 (Princeton 2015).

with the Dictum's historicity, but rather with its subsequent reception[80] (which is why the combined text extant since medieval times is more important than each individual scholion in isolation). As we have just seen, later rabbis have trodden two very different paths in construing the Dictum. To explain the discrepancy, it is helpful to sketch the types of categories into which the Dictum may be slotted.

B. A Bakhtinian Prism

1. Hail Mikhail

The Russian literary theorist Mikhail Bakhtin (1895–1975) bequeathed valuable insights regarding "dialogic" texts, namely "the creation within a single text of a plurality of independent and unmerged voices or consciousnesses, a genuine polyphony of fully valid voices."[81] Given that the Talmud is replete with dialogue, a rich literature reads its discourse through a Bakhtinian filter.[82] The dialogic nature of our own Three Stories leads naturally to tapping into that perspective.[83]

---

80 Our search here investigates "Jewish creativity … in a way that purely historicist knowledge about the Jewish past could never" reveal. David Stern, *Midrash and Theory: Ancient Jewish Exegesis and Contemporary Literary Studies* 10 (Northwestern 1996).

81 Christine E. Hayes, "Displaced Self-Perceptions: The Deployment of Mînîm and Romans in *B. Sanhedrin* 90b–91a," in *Religious and Ethnic Communities in Later Roman Palestine* 263 (Hayim Lapin, ed., Maryland 1998).

82 One example is Wimpfheimer, *supra* n. 1, which looks to Bakhtin along with another "scholarly father," *id.* at 13, namely Robert Cover. (Let me add that Cover was my professor at Yale Law School.) Another is Daniel Boyarin, *Socrates and the Fat Rabbis* 14 (Chicago 2009), which deploys Bakhtin to view the Talmud through a seriocomical prism. Boyarin credits David Stern (formerly my next-door neighbor in Los Angeles) as the first modern critic to hoist the Bakhtinian banner. *Id.* at 146.

83 In traditional terms, the stories form part of *aggada* rather than *halakha.* One legacy of the two books just cited is to abandon that distinction. *Id.* at 20, 28, 370 (citing Wimfpheimer). That trope has a venerable history: "An old *halachah*, abrogated, retires into the crucible of the heart, and is transmuted into an *aggadah*, [which later] again condenses into *Halachah*, but in an improved or wholly new form." Haim Nahman Bialik, *Revealment And Concealment : Five Essays* 49 (Jerusalem 2000).

2. Socratic Torah

Consider a famous midrash about the red heifer:[84]

> A certain *goy* questioned RYBZ saying, "These things that you do appear to be a kind of sorcery. You bring a heifer, slaughter it, burn it, grind it, take its ashes; [when] one of you is defiled by contact with a corpse, you sprinkle two or three drops on him and tell him, you are pure!'"
> Rabban Yoḥanan said, "Has the spirit of madness ever possessed you?"
> He replied, "No."
> "Have you ever seen a man whom the spirit of madness has possessed?"
> He said, "Yes."
> "And what do you do for such a man?"
> "We bring roots and make smoke under it and we throw water on it and it [the spirit] flees."
> Rabban Yoḥanan then said, "Do your ears not hear what your mouth is saying? So too that spirit is a spirit of impurity as it is written, *'And I will also make the prophets and the unclean spirit vanish from the land.'*" (Zech 13:2.)
> When he [the non-Jew] left, his [Rabban Yoḥanan's] disciples said: "Our master, you put off that non-Jew with a reed, but what answer will you give us?"
> Rabban Yoḥanan answered: "By your lives! The corpse does not defile, and the water does not purify; rather it is a decree of the Holy One, blessed be He. The Holy One, blessed be He, said, I have set it down as a statute, I have decreed a decree and you are not permitted to transgress my decree.' *'This is the statute of the Torah'* (Num. 19:2).[85]

The parallel with our Stories is striking—not only is RYBZ again the protagonist, but he gives an initial answer that fails to hit the nail on the head, and then has harsh words for his interlocutor ("Fools" in our Stories, "not hear[ing] what your mouth is saying" here). Only when challenged does he supply the correct explanation, replete with scriptural citation. All that is missing from our Stories is the familiar trope about the initial answer "putting off [his interlocutors] with a reed."

---

84 It is found, in almost identical form, in two places. See *Numbers Rabbah, Ḥukkat* 19:8; *Pesikta de-Rav Kahana* 4:7.

85 This English translation comes from Hayes, *supra* n. 79, at 277–78.

Jenny Labendz cites the above tale as an example of Socratic Torah in her book thus entitled.[86] Throughout rabbinic literature, rabbis respond to questions put to them by Gentiles. The distinctive feature of Socratic Torah is that "the non-Jew does not merely prompt engagement with the Torah; he participates in it."[87] In a nutshell, the thesis is that, like Plato, rabbis engaged in this sort of dialogue "because they believed that knowledge that comes from life experiences and intuitions even of non-Jews is relevant to Torah, and in fact may itself be a source of rabbinic knowledge."[88] The audience of these tales may justly conclude that listening to Gentiles is one productive vehicle towards ultimate truth.[89]

3. Isocratic Torah

What construct should we place in opposition to Socratic Torah? For this purpose, we can call upon the "true rival of Plato," namely Isocrates.[90] Thus, the converse label "Isocratic Torah" is apropos—plus it has the virtue of being euphonic, given that it happens to append the Hebrew prefix for negation to the very phenomenon whose opposite we wish to invoke.[91]

Nonetheless, it is not contended that the historical Isocrates was actually xenophobic[92]—any more than that the historical Socrates unfailingly dealt with his interlocutors in good faith to learn from their wis-

---

86 Jenny R. Labendz, *Socratic Torah: Non-Jews in Rabbinic Intellectual Culture* 61, 73–74, 104, 128 (Oxford 2013).

87 *Id.* at 107.

88 *Id.* at 75. An obvious distinction, however, is that Socrates always claimed at the end not to know anything, whereas the rabbis drew "advanced clear conclusions by the end of each dialogue of Socratic Torah." *Id.* at 84.

89 *Id.* at 93; "Readers who come to the Talmud after a long acquaintance with Plato cannot fail to be struck by the dialectical character of rabbinic thought." Jacob Howland, *Plato and the Talmud* 11 (Cambridge 2011).

90 Boyarin, *supra* n. 82, at 69, 85.

91 For instance, the negation of *efshar* (possible) in Hebrew is *i-efshar* (impossible). The usage here is whimsical rather than scientific; of course, in Greek itself, the prefix for negation is an alpha rather than the iota with which Isocrates' name begins, as we see in such English terms with Hellenic roots as *symmetric* versus *asymmetric.*

92 In composing *Busiris,* Isocrates admittedly has been charged with "Athenian ethnocentrism." Phiroze Vasunia, *The Gift of the Nile: Hellenizing Egypt from Aeschylus to Alexander* 184 (Berkeley 2001). But the better view acquits him of anything beyond satiric intent. Erich S. Gruen, *Rethinking the Other in Antiquity* 104-05 (Princeton 2011).

dom.[93] The typologies of Socratic Torah and Isocratic Torah simply qualify as useful labels, not as historical markers. Those labels allow us to slot our three stories of "idle chatter" below into their proper disposition.

As we have seen, one typical ingredient of Socratic Torah is putting off one's interlocutors initially with a reed. That crucial element reveals a different dimension to the dialogue, when "the author pulls the camera back, as it were, and we find that the rabbi's students had been present and listening all along."[94] The text thereby reveals two successive modes to the rabbi's discourse: "When speaking to the non-Jews, he bases his explanation of rabbinic law on the imagination and intuition of a non-Jew, but when speaking to his students, he cites a biblical verse. He changes gears in a matter of seconds."[95]

An alternative way to express the point is through Christine Hayes' invocation of "two incommensurate exegetical perspectives."[96] The answer to the outsider can be based on objective features, but when the disciples later invoke the familiar trope of "you have driven away these minim with a mere reed; but what will you answer us?", a different answer is required "for those who accept the hermeneutical assumption of omnisignificance," which is the fundamental basis for traditional rabbinic interpretation.[97]

Isocratic Torah lacks that stereo feature—its repetition is monophonic, with the rabbi never departing from his own self-contained perspective. More broadly still, "Socratic Torah reflects a cosmopolitan rabbinic self-perception as members of a broad intellectual community that includes non-Jews."[98] In this sense, the conflict between the two can be mapped as the difference between parochialism and universalism.[99]

4. Discussions with Sectarians

Apart from rabbis' conversations with Gentiles, the vast bulk of discussion recorded in rabbinic literature is with their fellow Jews. Three types of discussion along those lines are possible—(a) with learned adversaries who are equally devoted to the same underlying framework; (b) with learned adversaries, but who have descended into heresy; and (c) with

---

93 For a comprehensive debunking of Socrates' good faith, see Boyarin, *supra* n. 82.

94 Labendz, *supra* n. 86, at 103.

95 *Id.* at 127.

96 Hayes, *supra* n. 81, at 270 n. 49.

97 *Id.*

98 *Id.* at 213.

99 Labendz, *supra* n. 86, at 119.

the great unwashed. In all three instances, the text portrays the rabbis of the academy basically as living for the sake of sharp argumentation.[100] Discussions "in the Bavli routinely employ words connoting antagonism and physical struggle."[101] In terms of category (a), even discussions between fathers and sons or between teachers and disciples, when matters of Torah are at stake, are presented such that "they become enemies toward each other."[102] Such is the give-and-take of the oral exchanges recorded in the Talmud, where conversation is "unmediated, and often fast-paced, which can prompt tempers to flare and insults or fists to be hurled."[103] And yet, by the end, their friendship is restored.[104]

Turning to category (c), rabbinic tradition is filled with contempt towards the unlearned, to such an extent that "one is permitted to tear apart an *am ha-aretz* as (one would) a fish."[105] Taking the antagonism even further, the same *sugya* that condones fish-gutting continues:

> R. Eleazar said, "It is permitted to stab an *am ha-aretz* on Yom Kippur that falls on the Sabbath." His students said to him, "Master! Say 'to slaughter him.'" He said to them, "Slaughtering requires a blessing, stabbing does not require a blessing."[106]

Although it is admittedly perilous to judge what an ancient culture might have considered humorous,[107] those observations seem so over-the-top as to qualify.[108]

Nonetheless, as in category (a), ultimate reconciliation is also the goal here. The same individual who condoned fish-gutting "objected to the opinion that the *ammei ha-aretz* have no hope of resurrection."[109] The

---

100 For them, "the lack of intense dialectical debate was essentially a fate worse than death." Jeffrey Rubenstein, *The Culture of the Babylonian Talmud* 42–43 (Johns Hopkins 2003).

101 *Id.* at 59.

102 T.B. Kiddushin 30b. See Rubenstein, *supra* n. 100, at 60.

103 *Id.* at 63. This commentator explains the direction, "One may not enter the study-house with weapons," T.B. Sanhedrin 82b, with the explanation, "While metaphoric shields protect against metaphoric warfare, they might not help against real weapons and actual bloodshed." *Id.* at 61.

104 T.B. Kiddushin 30b.

105 Lee I. Levine, *The Rabbinic Class of Roman Palestine* 116 (JTS 1989).

106 Rubenstein, *supra* n. 100, at 129, quoting T.B. *Pesaḥim* 49a–b (omitting brackets from that author's translation).

107 Momigliano, *supra* n. 72, at 99 (lamenting "our deplorable ignorance of Carthaginian and Parthian jokes").

108 Rubenstein, *supra* n.100, at 201 n. 70.

109 *Id.*

end of the *sugya* counsels the *am ha-aretz* to marry off his daughter to a sage, thereby raising his own stature at the same time that he benefits the latter's property interests.[110]

Finally, we come to category (b). Adiel Schremer counsels that the essence of the *minut* that the rabbis opposed inheres in their social separation, rooted in the need for group unity.[111] Emblematic here is the famous episode of the Boethusians[112] suborning perjury over the advent of the new moon, to engender the chaos of calendrical confusion into the Jewish community[113]—a subversive tactic directly connected to their program of establishing Shavuot on Sunday, as discussed in Story 3. Michal Bar-Asher Siegal understands *minut* according to its more traditional interpretation of *heresy*.[114] She adds that they merit the label "fool" not so much as a measure of their intellectual deficiency so much as the peril of their salvific condition.[115]

Under either view, opposition to *minim* constituted an essential feature of protecting the community itself.[116] With them, there could be no compromise, thus warranting full-scale opposition.**[117]** When dealing with sectarians, Isocratic Torah reigns supreme.

---

110 *Id.* at 136.

111 Schremer, *supra* n. 41, at 16, 50. That author avoids the label *heresy*, which connoties a theological quarrel (and hence is more representative of views that Christians held of Jews than vice versa). *Id.* at 144 (debunking "the widespread scholarly assumption that *minut* is the rabbinic equivalent of the Christian 'heresy'").

112 With respect to the Sadducees, by contrast, their status is more contested. One view identifies them as *minim*, others do not. *Id.* at 259 n. 2, 167 n. 58. Various textual variations exist among the terms *minim*, Sadducees, and Pharisees. *Id.* at 173 n. 8, 175 n. 39.

113 T.B. Rosh Hashanah 22b, discussed in Schremer, *supra* n.41, at 79; Raymond Harari, *Rabbinic Perceptions of the Boethusians* 235–53 (UMI Microfilm 1995).

114 She pays her respects to Schremer, but reaches the opposite conclusion. Bar-Asher Siegal, *supra* n. 14, at 10, 14. Note further that "*min* in tannaitic sources refers to a heretical Jew, whereas in Talmudic literature it denotes a non-Jewish heretic." *Id.* at 19.

115 *Id.* at 46. A synonym for "fool" is "empty," which characterizes their understanding of scripture. *Id.* at 43-65 ("A Fool You Call Me?' On Insult and Folly in Late Antiquity"). See n. 145 *infra.*

116 From a psychological perspective, one may cite here the narcissism of small differences. Sigmund Freud, *Civilization, Society and Religion* 131, 305 (Penguin 1991).

117 "Towards gentiles, the rabbis could allow themselves the 'generosity' of practical tolerance, at times even a sense of brotherhood. Toward separatists, who had challenged the identity of the community, they were uncompromisingly hostile." Schremer, *supra* n. 41, at 141.

C. Slotting in Our Stories to that Framework

Based on those observations, our Stories should qualify as paradigmatic Isocratic Torah. Their concern is not universalistic, but instead particular.[118] Far from learning anything from the opponents, they are dismissed as fools. Rather than stereo presentation of initially the putting off the outsiders with a reed and then drawing back the curtain for the insiders, the presentation is monophonic, incessantly driving home the same conclusion: "You are so worthless that I won't even dignify your 'points' by engaging them."

And yet. On the surface, the Stories look like Socratic Torah. A quick perusal of the Red Heifer Midrash, which qualifies as vintage Socratic Torah, reveals a pattern identical to our Stories in numerous particulars—RYBZ as protagonist, who gives an initial answer that fails to hit the nail on the head, proceeding to harsh words for his interlocutor, and replete with the "real story" that concludes with the accurate verse from scripture. It appears to embody everything that Socratic Torah requires except the reed.

Indeed, so closely do our stories adhere to that paradigm that Rashi actually supplies that missing reed in his commentary—he explicates the phrase "our complete Torah" in Story 3 as "putting off a person with a reed or with straw like your idle chatter—for we have a proof but you lack any proof."[119] His grandson uses similar language to explicate that phrase in Story 2.[120] In their minds, no fundamental gap separated our Stories from those other incidents in which famous rabbis, including RYBZ, engaged in dialogue that we now characterize as Socratic.

But they actually are the opposite of Socratic, the hallmark of which is that, after invocation of the reed, the curtain is drawn back to make way for the different answer given to "those who accept the hermeneutical assumption of omnisignificance." In other words, when speaking to Gentiles, there can be no appeal to scripture—so Socratic Torah necessarily invokes logic. But, after retreating back to his own students, RYBZ gives a new answer based on the bedrock principal of scriptural omnisignificance.

---

118 The tension between those poles is perennial. James Loeffler, *Rooted Cosmopolitans* (Yale 2018).

119 Rashi to T.B. Menaḥot 65b (לדחות אדם בקנה ובקש כשיחה בטילה שלכם דלנו יש ראיה ולכם אין ראיה).

120 Rashbam to T.B. *Bava Batra* 115b (איני צריך לדחותך בקש). The doyenne of *Megilat Ta'anit* studies likewise characterizes RYBZ as "putting [them] off with straw by [citing] a verse that does not belong." Noam, *supra* n. 9, at 254.

We can now appreciate why the opposite framework is at work with his dispute with the Sadducees: Given that they accept the written Torah, they are equally committed to omnisignificance. That is why the curtain is not subsequently drawn back. It also accounts for the explanation of "complete Torah" as referring to the combination of Written Torah plus Oral Torah, as the Sadducees reject only the latter.

The above interpretation is how Maharsha explains Story 3—the Sadducees reject the Oral Torah (as opposed to the omnisignificance of the Written Torah).[121] Nonetheless, when we move to Story 2, that same commentator offers a radically different reading, which opens a new dimension here—perhaps the Sadducees accepted the binding nature of the Written Torah yet denied its omnisignificance.

To understand Maharsha's interpretation of Story 2, we must start with the tale told about how King Manasseh started down the path towards consummate evil.[122] He began by questioning whether it was really necessary for Moses to record such "worthless" details as "And the children of Lotan were Hori and Hemam; and Lotan's sister was Timna" (Gen. 36:22). Maharsha attributes to the Sadducees in Story 2 the view that "many words in the Torah are idle chatter that deserve to be burned,"[123] thus aligning their view with Manasseh's regarding such matters as the superfluity of Lotan's genealogy. That stance yields a perfect explanation for why RYBZ initially cited verses about Lotan and his brothers (Gen. 36:20, 36:24)—it sets up his position that this biblical passage is necessary to derive the proper lesson for rules of inheritance even before the giving of the Torah. The Sadducee cannot grasp the point from those bare citations and is incredulous: "With that you rebuff me!?" At that point, he earns the response, "Fool! Our complete Torah shall not be like your idle talk" in order to drive home the point that our complete Torah is perfect (following Ps. 19:8) and contains within it no "idle chatter" along the lines of "your claim that it does contain that idle chatter, G-d forfend."[124]

Given that wicked Manasseh specifically singled out Gen. 36:22 as extraneous, it was highly skillful, on this reading, for RYBZ to rely on Gen. 36:20 and 36:24. Story 2 is thus beautifully structured to exalt exe-

---

121 Maharsha, *Ḥidushei Agadot* to *Menaḥot* 65a (א"ל שוטה ולא תהא תורה שלימה שלנו עם קבלתה כשיחה בטילה שלכם).

122 T.B. Sanhedrin 99b.

123 Maharsha, *Ḥidushei Agadot* to *Bava Batra* 115b.

124 שאנו אומרים שהתורה שלמה תמימה ואין בה שיחה לבטלה כשיחה בטילה שלכם שאתם אומרים שיש בה שיחה בטילה ח"ו.

getical omnisignficance,[125] which we have already identified as the defining characteristic of the rabbinic outlook.[126] On that interpretation, it moves further in alignment with Socratic Torah, albeit still retaining elements of the opposite stance.[127]

The irony is rich. The Stories have the hallmark of particularistic Isocratic Torah. Yet they combine many of the elements of universalistic Socratic Torah. Story 2 commences, "In the days of the Greek kingdom, they used to rule by Gentile law," and uses the Dictum to celebrate the triumph when Gentile law is banished from the realm of Torah. Centuries later, however, Nathanson invokes the Dictum to construe Torah in light of Russian and Austrian law. How can the same phrase mean something and its opposite?

IV. On Autantonyms

A. Getting Nowhere Fast

Words function to convey meaning, which entails, at its most basic level, to exclude the opposite. Thus, the minimal denotation of "hot" tells us that the matter in question is not "cold." Yet some rare words fly free of their semantic straitjacket, conveying a given meaning plus, alternatively, its opposite. Consider the common noun "sanction"—it can mean either *a threatened penalty for disobeying* or alternatively *official permission for an action.* Those two meanings are almost directly opposed. To take another example, the adjective *fast* means *moving at high speed,* as in "a fast car." Yet an additional meaning is *firmly fixed or attached,* as in "being fast

125 Regardless of which of Maharsha's interpretations applies, both fall within the paradigm of calling the opponents a Fool as a measure of "fierce scriptural arguments in rabbinic literature." Bar-Asher Siegal, *supra* n. 14, at 61. It should be added that the epithet represents a rare slur in rabbinic literature used most notably "against specific groups, such as the Sadducees." *Id.* at 60.

126 "The Rabbis always undertake their study of the Bible with the assumption that every word in Scripture is both necessary and significant." Stern, *supra* n. 80, at 18. The technique extends even to every letter (sometimes all the way to every scribal flourish or enclitic). *Id.* at 29, 60.

127 It qualifies as Socratic Torah insofar as it ends on a theme of omnisignficance, but not in the respect that there is first one answer to outsiders and then a true answer to insiders. Instead, on this interpretation, RYBZ first articulated a "teaser" with Gen. 36:20 and 36:24. There is no curtain raised at the end for the disciples to revel in the common assumption of omnisignficance, but instead an ongoing debate throughout with the *minim* who consistently deny that proposition.

asleep." So the same word means *moving* or else *not moving*, depending on the context.[128]

These Janus-words are variously called *contranyms* or *autantonyms*.[129] Sigmund Freud, in a 1910 article, called them *Urworte* (primal words),[130] adducing the English word *cleave* as a prime example.[131] Though his article does not elaborate usages, the King James Version aptly bears him out as to that English-language usage: In the verse, "If I forget thee, O Jerusalem, … let my tongue *cleave* to the roof of my mouth" [Ps. 137:5–6], the word means "stick together," whereas in the verse, "And every beast that parteth the hoof, and *cleaveth* the cleft into two claws, and cheweth the cud among the beasts, that ye shall eat" [Deut. 14:6], it means "split apart."

In a previous article, I have exposited the fundamental term on which copyright law is premised as an example of this phenomenon[132]—the law protects only *original* works of authorship,[133] but what does that word mean? In context, it refers to something *new*—even though the law equally recognizes "original" in other contexts as something *old*: A scholar of constitutional law who composes an article today has created *original* expression (circa 2020)—concerning the subject matter of the Founders' *original* intent (circa 1789).[134] The same term in Hebrew (*meqori*) evinces an identical fluctuation.[135] Failure to appreciate the dif-

---

128 The Federal Trade Commission once defined the word "fast" synonymously with "fade-proof." 16 C.F.R. § 171.4 (1973). By contrast, current Coast Guard regulations detail the requirements for "a fast rescue boat." 46 C.F.R. § 160.156-7 (2018). The latter *fast* requires quick movement, the former none at all.

129 Even more ponderous terminology lurks here. Barbara Lewandowska-Tomaszczyk, "Dynamic Perspective on Antonymous Polysemy," in *Making Meaningful Choices in English* (Rainer Schulze, ed., Gunter Narr 1998) (examples from *handicap* to *weather*).

130 *The Antithetical Meaning of Primal Words*, Collected Papers vol. 4, 181–191 (translated by M.N. Searl 1925). His treatment ends with what we now call "Freudian slips": It is "the original antithetical meaning of words" that occasions people inadvertently blurting out the opposite of what they intend. *Id.* at 161 n. 3.

131 *Id.* at 159. Most of Freud's article concerns words in ancient Egyptian, but there is a generous mixture of German and Latin in the presentation. My thanks to David Stern for the Freud reference.

132 David Nimmer, *Copyright in the Dead Sea Scrolls*, 38 Hous. L. Rev. 1, 196 (2001).

133 17 U.S.C. § 102(a).

134 The same article investigates other building blocks of copyright to similar effect, showing the instability of numerous terms. Nimmer, *supra* n.132, at 193-96.

135 Israel's Copyright Act, חוק זכות יוצרים, התשס"ח, 2007 § 4 accords protection to expression that is יצירה מקורית, a reference denoting something new. Equally

ference led the Supreme Court of Israel into error in a famous copyright case decided in 2000.[136] Thus is Janus a constant, albeit unremarked, presence in our lives.

With that terminology under our belt, we are now ready to categorize the Talmudic phrase in question.

B. Idle Chatter as Its Own Opposite

"Our complete Torah shall not be like your idle talk" rests on two contrasting foundations. The first one is unambiguous. תורה שלמה reflects the high end of praise. By contrast, שיחה בטלה itself exhibits Janus-like qualities; in fact, that status pertains to both component words—it may be idle chatter or something near the other end of the spectrum.

Let us start with the first word of the phrase. At its most basic level, *siḥa* represents simply *talk*; the content of that talk can range from supernal to infernal. At the latter end, *Ethics of the Fathers* uses that noun as part of its direction, "Engage not in conversation with a woman."[137] The word is interpreted in that context to refer to *flirtation*.[138]

Nonetheless, the same word can carry the opposite valence. When Isaac meets Rebecca, the text describes him as לָשׂוּחַ בַּשָּׂדֶה—in other words, he engages in the verb form of that same word. (Gen. 24:63) What does the word mean? Although it is a hapax legomenon,[139] Rashi interprets it to mean *prayer*.[140] His interpretation faithfully reflects the tradition, which hangs Isaac's institution of the afternoon service on that precise phrase.[141] In sum, then, *siḥa* can range widely.

---

common usage refers to ancient writings as מקורות, transvaluing the same word into something old. Rakover, *supra* n. 60 (*Zekhut Ha-yotsrim Bemeqorot Ha-yehudi'im*).

136 Nimmer, *supra* n.132, 116–32, 193–96, citing *Eisenman v. Qimron*, C.A. 2790/93, 2811/93, 54(3) P.D. 817.

137 Mishnah *Avot* 1:5.

138 Rambam, ad loc: וידוע כי השיחה עם הנשים על הרוב אמנם היא בעניני הביאה. Another commentator interprets the unadorned word *siḥa* here to refer to *siḥa beteilah*. Meiri, *ad loc*. Admittedly, the end of the same Mishnah indicates that this conversation leads to neglect of Torah studies (*uvotel midivrei Torah*).

139 A modern translator guesses at the word's intent, as "no one is sure what it really means." Robert Alter, *The Hebrew Bible* (Norton 2019), comment to Gen. 24:63.

140 Rashi, ad loc., citing Psalms 102:1

141 The Talmud could not be more definitive identifying the mysterious verb *la'suaḥ* as deriving from our word *siḥa*: יצחק תקן תפלת מנחה - שנאמר ויצא יצחק לשוח בשדה לפנות ערב, ואין שיחה אלא תפלה T.B. *Berakhot* 26b.

Turning to *beteilah*, that adjective is one of *negation*. A *batlan* who does not engage in business affairs can justly be labeled *idle*.[142] Yet there is another meaning for that same term: one who refrains from commerce in order study Torah full time.[143] The meaning of *batlan* can therefore toggle[144] from *worthless bum* to *dedicated scholar*.[145] We thus meet Janus face-to-face (as it were) once again.[146]

In sum, *Torah shelaimah* always qualifies as the Best; *siḥa beteilah* may fall at the opposite end of the spectrum, namely the Worst; but it alternatively could fall simply at a lower level—the Very Good, shall we say. In other words, it could be *idle chatter* of no consequence at all, or it could be part of a *vital chat* by comparison to which *Torah shelaimah* reaches its crowning glory.

142 The Biblical verb itself carries that meaning. Eccl. 12:3 (וּבָטְלוּ הַטֹּחֲנוֹת). The King James Version loses that meaning by rendering it "the grinders cease," but Robert Alter preserves it in his translation: "the maids who grind grow idle."

143 "What city is big? One that has ten *batlanim*; less than that is a village." Mishnah *Megilla* 1:3, In his *Perush la-Mishnah*, Maimonides explains that this category refers to "having ten people in the synagogue who have no work outside the community and reading the Torah and being zealous for the synagogue."

144 See Avivah Gottlieb Zornberg, *The Particulars of Rapture* 113 (Schocken 2001) (noting Targum's use of *batlanim* as translation of term that can convey either *lax* or *medicinal*).

145 An alternative locution lacks that ambiguity—sometimes, the words of *minim* are derided as *davar req*, an "empty word." Bar-Asher Siegal, *supra* n.14, at 51–57. Had that term been used, it would have been much more difficult to interpret our Dictum as a contranym. By contrast, the word *beteilah* "on its own does not necessarily mean 'empty'" and instead depends on context. *Id.* at 58 n. 52.

146 Boyarin demonstrates that the parallel Greek term ἀπϱάγμονα likewise bears both of those conflicting meanings. Literally *a-pragmatic*, it refers to a person who is "useless" by one measure but a "philosopher" (one who does not strive for power, prestige, money) on another. Boyarin, *supra* n. 82, at 67. Avivah Zornberg has pointed me to the further anomaly that, in ancient Greek, "the word for business activity [ασχολειν] was formed by the prefixing of an a-privative to the word for enjoyment of leisure." Kenneth Burke, *Language as Symbolic Action* 471 (Berkeley 1966).

C. Explaining the Dictum's Two-Facedness

So how do these considerations explain our Janus-faced Dictum? The seeds planted above may sprout in several different directions, many of them interleaved. This final section pulls those explanations together.

1. Context

Several aspects of context come to the fore. One concerns the context in which the Stories themselves are set. The others deal with the context in which later rabbis have appropriated the Dictum from those Stories. We consider each in turn.

Fast Company—Let us look at the company our Stories keep. In general, tales throughout the Talmud at times qualify as Socratic Torah, at other times as its opposite. As explicated above, our Stories occupy a middle ground—they have many features characteristic of the universal outlook, but at base they evince a particularistic bent.

It therefore requires careful analysis to slot the Dictum into its proper compartment. But rabbis across the ages who have quoted the Dictum have not undertaken that exercise.

Thinking, Fast and Slow—An Israeli psychologist who won the Nobel prize has captured two modalities of thought: some is deliberate and plodding, the other arrives instantly.[147] A *poseq* writing about copyright protection of a book, inheriting from a predeceased daughter, or the permissibility of Gentiles laboring to build a synagogue on Saturdays requires deliberate concentration on the subject matter at hand—that aspect proceeds slowly. On the other hand, the act of composition requires fluid writing—one cannot devote endless time investigating the roots of each locution used, or the *teshuvah* will never get written.

We can therefore appreciate why sages across the ages have used the same locution, but in opposite senses. It was simply a useful slogan for the moment to express a point of view, not a considered reflection on the etymology of the words that comprise the slogan.

Pulling a Fast One. Or maybe, to the contrary, those using the Dictum as a defense of secular learning were thinking slowly, as they decided deliberately to invoke the quoted words "against the grain." Readers of *midrash* can grow dizzy as the Rabbis wrest a Biblical verse out of its setting and adduce it as essentially the opposite of its original meaning. Similarly, in the poetry of medieval Spain, a whole rhetorical strategy of

---

[147] Daniel Kahneman, *Thinking Fast and Slow* (Farrar, Straus & Giroux 2011).

shibutz (interweaving) developed.[148] When Ramban wrote a letter to French rabbis of his era who had pronounced a ban on the *Guide to the Perplexed*, that defense of his illustrious Spanish forebear incorporated many Biblical verses without citation, "pulling a phrase out of context, shockingly so at times."[149] Beyond enhancing (not incidentally) his own erudition, this process of *shibutz* was designed to win over adherents, as they recognized Ramban's densely packed allusions and appreciated new depth to his polemic.[150]

This explanation has some limited purchase here. On the one hand, it establishes a pedigree for the process of meaning-reversal, rendering the whole phenomenon less mysterious. On the other, though, it is doubtful that Nathanson credited readers of his responsum with the same depth that Ramban accorded his own correspondents, the French rabbis. So we have only half of the ingredients present of classical *shibutz*: we may presume that Nathanson knew the original Talmudic context of the Dictum when he invoked it against the grain—but not that he would thereby improve his luster with readers who would appreciate the reversal as a sparkling rhetorical device.

2. Narrative

Fast Acting—The most salient aspect of our three Stories is that they are narratives.[151] RYBZ acts as a character in them, as do his adversaries. That status is not inexorable—one could have drafted a legal code containing propositions, such as: "It is forbidden to consult any other legal system when reaching a Torah ruling."[152] Instead, our tradition embod-

---

148 David Stern, "Introduction" in *Rabbinic Fantasies* 26 (David Stern & Mark J. Mirsky, eds. Yale 1990) ("Sometimes, the intent … was to extend the connotation of a scriptural phrase to a new and original point; at other times, it was to shock the reader into seeing the sacred text in a profoundly profane setting"). See generally Raymond P. Scheindlin, *Wine, Women, & Death: Medieval Hebrew Poems on the Good Life* (JPS 1986).

149 Patricia Bizzell, "Shibutz as a Conciliatory Rhetorical Style in Nachmanides' 'Letter to the French Rabbis'," 17 *Advances in the History or Rhetoric*, 109, 123 (2014).

150 *Id.* at 114.

151 Talmudic exchanges with a *min* constitute "fictitious dialogue composed to express rabbinic thought". Bar-Asher Siegal, *supra* n. 14, at 22.

152 One is put in mind of the movement in the United States to ban courts from consulting *Sharia* as a source of law. Eugene Volokh, *Religious Law (Especially Islamic Law) In American Courts*, 66 Okla. L. Rev. 431 (2014).

ies a story with actors from which some readers derive that view—and others its opposite.

"A narrator tells a story because it is interesting, and legal narratives are almost always more interesting for describing protagonists whose actions trump the expectations established by rules of law."[153] It is no great surprise for readers to derive different lessons from the story, depending on their own times.

A Turn Towards the Menippean—In addition, an important register of our Stories is their humorous nature. In *Socrates and the Fat Rabbis*, Daniel Boyarin explicates those parts of the Talmud that paint our rabbinic heroes in Rabelaisian hues, with humor to spare.[154] The three tales about RYBZ are scarcely as over the top as the tales he explicates. Withal, they evidence an admixture of humor with seriousness, which is that book's leitmotif.[155]

The invocation of humor sheds valuable light on our Three Stories. In each instance, RYBZ initially brings forth seemingly irrelevant citations as a strategy to ridicule his opponents.[156] He exhibits what Christine Hayes labels "exegetical exuberance,"[157] which is particularly ironic in that the tradition subsequently rejected his exegesis (even as it accepted his bottom line).

In short, although RYBZ is a revered role model in general,[158] one may view his interchanges with the sectarians as less than his finest hour, punctuated as they were by calling his opponents fools for failing to accept propositions that were themselves wobbly. It is therefore not surprising to find future Nathansons and others who wished to invert the initial sense with which he pronounced the Dictum.

153 Wimpfheimer, *supra* n. 1, at 133.

154 Boyarin, *supra* n. 82, at 28 ("bodily glory and mess").

155 The following is representative: "Menippean satire, also known as spoudogeloion, is a peculiar type of literature produced by and for intellectuals in which their own practices are both mocked and asserted at one and the same time." *Id.* at 26. For more on humor and ridicule as polemical tools used in the rabbinic corpora against heretics, see Bar-Asher Siegal, *supra* n.14, at 189–90.

156 Neusner, *supra* n. 21, at 85.

157 Hayes, *supra* n. 81, at 282. Although the target of the text analyzed in that work consists of heretics, a variant reading is to Sadducees. *Id.* at 264.

158 Gedaliah Alon, *The Jews in Their Land in the Talmudic Age* 86–118 (Gershon Levi, trans. Harvard 1989).

3. Fast Forward

A lot can happen over the course of two thousand years. Things change. New sensibilities emerge. Moving from the time of RYBZ to Nathanson, let us look at significant currents in the Jewish world in the decades before his 1860 *teshuvah.*

As a young lad in Romania, Solomon Schechter learned that a place existed called "America." The cause was not a vibrant geography curriculum in his ḥeder, but instead that he read *Sefer haBrit*, a work that popularized science and other secular subjects on the theory that their understanding was needed for a proper appreciation of Torah.[159] Pinḥas Elijah Horowitz of Lithuania composed the work in 1797, with a Kabbalistic spin across a broad swath of subject matters.[160] From its publication through 1925, the book went through forty printings in Hebrew, Yiddish, and Ladino.[161] Jews throughout Eastern Europe read it, right down to characters in Yiddish novels.[162]

Sefer ha-Brit admonishes its readers, "Go and learn from that good and wise man, Socrates."[163] There follows a paean to copyright protection—Horowitz places a duty on his readers to support the works of authors by going out and buying their books, even if not of interest![164] The milieu in which Nathanson was writing militated in favor of his approach, both favoring works of authors and appreciating secular wisdom while refining Torah.[165]

---

159 Ira Robinson, *Kabbala and Science in Sefer Ha-Berit: A Modernization Strategy for Orthodox Jews*, 9 Modern Judaism 275, 275 (1989).

160 David B. Ruderman, *A Best-Selling Hebrew Book of the Modern Era: The Book of the Covenant of Pinḥas Hurwitz and its Remarkable Legacy* (Washington 2014).

161 *Id.* at 123-29. More recently, a hardcover edition published in Israel runs 779 pages with notes, commentaries, and indices. Rabbi Pinchas Eliyahu Horowitz, *The Complete Book of the Covenant* (Yitzhak Leqes, ed., Hen Le-Dodi 2014) (Hebrew).

162 Isaac Bachevis Singer, *Shosha* 8 (Farrar Straus & Giroux 1978).

163 *Sefer ha-Brit*, part 2, *Divrei Emet* 78a. Socrates "did not wish to flee from the prison and jailor to save himself from death, even though he had the chance afforded by his students who paid a bribe." *Id.*

164 "Don't say, 'Why do I need another book or invention?' That is not only failing to support but is actually causing harm to the author and to the whole world. It causes them monetary harm and to not wish to write anymore." *Id.* at 77b-78a. Hurwitz himself was a victim of copyright infringement in 1800, soon after the initial 1797 publication of *Sefer ha-Brit.* Ruderman, *supra* n. 160, at 7, 33.

165 It is no great leap to associate *Sefer ha-Brit* with Nathanson's composition of his copyright *teshuvah* in 1860—Hurwitz himself originally composed the first part of *Sefer ha-Brit* in Lemberg and a new edition of the work was published there in 1859. *Id.* at 22, 125.

On that note, our investigation concludes. Historians strive to avoid retrojecting modern sensibilities onto ancient texts.[166] Rabbis have no such compunctions. Given their freedom to adjust to their own times, it is almost natural to find Nathanson looking at Austrian copyright law when adjudicating Torah law about copyright protection.[167] Nor should it occasion surprise that, to express himself felicitously, he alighted on a pithy saying from the sources, without being bothered that he was using it in a manner at odds with its origin.

The standard interpretation of the "complete Torah" that RYBZ referenced in the Dictum is that it contains two branches: Written and Oral. The passage of two millennia allows us to reclassify those branches: Socratic Torah and Isocratic Torah. For the particularistic outlook exemplified in the Stories has never ceased—yet, the tradition has also witnessed powerful universalistic expressions throughout the ages. The dichotomy persists through today—one need not search far to locate current books with particularistic tendencies published in the Orthodox world[168] nor to find universalistic admonitions in that same literature.[169]

For that reason, we find one and the same slogan deployed by champions of particularism to support their viewpoint no less than by champions of universalism to support their contrary position. After all, our Torah is complete. Expecting anything less would just be idle chatter. ☙

---

166 Rubenstein, *supra* n. 100, at 198 n. 31.

167 Greater depths lurk here than can be fully explicated in this article. A vast corpus of doctrines exists whereby rabbis consider other legal systems in reaching their Torah rulings; we previously saw references to *minhag ha-medinah* and *dina d'malkhuta dina*. Although Rashba rejected application of those doctrines in the matter he faced in Perpignan, other situations call for different expedients. For a discussion of this aspect of Nathanson's ruling, see generally Netanel, *supra* n. 55.

168 Yitzhak Shapira &Yosef Elitzur, *Torat Ha-Melekh* (Od Yosef Chai 2009). The Israeli police investigated the authors and *haskamah* writers of that book for incitement in endorsing wanton murder of Arabs; but the state ultimately decided not to press charges. Jeremy Sharon, "A–G: 'Torat Ha-Melech' Authors will not be Indicted," *Jerusalem Post* (May 28, 2012).

169 One recent book condemns an ontological view of non-Jews as "tragic and extremely dangerous… the very antithesis of all that Judaism stands for." Nathan Lopes Cardozo, *Jewish Law as Rebellion* 87 (Urim 2018). It concomitantly celebrates "the universalistic mission, as expressed by the prophets…" *Id.* at 111.

The Original Understanding of Sea Sponges in mShabbat 21:3

By: STEVEN H. ADAMS

In popular Mishnaic texts *mShabbat* 21:3 reads "ספוג אם יש לו עור בית אחיזה מקנחין בו ואם לאו אין מקנחין בו וחכמים אומרים בין כך ובין כך ניטל בשבת". The anonymous redactor (*stamma*) of *bShabbat* 143a, followed by medieval halakhic scholars, understood this Mishnah as teaching that squeezing a handleless sponge violates a *melakhah*. However, this interpretation of the Mishnah has many problems. Equipped with the *stamma*'s understanding of the Mishnah, Avraham ben David ("Ravad," 12th century) doubted whether a sponge's handle can in fact prevent the sponge from being squeezed while scrubbing and wiping down a surface, and truly evade transgression of *melakhah*. A widespread medieval Mishnaic explanation, that the *melakhah* transgressed by squeezing a wet sponge is *dash*, is in direct conflict with Talmudic sources which permit squeezing materials if the fluid exudate is not intended for collection (הולך לאיבוד). Furthermore, as many as fifteen textual variants, many of which are contradictory to one another, exist for this clause of the Mishnah, suggesting that the manner in which the Mishnah was interpreted has adapted over time. It will be reasoned that the *stamma* of *bShabbat* 143a erroneously understood *mShabbat* 21:3 as discussing violation of a *melakhah*,[1] while in fact the Mish-

1 That the *stammaic* layer of the Talmud is a late addition which does not always reflect an accurate understanding of earlier teachings is described by David Weiss Halivni:

> I have determined that the majority of the discursive portions of the Talmud, which are overwhelmingly anonymous, ought to be treated as a later commentary, noncontemporaneous with the statements attributed by name to the Sages (Amoraim) of the Talmud. *The fact that this discursive matrix is not contemporaneous with the earlier and more carefully preserved rabbinic statements recorded in the Talmud, but is the product of later generations, entitles us to offer alternatives whenever the given explanation or understanding of an earlier statement seems unsatisfactory (either because it does not fit the words of the earlier statement or because it contradicts a parallel source).* Whereas the attributed opinions were scrupulously distilled into terse, apodictic statements, which were carefully preserved and

Steven (Tzvi) H. Adams is pursuing a medical degree at SUNY Upstate Medical University.

> which were intended to serve as authoritative dicta, the discursive material that now connects these statements was not so distilled, not so carefully preserved, and not intended to serve as authoritative pronouncements. The discursive material contains many suggestions and possibilities out of which legal data may be extracted, but which by themselves were never meant as final rulings or even tenable positions. Indeed, later generations—probably until the time of R. Hai Gaon (10th-11th century) —felt free to add their own comments to the discursive material (and perhaps also to alter or subtract from this material). Maimonides apparently did not regard the discursive turns of the Talmud as the final word in matters of law. In his famous legal code, the *Mishneh Torah*, he often codifies positions contrary to those that seem to prevail in the argumentation of the Gemara, its "give and take," as this discursive material is traditionally called. Such contradiction can be accounted for only if we understand that Maimonides related to the discursive disputations of the Talmud, not as a passive spectator, but as almost an active participant ... Maimonides evidently recognized the anonymous "give and take" of the Gemara as a guide and a commentary to the earlier Ammoraic statements, but he did not interpret this framework… as being itself a closed or final legal code. (italics added for emphasis) (David Weiss Halivni, *Revelation Restored: Divine Writ and Critical Responses* [Boulder: Westview Press, 1997], p. 95, note 1.)

Besides Maimonides, other medieval scholars including R. Tam, shared this dismissive attitude towards the *stamma* (see Adams, "The Development of a Waiting Period Between Meat and Dairy: 9th – 14th Centuries" *Oqimta: Studies in Talmudic and Rabbinic Literature* 4 [2016], pp. 112-114).

This paper aligns well with a premise that even the Talmud (preceding the late *stammaic* additions) could have misunderstood the true meaning of the Mishnah, or often did not strive to present the authentic original meaning of the Mishnah. This approach has been attributed to rabbinic scholars including Eliyahu of Vilna and Menashe of Ilya (see Yaakov Elman, "Progressive Derash and Retrospective Peshat: Nonhalakhic Considerations in Talmud Torah," ed. Shalom Carmy, *Modern Scholarship in the Study of Torah* [Jason Aronson, 1996], pp. 240-250; Yisroel Sklov, *Pe'at ha-shulḥan*, Intro. [Jerusalem: Pardes, 1958], p. 5b column 1: "וגמ' ס"ל כאידך תנא ואליבי' קאמרה הגמ' חסורי מחסרי"). It is further noteworthy that modern scholarship has demonstrated that portions of Rashi's and Ḥananel's commentaries entered standard Talmud editions because later copyists mistook the teachers' words for their version of the text (Saul Lieberman, *Tosefeth rishonim: seder Nashim* vol. 2 [Palestine, 1936], p. 13-15; David Rosenthal, *Sefer hayovel le-rav Mordechai Breuer: asufat ma'amarim be-made'ei ha-Yahadut*, eds. M. Ahrend and M. Bar-Asher [Jerusalem: Akedemon, Hebrew University, 1992], pp. 596-600, notes 29-30).

nah describes sea sponges as they pertain to the laws of *muktzeh*—an interpretation supported by the context of the Mishnah's chapter.[2] Specifically, the Mishnah teaches that without its handle the sea sponge is considered an incomplete tool (*keli*), thereby subject to *muktzeh* restrictions. The comments of the *stamma* were likely a very late stratum added to the Talmud.[3] The Babylonian redactor's error may possibly be attributed to his limited familiarity with the manufacture of sea sponges, an industry historically centered in the Mediterranean Sea. The impact of this *stamma* upon the development of halachic stringencies in the laws of Shabbat will be described.

The *stamma*, Mishnah Shabbat 21:3, reads:

> ספוג אם יש לו [עור] בית אחיזה מקנחין בו ואם לאו אין מקנחין בו וחכמים אומרים בין כך ובין כך ניטל בשבת.
>
> As for a sponge, if it has a [leather] handle, one may wipe [the board] with it; if not, one may not wipe [the board] with it. The Sages maintain in either case it may be handled on Shabbat.[4]

---

2 The term "*muktzeh*" is used here as it was in the Talmudic era: items that may be touched though not moved during Shabbat (see Ephraim Urbach, *ha-Halakha, mekoroteha ve-hitpathutah* [Givatayim, Israel: Yad la-Talmud, 1984], pp. 124-127).

3 It should not be assumed that this piece of *stammaic* commentary was present in the Talmud as early as the sixth century, when the bulk of the Talmudic corpus was assembled. It is well established that much of the anonymous layer throughout the Talmud was added at a much later date. Weiss Halivni postulates that the general editing activity of the *stammaim* continued until the mid-ninth century (Halivni, *The Formation of the Babylonian Talmud*, trans. to English by Jeffrey Rubinstein [Oxford: Oxford University Press, 2013], p. 9), but he believes small insertions may have continued to be added afterwards:

> ...later generations—probably until the time of R. Hai Gaon (10th – 11th century)—felt free to add their own comments to the discursive material (and perhaps also to alter or subtract from this material) (Halivni, *Revelation Restored*, p. 95 n. 1.).

Indeed, Hai's numerous textual amendments to the Talmud (and to its anonymous layer) have been confirmed by recent scholarship (see Uziel Fuchs, "*Haga'otav shel rav Hai gaon ba-Talmud*," *Ta-Shma: mehkarim be-ma`adei ha-yahadut le-zikhro shel Yisrael Ta-Shma*, ed. Avraham Reiner, vol. 2 [Alon Shvut, 2011], pp. 601-626). Hai's editing demonstrates that the Talmudic text was perceived to have some degree of fluidity even in the 11th century (Fuchs, ibid., 626; idem., "*Mekomum shel geonei Bavel be-mesoret ha-nusah shel ha-Talmud ha-Bavli*," [Ph.D. Thesis, Hebrew University of Jerusalem, 2003], p. 66).

4 Translation is adapted from *The Soncino Babylonian Talmud, Book V*, trans. by H. Freedman, reformatted by Reuven Brauner, *Shabbat* 143a (Raa`nana, 2011), p. 45.

The anonymous speaker of the Talmud (*bShabbat* 143a) understood the Mishnah as teaching a law regarding *melakhah*: Unless the sea sponge is fastened to its handle it may not be used to wipe down a surface, lest such usage squeezes the sponge:

> שער של אפונין: מני ר"ש היא דלית ליה מוקצה. אימא סיפא ספוג אם יש לו בית אחיזה מקנחין בו ואם לאו אין מקנחין בו אתאן לר' יהודה דאמר דבר שאין מתכוין אסור בהא אפילו ר"ש מודה דאביי ורבא דאמרי תרוייהו מודה ר"ש בפסיק רישיה ולא ימות.
>
> "Panicles of beans." Who is the authority? [Apparently] R. Shimon, who rejects [the interdict of] *muktzeh*? Then consider the final clause: "As for a sponge, if it has a leathern handle, one may wipe [the board] with it; if not, one may not wipe with it": this agrees with R. Yehudah, who maintains, That which is unintentional is forbidden?—Here even R. Shimon agrees, for Abaye and Raba both maintained: R. Shimon admits in a case of 'cut off his head but let him not die.'[5]

According to the *stamma* the Mishnah can be understood as follows:

> [Regarding the usage of] a sponge [to wipe off the table]; if it has a [leather] handle [so that by handling it *one will not necessarily squeeze the sponge*], one may wipe [the table] with it; if not [and therefore *one would certainly squeeze the sponge*], one may not wipe [the table] with it.

Ravad's Practical Difficulty

Understanding *mShabbat* 21:3 through the lens of the *stamma*, Avraham ben David wondered how the addition of a handle can aid in avoiding compression of the sponge. Whether the force upon the sponge is exerted via one's hand, or via a handle, the sponge will inescapably be squeezed:

> אמר אברהם – הצרפתים מפרשים כן וקשיא לי כי יש לו בית אחיזה מאי הוי, אי אפשר לקנוח בלא סחיטה...[6]
>
> Avraham (Ravad) states: The French sages likewise explained this law like Maimonides, however, I am bothered—if a handle is affixed to the sponge what good is done? It is still impossible to use the sponge without squeezing…

---

5 Translation is adapted from *Soncino*, ibid.

6 *Hasagot ha-Ravad* to Maimonides, *Mishneh Torah*, *Laws of Shabbat* 22:15.

Melakhat Dash

Tosafists and others understood that the *melakhah* proscribed by *mShabbat* 21:3 (through its *stamma bShabbat* 143a commentary) is that of *dash*.[7] By this explanation, even though the soiled table water collected into the pores of the sponge is discarded and ultimately goes to waste (הולך לאיבוד), pressing a sea sponge in the act of wiping down a table surface is forbidden.[8] However, this understanding of the scope of the laws of *dash* is problematic as it contradicts *dash* guidelines described in other Talmudic sources. For example, *bShabbat* 145a states:

> כבשים שסחטן אמר רב לגופן מותר למימיהן פטור אבל אסור.
>
> If one presses out [pickled] preserves,—Rav said: If for their own sake,[9] it is permitted; if for their fluid,[10] he is not culpable, nevertheless it is forbidden.[11]

This teaches that if the squeezed liquid is not for collection *dash* is not violated. Similarly, *bShabbat* 50b discusses which detergents one is not permitted to wash oneself with on Shabbat lest such washing causes one's hair to fall out—triggering a transgression of *melakhat gozez*, shearing. Thereafter, a question is posed whether olives may be crushed on Shabbat:

> בעו מיניה מרב ששת מהו לפצוע זיתים בשבת אמר להו וכי בחול מי התירו קסבר משום הפסד אוכלין.

---

7 See *Sefer ha-terumah, Laws of Shabbat* 244 (Warsaw, 1897), p. 149; Moshe of Coucy, *Sefer mitzvot gadol ha-shalem* vol. 1, negative commandment 65 (Jerusalem: Machon Yerushalayim, 2003), p. 117-118; *Mordekhai bShabbat* 20:428; Asevilli, *Ḥiddushei ha-Ritva, bShabbat* 143a (Jerusalem: Mossad Harav Kook, 2008), p. 934; Aaron of Lunel, *Orḥot Ḥayyim, Laws of Shabbat* 1:23 (Florence, 1750), p. 45b; *Kolbo*, ed. David Avraham, vol. 2, *Laws of Shabbat* 31 (Jerusalem: Feldheim Publishers, 2009), p. 73; *Tur* O.Ḥ. 320: *Tur* includes the sponge law in the rules of *dash* in section 320, not amongst laws of laundering in section 302.

8 Tosafists state so explicitly: "ומורי רבי' מפרש דאיסורא דרבנן מיהא איכא אע"ג דהמש' הולך לאבוד כגון ספוג שאין לו בית אחיזה אין מקנחין בו הקערה מן השמן ומן המאכל", (*Sefer ha-terumah* Laws of Shabbat 244 [Warsaw, 1897], p. 149; other sources below in note 80).

9 I.e., he wishes to eat them, and they bear too much moisture at present.

10 He actually wishes to drink its fluid.

11 Translation and previous two notes are adapted from *Soncino, Shabbat* 145a, p. 51.

R. Sheshet was asked: Is it permissible to bruise olives on the Sabbath? He answered them: Who permitted it then on weekdays? (He holds [that it is forbidden] on account of the destruction of food).[12]

The medieval Talmudic commentaries, geonim and rishonim,[13] explained that the intent of the question posed to R. Sheshet is whether the acidic olive juice can be used for washing the hands (and face), as suggested by the context of the entire Talmudic passage. Yitzchak Alfasi wrote:

> בעו מיניה מרב ששת: מהו לפצוע זיתים בשבת? פירוש, למימשא ביה ידיה. אמר: וכי בחול מי התירו? קסבר משום הפסד אוכלין.
>
> [Talmud:] R. Sheshet was asked: Is it permissible to bruise olives on the Sabbath? [Alfasi interjects:] The meaning is: [Is it permissible to bruise olives] to rinse one's hands? [Talmud:] He answered: Who permitted it then on weekdays? (He holds [that it is forbidden] on account of the destruction of food.)

Neither the questioners nor R. Sheshet saw a problem with squeezing olives, in the context of violating Shabbat laws, other than the possibility that using the juice yield for a face-and-hand scrub might have an inadvertent depilatory effect. Yom Tov Asevilli (Spain, 1260s – 1320s) makes clear why *melakhat dash* was not of concern to the rabbis:

---

12 Translation adapted from *The Soncino Babylonian Talmud, Book II*, trans. by H. Freedman, reformatted by Reuven Brauner, *Shabbat* 50b (Raa`nana, 2011), p. 51.

13 See B. M. Levin, ed., *Otzar ha-geonim Shab., peirushim* 90 (Jerusalem: Hebrew University Press Association, 1930), p. 21, citing Hai and "the geonim"; see ibid. note 8 citing Aaron ha-Levi; Rabbeinu Ḥananel (printed in the margin of standard Talmud editions); Tosafot *bShabbat* 50b s.v. *mahu liftzoa*; Asher b. Yehiel, *Rosh bShabbat* 4:9; Isaac b. Moses of Vienna, *Or zarua'* 1:205 (Jerusalem: Machon Yerushalayim, 2009), p. 180; Nahmanides, *Ḥiddushei ha-Ramban Shabbat, Eiruvin, Megillah*, ed. Hershler, Shabbat 50b (Jerusalem: Machon Ha-Talmud Ha-Yisraeli Ha-Shalem, 1973), pp. 177-178; Shlomo b. Aderet, *Ḥiddushei ha-Rashba* Shabbat, ed. Yair Broner 50b (Jerusalem: Mossad Harav Kook, 2008), p. 248; Nissim of Gerona, *Ḥiddushei ha-Ran Shabbat* 50b (Jerusalem: Mossad Harav Kook, 2008), pp. 246-247; *Piskei ha-Rid u-piskei he-Riaz Brakhot ve-Shabbat, Shabbat* 50b (Jerusalem: Machon HaTalmud HaYisraeli HaShalem, 1992), p. 292; Menachem ha-Meiri, *Beit ha-beḥirah*, ed. Isaak Lange, Shabbat 50b (Jerusalem, 1976), pp. 183-184. Rashi and Yehonatan of Lunel, though, are exceptions (Rashi, *bShabbat* 50b s.v. *liftzoa zeiti*; *Ḥiddushei ha-Ri meLunel, Shabbat* 50b [Jerusalem: Yad Harav Herzog, 2011], p. 301). They understood the Talmud's query as asking whether it is permissible to crush olives against a stone to weaken the olive's bitter taste.

> פר"י ז"ל לפצוע זתים לחוף בהן פניו וידיו קאמר ומשום הסרת שער וכעין סוגיין דלעיל, אבל משום סחיטה ליכא כיון שאינו צריך למימיהן והולך לאיבוד.
> … the crushing of olives was for scrubbing one's face and hands with their juice. [The problem being addressed was the possibility of causing] one's hair to fall out, like the context of the [Talmud's] discussion above. *Melakhat dash* is not pertinent here because one does not need the juice as it goes to waste ….

Asevilli tells us that although the pressed olive juice serves an important function as a toiletry aid, *dash* is avoided because the juice ultimately goes to waste (הולך לאיבוד).[14]

We should recognize that crushing olives (the topic of *bShabbat* 50b) represents the fundamental case of the *melakhah* of squeezing on Shabbat as explained in *bShabbat* 145a,

> אמר רב חייא בר אשי אמר רב דבר תורה אינו חייב אלא על דריסת זיתים וענבים בלבד וכן תני דבי מנשה דבר תורה אינו חייב אלא על דריסת זיתים וענבים בלבד.
> R. Hiyya b. Ashi said in Rav's name: By the words of the Torah one is culpable for the treading out of olives and grapes alone. And the School of Menasheh taught likewise: By the words of the Torah one is culpable for the treading out of olives and grapes alone,[15]

and even so *dash* is not violated if the exudate goes to waste, per *bShabbat* 50b.

---

14 An assumption is made here that Hai, Alfasi, and the other medieval authorities cited in the previous note understood that *melakhat dash* was not a concern for squeezing olives in *bShabbat* 50b for this same reason that Asevilli gives (כיון שאינו צריך למימיהן והולך לאיבוד). Asevilli (on *bShabbat* 50b) merely spelled out a fine detail which was obvious to his medieval predecessors. Shlomo b. Aderet and Meiri specify elsewhere that if the squeezed liquid goes to waste *melakhat dash* cannot apply (*Ḥiddushei ha-Rashba, Shabbat*, ed. Yair Broner 111a [Jerusalem: Mossad Harav Kook, 2008], pp. 405-406; Aderet cited in Vidal of Tolosa, *Maggid Mishnah* on Maimonides, *Mishneh Torah*, *Laws of Shabbat* 9:11; *Beit ha-beḥirah, Beitzah* 30a [Jerusalem, 1969], p. 180). Rashba's words, "וזו אינה ראיה דודאי נהנה הוא במים הנסחטין דצריך לו לקנח ולנקות", (*Ḥiddushei ha-Rashba, Ketubot* 6a [Jerusalem: Mossad Harav Kook, 2010], p. 33), appear to contradict his commentary to *bShabbat* 50b. See also the comments of Tosafot (*bBeitzah* 30a s.v. *zimnin de-matmish*) "אבל התם מיירי ביין דסחיטה שלו אסורה משום דש וא"כ כי נפיל לארעא הולך לאיבוד ולא חיישינן לסחיטה", and "והכא אומר ר"ת דליכא למימר דאסור משום מפרק כיון שהנסחט הולך לאיבוד אע"ג דהוי פסיק רישיה" (*Ketubot* 6a s.v. *hai mesucharayata*).

15 Translation is adapted from *Soncino, Shabbat* 145a, p. 51.

As R. Sheshet was being asked a practical question, clearly such squeezing is allowed, within the parameters of *dash*, even according to rabbinic law.[16]

Tosafot's reading of the *stamma*'s rendering of *mShabbat* 21:3, which would apply *dash* even if the squeezed sponge liquid goes to waste, is contradicted by these cited early Talmudic sources.[17,18,19]

---

16 *bShabbat* 50b's permit to use olive juice in such a manner on Shabbat is found in *Tur* and *Beit Yosef* O.Ḥ. 326:10.

17 Rav (*bShabbat* 145a) and R. Sheshet (*bShabbat* 50b) were 3rd-century Amoraim, while the anonymous redactor of the Talmud (*stamma*) of *bShabbat* 143a may have lived as late as the 11th century (see notes 1 and 3 above).

18 Even if the squeezed sponge liquid aids in cleaning the table surface, it is still considered "going to waste" as is clear from the cited *bShabbat* 50b regarding pressed olive juice, where the acidic juice cleans one's face and hands before going to waste.

19 YomTov Asevilli's unique reading of *mShabbat* 21:3 avoids any contradiction to *bShabbat* 50b or *bShabbat* 145a. Asevilli suggests that the sponge described in *mShabbat* 21:3 was used to soak up spilled wine in order to collect it—it was not going to waste—and therefore it is subject to *melakhat dash* (*Ḥiddushei ha-Ritva bShabbat* 143a [Jerusalem: Mossad Harav Kook, 2008], p. 934). However, Asevilli's reading of the Mishnah is problematic. The previous Mishnah (*mShabbat* 21:2) discusses cleaning up peels and crumbs, and wiping spittle (*lashleshet*) off leather. This context suggests that the sponge of our Mishnah (*mShabbat* 21:3) was similarly used for wiping down a soiled surface. See Homer, *Odyssey* Book 22, lines 450-455 trans. by Samuel Butler (London, 1900), p. 297: "they cleaned all the tables and seats with sponges and water, while Telemachus and the two others shovelled up the blood and dirt from the ground." Furthermore, the meaning of the word קנח (used in *mShabbat* 21:3) is "to wipe off, cleanse" (Jastrow, *A Dictionary of the Targumim, Talmud Babli, Talmud Yerushalmi and Midrashic Literature*, entry, קנח [New York: G.P. Putnam's Sons, 1903], p. 1389). קנח is commonly used to convey meaning of cleaning off a soiled surface. See *mBrachot* 8:3: "מקנה ידיו במפה"; *bḤullin* 105a: "אין קינוח פה אלא בפת"; *bSanhedrin* 94b: "שהיה אוכל ארבעים סאה גוזלות בקינוח סעודה"; *bShabbat* 82a: "מקנה בצרור ואין מקנה בחרס". If wiping for the purpose of soaking up and collecting were the intent of the *mShabbat* 21:3, a different verb such as ספג found in the following Mishnah (*mShabbat* 22:1) would have been used: "חבית שנשברה, מצילין הימנה מזון שלש סעודות. ואומר לאחרים: בואו והצילו לכם, ובלבד שלא יספג". Rashi there (*bShabbat* 143b s.v. *u-bilvad shelo yispog*) comments, "ובלבד שלא יספוג. שלא ישים ספוג במקום היין לחזור ולהטיפו בכלי גזירה שמא יסחוט". (Similarly, see *bZevaḥim* 40b וטבל ולא מספג.) Asevilli stretched the meaning of קנח in *mShabbat* 21:3 in order to reconcile the Mishnah (as understood by the *stamma* in terms of *melakhah*) with the laws of *dash* which do not apply in cases of fluid going to waste (as Asevilli explained in his comments to *bShabbat* 50b and elsewhere).

Melakhat Melabein

Perhaps because of the conflict to *bShabbat* 50b and *bShabbat* 145a posed by Tosafot's *dash* interpretation, Maimonides chose to read *mShabbat* 21:3 and its *stamma* differently.[20] Maimonides teaches the law of the sea sponge amongst the rules of *melabein*, laundering, not *dash*.[21] Including the prohibition against squeezing the sponge under laundering obviates any contradiction from the *stamma* of *bShabbat* 143a to *bShabbat* 50b/145a because the fate of a sponge's exudate is of no significance for the *melakhah* of *melabein*.

Maimonides' opinion, however, is difficult to accept. While wiping down a soiled surface, one's intention is for the sponge to become less clean by absorbing the spills, food particles, and filth from the surface.[22] As the kitchen sponge's function is to absorb dirty fluids,[23] it is difficult to recognize its use as a transgression of the *melakhah* of *melabein*.[24]

Context

The difficulties presented above (Ravad's practical question, and the problems with the explanations of Tosafot and Maimonides) hint that the

---

20 The teaching on *bShabbat* 145a, "כבשים שסחטן אמר רב לגופן מותר", is codified by Maimonides in *Mishneh Torah*, *Laws of Shabbat* 21:13.

21 *Mishneh Torah*, *Laws of Shabbat* 22:15. This is also the understanding of the Mishnah according to the Parma Ms cited in *Midrash Tanḥuma*, ed. Solomon Buber, *Vayetzei* 17 (Vilna: Rom, 1885), p. 155 n. 108.

22 Note that the previous Mishnah (*mShabbat* 21:2) discusses cleaning up peels and crumbs, and wiping spittle (*lashleshet*) off leather. This context suggests that the sponge of our Mishnah (*mShabbat* 21:3) was similarly used for wiping down a soiled surface. קנח (used in *mShabbat* 21:3), which means "to wipe off, cleanse" (Jastrow, *Dictionary*, p. 1389), is commonly used to convey meaning of cleaning off a soiled surface, thereby dirtying the item used for wiping. See examples cited in note 19 above. Maimonides writes (*Mishneh Torah*, *Laws of Shabbat* 22:18), "כר או כסת שהיה עליהן צואה או טנוף מקנחו בסמרטוט", and on the Mishnaic source for this law he comments, "לשלשת, לכלוך וטנוף. מקנחה, מסירה. סמרטוט, בלויי בגד" (*Mishnah im peirush rabbeinu Moshe ben Maimon*, *Moed, Shabbat* 21:2 ed. Yosef Qafih [Jerusalem: Mossad Harav Kook, 1963], p. 85), showing no concern for transgression of *melabein*.

23 This argument is similar to Avraham Gombiner's logic, "ונ"ל דבסמרטוט המיוחד לכך שרי דלא גזרינן שמא יסחוט" (*Magen Avraham* O.Ḥ. 302:27).

24 Compare the position of Rabbeinu Tam, regarding simple clean water, that "לא אמרינן שרייתו זהו כיבוסו היכא שהוא דרך לכלוך" (Tosafot, *bShabbat* 111b s.v. *hai mesuchrayata*; *Tur* O.Ḥ. 302). Certainly soiled liquids on a surface after a meal cannot cause a violation of *melabein*.

sea sponge teaching of *mShabbat* 21:3 formerly had a different meaning than that of *melakhah* attributed to it by the *stamma* of *bShabbat* 143a of a later era.[25,26] The context of the chapter in which this Mishnah appears may provide an important clue as to the original meaning of the sea sponge passage. The 21st chapter of *mShabbat*, with small exception, discusses the laws of *muktzeh*, items that may not be moved on Shabbat.[27] It

---

25 All extant manuscripts, Ms. Vat. Ebr. 108 (square Sephardic script, end of 13th century, early 14th century), Ms. Munich, Cod. hebr. 95 (1342, probably in France), Ms. Nuremberg Fr. 51-68 (France, 14th century), available on *The Friedberg Project for Talmud Bavli Variants* website contain the *stammaic* passage (dates and locations from "The complete manuscripts of the Babylonian Talmud," ed. by Menachem Katz, Asael Shmeltzer, Hillel Gershuni, Sarah Prais, The Friedberg Project for Talmud Bavli Variants [June 2017], pp. 8, 11, 12, https://bavli.genizah.org/Content/pdfFile/Introductions_B/Introductions_Eng/Background%20to%20complete%20mss.pdf). The earliest extant sources in which the *stamma* is found are the commentaries of Ḥananel and Nissim of Kairouan (11th century), albeit in terse form (Nissim, *ha-Mafte'aḥ, Shabbat* 143a ed. Jacob Goldenthal [Wien, 1847], p. 53b; Ḥananel's commentary appears in the margin of standard Talmud editions). (There are limited extant writings of the Babylonian geonim to *bShabbat* 143a, see Levin, *Otzar ha-geonim, Shab.*, p. 89). Nissim's brief comments to our *sugya*, "אתאן לרבי יהודה דאמר דבר שאין מתכוין אסור עיקר דבריו של ר' יהודה במשנה במסכת בכורות (דף לג) ובמס' יום טוב (דף כג) וכבר פירשנו דבריו גם במס' זו בפ' כירה", indicate that the Talmud text in his possession already contained the *stamma*. Most likely, the *stamma* was inserted by Babylonian scholars in generations prior to Nissim and Ḥananel.

26 Our *stamma*'s additions to the Talmud can be detected elsewhere as well: In *bShabbat* 134b we find the *stamma* saying, "התם משום סחיטה", a response only possible if *dash* can apply even in an instance where the squeezed fluid goes to waste. (However, one can argue that the oil used in *bShabbat* 134b is not deemed "going to waste" because it aids in healing the wound under the bandage, and all would agree that rules of *dash* apply. See *Y. Shabbat* 6:5 (37b): "שמן הוא שהוא מרפא").

27 *mShabbat* chapter 21:

משנה א: נוטל אדם את בנו והאבן בידו, וכלכלה והאבן בתוכה. ומטלטלין תרומה טמאה עם הטהורה ועם החולין. רבי יהודה אומר, אף מעלין את המדומע באחד ומאה.

משנה ב: האבן שעל פי החבית, מטה על צדה והיא נופלת. היתה בין החביות, מגביהה ומטה על צדה והיא נופלת. מעות שעל הכר, נוער את הכר והן נופלות. היתה עליו לשלשת, מקנחה בסמרטוט. היתה של עור, נותנין עליה מים עד שתכלה.

משנה ג: בית שמאי אומרים, מגביהין מן השולחן עצמות וקליפין. ובית הלל אומרים, נוטל את הטבלה כולה ומנערה. מעבירין מלפני השולחן פירורין פחות מכזית ושער של אפונין ושער של עדשים, מפני שהוא מאכל בהמה. ספוג, אם יש לו עור בית אחיזה, מקנחין בו, ואם לאו, אין מקנחין בו. (וחכמים אומרים) בין כך ובין כך, ניטל בשבת, ואינו מקבל טומאה.

mShabbat 21:3's unfinished sponge tool *muktzeh* teaching was likely included in chapter 21 rather than chapter 17 (with other specific *muktzeh* laws regarding

is reasonable to say that this item is likewise part of that discussion.[28] The Mishnah's first speaker's (*tanna kamma*) intention was that until a handle is affixed to the sponge it is not considered a functional completed item, *keli,* and is thus *muktzeh*.[29] The Sages dissented, maintaining that the

---

unfinished or incomplete vessels) because 21:3 deals with cleaning tables and dining surfaces ("נוטל את הטבלה כולה ומנערה", "מגביהין מן השולחן עצמות וקליפין").

28 The usage of the verb, מקנחים, the appropriate verb for the action performed with the sponge, merely intended that the sponge is not *muktzeh* and may be used in its normal fashion. This choice of language is like that in *mShabbat* 17:6:

האבן שבקירויה אם ממלאין בה ואינה נופלת ממלאין בה ואם לאו אין ממלאין בה.

> If a stone [is placed] in a gourd shell, and one can draw [water] in it and it [the stone] does not fall out, one may draw [water] in it; if not, one may not draw water in it. (*Soncino*)

The verb ממלאין, "fill," merely teaches that the stone embedded into the gourd-vessel is not *mukzta* and does not relate to a conceivably forbidden *melakhah* being performed.

Another example is from *mShabbat* 20:5, "לא ינענעו בידו", where the Mishnah chooses the appropriate verb for the item discussed rather than using a generic term such as "לא יטלנו בידו".

29 There are historical records of sponges with handles being used in ancient times. Paleopathologist Philippe Charlier writes that "during the Greco-Roman period, a sponge fixed to a stick (tersorium) was used to clean … after defecation…." (Philippe Charlier, et al, "Toilet Hygiene in the Classical Era," *BMJ* [2012]: 345). An early source is from Seneca the Younger (4 BCE – 65) who wrote:

> secessit ad exonerandum corpus — nullum aliud illi dabatur sine custode secretum; ibi lignum id quod ad emundanda obscena adhaerente spongia (*Moral letters to Lucilius [Epistulae morales ad Lucilium] by Seneca*, trans. by Richard Mott Gummere vol. 2, Letter 70, line 20 [A Loeb Classical Library, 1920], p. 66)

Translation:

> he withdrew in order to relieve himself, — the only thing which he was allowed to do in secret and without the presence of a guard. While so engaged, he seized the stick of wood, tipped with a sponge, which was devoted to the vilest uses…
>
> (*Moral letters*, p. 67)

This item, called a xylospongium (= wood-sponge) in Greek, likely functioned as a toilet brush and general-purpose mop as well. In Book XII of *Epigrams* of the Roman poet, Martial (published in Spain, c. 102 CE) is written:

> Lauta tamen cena est: fateor, lautissima, sed cras
> Nil erit, immo hodie, protinus immo nihil,
> Quod sciat infelix damnatae spongia virgae
> Vel quicumque canis iunctaque testa viae
> (Marcus Valerius Martialis, *Epigrammaton libri*, ed. Wilhelm Heraeus, Jacobus Borovskij, Book XII, poem XLVIII, lines 5-8 [Leipzig. 1925/1976])

sponge is considered fully functional prior to the addition of a handle. This is comparable to the law that wood and stones are *muktzeh* until they are fashioned into usable and finished tools.[30] Elsewhere in the Mishnah it is taught that the addition of a handle to an item is a sure way to remove its prior *muktzeh* status.[31] Alternatively, several variants read, "ספוג אם יש

Translation:

> Yet your dinner is a handsome one, I admit, most handsome, but tomorrow nothing of it will remain; nay, this very day, in fact this very moment, there is nothing of it but what a common sponge at the end of a mop-stick, or a famished dog, or any street convenience can take away. (*The Epigrams of Martial*, tr. into Engl. prose [London: Bohn's Libraries, 1860], p. 565)

An inscription on the fresco *Baths of the Seven Sages*, from 2nd-century Ostia Antica, Italy, contains the words, "(u)taris xylosphongio," "use the sponge on wood" (John R. Clarke, *Art in the Lives of Ordinary Romans: Visual Representation and Non-Elite Viewers in Italy, 100 B.C.–A.D. 315* [Berkeley: University of California Press, 2006], p. 171, 311). For further uses of the sponge in ancient times see Roberto Pronzato and Renata Manconi, "Mediterranean commercial sponges: Over 5000 years of natural history and cultural heritage," *Marine Ecology* 29 (2008): pp. 146–150. Some variants of *mShabbat* 21:3 read עור בית אחיזה indicating a leather handle rather than a wooden stick handle.

30 See *mShabbat* 17:6, *bShabbat* 125b; Maimonides, *Mishneh Torah*, *Laws of Shabbat* 25:6.

31 See *mShabbat* 17:8:

> כל כיסויי הכלים שיש להן בית אחיזה ניטלין בשבת א"ר יוסי במה דברים אמורים בכיסויי הקרקעות אבל בכיסויי הכלים בין כך ובין כך ניטלין בשבת.
>
> All lids of utensils which have a handle may be handled on the Sabbath. Said R. Yose, when is that said? In the case of lids of ground [buildings], but the lids of utensils may in any case be handled on the Sabbath. (*Soncino*, p. 84)

Though *mShabbat* 17:8 strongly resembles *mShabbat* 21:3, 17:8 primarily discusses how to resolve a *melakhat boneh* issue, as the *muktzeh* status of lids without handles is due to a possible *boneh* violation (see *bShabbat* 126b and rishonim). However, some understood *mShabbat* 17:8 as discussing *muktzeh* even unrelated to *boneh* (see Moshe Margalit, *Pnei Moshe*, *Y. Shabbat* 6:5 [37b]). According to *Y. Shabbat* 17:8 (84a) the *tanna kamma*'s view applies to all vessel lids, not merely those affixed to the ground—unlike the explanation of Bavli 126b. Also, see Ritva's comment, "בעי ת"ק בית אחיזה להיכירא דלהוי עליו תורת כלי", (*Ḥiddushei ha-Ritva bShabbat* 125a [Jerusalem: Mossad Harav Kook, 2008], p. 815). It should be noted that *mShabbat* 17:8 was included in a chapter teaching laws of *muktzeh*. Likewise, Maimonides and Yaakov ben Asher codified the rulings from *mShabbat* 17:8 in their sections on *muktzeh* (Maimonides, *Mishneh Torah*, *Laws of Shabbat* 25:13; *Tur* O.Ḥ. 308:10). The position of *tanna kamma* of *mShabbat* 21:3 may be similar to other views found in the Talmud which required a change or act performed unto an incompletely processed item in order that it not be *muktzeh*: See *bShabbat* 125b:

"לו עוֹד בית אחיזה מקנחין בו ואם לאו אין מקנחין בו",[32] telling that the Mishnah discusses the case of a sponge whose handle had fallen off. The *tanna kamma* considered the sponge *no longer* a proper tool. The Sages opined that the sponge *remains* fully functional even without its handle.[33]

> פעם אחת הלך רבי למקום אחד ומצא נדבך של אבנים ואמר לתלמידיו צאו וחשבו כדי שנשב עליהן למחר ולא הצריכן רבי למעשה ור' יוחנן אמר הצריכן רבי למעשה מאי אמר להו רבי אמי אמר צאו ולמדום אמר להו רבי אסי אמר צאו ושפשפום.
>
> Rabbi once went to a certain place and found a course of stones, whereupon he said to his disciples, Go out and intend [them,] so that we can sit upon them to-morrow; but Rabbi did not require them [to perform] an act of labor. But R. Johanan said, Rabbi did require them [to perform] an act of labor. What did he say to them? — R. Ammi said: He said to them, Go out and arrange them in order. R. Assi said: He said to them, 'Go out and scrape them' [free of mortar, etc.] (Brauner, *Soncino*, p. 82)

Similarly, *Mordechai* writes that in order to use rocks and wood blocks on Shabbat one must perform an "act of *tikkun*" to them prior to the start of Shabbat: "הרוצה להשתמש באבן או בבקעת בשבת לסגור בהם הדלת או להכות בהם הברזא צריך שיעשה שום מעשה של תיקון מבעוד יום ואם לאו אסור" (*bShabbat* 126b remez 416). On *bShabbat* 50a,

> יוצאין בפקורין ובציפא בזמן שצבען (בשמן) וכרכן במשיחה לא צבען (בשמן) ולא כרכן במשיחה אין יוצאין בהם.
>
> One may go out on Shabbat with combed flax or combed wool when he previously dipped them in oil and tied them with twine. If he did not dip them in oil or tie them with twine, he may not go out with them.

Tosafot (s.v. *aval lo*) comments, "אבל לא צבען בשמן אין יוצאין בהן. לאו דוקא אין יוצאין דאפילו לטלטלם אסור לפי שאינם מוכנים". Wool and flax, which had already reached the stage of combing (comparable to sea sponge which was cleaned but not yet fitted with a handle), needed additional preparation to be permitted to be moved on Shabbat.

32 This version of *mShabbat* 21:3 appears in the Cambridge Ms (*Catalogue of the Hebrew Manuscripts Preserved in the University Library, Cambridge*, Volume 2 [Brockhaus, Univ. Libr., 1876], p. 4), as well as in printed *Mishnayot* and liturgy books (see *Seder tefilot Śifte renanot mi-kol ha-shanah ke-minhag ashkenaz: ... hen bi-leshon ha-kodesh u-vi-leshon Ashkenaz ...* [Petschau, 1769], p. 86a; *Seder Tefilot mi-kol ha-shanah: ke-minhag Pehm Polin u-Mehrin* [Seckel b. Ahron, 1797], p. 107(?); *Mishnayot Seder Mo'ed, Shabbat* 21:3 [Furth: Zirndorfer, 1814], p. 28a.) Codex Kaufmann (MS Kaufmann A 50, fol. 49v) seems to read "עוֹד בית אחיזה" as well (see Figure 1). While late printings containing עוֹד may be attributed to printer's errors, one wonders if the עוֹד became עוֹר in early centuries due to scribal errors. This possibility is strengthened when we consider that early historical descriptions of the sponge tool depict a sponge on a stick, not a sponge affixed to a leather handle (see note 29).

33 Accordingly, the dispute in *mShabbat* 21:3 resembles the discussion regarding broken vessels in *mShabbat* 17:5.

Mishnaic Variants

Authoritative texts of the Mishnah, including Codex Kaufmann, Oxford and Cambridge manuscripts, as well as Alfasi's *Halakhot* and the di Trani family commentaries, indicate that *melakhah* (*dash* or *melabein*) is not the Mishnah's topic. According to these variants, the Mishnah concludes by stating that the Sages disagreed with the *tanna kamma* in regard to the distinction between a sponge with and without a handle and allowed compression (not merely handling) of the sponge regardless: "וחכמים אומרים בין כך ובין כך מקנחים בו", or "וחכמי' אומ' בין כך ובין כך מקנחין בשבת" according to Alfasi, and "וחכמים אומרים בין כך ובין כך מקנחין ניטל בשבת" in the Oxford Ms. As the Sages certainly did not intend to allow violation of the Shabbat laws, the Mishnah must not have been addressing violation of a *melakhah*.[34]

Variants of mShabbat 21:3

Group 1	Codex Kaufmann,[35]	ספוג אם יש לו עו?ד? בית אחיזה מקנחים בו ואם לאו אין מקנחין בו וחכמ' אומ' בין כך ובין כך מקנחים בו
	Cambridge Ms[36]	ספוג אם יש לו עוד[37] בית אחיזה מקנחין בו ואם לאו אין מקנחין בו וחכ' אומ' בין כך ובין כך מקנחין בו

---

34 It is superior to ascribe to both the *tanna kamma* and the Sages positions which are logical and easily defendable (whether *muktzeh* can apply to a sea sponge after it is cleaned and mostly processed but yet prior to its very final completion, the addition of a handle) than to suggest that basic principles of *melakhah* (whether *dash* can apply even when the juice goes to waste, or whether *melabein* can apply even to an item one is making filthy) were a matter of dispute in the Mishnah.

35 MS Kaufmann A 50, fol. 49v ("Mishnah MS A 50 – Italy, late 11th – mid 12th c.: fol. 49v Shabbat XIX.5 - XXI.3," David Kaufmann and His Collection, Accessed March 30, 2018, http://kaufmann.mtak.hu/en/ms50/ms50-049v.htm).

36 The Mishnah on which the Palestinian Talmud Rests: Edited for the Syndics of the University Press from the Unique Manuscript Preserved in the University Library of Cambridge, Add. 470. 1, ed. by William Henry Lowe, Shabbat 21:3 (Cambridge: University Press, 1883), p. 38b.

37 This variant suggests that the Mishnah is discussing the case of a sponge whose handle had fallen off. The *tanna kamma* considered the sponge no longer a proper tool. The Sages opined that the sponge remains fully functional without its handle.

Isaiah di Trani the Elder[38]	ספוג אם יש לו עור בית אחיזה מקנחין בו ואם לאו אין מקנחין בו וחכמים אומרים בין כך ובין כך מקנחין בו
Alfasi's Halakhot[39]	ספוג אם יש לו בית יד מקנחין בו ואם לאו אין מקנחין בו וחכמי' אומ' בין כך ובין כך מקנחין בשבת
Tosafot[40]	ספוג אם יש לו עור בית אחיזה מקנחין ואם לאו אין מקנחין בו וחכמים אומרים בין כך ובין כך מקנחין בו
Menaḥem haMeiri[41]	ספוג אם יש לו עור בית אחיזה מקנחין בו וחכ"א בין כך ובין כך מקנחין בו

38 *Piskei ha-Rid u-piskei he-Riaz Berakhot ve-Shabbat, Shabbat* 143a (Jerusalem: Machon HaTalmud HaYisraeli HaShalem, 1992), pp. 510-511. Many of the rishonim cited in this table, who possessed the ancient text showing the Sage's permissive attitude towards squeezing sponges, replaced the simplest meaning of the Mishnah's words (namely, that one is permitted to squeeze a wet sponge) with a clever reinterpretation in order to reconcile their Mishnah's text with the *stamma*'s interpretation. To be fair, their reconciliations will be cited in the footnotes. The relevant comments of di Trani are as follows:
וחכמ' אומ' בין כך ובין כך מקנחין בו. פי' משום דקסברי אין תורת סחיטה בספוג, דתורת סחיטה יש בענבים וזיתים וכיוצא בהן לסוחטן ולהוציא מהן משקין שהיא תולדה דדש, ותורת סחיטה יש נמי בבגדי', והיא תולדה דמכבס שהוא חפץ בליבונן, אבל הספוג אין בו לא זה ולא זה, משום מפרק אינו חייב שאין המשקין מגופו כמו הפירות שתהא סחיטתו תולדה דדש, ולליבונו נמי אינו צריך שתהא תולדה דמכבס, והילכך מותר לקנח בו, ואין בו משום סוחט. והכי נמי אמרי' בפרקין דלקמן בפרק חבית שנשברהא, תנא לא יספג ביין ולא יטפח בשמן, שלא יעשה כדרך שהוא עושה בחול, אלמא לא אסר הסיפוג אלא משום מעש' חול ולא משום סחיטה, וההיא אתיא כחכמ' דהכא.

39 *Hilkhot Rav Alfas*, vol. 1, ed. Nissan Zacks (Jerusalem: Mossad Harav Kook, 1969), p. 146. Zacks reprinted the first printed edition of Alfasi's *Halakhot* which appeared in Constantinople in 1509. A later printing of *Halakhot* which appears in the back of standard Talmud editions reads, "וחכמים אומרים, בין כך ובין כך, ניטל בשבת". Alfasi omits the comments of the *stamma* and therefore possibly understood the Mishnah as suggested in this essay. (Though one may argue that Alfasi did not consider the *stamma*'s comment to contain practical value and therefore omitted it from his halakhic digest.)

40 Tosafot *bShabbat* 143a s.v. *ve-im lav ein*: "...איח ספרים דגרסי ספוג אם יש".

41 Menachem ha-Meiri, *Beit ha-beḥirah*, ed. Isaak Lange, *Shabbat* 143a (Jerusalem, 1976), p. 566. Meiri explains the text as follows:
ספוג והוא שהיה מנהגם לטבלו במים ולקנח בו את הטבלא אם יש לו עור בית אחיזה ר"ל בית אחיזה של עור לאחזו בו מקנחין בו אבל אם אין לו בית אחיזה אסור אחר שהוא טבול במים שהרי כשאוחזו נסחט בין אצבעותיו ויש כאן איסור סחיטה ואף לר' שמעון שהרי פסיק רישיה הוא בין כך ובין כך ר"ל אע"פ שאין לו בית אחיזה אם הוא נגוב ניטל בשבת מפני שתורת כלי עליו ואין גוזרין נגוב אטו טבול.

	Yeshayah ben Eliyah di Trani the Younger[42]	ספוג בין יש לו בית אחיזה בין שאין לו בית אחיזה מותר לקנח בו, ובלבד שלא יתכוין לסוחטו...
	Yehudah haRofe Anav[43]	בין כך ובין כך מקנחין בו
Group 2	Meir ben Shimon haMe`ili of Narbonne[44]	ספוג בין שיש לו עור בית אחיזה בין שאין לו ניטל בשבת ומקנחין בו
	Oxford Ms[45]	ספוג אם יש לו עור בית אחיזה מקנחין בו ואם לאו אין מקנחין בו וחכמים אומרים בין כך ובין כך מקנחין ניטל בשבת ואין מקבל טומאה
	Meir Lublin[46]	וחכמים אומרים בין כך ובין כך מקנחים בו וניטל בשבת וכו' כצ"ל
Group 3	Maimonides's Commentary to the Mishnah[47]	ספוג--אם יש לו עור בית אחיזה, מקנחין בו; ואם לאו, אין מקנחין בו. וחכמים אומרים, בין כך ובין כך, ניטל בשבת
	Babylonian Talmud: first print, Venice 1520–1523	ספוג אם יש לו עור בית אחיזה מקנחין בו ואם לאו אין מקנחין וחכמי' או' בין כך ובי' כך נוטל בשבת
Group 4	Parma Ms	ספוג אם יש לו עור בית אחיזה מקנחין ואם לאו אין מקנחין בו וחכמים אומרים בין כך ובין כך אין מקנחין בו

42 *Piskei Ri"az Shabbat ve-Eiruvin*, ed. B. Rotenberg (New York, 1962), p. 104. The work contains Yeshayah's final rulings rather than his version of the text. However, his ruling suggests that the Mishnah variant in his possession was similar to that of Codex Kaufmann.

43 Yehuda haRofe Anav, *Shitat ha-kadmonim al masekhet Shabbat*, ed. Moshe Yehuda Blau (Brooklyn, New York, 1987), p. 238. The full commentary reads: הספוג. שעשוי לקנח בו את הקערה ויש לו בית אחיזה: מקנחין בו. דאינו נסחט הואיל ואינו אוחז הספוג שאם היה אוחזו ודאי סוחטו ומודה רבי שמעון בפסיק רישיה: בין כך ובין כך מקנחין בו. דתבשיל לא חשיב משקה דלא חשיבא סחיטה דידיה:.

44 Meir ben Shimon ha-Me`ili, *Ha-Meorot, bShabbat* 143a, ed. Moshe Yehuda Blau (Brooklyn, New York, 1964), p. 192-193. The commentary reads: ספוג בין שיש לו עור בית אחיזה בין שאין לו ניטל בשבת פירוש דתורת כלי עליו ... ומקנחין בו פירוש את הטבלא בשבת כשיש לו בית אחיזה ואע"פ שאינו נגוב אבל אי לית ליה בית אחיזה אתי לידי סחיטה ואסור.

45 Cited by *Shinui nus`haot* in *Mishnayot zekher Ḥanokh* vol. 3 (Jerusalem: Hotza'at Vagshal, 1999), p. 161.

46 Meir Lublin, *Meir Einei Ḥakhamim* (*Maharam*), *bShabbat* 143a (printed in the back of standard Talmud editions).

47 *Mishnah im peirush rabbeinu Moshe ben Maimon*, Moed, ed. Yosef Qafih (Jerusalem: Mossad Harav Kook, 1963), p. 86: וספוג, צמר ים שמנגבין בו... ואפילו ר' שמעון מודה שאסור לנגב בו אם אין לו בית אחיזה ... ומה שאמרו חכמים בין כך ובין כך ר"ל בין שיש לו בית יד שמותר לנגב בו בין שאין לו מותר לטלטלו בשבת והלכה כחכמים.

	Tosafist Yitzchak of Dampierre[48]	בין כך ובין כך אין מקנחין בו
Group 5	Ms. Vat. Ebr. 108, Bezalel Ashkenazi's preferred variant[49]	ספוג אם יש לו בית אחיזה מקנחין בו ואם לאו אין מקנחין בו בין כך ובין כך ניטל בשבת ואינו מקבל טומאה
	Soncino Talmud, first print, 1489-1498	ספוג אם יש לו עור בית אחיזה מקנחין בו ואם לאו אין מקנחין בין כך ובין כך נוטל בשבת ואינו מקבל טומאה
Group 6	Tosafot (alternate opinion)[50]	ספוג אם יש לו עור בית אחיזה מקנחין ואם לאו אין מקנחין בו...
	Ms. Munich, Cod. hebr. 95	ספוג אם יש לו בית אחיזה מקנחין ואם לאו אין מקנחין בו *סליק פירקא*

Figure 1 – Codex Kaufmann

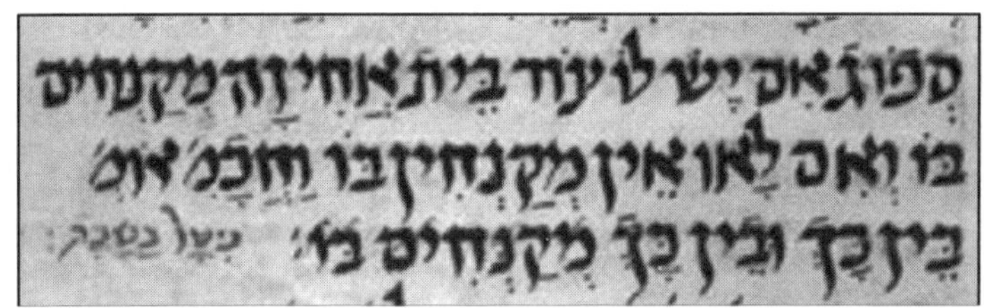

ספוג אם יש לו עור בית אחיזה מקנחים
בו ואם לאו אין מקנחין בו וחכמ' אומ'
בין כך ובין כך מקנחים בו:

The Mishnah Text's Evolution

A possible explanation for the existence of so many Mishnaic variants is that the text evolved in several phases over many centuries.

<u>Stage 1:</u>

It is generally accepted that Codex Kaufmann (Group 1), the oldest of extant complete Mishnah manuscripts, which here reads, "וחכמ' אומ' בין כך ובין כך מקנחים בו", conserves the language of the Mishnah in its most authentic form.[51] Other variants (Group 3), such as Maimonides's text, read, "וחכמים אומרים בין כך ובין כך ניטל בשבת". Both texts can be interpreted in the same manner: The Sages opined that whether with or without a handle, one may "מקנחין בו", "wipe with" the sponge, or "ניטל בשבת," the sponge may be "moved on Shabbat"—the teaching being that a sponge,

48 Tosafot *bShabbat* 143a s.v. *ve-im lav ein*: "וה"ר יצחק מדלפירא גרס בין כך...".

49 Cited by Shelomo Adeni, *Melekhet Shlomo*, *mShabbat* 21:3 in *Mishnayot zekher Ḥanokh* vol. 3, p. 161.

50 Tosafot *bShabbat* 143a s.v. *ve'im lav ein.* This view deletes from "וחכמים אומרים"..., and onwards.

51 See Michael Ryzhik, "The Language of the Mishnah: From Late Manuscripts to the Printed Editions," *The Edward Ullendorff Lectures in Semitic Philology*, Third Lecture (Bar Ilan University, 2016), p. 2.

even though it has no handle, is not *muktzeh*. The *tanna kamma* regarded the sea sponge as incomplete and not fully purposeful without its handle. The Sages dissented, deeming the sea sponge fully functional even before a handle is affixed (or even after the handle has fallen off—according to the "אם יש לו עוד בית אחיזה" variant). Later, Meir Lublin and the Oxford manuscript (Group 2) combined both these variants as "וחכמים אומרים בין כך ובין כך מקנחין ניטל בשבת", as did a late inscription penned into the margin of Codex Kaufmann (see Figure 1).

Stage 2:

In the late anonymous Bavli stratum the contextual *muktzeh* reading was abandoned. Because the sponge is used for squeezing and because the verb ספג means "to soak up,"[52] the dispute between *tanna kamma* and the Sages came to be understood as a conversation regarding *melakhah* (*dash* or *melabein* as discussed above). (A historical explanation for a transition in understanding of the Mishnah is suggested below.) The Mishnaic variant reading of "וחכמים אומרים בין כך ובין כך ניטל בשבת" (Maimonides's version—Group 3), was preferred (or created) over the alternate "וחכמים אומרים בין כך ובין כך מקנחין בו", (Group 1) as the latter posed a serious problem for it suggested the Sages allowed transgression of a *melakhah* (*dash* or *melabein*).

However, the original text, "בין כך ובין כך מקנחין בו", survived especially in Italian writings, such as the Codex Kaufmann,[53] and Anav and de Trani family commentaries, likely under the influence of the Palestinian Sages (see below).[54]

---

52 Michael Sokoloff, *A Dictionary of Jewish Babylonian Aramaic of the Talmudic and Geonic Periods*, entry – ספג (Ramat Gan: Bar Ilan University Press, 2002), p. 824. Sokoloff notes the word's Greek origins. Marcus Jastrow (*Dictionary*, entry, ספג, p. 1011), translates "to absorb."

53 Malachi Beit-Arié argues that the Kaufmann Manuscript was written in 12th-century Italy (Malachi Beit-Arié, "Ktav yad Kaufmann shel haMishnah – motze'o u-zmano," *Kovetz ma'amarim be-lashon Ḥazal*, II [Jerusalem: Hebrew University of Jerusalem, 1980], p. 88.)
Others suggest that the manuscript comes from Palestine as, "It has kept older forms of the Palestinian type of text and it often reflects the spoken language of second-century Palestine" ("3.2. Mishnah [MS A 50]," *David Kaufmann and His Collection*, accessed March 30, 2018, http://kaufmann.mtak.hu/en/study04.htm).

54 Moshe Sofer's assessment is that Nathan of Rome, author of *Arukh*, used a Mishnaic text which read "וחכמים אומרים בין כך ובין כך מקנחין בו" (Moshe Sofer, *Ḥiddushei Ḥatam Sofer*, *Shabbat* 143a [Jerusalem, 2006], p. 240) like is found in the

Stage 3:

The authors of Tosafot in northern France still possessed the suggested original variant but regarded it as faulty because it contradicted the *stamma*'s understanding of the Mishnah. Tosafot wrote, "אית ספרים דגרסי וחכ"א בין כך ובין כך מקנחין בו ולא יתכן דאמר בגמרא דבאין לו עור בית אחיזה אפילו ר"ש מודה דאסור משום דפסיק רישיה הוא", wondering how there possibly could have been a view amongst the Sages that squeezing is allowed on Shabbat.[55] Tosafot understood the Mishnah through the lens of the s*tammaic* stratum, that laws of a *melakhah* (*dash* according to Tosafot) were discussed. Tosafot (and the Parma Ms) chose to amend the ancient original text of the Mishnah to fit the new understanding of the Mishna's logic: וחכמים אומרים בין כך ובין כך אין מקנחין בו, adding the word אין (Group 4).

Stage 4:

Others (Group 5), like Bezalel Ashkenazi[56] and the scribe of the Vatican manuscript, took matters a step further by choosing to omit "וחכמים אומרים", leaving only "בין כך ובין כך ניטל בשבת"—as they reasoned that the *tanna kamma* surely did not dispute the non-*muktzeh* status of a sea sponge.[57]

Stage 5:

Some Tosafot authors suggested an emendation omitting the entire rejoinder of the Sages (Group 6), thereby resolving any difficulties the passage may have presented.[58]

Persian Gulf Marine Products

The reason for the anonymous Babylonian redactor's revisionist interpretation of *mShabbat* 21:3 may be related to geography and social economic

---

other mentioned Italian works. It is significant that Italian rishonim were not aware of an alternate text.

55 Tosafot *bShabbat* 143a s.v. *ve'im lav ein.*

56 Cited in Adeni, *Melekhet Shlomo*, *mShabbat* 21:3. Eliezer ben Yoel HaLevi's text also appears to leave out "וחכמים אומרים": "ספוג אם יש לו עור בית אחיזה מקנחים בו ואם לאו אין מקנחין בו. ובהא אפילו רבי שמעון מודה, דפסיק רישיה הוא. בין כך ובין כך ניטל בשבת", (*Ra'avyah*, ed. David Deblinski, vol. 1, Shabbat 327 [Bnei Brak, 2005], p. 281).

57 This reasoning for choosing a preferred Mishnaic variant is given in Adeni, *Melekhet Shlomo mShabbat* 21:3.

58 Tosafot *bShabbat* 143a s.v. *ve-im lav ein.*

history. The Jews of Babylonia were removed from the centers of the sponge diving industry in the Mediterranean Sea. Divers in the Persian Gulf were interested in a far more precious commodity—pearls, as the Gulf was famous in the old world for its pearls.[59] There are extensive reports from travelers and historians, as well as archeological evidence, dating from antiquity through the 20th century—including the period of Babylonian Talmud and its late redaction—that the Persian Gulf was prized for its valuable pearl industry.[60] Interestingly, the Babylonian Talmud discusses what marine products were sought after in the Persian Gulf with some detail, but fails to mention sea sponges:

> היכי עבדו מייתו שית אלפי גברי בתריסר ירחי שתא ואמרי לה תריסר אלפי גברי בשיתא ירחי שתא וטעני לה חלא עד דשכנא ונחית בר אמוראי וקטר אטוני דכיתנא בכסיתא וקטר להו בספינתא ונטלי חלא ושדו לבראי וכמה דמדליא עקרא ומתיא ומחליף על חד תרין בכספא תלת פרוותא הויין תרתי בי ארמאי וחדא דבי פרסאי דבי ארמאי מסקן כסיתא דבי פרסאי מסקן מרגנייתא ומקרייא פרוותא דמשמהיג.[61]
>
> How do they perform this collection of coral? They bring there six thousand men for twelve months (or according to others twelve thousand men for six months) and load the boat with sand until it rests on the sea-bottom. Then a diver goes down and ties a rope of flax to the coral while the other end is tied to the ship, and the sand is then taken and thrown overboard, and as the boat rises it pulls up the coral with it. The coral is worth twice its weight in silver. There were three ports, two belonging to the Romans and one belonging to the Persians. From the Roman side they brought up coral, from

---

59 Furthermore, it is not clear whether the coasts of the Persian Gulf possessed varieties of sponge fit for preparation for household use, as only select sponge species are of such quality. See Ernest J.J. Cresswell, *Sponges — their nature, history, modes of fishing, varieties, cultivation, etc.* (London: Sir I. Pitman & sons, 1922), p. 11:

> Hard sponges were of no value to the trade, and were called "wild" or "mud."… Aristotle also informs us precisely where the best sponges were to be found. On the eastern side of Cape Matapan there are beautiful sponges, but beyond that region they are of lower grade.

See also Pronzato and Manconi, "Mediterranean commercial sponges," *Marine Ecology*, p. 151.

60 Robert Carter, "The History and Prehistory of Pearling in the Persian Gulf," *Journal of Economic and Social History of the Orient* 48, no. 2 (2005): pp. 139-209, esp. pp. 143-146.

61 *bRosh haShanah* 23a.

the Persian side pearls. This [the Persian] one was called the port of Mashmahig.[62]

If the Babylonian authors of the *stamma* (approx. 6th – 9th centuries) did use sponges, it was likely an imported item from the Mediterranean Sea that arrived completely processed and ready for use.[63] It is difficult to find an instance in the Babylonian Talmud where sponges are clearly mentioned as a familiar item to its writers.[64] Babylonian Jews may have lacked familiarity with the extensive processing sea sponges underwent once harvested from the sea until they became usable as household items. To their knowledge the sea sponge had little relevance to *muktzeh* matters.

---

62 Maurice Simon, *Rosh Hashanah. Translated into English with notes, glossary and indices by Maurice Simon,* 23a (London: The Soncino Press, 1938); in *The Soncino Babylonian Talmud Rosh haShanah*, reformatted by Reuven Brauner (Raa`nana, 2011); this appears on pp. 62-63. Mashmahig is identified with Muharraq Island, Bahrain (Carter, "The History and Prehistory of Pearling," p. 191) or "an island in the Persian Gulf between 'Oman and al-Bahrin" (Simon, *Rosh haShanah*, p. 63 in Brauner's *Soncino*). Alternatively, according to Rashi "ומקרייא פרוותא דמשמהיג", means "the Persian ports are called royal ports."

63 Raw and unprocessed sponges could not be transported long distances as they would rot and lose their tactile strength along the way (see Cresswell, *Sponges*, pp. 43-45). The only form of sponge with which the rabbis living in Persia could have been familiar was the ready-made finished product. Preparing a raw sponge was a skilled task which was likely unknown to people living far from any sponge industry.

64 The existences of a thriving pearl industry in the Persian Gulf and a similar sponge industry in the Mediterranean in ancient times are both well documented. However, I was unable to find evidence of sponge fishing and processing in the Persian Gulf of ancient times. For example, the *Encyclopædia Iranica* website's search tool yields no relevant results for the words "sponge," "dive," and "diving." Lack of evidence for an Iranian sponge industry in the times of the Talmud does not prove for certain that none existed. In the words of Zohar Amar, "לפי שעה, אין לי ראיות לשימוש בספוג בבלי, אבל עדיין אין זה פוסל לחלוטין את האפשרות שהם הכירוהו, רק שלא נזכר", (e-mail message to author, April 3, 2018). However, it is recorded that during the era of the geonim, Persian physicians used drug-impregnated sponges for inhalation anesthesia in surgical operations (Ali Dabbagh, Samira Rajaei, Samad EJ Golzari, "History of Anesthesia and Pain in Old Iranian Texts," Anesthesiology and Pain Medicine 4:3 (2014): p. 3; Alireza Salehi, Faranak Alembizar, Ayda Hosseinkhani, "Anesthesia and pain management in traditional Iranian medicine," *AMHA - Acta Medico-Historica Adriatica* 14:2 [2016]: p. 320).

Extensive Processing

Descriptions from the early 20th century of sea sponge preparation from harvest to dealer's counter depict an extensive and careful process:

> When first taken from the water, the sponge presents a very different appearance to when it is seen on the dealer's counter. The entire body, including the canals and osculums, are coated with a fine, black gelatinous substance. This is the flesh of the invertebrate and has to be removed before the sponge is fit for market. The process of cleaning takes from five to eight days. The sponge is allowed to die on the deck of the vessel and is then thrown into a "crawl," an enclosure made of stakes in shallow water. There the natural process of decay ensues, and the flesh drops from the fibrous skeleton and is carried off by the tide flowing through the enclosure. In a short time the sponge is ready for beating and the spongers, armed with "gluts" (short thick clubs), spring into the "crawl" and pound the sponges vigorously, thereby expelling all the disintegrated matter in the pores of the sponge. This thorough beating is very necessary, as an improperly cleaned sponge is nearly worthless in the market. The buyers are very keen about "dead meat," as it is known to the trade, that is to say, portions of black jelly remaining in the centre of the sponge, not discernible to the untrained eye, but which is quickly detected by the expert, who will shun the sponge containing it.[65]

Because of their limited familiarity with the sponge manufacturing process, Babylonian Sages may have had difficulty understanding *mShabbat* 21:3 in the context of *muktzeh*, which commonly applies to unfinished tools before their construction is complete, and therefore sought out an alternative explanation. As the verb ספג means "to soak up," it was easy to view the Mishnah's words as a limitation against transgressing a *melakhah* often violated by soaking or squeezing (such as *dash* or *melabein*).

---

65 Cresswell, *Sponges*, pp. 43-45. Aristotle writes, "Whilst they are still alive and before they are washed and cleaned, they are blackish in colour" (*The Works of Aristotle: Vol. IV: Historia Animalium*, trans. by D'Arcy Wentworth Thompson, 5:16 [Oxford: Clarendon Press, 1910], p. 548b). For a brief video of sea sponge harvesting and processing see BlueWorldTV, "Jonathan Bird's Blue World: Sponges!" YouTube Video, 1:05-3:06, March 11, 2014, https://www.youtube.com/watch?v=m8a0oNsDEx8&vl=en.

Mediterranean Sponge Fishing

Unlike their Persian counterpart, the Jews of the Mediterranean Basin of antiquity and the medieval era were intimately familiar with the production of sea sponges because the Mediterranean was the world center of the sea sponge industry for millennia—especially at its eastern end along the coast of the Levant.[66] Jewish merchants regularly sailed these waters:

> בני ביישן נהוג דלא הוו אזלין מצור לצידון במעלי שבתא.[67]
>
> The citizens of Beyshan were accustomed not to go from Tyre to Sidon [for market day—Rashi] on the eve of the Sabbath.[68]

The Jerusalem Talmud reveals that Jews even participated in sponge diving:

> ההן דגזז ספוג גומי קרולין חייב משום קוצר ומשום נוטע.[69]
>
> One who harvests a sea sponge, *gomi*, or coral is accountable for the *melakhah* of harvesting and the *melakhah* of planting.[70]

---

66 From Cresswell's *Sponges*:

> Phoenicians, Egyptians, Greeks, Romans, Byzantines and Venetians ...All these peoples during the height of their civilization consumed large numbers of sponges (p. 12). The very finest grades come from the south-eastern part of the Mediterranean, and the quality deteriorates as one goes westward along both the north and south shores. ...In the Red Sea there are many sponges, but their quality is so inferior as to make them even not worth the freight that has to be paid for their transference... (pp. 22-23)... from an imaginary line drawn from about Tunis to Italy, sponges become very prolific, and as the eastern part of the Mediterranean is reached, both in the north and south, sponges become more abundant and better in quality. From these waters by far the largest quantity of useful sponges are obtained, and no other waters produce anything like such valuable supplies of equal or perhaps greater bulk (p. 16).

In general, all commercial sponge species are considered to be common and are widely distributed in the Mediterranean Sea along the coast of Dalmatia, Greece, the Aegean islands, Turkey, Cyprus, Syria, Egypt, Libya, and Tunisia. Although the presence of conspicuous populations of bath sponges has been determined along northern coasts of the Western Mediterranean basin (peninsular Italy, France and Spain), they are generally considered not to be economically exploitable.(Pronzato and Manconi, "Mediterranean commercial sponges," *Marine Ecology*, p. 157)

67 *bPesaḥim* 50b.

68 Translation from *Soncino, Pesaḥim* 50b (Raa`nana, 2011), p. 60.

69 *Y. Talmud, Shabbat* 7:2, (48b).

70 For why severing a sponge is considered an act of planting see Cresswell, *Sponges*, pp. 95-101.

> אמר רבי אבהו אם הים גליני והביט לארבע רוחותיו וראה שאין שם בריה משיאין את אשתו. ושוב מעשה באסיא באחד ששלשלתו לים ולא עלת בידם אלא רגלו. תני רצו לחתוך ספוגים ובאו ומצאו אותו שולחני בעכו.[71]
>
> R. Abahu taught: [If a man did not resurface from the sea and] the sea is clear and calm, and after searching in all directions the man is not seen [we can assume he drowned and perished] and his wife can remarry. Then there was an incident in Assi[72] in which [a diver] was lowered by rope into the sea and only his foot returned.[73] [The rabbis] taught: [the diver's mission] was to harvest sponges. [Later, this diver] was located in Acco, working as a moneychanger.[74]

Because the Jews of Palestine and its environs knew of the processing stages of the sponge they presumably had no difficulty understanding *mShabbat* 21:3 as a law regarding *muktzeh* which taught that until the sponge tool is completed it is to be treated as an unfinished item and remains *muktzeh* like unprocessed rocks and stones.[75] In possession of the former authentic understanding of the Mishnah, early medieval scholars of Palestine were not tempted to alter the words of the Sages, וחכמים אומרים בין כך ובין כך מקנחין בו. This statement of the Sages was simply an alternate view that the sea sponge is functional prior to the attachment of a handle, but *after* the cleaning and beating processing, and accordingly is not *muktzeh*. Therefore, textual variants extant from areas more heavily influenced by the Palestinian Sages (such as the Italian Mishnaic texts) retained the original reading of the Mishnah.

---

71 *Y. Talmud, Yevamot* 16:4, (83b).

72 Some suggest that Assi was located in the vicinity of the Greco-Roman cities Apamea and Antioch on the Orontes River (*Arukh ha-shalem*, ed. Kohut, vol. 1 [Vienna, 1878], p. 179).

73 It was presumed the diver drowned or had an unfortunate encounter with a shark or other sea creature.

74 The translation, my own, is in line with the explanation of Moshe Frishko: "תני רצו לחתוך ספוגים ובאו ומצאו אותו שולחני בעכו משמע שהם הורידוהו לים כדי לחתוך ספוגים" (*Yadav Shel Moshe* [Salonika, 1812], p. 103b). Marcus Jastrow translates "רצו לחתוך ספוגים", as "(divers) wanted to cut sponge" (Jastrow, *Dictionary*, entry – ספוג m, p. 1012). Alternatively, the passage can be understood as saying that the sailors, who had lowered the person who went missing into the water, subsequently went sponge fishing "אי נמי שהם היו רצין כדרכן ולחתוך ספוגים מהים ועל ידי זה באו לעכו שהיא על שפת הים ומצאו אותו. ועיקר" (Moshe Margalit, *Pnei Moshe, Yevamot* 16:4, 83b, found in *Talmud Yerushalmi* vol. 26, *Yevamot* 16 [Israel: Oz ve-Hadar, 2016], p. 86b).

75 The Jerusalem Talmud provides no comment to *mShabbat* 21:3 and thus speculation is resorted to here.

Avraham ben David's confusion regarding how the addition of a handle to a sponge can prevent squeezing the sponge was justified. Affixing a handle to the sea sponge in no way changes its compressible and absorptive nature. The Mishnah only discussed a sponge's *muktzeh* status.

Impact on Halakhic Thought

The textual error and misunderstanding of *mShabbat* 21:3 gradually entered rabbinic study halls and caused the emergence of new stringencies in the laws of Shabbat. Found in medieval to modern rabbinic Shabbat law literature is an often-repeated dispute regarding whether it is permitted to perform an action which produces a sure unintended side effect which violates Shabbat laws, "פסיק רישיה דלא ניחא ליה".[76] Nathan of Rome permitted such an action,[77] but Ri ha-Zaken considered it forbidden by rabbinic law.[78] The debate began regarding snugly fitting a cloth-wrapped spigot into its hole in a wine barrel. As the spigot would press some wine out of the cloth Ri argued such an act is forbidden by the rules of *melakhat dash*. Nathan opined that pressing the cloth with the spigot's insertion to the barrel is permitted because the pressed wine falls to the floor, and is לא ניחא ליה, of no interest to the person. Though in later centuries the discussion became more extensive, the primary basis for Ri ha-Zaken's position was *mShabbat* 21:3 which seemingly teaches that squeezing a wet dirtied sea sponge is forbidden even though the dirty water goes to waste. Ri's disciple, Barukh ben Yitzḥak from Worms, records his teacher's words:

> ומורי רבי' מפרש דאיסורא דרבנן מיהא איכא אע"ג דהמש' הולך לאבוד כגון ספוג שאין לו בית אחיזה אין מקנחין בו הקערה מן השמן ומן המאכל א"כ אסור למשוך בברזא הכרוכה במוכין אפי' היא מן הצד וגם אין כלי תחת החבית.[79]
>
> My teacher [Ri ha-Zaken] explained that a rabbinic prohibition applies even in scenarios in which the liquid goes to waste, as [observed in *mShabbat* 21:3] that a sponge with no handle may not be used to wipe a plate from oil and food. Therefore, it is forbidden to press the spigot wrapped in cloth even if [the spigot] is placed into the barrel from the side and no collecting vessel is placed beneath the

---

76 See *Tur* and *Shulḥan Arukh* O.Ḥ. 320:18; Kagin, *Mishnah Berurah* 321:57; ibid. 253 *sha`ar hatziyon* 43; ibid. 259 *sha`ar hatziyon* 16, 21.

77 *Sefer he-Arukh*, ed. S. Schlesinger, entry, סבר (Tel Aviv: Lipa Friedman Publications, n.d.), p. 371.

78 *Tur* O.Ḥ. 320.

79 *Sefer ha-terumah, Laws of Shabbat* 244 (Warsaw, 1897), p. 149.

barrel [in which case the pressed wine drops to the floor and is wasted].

Other medieval scholars also record that *mShabbat* 21:3 was the source for Ri ha-Zaken's position.[80] However, Ri's argument is only valid if *mShabbat* 21:3 describes laws of *dash*. As has been argued above, *dash* was not the intent of the Mishnah, and thus Ri ha-Zaken's proof falls apart.[81] It is likely that Nathan of Rome was not concerned by *mShabbat* 21:3 because he understood it in its proper *muktzeh* context. The text of Nathan's Mishnah was probably similar to that of Codex Kaufmann and of his Italian colleagues.[82] It is possible that Nathan's Talmud manuscript did not contain the added words of the *stamma* which interpreted the Mishnah in terms of *melakhah*.

Another stringency which arose because of the late flawed understanding of *mShabbat* 21:3 is refraining from swimming or bathing (even in cold water) on Shabbat, due to a concern that one might squeeze out water from one's hair after the bath. A ruling in *bShabbat* 128b teaches that *melakhat dash* does not apply to wet hair:

> רבה ורב יוסף דאמרי תרווייהו אין סחיטה בשיער.
> Rabba and Rav Yosef who both said: [The prohibition of] wringing out does not apply to hair [since hair fibers are nonabsorbent—Rashi].[83]

---

80 Moshe of Coucy, *Sefer mitzvot gadol ha-shalem,* vol. 1, negative commandment 65 (Jerusalem: Machon Yerushalayim, 2003), p. 117-118; *Maḥzor Vitri*, vol. 1, ed. Aryeh Goldschmidt, *Laws of Shabbat* 40 (Jerusalem: Machon Otzar Ha-poskim, 2009), p. 249, this portion of *Maḥzor Vitri* was borrowed from *Sefer ha-terumah* (see Goldschmidt's comments p. 238 n. 1); *Mordekhai, bShabbat* chapters 18-19, 143a; *Mordekhai, bShabbat* 141a *remez* 428. Aaron of Lunel and *Kolbo* likewise cite *mShabbat* 21:3 as the source for the stringent position (Aaron of Lunel, *Orḥot Ḥayyim*, *Laws of Shabbat* 1:23 [Florence, 1750], p. 45b; *Kolbo*, ed. David Avraham, vol. 2, *Laws of Shabbat* 31 [Jerusalem: Feldheim Publishers, 2009], p. 73). Also see Shlomo b. Aderet, *Ḥiddushei ha-Rashba, Ketubot* 6a (Jerusalem: Mossad Harav Kook, 2010), pp. 32-33. It may be that Ri ha-Zaken's sole source for his position was *mShabbat* 21:3 and only later scholars saw support from other Talmudic passages as well.

81 Maimonides's unique *melabein* understanding of the Mishnah similarly does not allow for conclusions regarding "פסיק רישיה דלא ניחא ליה" to be drawn.

82 Moshe Sofer writes that Nathan of Rome likely used a Mishnaic text which read "וחכמים אומרים בין כך ובין כך מקנחין בו" (*Ḥatam Sofer, Shabbat* 143a, p. 240).

83 Translation adapted from *Soncino.*

Most medieval authorities understood this ruling as absolute,[84] while some insisted that the Talmud only intended that a biblical prohibition does not exist, but a rabbinic prohibition does still apply.[85] Regardless of the interpretation one chooses, it is clear from the context of the Talmud's ruling that wringing for the purpose of collecting the squeezed liquid is discussed.[86] If the wringed liquid were to go to waste no prohibition should apply. However, when halachic scholars juxtaposed the medieval-era opinion that rabbinic prohibition does apply to hair, "יש סחיטה בשיער מדרבנן", with the view of Ri ha-Zaken (which, as explained above, was based upon a late-era interpretation of *mShabbat* 21:3) that an action which produces a sure unintended side effect which violates Shabbat laws is forbidden, "פסיק רישיה דלא ניחא ליה אסור", they concluded that wringing out wet hair is forbidden even if the fluid is not for collection.[87] This thought process gave rise to practical guidance promoted by halakhists that bathing and *mikveh* immersion must be avoided on Shabbat lest one come to squeeze out the water in one's hair afterwards.[88] Already in the 12th century, Avraham ben David (Ravad) wrote that women must not immerse

---

84 Menachem ha-Meiri, *Beit ha-beḥirah*, ed. Avraham Sofer, *Niddah* 67b (Jerusalem, 1949), p. 302; Shlomo b. Aderet as clarified by *He`arot hagaon Rabi Yosef Shalom Elyashiv, Shabbat* 128b (Jerusalem, 2014), p. 650; Yehonatan of Lunel, *Peirushei rabbeinu Yehonatan me-Lunel*, Shabbat 51b in Alfasi pagination (Jerusalem, 1985), p. 26; *Ḥiddushei ha-Ran* (attributed to Ran) Shabbat 128b (Warsaw, 1862), p. 76b, citing and agreeing with Aaron ha-Levi in regard to water in hair.

85 Vidal of Tolosa, *Maggid Mishnah* on Maimonides, *Mishneh Torah*, *Laws of Shabbat* 9:11; a view cited in *Beit ha-beḥirah, Niddah* 67b; Avraham ben David, *Ba`alei hanefesh*, ed. Yosef Qafih, *sha`ar ha-Tevilah: ḥafifah* (Jerusalem: Mossad Harav Kook, 2007) p. 83.

86 The Talmud discusses transporting oil for the needs of a woman giving birth.

87 An example of such juxtaposition is seen in Yeḥiel Michel Epstein, *Arukh ha-shulḥan* O.Ḥ. 320:34-35.

88 In later centuries, further reasons for the then prevalent custom amongst Ashkenazi Jewry to refrain from bathing were suggested by halakhists. However, concern for squeezing hair remained the primary and emphasized reason in many halachic guides (see Maharil cited in *Magen Avraham* O.Ḥ. 326:8; Schneur Zalman of Liadi, *Shulḥan arukh ha-rav* vol. 2, O.Ḥ. 326:6 [Jerusalem: Oz veHadar, 1992], p. 298; Epstein, *Arukh ha-shulḥan* O.Ḥ. 326:8-9; Kagin, *Mishnah Berurah* 326:21), while in other sources it is the only reason given to refrain (see Eliyahu of Vilna, *Ma`aseh rav*, ed. Y. Zelushinski, *Laws of Shabbat* 125 [Jerusalem, 2011], p. 138-139: "טבילה בשבת אם צריך לקרי מוטב לטבול במ"ש ולא בשבת כי א"א להזהר שלא יבא לידי סחיטה ויוצא שכרו בהפסדו"). Bathing in cold water on Shabbat remained permissible in the Sephardic world (see Karo, *Shulḥan Arukh* O.Ḥ. 326:1; Ben Tzion Abba Shaul, *Ohr le-tzion* 2:35 [Jerusalem: Ohr leTzion, 1992], p. 251;

in their ritual bath on Shabbat as they will surely come to wring out their wet hair:

> ואני תמה היאך אשה יכולה לטבול בלילי שבת ולילי יום טוב ואיך תנצל מסחיטת שער, ולכן אני אומר כי ראויה הטבילה לדחות עד מוצאי שבת או מוצאי יום טוב.[89]
>
> I wonder how a woman is permitted to immerse during the nights of Shabbat or Yom Tov, for how can she avoid wringing her hair? Therefore, I say that the immersion be delayed until after Shabbat or Yom Tov.

Subsequent scholars have noted that such a ruling does not match the historical halakhic record.[90] Meiri, commenting on view of Ravad, wrote, "וכן מה שכתבו מסחיטת שער לדבריהם היאך לא חששו בתלמוד בכך", "regarding what [some scholars forbade immersion on Shabbat because of it possibly leading] to squeezing hair, why is it that such a concern is not found in the Talmud?"[91] Because of this perceived squeezing hair problem some authorities in recent centuries permitted immersion but cautioned to refrain from wringing one's wet hair.[92] Many Ashkenazi halakhists, including Vilna Gaon and the author of *Mishnah Berurah*, instructed that bathing and *mikveh* immersion should be avoided altogether on Shabbat, lest one come to squeeze out the water in one's hair afterwards.[93]

Yitzhak Yosef, *Kitzur Shulḥan Arukh Yalkut Yosef* [2006] O.Ḥ. 326:4). Islamic hygienic expectations (and Middle Eastern climate) prevented development of Sephardic customs which would limit bodily cleanliness.

89 *Ba`alei hanefesh*, p. 83. *Beit Yosef* (to *Tur* vol. 9, YD 199:6 [Tel Aviv: Machon Shirat Devorah, 1993], p. 217) writes that *Kolbo* repeats Ravad's words.

90 See *mShabbat* 3:4, 22:5; *bShabbat* 57a; *mBeitzah* 2:2.

91 Meiri, *Beit ha-behirah, Niddah* 67b, p. 302. In *Ḥiddushei ha-Ran* (attributed to Ran) *Shabbat* 128b we find the argument that as ritual immersion is permitted on Shabbat surely one is permitted to wring out hair without violating the Shabbat laws. Yosef Karo (*Beit Yosef* Y.D. 199:6) notes that Ravad's position contradicts the Talmud; Yisroel Isserlein writes, "אע"ג דלא מצינו איסור מפורש על זה" (*Trumat ha-deshen* vol. 1, 255 [Jerusalem: Ohr ha-Ḥayyim, 2015], p. 254). Meiri concludes with an unconvincing argument, "ואע"פ שאפשר לומר שבזמן התלמוד לא היו מגדלות שער כל כך אבל עכשו שנוהגות בשערות ארוכות יש לחוש מ"מ הואיל ומצות עונה בטבילה אין חוששין לכך אלא שמזהירין אותן בכך כמה שאפשר".

92 Yisroel Lifschitz, *Tiferet Yisroel: hilkhita gevirta*, *Shabbat* 3 in *Mishnayot zekher Ḥanokh* vol. 3, p. 44; Avraham Danzig, *Haye adam*, *Laws of Shabbat* 22:12 (Frankfurt am Main, 1860), p. 197.

93 Kagin, *Mishnah Berurah* 326:21; Epstein, *Arukh ha-shulḥan* O.Ḥ. 326:8-9; Eliyahu of Vilna, *Ma`aseh rav*, ed. Y. Zelushinski, *Laws of Shabbat* 125 (Jerusalem, 2011), pp. 138-139.

The suggestion put forth here is that the *stamma* of *bShabbat* 143a misled many readers of *mShabbat* 21:3 to understand that *melakhat dash* applies even when the fluid squeezed out is not intended for collection. The *stamma*'s Mishnah interpretation was the foundation of Ri ha-Zaken's novel view that "פסיק רישיה דלא ניחא ליה אסור". Later authorities who maintained that a rabbinic prohibition of wringing is applicable to hair, "יש סחיטה בשיער מדרבנן", logically extended the squeezing hair restriction to include scenarios in which the squeezed liquid goes to waste. What followed from this reasoning was that bathing must be avoided lest one squeeze out the water from the resultant wet hair. Some scholars noted that such a halakhic recommendation is incongruent with historical Talmudic tradition of permitting immersion on Shabbat. However, as both "פסיק רישיה דלא ניחא ליה אסור", and "יש סחיטה בשיער מדרבנן", were independent positions upheld by respected medieval scholars, refraining from squeezing one's hair and even abstaining from bathing at all gradually became standard Shabbat halakhic guidance in recent centuries.

ꙮ

On the Meaning of the Word Ḥem'ah in Biblical Hebrew

By: YISROEL ASHER COLEMAN

The word *ḥem'ah* (חמאה) occurs in the Pentateuch twice (Genesis 18:8, Deuteronomy 32:14), in Judges once (5:25), in 2 Samuel once (17:29), in Isaiah twice (7:15, 7:22), in Job once (20:17) and in Proverbs once (30:33). Its meaning, while generally assumed to be "butter," is a matter of some obscurity, as this short article will demonstrate. Here the earliest source will be examined, that of Genesis 18. There Abraham hastens to greet his angelic guests with delicacies, some of which have been produced by his cattle. The verse reads:

וַיִּקַּח חֶמְאָה וְחָלָב וּבֶן־הַבָּקָר אֲשֶׁר עָשָׂה וַיִּתֵּן לִפְנֵיהֶם וְהוּא־עֹמֵד עֲלֵיהֶם תַּחַת הָעֵץ וַיֹּאכֵלוּ.

In the Septuagint, the word *ḥem'ah* is rendered as βούτυρον (*bouturon*). The word βούτυρον is understood to mean "butter."[1] Later translations of the Bible seem to follow this translation: the Vulgate renders *butyrum*; the King James Version reads "butter." An attempt must be made to ascertain if this translation is equivalent to modern-day butter, which for the purposes of this article shall be generally characterized as churned, unclarified butter.

Pliny the Elder remarks: "From milk, too, butter (*butyrum*) is produced; held as the most delicate of food among barbarous nations, and one which distinguishes the wealthy from the multitude at large. It is mostly made from cows' milk, and hence its name; but the richest butter is that made from ewes' milk." Here Pliny makes reference to the origin of the Greek word: *bous* (cow) and *tyros* (curds or cheese). This may be a clue as to the different nature of this ancient butter: in the process of

---

1 H. G. Liddell and R. Scott, *A Greek-English Lexicon* (Oxford: Clarendon Press, 1940).

Yisroel Asher Coleman is an *avrekh kollel* and rabbinical student. He currently resides in Palo Alto, CA, where he is a member of the Jewish Study Network.

churning butter, the maker should see neither curds nor cheese.[2] This supposition is confirmed by Pliny's explanation of the process:

> There is a butter made also from goats' milk; but previously to making it, the milk should first be warmed, in winter. In summer it is extracted from the milk by merely shaking it to and fro in a tall vessel, with a small orifice at the mouth to admit the air, but otherwise closely stopped, a little water being added to make it curdle the sooner. The milk that curdles the most, floats upon the surface; this they remove, and, adding salt to it, give it the name of "*oxygala*." They then take the remaining part and boil it down in pots, and that portion of it which floats on the surface is butter, a substance of an oily nature. The more rank it is in smell, the more highly it is esteemed.[3]

The process Pliny describes is markedly similar to that used to this day in the Middle and Far East for the production of clarified butter. Pliny may have erred in his characterization, for the solids that are produced and float to the surface are in these methods discarded and the remaining liquid preserved, coagulated and consumed. This possibility has already been remarked upon by John Bostock and H.T. Riley, Pliny's translators.[4] The historian and linguist Andrew Delby argues that unclarified butter of the churned sort was rare in Ancient Mesopotamian cuisine, because the climate would have rendered it rancid within hours. He claims that references to butter in Near Eastern literature must be references to ghee.[5] His claim is partially supported by the translation of Onkelos *ad loc*, who renders the word *ḥem'ah* as שְׁמַן, a word it is same to assume is a cognate of the Arabic *smen* or *samneh*. Indeed, Saadya Gaon in his *Tafsir* renders the translation "סמנא," while in Deuteronomy he translates "סמן." Smen is quite similar to ghee.[6]

It is necessary, however, to take literary context into account. In the scene portrayed by the Bible, Abraham rushes to his cattle and "*takes butter*

---

2 See also https://www.uoguelph.ca/foodscience/book-page/overview-butter-making-process

3 John Bostock, Pliny the Elder and Henry Thomas Riley, *The Natural History of Pliny* (1855) 28:35.

4 Ibid., Note 5.

5 Andrew Dalby, *Food in the Ancient World from A to Z* (London: Routledge, 2003).

6 It seems unlikely that the butter described in the Biblical account is whey butter, as some have suggested. Whey butter is a product that requires excessive labor, and the process required to create it is extremely inefficient, yielding as little as three pounds of butter per 1,000 pounds of milk. See Charles Francis Doane, *Whey butter* (Washington, DC: US Dept. of Agriculture, Bureau of Animal Industry, 1910).

and milk." The implication is strong that the "butter" Abraham takes is produced quickly or immediately, a scenario that in the case of smen or ghee loses credibility. The Biblical narrative is clearly intended to convey an impression of great haste. This point is hammered home by the French medieval commentator Rabbi Shlomo Yitzhaki ("Rashi"), who goes so far as to suggest that *ḥem'ah* here refers to nothing more than cream, skimmed from the freshly produced milk. While this reading is quite compelling, it is possible to explain the alternative translation offered by most versions of the Bible.

It is entirely likely that in this case, *ḥem'ah* means curds. The process of curdling may be effectuated by adding a curdling agent or even by the mere application of heat. The resulting product is then strained, and may be eaten immediately if absolute dryness is not required. This translation is followed by later editions of the Bible, such as the English Standard Version. It is also the translation rendered by Gesenius.[7] This would explain how Abraham is able to quickly produce the dairy product in the Bible's description.[8] ☙

7 H.W.F. Gesenius and Samuel Prideaux Tregelles (transl.), *Gesenius' Hebrew and Chaldee Lexicon to the Old Testament Scriptures* (Grand Rapids: Eerdmans, 1957).

8 It is noteworthy that the Pentateuch's choice of חמאה to refer to curds may point to a relatively late date of origin for the word גבינה, used generally in rabbinic literature and once in the Book of Job to mean "cheese."

BRCA Testing for All Ashkenazi Women: A Halakhic Inquiry

By: SHARON GALPER GROSSMAN

I recently underwent testing for the BRCA mutation. Thank G-d, neither I nor anyone in my family has ever had breast or ovarian cancer. So, why would a woman who has never been diagnosed with cancer and has no family history of it undergo BRCA testing? This article presents the halakhic issues around offering BRCA testing to all Ashkenazi women regardless of family history, and introduces views of several modern poskim, who have not, until now, rendered an opinion on this topic.

Inherited mutations in BRCA1 and BRCA2 predispose one to extremely high risks of breast and ovarian cancer. Carriers of a BRCA1 mutation face a lifetime breast cancer risk of approximately 70% and an ovarian cancer risk of 30% to 40%.[1] For carriers of the BRCA2 mutation the breast cancer risk is approximately 50%, while the ovarian cancer risk is approximately 20%.[2] One in 40 Ashkenazi Jews carries a BRCA mutation.[3] BRCA mutations account for 11% of all breast cancer[4] and 40% of

1 Moslehi, R., Chu, W., Karlan, B., et al. "BRCA1 and BRCA2 Mutation Analysis of 208 Ashkenazi Jewish Women with Ovarian Cancer," *American Journal of Human Genetics* vol. 66 (Cambridge: 2000) pp. 1259–1272.

2 Ibid.

3 Roa, B.B., Boyd, A.A., Volcik, K., Richards, C.S. "Ashkenazi Jewish Population Frequencies for Common Mutations in BRCA1 and BRCA2," *Nature Genetics* vol. 14(2) (New York: 1996) pp. 185–187.

4 King, M.C., Marks, J.H., Mandell, J.B.: "New York Breast Cancer Study Group Breast and Ovarian Cancer Risks due to Inherited Mutations in BRCA1 and BRCA2." *Science* vol. 302(5645) (Washington, DC: 2003) pp. 643–646.

Sharon Galper Grossman, MD, MPh, is a radiation oncologist and former faculty member of Harvard Medical School where she also obtained a Master's in Public Health. She is a graduate of the Morot L-Halakha program for women's advanced halakhah learning at Matan Hasharon. She writes and lectures on women's health and halakhah and teaches for Matan, Machon Puah and the Eden Center where she is the director of community health programming. The preparation and publication of this article was made possible by a grant from the Memorial Foundation for Jewish Culture.

all ovarian cancer in the Jewish population.[5,6] Men who carry these mutations have a 5-25% risk of prostate cancer.[7,8,9,10,11]

Initially, only women already diagnosed with cancer underwent BRCA testing. However, testing prior to a cancer diagnosis enables women with positive results to pursue risk-reducing interventions including early-onset screening with breast MRI/mammogram, pelvic ultrasound and CA-125, chemoprevention, and risk-reducing surgeries such as mastectomy and oophorectomy. In BRCA carriers, MRI surveillance of the breast increases breast cancer detection rates and the number of pa-

5 Hirsh-Yechezkel, G., et al. "Population Attributes Affecting the Prevalence of BRCA Mutation Carriers in Epithelial Ovarian Cancer Cases in Israel," *Gynecologic Oncology* vol. 89(3). (Elsevier): 2003, pp. 494–498.

6 Risch, H.A., et al. "Prevalence and Penetrance of Germline BRCA1 and BRCA2 Mutations in a Population Series of Women with Ovarian Cancer," *American Journal of Human Genetics* vol. 68(3) (Cambridge: 2001) pp. 700–710.

7 Antoniou, A., Pharoah, P.D., Narod, S., et al. "Average Risks of Breast and Ovarian Cancer Associated with BRCA1 or BRCA2 Mutations Detected in Case Series Unselected for Family History: A Combined Analysis of 22 Studies," *American Journal of Human Genetics* vol. 72(5) (Cambridge: 2003) pp. 1117–1130.

8 Antoniou, A.C., Pharoah, P.D., Narod, S. et al. "Breast and Ovarian Cancer Risks to Carriers of the BRCA1 5382insC and 185delAG and BRCA2 6174delT Mutations: A Combined Analysis of 22 Population-Based Studies," *Journal of Medical Genetics* vol. 42(7) (London: 2005) pp. 602–603.

9 Chen, S., Parmigiani, G. "Meta-analysis of BRCA1 and BRCA2 Penetrance," *Journal of Clinical Oncology* vol. 25(11) (Alexandria: 2007) pp. 1329–1333.

10 Struewing, J.P., Hartge, P., Wacholder, S., et al. "The Risk of Cancer Associated with Specific Mutations of BRCA1 and BRCA2 Among Ashkenazi Jews," *New England Journal of Medicine* vol. 336(20) (Waltham: 1997) pp. 1401–1408.

11 Finkelman, B.S., Rubinstein, W.S., Friedman, S., et al. "Breast and Ovarian Cancer Risk and Risk Reduction in Jewish BRCA1/2 Mutation Carriers," *Journal of Clinical Oncology* vol. 30(12) (Alexandria: 2012) pp.1321–1328.

tients diagnosed at an earlier stage of disease, and is cost effective[12,13,14,15,16] and supported in multiple guidelines.[17,18] However, the impact of surveillance with breast MRI on mortality is not clear. Surveillance for early detection of ovarian cancer in BRCA carriers has not proven beneficial. Some BRCA carriers may opt for chemoprevention, taking tamoxifen or oral contraceptive pills as a way to reduce the risk of developing breast and ovarian cancer. However, only limited data are available regarding the preventive benefit of tamoxifen in BRCA mutation carriers. And although studies show that oral contraceptive pills reduce risk of ovarian cancer, they may theoretically increase the risk of breast cancer.[19] Prophylactic mastectomy reduces the risk of developing breast cancer by 90% and might increase survival, especially when performed at a younger

---

12 Grann, V.R., Jacobson, J.S., Thomason, D., et al. "Effect of Prevention Strategies on Survival and Quality-Adjusted Survival of Women with BRCA1/2 Mutations: An Updated Decision Analysis," *Journal of Clinical Oncology* vol. 20 (Alexandria: 2002) p. 2520.

13 Kurian, A.W., Sigal, B.M., Plevritis, S.K. "Survival Analysis of Cancer Risk Reduction Strategies for BRCA1/2 Mutation Carriers," *Journal of Clinical Oncology* vol. 28 (Alexandria: 2010) p. 222.

14 Kriege, M., Brekelmans, C.T., Boetes, C., et al. "Efficacy of MRI and Mammography for Breast-Cancer Screening in Women with a Familial or Genetic Predisposition," *New England Journal of Medicine* vol. 351 (Waltham: 2004) p. 427.

15 Warner, E., Hill, K., Causer, P., et al. "Prospective Study of Breast Cancer Incidence in Women with a BRCA1 or BRCA2 Mutation under Surveillance With and Without Magnetic Resonance Imaging," *Journal of Clinical Oncology* vol. 29 (Alexandria: 2011) p. 1664.

16 Plevritis, S.K., Kurian, A.W., Sigal, B.M., et al. "Cost-Effectiveness of Screening BRCA1/2 Mutation Carriers with Breast Magnetic Resonance Imaging," *JAMA: The Journal of the American Medical Association* vol. 295 (Chicago: 2006) p. 2374.

17 NCCN Clinical Practice Guidelines in Oncology (NCCN Guidelines). Genetic/Familial High-risk Assessment: Breast and Ovarian. Version 2.2019. www.nccn.org/professionals/physician_gls/pdf/genetics_screening.pdf (Accessed on September 10, 2018).

18 Saslow, D., Boetes, C., Burke, W., et al. "American Cancer Society Guidelines for Breast Screening with MRI as an Adjunct to Mammography," *CA: A Cancer Journal for Clinicians* vol. 57(2) (Hoboken: 2009).

19 Iodice, S., Barile, M., Rotmensz, N., et al. "Oral Contraceptive Use and Breast or Ovarian Cancer Risk in BRCA1/2 Carriers: A Meta-Analysis," *European Journal of Cancer* vol. 46 (Elsevier): 2010 p. 2275.

age.[20,21,22,23] Compared to BRCA carriers who opt for surveillance alone, BRCA carriers who undergo risk-reducing oophorectomy decrease their risk of death by 77%, in large part due to a reduction in the incidence of ovarian cancer, but also due to a significant reduction in the incidence of breast cancer (oophorectomy reduces the incidence of breast cancer by 48%) and of breast cancer mortality.[24] Prophylactic oophorectomy is most effective at reducing the risk of cancer if a woman undergoes surgery before she turns 40. Additionally, risk-reducing surgeries have been shown to be the most cost-effective measures. Using costs, life-years (LY), and quality-adjusted life-years (QALY) as outcomes, a study that compared preventive surgery, chemoprevention, MRI, and mammography showed that prophylactic surgeries were associated with the lowest overall cost and the longest survival in LYs, dominating all other strategies.[25] Most modern *poskim* permit and some even require prophylactic surgery in BRCA carriers.[26] Identifying BRCA carriers prior to cancer diagnosis in order to initiate early surveillance and risk-reducing surgery saves lives.

---

20 Domchek, S.M., Friebel, T.M., Singer, C.F., et al. "Association of Risk-Reducing Surgery in BRCA1 or BRCA2 Mutation Carriers with Cancer Risk and Mortality," *JAMA: The Journal of the American Medical Association* vol. 304(9) (Chicago: 2010) pp. 967–975.

21 Kurian, A.W., Sigal, B.M., Plevritis, S.K. "Survival Analysis of Cancer Risk Reduction Strategies for BRCA1/2 Mutation Carriers," *Journal of Clinical Oncology* vol. 28(2) (Alexandria: 2010) pp. 222–231. doi:10.1200/JCO.2009.22.7991.

22 Carbine, N.E., Lostumbo, L., Wallace, J., Ko, H. "Risk-Reducing Mastectomy for the Prevention of Primary Breast Cancer," Cochrane Database System Review 2018;4:CD002748.

23 https://www.health.gov.il/hozer/mk03_2020.pdf.

24 Ibid.

25 Grann, V.R., Patel, P.R., Jacobson, J.S., et al. "Comparative Effectiveness of Screening and Prevention Strategies Among BRCA1/2 Affected Mutation Carriers," *Breast Cancer Research and Treatment* vol. 125. (Springer): 2011, pp. 837–847.

26 Grossman, S.G. "The Angelina Jolie Effect in Jewish Law: Prophylactic Mastectomy and Oophorectomy in BRCA Carriers," *Rambam Maimonides Medical Journal* vol. 6(4) Haifa: 2015. e0037. doi:10.5041/RMMJ.10222. Willig MI. Catching cancer before it catches you: Medical and Halakhic implications of BRCA gene testing (Audio Lecture) Yeshiva University Medical Ethics Forum. 2008. [Accessed September 1, 2015]. Macros and Adina Katz YUTorah Online. Rabbi Willig addresses this issue 99 minutes into the recording.

1. Who Should Undergo BRCA Testing Prior to Cancer Diagnosis?

Until very recently, no one would have offered BRCA testing to someone like me, a woman with no family history of cancer. Among cancer-free women, referral for genetic assessment has been limited to those with a family history of breast and ovarian cancer. In 2014, the U.S. Preventive Services Task Force (USPSTF) reiterated its recommendation against BRCA testing for healthy women in the absence of family history of cancer.[27] This recommendation was based on the lack of data on cancer risks among BRCA carriers in the general population, as opposed to mutation carriers in severely affected families.[28] Three recent studies argue for a reassessment of this policy as they confirm that limiting BRCA testing to women with a family history of breast or ovarian cancer fails to identify the vast majority of BRCA carriers in the Ashkenazi population. In a Canadian study of 2,000 unselected[29] Ashkenazi Jewish women,[30] an Israeli study of 8,105 unselected Ashkenazi Jewish men,[31] and a British study that randomly assigned 1,034 unselected Ashkenazi Jewish men and women either to testing based on family history or testing regardless of family history,[32] BRCA testing based on family history alone failed to

---

27 Moyer, V.A. "Risk Assessment, Genetic Counseling, and Genetic Testing for BRCA-Related Cancer in Women," U.S. Preventive Services Task Force recommendation statement. *Annals of Internal Medicine* vol. 160(4) (Philadelphia: 2014) pp. 271–281.

28 "Genetic Risk Assessment and BRCA Mutation Testing for Breast and Ovarian Cancer Susceptibility: Recommendation Statement," *Annals of Internal Medicine* vol. 143(5) (Philadelphia: 2005) pp. 355–361.

29 In this context, the term "unselected" refers to Jewish women or men who participated in a study because of their Ashkenazi ancestry, regardless of their family history.

30 Metcalfe, K.A., Poll, A., Royer, R., et al. "Screening for Founder Mutations in BRCA1 and BRCA2 in Unselected Jewish Women," *Journal of Clinical Oncology* vol. 28(3) (Alexandria: 2010) pp. 387–391.

31 Gabai-Kapara, E., Lahad, A., Kaufman, B., et al. "Population-Based Screening for Breast and Ovarian Cancer Risk Due to BRCA1 and BRCA2," *Proceedings of the National Academy of Sciences of the United States of America* vol. 111(39) (Washington, DC: 2014) pp. 14205–14210.

32 Manchanda, R., Loggenberg, K., Sanderson, S., et al. "Population Testing for Cancer Predisposing BRCA1/BRCA2 Mutations in the Ashkenazi-Jewish Community: A Randomized Controlled Trial," *Journal of the National Cancer Institute* vol. 107 (Oxford: 2015) doi:10.1093/jnci/dju379, p. 379.

identify more than half the carriers of the mutation.[33] These studies support population-based testing for all Ashkenazi women regardless of family history.

These three studies reveal that BRCA mutations in individuals screened from the general population are no less harmful than those of carriers who were referred for screening based on family history. In the Israeli study, BRCA carriers identified from the general population, regardless of family history of breast or ovarian cancer, had very high risks of developing cancer; by age 80, their risk for either breast or ovarian cancer was 83% for BRCA1 carriers and 76% for BRCA2 carriers. These risks were even higher in more recent birth cohorts.[34] In addition, these studies confirm that women who test positive act on the results. Investigators from Ontario reported uptake of screening and prevention options in women with a BRCA mutation identified through Jewish population genetic testing and confirmed that such women do in fact seek intervention.[35] Before genetic testing, none of these women had undergone breast MRI screening, or risk reducing surgery, or had taken a chemo-preventive drug. By one year after testing, 100% of them had undergone MRI. Within two years of receiving a positive genetic test result, 16% of the women had taken a chemo-preventive drug, 11.1% had undergone prophylactic mastectomy, and 90%, a prophylactic oophorectomy. These results show that women who undergo population-based BRCA testing and are found to be carriers of the mutation, process this information and take steps to reduce their risk of developing cancer.

Mary-Claire King (the scientist who discovered the BRCA mutation) has highlighted the results of the Israeli study to support the position that all women, and not just Ashkenazi Jews, should receive genetic testing for BRCA1 and BRCA2.[36] She based her recommendation on the finding that the cancer risks associated with a BRCA mutation are high even in the

---

33 Ibid. pp. 1–19.

34 Gabai-Kapara, "Population Based Screening for Breast and Ovarian Cancer Risk Due to BRCA1 and BRCA2."

35 Metcalfe, K.A., Poll, A., Llacuachaqui, M., et al. "Patient Satisfaction and Cancer-Related Distress Among Unselected Jewish Women Undergoing Genetic Testing for BRCA1 and BRCA2," *Clinical Genetics* vol. 78. (Wiley Online Library): 2010, pp. 411–17.

36 King, M.C., Levy-Lahad, E., Lahad, A. "Population-Based Screening for BRCA1 and BRCA2," 2014 Lasker Award. *JAMA: The Journal of the American Medical* Association vol. 312(11) (Chicago: 2014) pp. 1091–1092.

absence of a family history of cancer.[37] Although population-based testing might not be feasible for the entire U.S. population, these studies support population-based testing for all Ashkenazi women in Israel as a rational approach to identifying BRCA carriers, especially since there are two mutations in BRCA1 and one mutation in BRCA2 that together are present in up to 2.5% of Ashkenazi Jewish women. One of the three mutations is present in 12% of unselected patients with breast cancer[38] and in 35% of unselected patients with ovarian cancer.[39] Given that these three mutations comprise the majority of the deleterious mutations in the Jewish population, genetic testing among healthy Ashkenazi Jews without a family history of breast or ovarian cancer can be focused and limited to these three founder mutations, making such testing more straightforward and cost-effective. To this end, Efrat Levy-Lahad, director of the Medical Genetics Institute at Shaare Zedek Medical Center, has argued vociferously for offering BRCA testing to all Ashkenazi women in Israel.

Why does screening based on family history alone fail to detect such a significant number of women who carry the BRCA mutation? There are many possible answers. Families in the Israeli study were small and included few females with mutations who had reached the ages of highest cancer risk.[40] Young women in these families would not have been tested in the absence of a general screening program. Incomplete family histories might be due to limited communication within the family, lack of awareness, inaccuracies in family history, family lost in the Holocaust, family migration, paternal transmission, male preponderance, few women inheriting the mutation, and chance. Furthermore, BRCA risk prediction models are imperfect and underestimate the probability of detecting mutations at low (≤10%) and intermediate (10%–40%) probability levels, while

---

37 Gabai-Kapara, "Population Based Screening for Breast and Ovarian Cancer Risk Due to BRCA1 and BRCA2."

38 Warner, E., Foulkes, W., Goodwin, P., et al. "Prevalence and Penetrance of BRCA1 and BRCA2 Gene Mutations in Unselected Ashkenazi Jewish Women with Breast Cancer," *Journal of the National Cancer Institute* vol. 91 (Oxford: 1999) pp. 1241–1247.

39 Moslehi, "BRCA1 and BRCA2 Mutation Analysis of 208 Ashkenazi Jewish Women with Ovarian Cancer."

40 Gabai-Kapara. "Population Based Screening for Breast and Ovarian Cancer Risk Due to BRCA1 and BRCA2."

overestimating mutations at high-probability thresholds.[41,42,43] Population screening enables us to identify carriers regardless of their relatives' willingness to divulge information on cancer diagnosis or genetic test results. This is a factor that can limit testing in ultra-Orthodox communities, which tend to discourage disclosure.[44] Population-based testing also identifies carriers independent of physician referral, a potentially important consideration as a recent study demonstrated that only 19% of U.S. primary care physicians accurately assessed family history for BRCA testing.[45] In families of BRCA carriers in France, most eligible relatives are not referred for testing.[46] In the population-based trial in Israel, only 35% (29 of 82) of high-cancer-incidence families had received a referral for genetic counseling, despite its availability to all Israelis through the universal health care system. Although there is an equal risk of maternal and paternal transmission of BRCA1 and BRCA2, there is often a misperception about paternal transmission of breast cancer risk. In the Ontario study, the majority of families demonstrated paternal transmission of the BRCA mutation.[47] Many women and their physicians underestimate the significance of a family history of breast cancer on the father's side of the

---

41 Marroni, F., Aretini, P., D'Andrea, E., et al. "Evaluation of Widely Used Models for Predicting BRCA1 and BRCA2 Mutations," *Journal of Medical Genetics* vol. 41(4) (London: 2004) pp. 278–285.

42 Barcenas, C.H., Hosain, G.M., Arun, B., et al. "Assessing BRCA Carrier Probabilities in Extended Families," *Journal of Clinical Oncology* vol. 24(3) (Alexandria: 2006) pp. 354–360.

43 Antoniou, A.C., Hardy, R., Walker, L., et al. "Predicting the Likelihood of Carrying a BRCA1 or BRCA2 Mutation: Validation of BOADICEA, BRCAPRO, IBIS, Myriad and the Manchester Score," *Journal of Medical Genetics* vol. 107(1). (London: 2008), pp. 425–431. Downloaded from https://academic.oup.com/jnci/article-abstract/107/1/dju379/907914 by guest on 13 December 2018 11 of 11 | JNCI J Natl Cancer Inst, 2015, Vol. 107, No. 1 articling system using data from UK genetics clinics.

44 Freund, A., Cohen, M., Faisal, A. "The Doctor Is Just a Messenger: Beliefs of Ultra-Orthodox Jewish Women in Regard to Breast Cancer and Screening," *Journal of Religion and Health* vol. 53 (Springer): 2014, pp. 1075–1090.

45 Bellcross, C.A., et al. "Awareness and Utilization of BRCA1/2 Testing Among U.S. Primary Care Physicians," *American Journal of Preventive Medicine* vol. 40(1) (Elsevier): 2011, pp. 61–66.

46 Pujol, P., et al. "Lack of Referral for Genetic Counseling and Testing in BRCA1/2 and Lynch Syndromes: A Nationwide Study Based on 240,134 Consultations and 134,652 Genetic Tests," *Breast Cancer Research and Treatment* vol. 141(1) (Springer): 2013, pp. 135–144.

47 Metcalfe, "Screening for Founder Mutation in BRCA1 and BRCA2 in Unselected Jewish Women."

family. Only 34% of women diagnosed with breast cancer knew that a father can pass an abnormal breast cancer gene to his children[48] and less than half of all physicians (including oncologists) were aware that the gene can be passed through the father.[49,50] Population-based testing obviates the need to rely on family history, family disclosure, knowledge regarding paternal transmission, or physician referral.

2. What is the Ideal Age to Undergo BRCA Testing?

Proposed ages for BRCA testing include in utero, childhood, adolescence, prior to marriage, prior to conceiving the first child, age 25–30, upon completion of childbearing, and menopause. The ideal age for testing depends on how one intends to use the results. BRCA testing is performed to initiate early screening, prevent cancer with prophylactic surgery or chemoprevention, and to identify carriers who might undergo preimplantation gestational diagnosis (PGD) to prevent transmission of BRCA to potential offspring. To prevent cancer, predisposed individuals must be identified before cancer develops. BRCA-related cancers do not typically develop in childhood and rarely occur before the age of 25.[51] Thus, it is pointless to screen for the gene in utero or in children, decades before the disease manifests itself or screening is initiated. Conversely, testing after completion of childbearing or menopause is sub-optimal because the beneficial effects of risk-reducing surgery are attenuated after age 40, there is a risk of developing cancer between age 40 and menopause, and many years of potential intensive surveillance for early detection will have been lost. This leads to the conclusion that BRCA testing should ideally be performed between the ages of 25 and 30, ages at which screening is initiated and chemoprevention can be considered. Testing at age 25 allows women to plan their families with an eye to completing childbearing by age 40, to maximize the risk-reducing benefits of prophylactic oophorectomy.

---

48 Miesfeldt, S., Cohn, W., Ropka, M., et al. "Knowledge about Breast Cancer Risk Factors and Hereditary Breast Cancer Among Early-Onset Breast Cancer Survivors," *Familial Cancer* vol. 1 (Springer): 2001, pp. 135–141.

49 Pichert, G., Dietrich, D., Moosmann, P., et al. "Swiss Primary Care Physicians' Knowledge, Attitudes and Perception Towards Genetic Testing for Hereditary Breast Cancer," *Familial Cancer* vol. 2 (Springer): 2003, pp. 153–158.

50 Mouchawar, J., Klein, C.E., Mullineaux, L. "Colorado Family Physicians' Knowledge of Hereditary Breast Cancer and Related Practice," *Journal of Cancer Education* vol. 16 (Springer): 2001, pp. 33–37.

51 Metcalfe, K.A. et al. "Is It Time to Offer BRCA1 and BRCA2 Testing to All Jewish Women?" *Current Oncology* [S.l.] vol. 22 (Milton, Ontario: 2015) n. 4, p. e233-e236, June 2015. ISSN 1718–7729.

Mary-Claire King advocates BRCA testing for every woman, "at about age 30, in the course of routine medical care."[52] Rabbi Yair Hoffman proposes that *kallah* teachers instruct all women to undergo BRCA testing at age 25 or upon the first birthday of their first child.[53] He recommends testing upon reaching either of these two milestones because by age 25 many women will be married and can thus avoid discrimination in dating, and testing near marriage or near a birth might increase anxiety, and because this is the age at which intensive medical surveillance should begin. Rabbi Moshe Tendler disagrees, arguing that one should not wait until age 25 to undergo testing.[54] He believes that if you are old enough to marry, you are old enough to know your genetic future.

Should one undergo BRCA testing prior to marriage? Genetic testing before marriage for Tay Sachs has become routine. Couples can use the results of Tay Sachs testing to avoid marriage between two carriers of the mutation or to perform PGD to select embryos that do not carry both copies of the mutation. At first glance, one might consider applying this premarital testing model to BRCA screening. However, the differences in inheritance and in the diseases associated with these mutations suggest that doing so might not make sense. The Tay Sachs mutation is recessive, it does not affect the carrier, and concern arises only when two carriers marry each other and give birth to a child who harbors both copies of the recessive gene. The penetrance of Tay Sachs is 100%; all offspring who inherit both copies of the mutation will develop the disease in infancy. Tay Sachs is universally fatal in childhood. In contrast, the BRCA mutation is autosomal dominant, putting carriers themselves at increased risk of developing BRCA-related cancers. However, not all carriers of the mutation will develop BRCA-related cancers and if a BRCA-related cancer does develop, it will not do so until adulthood. Furthermore, there are screening interventions for early detection, and effective prophylactic treatments to prevent the development of BRCA-related cancers. In addition, BRCA-related cancers are curable. For the above reasons, the current model of screening the entire Ashkenazi population for Tay Sachs prior to marriage might not be appropriate for screening for the BRCA mutation.

Couples who would like to pursue pre-implantation genetic diagnosis (PGD) to prevent the birth of a child with the BRCA mutation must do BRCA testing prior to having children. However, testing before marriage

---

52 King, "Population Based Screening for BRCA1 and BRCA2."

53 http://www.5tjt.com/kallah-teachers-brca-testing-and-surgery/.

54 Personal communication, phone conversation, January 17, 2019, Israel.

can lead to discrimination in dating. In addition, because dating and marriage in the religious world can occur many years before surveillance for BRCA carriers is initiated, testing before marriage introduces anxiety over the mutation at a much earlier date than necessary. PGD is a challenging process financially, psychologically, and physically. PGD for all BRCA carriers might also be impractical. Modern *halakhic* decisors debate the use of PGD to select embryos that do not carry the mutation. Some permit but do not require PGD in this situation, as the parents would fulfill the *mitzvah* of having children even by bearing a child with the BRCA mutation.[55,56] There are others who believe that PGD should be reserved for the prevention of life-threatening diseases like Tay Sachs, and forbid this approach with regard to the birth of a child with the BRCA mutation. Machon Puah advocates dealing with each case individually. In families with known carriers of the BRCA mutation or a strong family history of breast (including in males) and ovarian cancer, testing for a BRCA mutation prior to marriage to prevent the birth of a BRCA carrier might be advisable. However, in light of the lower risk of harboring a BRCA mutation in the general Ashkenazi population, the reality that not all BRCA carriers will develop cancer, the fact that these cancers can be prevented and cured, and that such testing would further complicate *shiddukhim*/marriageability, offering population-based BRCA testing prior to marriage so that couples can choose to perform PGD on potential offspring is not recommended.

3. Arguments against Ashkenazi-Based Population Testing for BRCA Mutation

Population-based screening of the Ashkenazi population does not appear to be harmful. Arguments against such testing include uncertainty regarding the management of variants of unknown significance (VUS); the claims that BRCA testing causes anxiety, raises confidentiality issues, and fosters transmitter guilt; and cultural, work-related, and racial discrimination against BRCA carriers. In addition, critics contend that women without a family history of cancer are not interested in BRCA testing; that current models of genetic counseling cannot meet the increase in patient volume of population-based testing; and that the approach is not cost-effective. Finally, there is the misperception that there is no reason to undergo BRCA testing if one would not consider prophylactic surgery.

55 Steinberg, Avraham. *Ha-Refuah K-Halacha* vol. 2 (Schlesinger: Jerusalem, 1988) pp. 116–7.

56 Machon Puah. "*Treatment for BRCA*." http://www.ouisrael.org/tidbits/detail/Machon-Puah-Treatment-for-BRCA, 27 Dec. 2011.

However, outcomes data from studies of population-based BRCA testing in Ashkenazi women invalidate these arguments.

3a. Uncertainty Regarding Management of Variants of Unknown Significance

Variants of unknown significance (VUS) are DNA alterations of unknown pathogenicity. A diagnosis of VUS can be particularly anxiety provoking as the appropriate management of these genetic alterations is unknown. To avoid this problem, proponents of population-based testing for BRCA do not recommend reporting VUS. Testing should focus only on those BRCA mutations with known deleterious effects. In the Ashkenazi population, limiting testing to known founder mutations makes sense because the founder mutations account for 90% of the mutations identified.[57,58,59,60,61] If VUS focused founder mutation testing is performed in an Ashkenazi population, VUS are rare, eliminating this concern.[62] In addition, the increased number of test results should lead to the classification of many additional variants.

3b. Population-Based Testing Increases Anxiety

One of the reasons that Rabbi Moshe Tendler previously objected to population-based BRCA testing was his concern that mass screening might

---

57 King, "Population Based Screening for BRCA1 and BRCA2."

58 Kauff, N.D., Perez-Segura, P., Robson, M.E., et al. "Incidence of Non-Founder BRCA1 and BRCA2 Mutations in High Risk Ashkenazi Breast and Ovarian Cancer Families," *Journal of Medical Genetics* vol. 39 (London: 2002) pp. 611–614.

59 Phelan, C.M., Kwan, E., Jack, E., et al. "A Low Frequency of Non-Founder BRCA1 Mutations in Ashkenazi Jewish Breast-Ovarian Cancer Families," *Human Mutation* vol. 20. (Wiley Online Library): 2002, pp. 352–357.

60 Frank, T.S., Deffenbaugh, A.M., Reid, J.E., et al. "Clinical Characteristics of Individuals with Germline Mutations in BRCA1 and BRCA2: Analysis of 10,000 Individuals," *Journal of Clinical Oncology* vol. 20 (Alexandria: 2002) pp. 1480–1490.

61 Rosenthal, E., Moyes, K., Arnell, C., et al. "Incidence of BRCA1 and BRCA2 Non-Founder Mutations in Patients of Ashkenazi Jewish Ancestry," *Breast Cancer Research and Treatment* vol. 149 (Springer): 2015, pp. 223–227.

62 Spearman, A.D., Sweet, K., Zhou, X.P., McLennan, J., Couch, F.J., Toland, A.E. "Clinically Applicable Models to Characterize BRCA1 and BRCA2 Variants of Uncertain Significance," *Journal of Clinical Oncology* vol. 26 (Alexandria: 2008) pp. 5393–5400.

cause mental anguish.[63] However, compelling scientific data proves that population-based testing has a transient and minimal impact on anxiety.

Most women who present for clinical genetic testing already have significant family or personal histories of breast or ovarian cancer, and might expect a positive genetic test result. Studies show that among women referred for BRCA testing based on family history, the discovery of a BRCA mutation does not have a negative impact on their psychosocial functioning.[64,65,66,67] To the contrary, several studies report that the testing imparts important psychological benefits,[68,69,70,71] although a few noted increased distress.[72] However, women participating in a population-based genetic

---

63 Mosenkis, Ari. "Genetic Screening for Breast Cancer Susceptibility: A Torah Perspective," *Journal of Halacha and Contemporary Society* vol. 34 (Fall) (New York: 1997) pp. 5–26.

64 Schwartz, M.D., Peshkin, B.N., Hughes, C., Main, D., Isaacs, C., Lerman, C. "Impact of BRCA1/BRCA2 Mutation Testing on Psychologic Distress in a Clinic-Based Sample," *Journal of Clinical Oncology* vol. 20 (Alexandria: 2002) pp. 514–20.

65 Watson, M., Foster, C., Eeles, R., et al., on behalf of the psychosocial study collaborators. "Psychosocial Impact of Breast/Ovarian (BRCA1/2) Cancer–Predictive Genetic Testing in a UK Multi-Centre Clinical Cohort," *British Journal of Cancer* vol. 91 (Springer): 2004, pp. 1787–94.

66 Smith, A.W., Dougall, A.L., Posluszny, D.M., Somers, T.J., Rubinstein, W.S., Baum, A. "Psychological Distress and Quality of Life Associated with Genetic Testing for Breast Cancer Risk," *Psycho-Oncology* vol. 17 (Wiley Online Library): 2008, pp. 767–73.

67 Meiser, B., Butow, P., Friedlander, M., et al. "Intention to Undergo Prophylactic Bilateral Mastectomy in Women with an Increased Risk of Developing Hereditary Breast Cancer," *Journal of Clinical Oncology* vol. 18 (Alexandria: 2000) pp. 2250–7.

68 Nelson, H.D., Huffman, L.H., Fu, R., et al., "Genetic Risk Assessment and BRCA Mutation Testing for Breast and Ovarian Cancer Susceptibility: Systematic Evidence Review for the U.S. Preventive Services Task Force," *Annals of Internal Medicine* vol. 143(5) (Philadelphia: 2005) pp. 362–379.

69 Sivell, S., Iredale, R., Gray, J., et al. "Cancer Genetic Risk Assessment for Individuals at Risk of Familial Breast Cancer," *Cochrane Database Syst Review* vol. 2. (Wiley): 2007, CD003721.

70 Schlich-Bakker, K.J., ten Kroode, H.F., Ausems, M.G. "A Literature Review of the Psychological Impact of Genetic Testing in Breast Cancer Patients," *Patient Education and Counseling* vol. 62(1) (Elsevier): 2006, pp. 13–20.

71 Meiser, B., Butow, P., Friedlander, M., et al. "Psychological Impact of Genetic Testing in Women from High-Risk Breast Cancer Families," *European Journal of Cancer* vol. 38(15) (Elsevier): 2002, pp. 2025–2031.

72 Smith, K.R., West, J.A., Croyle, R.T., et al. "Familial Context of Genetic Testing for Cancer Susceptibility: Moderating Effect of Siblings' Test Results on Psychological Distress One to Two Weeks after BRCA1 Mutation Testing," *Cancer*

testing program often have no family history of cancer, and a positive genetic test comes as a surprise. In 98% of such women, the results of BRCA testing are negative, therefore the testing does not increase anxiety.[73] The concern is that women who test positive will experience psychological distress. A Canadian study found that in unselected Jewish women who underwent population-based genetic testing, cancer-related distress was low before testing and increased significantly by one year after receipt of positive test results (no such effect was seen after a negative test result).[74] For women who received a positive test result, distress levels decreased significantly two years after testing[75] and returned to baseline **in women who then chose preventive surgery**. Women who tested positive and decided against prophylactic surgery had high baseline anxiety prior to testing and continued to experience high levels of distress two years after testing. Future studies will determine the long-term impact of population-based testing in women who test positive and decline prophylactic surgery. Nevertheless, 92% of women were satisfied with the testing process. This study was not randomized and did not compare distress levels among women who were tested due to family history with those who underwent population-based screening. In addition, none of the women received pretest genetic counselling. In a randomized trial comparing the psychological impact of BRCA testing in women who underwent population-based testing with those who were tested based on family history, there was no difference in anxiety levels, depression, or physical/mental well-being between these two populations.[76] These results suggest that women who undergo population-based testing and receive a positive result experience a transient increase in anxiety similar to that of women who are tested based on family history. In those who opt for prophylactic surgery, distress returns to baseline at two years. Collectively, these findings confirm that for the majority of women, population-based testing does not harm their quality of life or psychological well-being and ameliorate concerns regarding the impact of population-based testing on

---

Epidemiology Biomarkers and Prevention vol. 8(4, part 2) (Philadelphia: 1999) pp. 385–392.

73 Metcalfe, "Patient Satisfaction and Cancer-Related Distress."

74 Ibid.

75 Metcalfe K.A., Mian, N., Enmore, M., et al. "Long-Term Follow-Up of Jewish Women with a BRCA1 and BRCA2 Mutation Who Underwent Population Genetic Screening," *Breast Cancer Research and Treatment* vol. 133 (Springer): 2012, pp. 735–40.

76 Manchanda, "Population Testing for Cancer Predisposing BRCA1/BRCA2 Mutations in the Ashkenazi-Jewish Community," pp. 1–19.

distress and anxiety. Future studies will further our understanding of the psychological impact of population-based testing especially in women who test positive and decline prophylactic surgery. However, even if population-based BRCA testing increases anxiety, one could argue in its favor because such testing leads to *pikuaḥ nefesh*.[77]

3c. Population-Based Testing Causes Discrimination

A woman who learns that she carries a BRCA mutation might confront group stigmatization, as well as discrimination in health, life, and disability insurance; in the workplace; and in *shiddukhim*.

Concerns regarding employment and legal discrimination against BRCA carriers are well founded. Although in the United States the Genetic Information Non-Discrimination Act provides federal protection against genetic discrimination of unaffected carriers, it is neither comprehensive nor easily actionable.[78] The Act protects the health insurance and employment status of individuals with hereditary cancer risks,[79] but excludes military members and veterans, and does not protect against discrimination regarding the availability of life, disability, and long-term care insurance. Even if legal protections were comprehensive and airtight, perception alone might be enough to create social stigma.

The concern that testing positive for BRCA will affect *shiddukhim* is also legitimate. Population-based genetic testing prior to marriage introduces many ethical dilemmas. Specifically, is there an obligation to disclose the results to a potential suitor? If so, what is the appropriate time frame? Before the *shiddukh* is made? On the first date? As the relationship begins to intensify? After the engagement? After marriage? If one waits until after marriage, would failure to disclose this information invalidate the marriage from a *halakhic* perspective? In one situation, where a young

---

77 In a forthcoming edition of *Ha-Refua K-Halacha,* which Rav Professor Avraham Steinberg shared with the author in a personal communication in January 2019, Rav Steinberg lists all of the potential arguments against population-based testing, including the possibility that testing will cause anxiety and psychological distress, and states, "When weighing the pros and cons of population-based testing, the pros ultimately outweigh the cons because *pikuaḥ nefesh*, the value of saving a life, overrides all other concerns."

78 Baruch, S., Hudson, K. "Civilian and Military Genetics: Nondiscrimination Policy in a Post-GINA World," *American Journal of Human Genetics* vol. 83. (Elsevier): 2008, pp. 435– 444.

79 Hudson, K.L., Holohan, M.K., Collins, F.S. "Keeping Pace with the Times: The Genetic Information Nondiscrimination Act of 2008," *New England Journal of Medicine* vol. 358 (Waltham: 2008) pp. 2661–2663.

girl whose mother died of breast cancer was in the early stages of dating, the boy's family insisted that she undergo BRCA testing before it would allow the relationship to progress, although his family promised to continue the relationship even if she tested positive. The woman did not want to know her BRCA status because she feared that a positive result would cause tremendous anxiety, leading her to spend the rest of her life waiting for cancer. Rav Chaim Kanievsky ruled that she was not required to undergo genetic testing.[80] Questions such as this might proliferate if BRCA testing were offered to all Ashkenazi women. However, delaying testing until after marriage (assuming marriage occurs before the age of 30) could obviate many of these dilemmas. In addition, population-based testing would require the development of an accompanying educational initiative to inform the public of the risks of carrying a BRCA mutation and of the existence of effective interventions to reduce the risk of developing cancer. Such a campaign could reduce stigmatization of and discrimination against BRCA carriers in *shiddukhim.*

3d. Population-Based Testing Violates Confidentiality

Population-based screening for BRCA raises numerous problems relating to confidentiality. If a woman tests positive, whom should she inform? Family members? Employers? It makes sense for her to tell her immediate family members, as they are at the most risk of carrying the gene and later developing breast cancer, and because she is likely to need their emotional support. However, Nishmat Avraham asked Rabbi Elyashiv whether a third party is obligated to disclose to close relatives the BRCA status of a woman who tested positive and refused to inform her immediate family, now at increased of developing cancer. Rabbi Elyashiv permitted the woman to maintain her confidentiality because the risk to other family members is not definite; even if a relative does carry the gene, it is not certain that he/she will develop cancer; and there is no completely preventative or curative treatment for cancer in those relatives who test positive. Therefore, he found no obligation to inform other family members.[81] It is possible that Rav Elyashiv might rule differently today, given the existence of effective potentially life-saving interventions to reduce the risk of developing breast and ovarian cancer. The argument for informing distant relatives is still less compelling. Although population-based testing raises confidentiality issues that must be addressed, these

80 https://drive.google.com/file/d/0B6Vpm_W8m0xMbmtxY1VvZFBVQk0/view.

81 *Nishmat Avraham* (*Even Ha-Ezer* and *Ḥoshen Mishpat*) vol. 3 (Brooklyn: Mesorah Publications, 2004) p. 302.

should not discourage population-based testing, which facilitates *pikuaḥ nefesh*.

3e. Population-Based Testing Causes Transmitter Guilt

Feelings of transmitter guilt can plague parents who have passed on a harmful mutation to their children.[82,83,84,85]

3f. Women Who Are BRCA Negative Might Mistakenly Believe that They Are Not at Risk of Breast or Ovarian Cancer

Some BRCA negative women might assume that they are at no risk of developing cancer. They might fail to recognize the possibility that other factors, including mutations in other susceptibility genes and in established environmental, reproductive, and lifestyle factors can increase the risk of breast and ovarian cancer. Without appropriate counseling, women might even avoid routine screening, since they incorrectly interpret negative test results to mean that they are at zero risk of breast or ovarian cancer. A public health campaign educating Israelis about the risk of breast and ovarian cancer in women who are BRCA negative must accompany any population-based testing.

3g. Women Do Not Want to Undergo BRCA Testing

Critics of population-based BRCA testing argue that women without a family history of breast or ovarian cancer are not interested in BRCA testing. However, Ashkenazi Jews' high participation levels in genetic screening programs for Tay Sachs disease and other genetic disorders refute this

---

82 Mellon, S., Gauthier, J., Cichon, M., et al. "Knowledge, Attitudes, and Beliefs of Arab-American Women Regarding Inherited Cancer Risk," *Journal of Genetic Counseling* vol. 22. (Springer): 2013, pp. 268–276.

83 Weitzel, J.N., Blazer, R.K., Macdonald, D.J., et al. "Genetics, Genomics, and Cancer Risk Assessment: State of The Art and Future Directions in the Era of Personalized Medicine," *CA Cancer: A Cancer Journal for Clinicians* vol. 61. (Wiley Online Library): 2011, pp. 327–359.

84 Allford, A., Qureshi, N., Barwell, J., et al. "What Hinders Minority Ethnic Access to Cancer Genetics Services and What May Help?" *European Journal of Human Genetics* vol. 22 (Springer): 2014, pp. 866–874.

85 Strømsvik, N., Råheim, M., Oyen, N., et al. "Men in the Women's World of Hereditary Breast and Ovarian Cancer: A Systematic Review," *Familial Cancer* vol. 8 (Springer): 2009, pp. 221–229.

claim.[86] An early study of women at high risk of carrying a BRCA mutation reported that 79% would "definitely" choose to undergo BRCA testing and 16% would "probably" do so, attesting to a substantial interest in such testing.[87] Ashkenazi Jews' widespread participation in a variety of BRCA research studies provides further evidence of women's support for population-based testing.[88] In Ontario, enthusiasm for population-based testing among Ashkenazim was overwhelming, as 2,000 women enrolled in the study within two weeks of the publication of a single newspaper article calling for participants.[89] 93% of the participants reported satisfaction with population-based testing.[90] In Israel, participation in population-based testing among Ashkenazi women is high, averaging 67%.[91]

3h. Population-Based Testing Promotes Racial Discrimination

A pitfall of population-based testing of Ashkenazi women is that this approach excludes two other groups that are at an increased risk of carrying a BRCA mutation—Ashkenazi men and Sephardim. The frequency of the BRCA mutation in men is no different than it is in women, and sons are just as likely to inherit BRCA as daughters. In men, the mutation is associated with an increased risk of prostate and male breast cancer. National Comprehensive Cancer Network (NCCN) recommends screening for breast and prostate cancer in male carriers.[92] However, the risk of cancer in male BRCA carriers is substantially lower than the risk in female carriers. In addition, there are no proven risk-reducing surgical options for

---

86 Kaback, M.M. "Population-Based Genetic Screening for Reproductive Counseling: The Tay-Sachs Disease Model," *European Journal of Pediatrics* vol. 159(suppl.3) (Springer): 2000, pp. S192–S195.

87 Struewing, J.P., Lerman, C., Kase, R.G., Giambarresi, T.R., Tucker, M.A. "Anticipated Uptake and Impact of Genetic Testing in Hereditary Breast and Ovarian Cancer Families," *Cancer Epidemiology Biomarkers and Prevention* vol. 4 (Philadelphia: 1995) pp. 169–173.

88 Rubinstein, W.S. "Hereditary Breast Cancer in Jews," *Familial Cancer* vol. 3 (Springer): 2004, pp. 249–257.

89 Metcalfe, "Screening for Founder Mutation in BRCA1 and BRCA2 in Unselected Jewish Women."

90 Metcalfe, K.A., et al. "Is it Time to Offer BRCA1 and BRCA2 Testing to All Jewish Women?" *Current Oncology* vol. 22, n.4 [S.l.] (Ontario: 2015) pp. e233–e236. ISSN 1718–7729.

91 Personal communication, Professor Efrat Levy-Lahad, January 23, 2019, Israel.

92 NCCN Clinical Practice Guidelines in Oncology (NCCN Guidelines). Genetic/Familial High-risk Assessment: Breast and Ovarian. Version 2.2019. www.nccn.org/professionals/physician_gls/pdf/genetics_screening.pdf (Accessed on September 10, 2018).

male carriers. In men, current recommendations for BRCA testing are limited to those with a strong family history of such cancers.[93]

Emphasis on Ashkenazi ancestry as a risk factor for BRCA mutations could lead to misperceptions and complacency in non-Ashkenazi Jews, and population-based BRCA testing could amplify differential access to care.[94,95] In addition, some argue that targeted screening for Tay-Sachs disease in Ashkenazim has detracted attention from diseases in non-Ashkenazi Jewish populations.[96] Although specific Sephardi populations such as 'pure' Sephardim who originated in Spain and Portugal and immigrated to Israel from Iraq, Yemen, Iran, and Afghanistan appear to be at increased risk of carrying a BRCA mutation,[97] current scientific evidence does not currently support BRCA testing for the entire Sephardi population.[98] More comprehensive research is needed before a recommendation can be made regarding testing the entire Sephardi population. Ashkenazi-based population testing for the BRCA mutation should include genetic counseling for non-Ashkenazi populations.

3i. It Is Impossible to Offer Genetic Counseling to the Entire Ashkenazi Population

Traditional cancer genetic counseling, including both pre-test and post-test counseling, is impractical on a large scale. Offering intensive genetic counseling to 100 women who have no family history, with the expectation that only two will be positive, would be an inefficient allocation of limited genetic counseling resources. Population-wide BRCA screening

93 NCCN Clinical Practice Guidelines in Oncology (NCCN Guidelines). Genetic/Familial High-risk Assessment: Breast and Ovarian. Version 2.2019. www.nccn.org/professionals/physician_gls/pdf/genetics_screening.pdf (Accessed on September 10, 2018).

94 Cancer screening: United States, 2010 MMWR Morb Mortal Wkly Rep 61: 41–45, 2012 Centers for Disease Control and Prevention (CDC) Medline.

95 Liao, Y., Bang, D., Cosgrove, S., et al. "Surveillance of Health Status in Minority Communities: Racial and Ethnic Approaches to Community Health Across the U.S." (REACH U.S.) Risk Factor Survey, United States, 2009 *MMWR Surveillance Summaries* vol. 60 (Atlanta: 2011) pp. 1– 44.

96 Brandt-Rauf, S.I., Raveis, V.H., Drummond, N.F., Conte, J.A., Rothman, S.M. "Ashkenazi Jews and Breast Cancer: The Consequences of Linking Ethnic Identity to Genetic Disease," *American Journal of Public Health* vol. 96 (Washington: 2006) pp. 1979–1988.

97 Sagi, M., Eilat, A., Ben Avi, L., Goldberg, Y., Bercovich, D., Hamburger, T., Peretz, T., Lerer, I. "Two BRCA1/2 Founder Mutations in Jews of Sephardic Origin," *Familial Cancer* vol. 10(1) (Springer): 2011, pp. 59–63.

98 Personal communication, Professor Efrat Levy-Lahad, January 23, 2019, Israel.

would generate a demand that would overwhelm the capacity of current genetic counseling practices.

All three studies of Ashkenazi-based testing offered a streamlined approach to genetic testing, limiting pre-test counseling to written educational materials and reserving post-test genetic counseling for women who tested positive or had a strong family history of breast or ovarian cancer. Women reported high levels of satisfaction with this approach.[99] Selective genetic counseling did not reduce the increase in risk-reducing interventions after a BRCA diagnosis. One year after testing, 100% of women had undergone MRI screening examination. Within two years of receiving a positive genetic test result, 11.1% had undergone prophylactic mastectomy and 90%, prophylactic oophorectomy.[100] In the Israeli study, although the pretest written materials included the phone number of a genetic counselor, only three out of 1,800 women contacted her.[101] These results confirm that Ashkenazi-based population testing can be successfully implemented using a more tailored approach to genetic counseling. To this end, future studies of population-based testing including the Screen Project in Canada, the BFOR trial in the United States, and the current proposal for population-based testing submitted to the Israel Ministry of Health, all offer selective genetic counseling.[102,103]

3j. Population-Based Screening Is Not Cost-Effective

Outcome data from two studies, including the randomized U.K. trial, strongly refute the claim that BRCA testing is not cost-effective. They show that population-based BRCA is highly cost-effective across a broad range of parameters, confirming that it would be cost-effective in the Israeli health-care system.[104,105]

---

99 Metcalfe, "Patient Satisfaction and Cancer-Related Distress Among Unselected Jewish Women."

100 Ibid.

101 Personal communication, Professor Efrat Levy-Lahad, January 23, 2019, Israel.

102 Akbari, M.R., Gojska, N., Narod, S.A. "Coming of Age in Canada: A Study of Population-Based Genetic Testing for Breast and Ovarian Cancer," *Current Oncology* vol. 24(5) [S.l.] (Ontario: 2017) pp. 282-283.

103 Personal communication, Professor Efrat Levy-Lahad, January 23, 2019, Israel.

104 Rubinstein, W.S., Jiang, H., Dellefave, L., Rademaker, A.W. "Cost-Effectiveness of Population-Based BRCA1/2 Testing and Ovarian Cancer Prevention for Ashkenazi Jews: A Call for Dialogue," *Genetics in Medicine* vol. 11(9) (Springer): 2009, pp. 629–639.

105 Manchanda, R., Legood, R., Burnell, M., McGuire, A., et al. "Cost Effectiveness of Population Screening for BRCA; Mutations in Ashkenazi-Jewish Women

3k. There Is No Reason to Undergo BRCA Testing if One Will Not Pursue Prophylactic Surgery

A growing number of *poskim* believe that prophylactic surgery is *halakhically* permitted. Some even posit that a BRCA carrier is required to undergo prophylactic surgery.[106] Even if a person with a positive result does not pursue prophylactic surgery, population-based screening is still important because it will enable women who test positive to initiate intensive surveillance to facilitate early diagnosis of breast and ovarian cancer or chemoprevention.

4. How Does *Halakhah* View BRCA Testing?

Answering this question is critical to any public health initiative in Israel, as a large percentage of the population would not undergo BRCA testing without rabbinic endorsement. While one can debate the appropriateness of seeking a rabbi's guidance before undergoing a medical intervention, the recent measles epidemic illustrates the power of modern *poskim* to facilitate disease prevention: The joint statement of leading *charedi* rabbis exhorting the Israeli population to get vaccinated against measles, and referring to those who refuse as *shofekh damim,* murderers, had a profound impact on vaccine increase in the *charedi* community.[107]

Given the scientific evidence supporting BRCA testing for all Ashkenazi women, is there a *halakhic* obligation for such women to undergo BRCA testing? Am I, an Ashkenazi woman without family history of breast or ovarian cancer, obligated to undergo BRCA testing?

The *halakhic* obligation to prevent disease is based on several Biblical sources including "*ve-nishmartem me'od le-nafshoteikhem*—And you shall protect your souls exceedingly," (*Devarim* 4:15) and "*rak hishamer le-kha u-shemor nafshekha*—only guard yourself and protect your soul" (*Devarim* 4:9). Rambam *Hilkhot De'ot* explains that we are obligated to prevent disease because a healthy body is a necessary precondition to performing the commandments and serving G-d.[108] In addition, in his *Hilkhot Rotze'aḥ*

Compared to Family-History Based Testing," *Journal of the National Cancer Institute* vol. 107(1) (Oxford: 2015) pp. 1-14.

106 Grossman, S.G., "The Angelina Jolie Effect in Jewish Law: Prophylactic Mastectomy and Oophorectomy in BRCA Carriers," *Rambam Maimonides Medical Journal*, vol. 6(4) (Haifa: 2015) p. e0037. https://www.yutorah.org/lectures/lecture.cfm/730940/rabbi-mordechai-i-willig/catching-cancer-before-it-catches-you-medical-and-halachic-implications-of-brca-gene-testing/. Rabbi Willig addresses this issue 99 minutes into the recording.

107 http://rotter.net/forum/scoops1/511727.shtml.

108 Maimonides (1138–1204), *De'ot* 4:2.

11:4, Rambam lists a series of medical interventions to prevent disease, including eating only when hungry, drinking only when thirsty, and going to the bathroom when necessary. This is not an exclusive or exhaustive list but a broad one with general applicability and fluidity. Presumably, as medical knowledge evolves, the list of interventions that we are required to perform to prevent disease might expand to include a *halakhic* obligation for all Ashkenazi women to undergo BRCA testing as it helps identify women who can take steps to reduce their risk of cancer and chances of dying.

4a. Extrapolating from Tay Sachs

There are, however, two *halakhic* principles that could potentially invalidate any *halakhic* obligation to undergo genetic testing in general and BRCA testing in particular. The first principle is based on *Devarim* 18:13, "You shall be perfect in the eyes of G-d," about which Rashi writes, "and do not search after the future," which has been interpreted as a prohibition on visiting fortunetellers and seeking the future. Does genetic testing that determines our genetic future qualify as a form of fortune telling?

The second *halakhic* principle at issue is that of *"shomer peta'im, Hashem,"* or "G-d watches over the simple."[109] The implication of this verse is that one should not investigate the dangers around him or within him but ought instead to leave his fate in the hands of G-d. This verse appears throughout the Talmud as a justification for engaging in risky behavior. Why is a woman allowed to become pregnant even though doing so can be dangerous to her? Why is a woman permitted to engage in intercourse after bloodletting or on the ninetieth day of pregnancy (intercourse under these circumstances was considered dangerous)? The answer in each of these cases is that they are permitted because "G-d watches over the simple." This principle also permits us to drive cars even though there is danger of an accident and to cross streets even though there is a risk of being hit by a car. Does *shomer peta'im Hashem* override the obligation to undergo BRCA testing? Should we forgo testing and rely on G-d to prevent breast and ovarian cancer? We should not, because multiple sources suggest that the verse does not apply when the danger is easy to detect, and that instead, there is an obligation to investigate.[110]

In the early days of Tay Sachs testing, Rav Moshe Feinstein was asked about the permissibility of Tay Sachs testing. In his *teshuva,* he weighs the competing values of *ve-nishmartem*, the obligation to prevent disease, and

---

109 *Psalms* 116:6.

110 *Proverbs* 14:115, *Sanhedrin* 110b, *Niddah* 31a, *Avodah Zarah* 30b, *Yevamot* 72a, *Shabbat* 129b; *Tosefta, Niddah* 2:4.

shomer peta'im, the apparent obligation to rely on G-d for a cure and the prohibition against searching after the future, including the possibility that genetic testing constitutes a form of seeking our genetic future.[111] He concludes that the prohibition against searching after the future and the principle of *shomer peta'im Hashem* do not apply to Tay Sachs testing since such testing is simple to do and refusal to test is equivalent to "closing our eyes to what one can see." Therefore, he advocates genetic testing for Tay Sachs. Can one derive an obligation for Ashkenazi women to undergo BRCA testing from Rav Moshe's mandate for Tay Sachs testing? As I noted earlier, there are significant differences in the transmission, penetrance, and prognosis of the two genetic diseases, making extrapolation from Tay Sachs testing to BRCA testing problematic. Because BRCA-related cancers occur in adulthood and not infancy, do not develop in all carriers, and are potentially preventable and curable, perhaps there is less urgency to BRCA testing. Rabbi Moshe Tendler, Rav Moshe Feinstein's son-in-law, speculates however that had his father-in-law been asked specifically about the obligation of all Ashkenazi women to undergo BRCA testing, he would have unequivocally endorsed BRCA testing for all women with the same enthusiasm that he endorsed Tay Sachs testing.[112] Nonetheless, Rabbi Moshe Tendler emphasizes that since no one ever posed the question regarding BRCA testing directly to Rav Moshe Feinstein, that conclusion is theoretical; it is impossible to discern what Rav Moshe Feinstein's true position on BRCA testing would have been.

4b. How Do Modern *Poskim* View Population-Based BRCA Testing of Ashkenazi Women?

In 2000, even before medical data confirmed that risk-reducing surgery or surveillance had life-saving potential, Rabbi J.D. Bleich wrote, "Genetic testing, including testing for BRCA1 and BRCA2, should be regarded as halakhically mandated in circumstances in which medical science believes that the results are likely to affect treatment in a manner that will enhance longevity anticipation or well-being. Certainly, a person identified as being at risk for a specific disease is obligated to pursue all available measures in order to ward off the disease or to diagnose its presence while the disease is yet in an incipient stage and still amenable to cure."[113] He bases this "halakhic mandate" to undergo BRCA testing on the verse "*Ve-nishmartem me'od le-nafshoteikhem,* And you shall be exceedingly watchful of your

---

111 *Iggerot Moshe, Even He-Ezer* IV, no. 10.

112 Personal communication, Rabbi Moshe Tendler, January 16, 2019, Israel.

113 Bleich, J.D. "Genetic Screening: Survey of Recent *Halachic* Periodical Literature," *Tradition* vol. 34 (Brooklyn: 2000) pp. 63–87.

lives" (*Devarim* 4:15) and concludes that BRCA testing should be included in Rambam's *Hilkhot Rotze'aḥ* list of interventions to pursue to maintain health, because a doctor who knows that he is examining a BRCA carrier might examine her breasts a little more carefully to look for a lump. In light of recent scientific data that confirm that BRCA testing saves lives and that the benefits of testing are far greater than a more thorough breast exam, if one asked him today about the obligation of all Ashkenazi women to undergo BRCA testing, Rabbi Bleich would in all likelihood offer an even stronger endorsement. In a 2008 Yeshiva University Conference on Medical Ethics, Rabbi Mordechai Willig also supported BRCA testing in all Ashkenazi women.[114]

Until recently, few other *poskim* had weighed in on the obligation of Ashkenazi women to undergo population-based testing for the BRCA mutation. However, because of their lengthy discussions with this author, several modern *poskim* have begun to consider this issue. In the forthcoming edition of *Ha-Refua K-Halakha*, Rav Professor Avraham Steinberg writes that there is a *halakhic* obligation for women with a family of history of breast and ovarian cancer to undergo BRCA testing and that testing in such women is strongly recommended. Rav Steinberg strongly recommends that all women with a strong family history of breast or ovarian cancer undergo BRCA testing before their first pregnancy. This will give those who test positive the opportunity to consider PGD in order to avoid the birth of a child who will carry the mutation. He also recommends BRCA testing for all Ashkenazi women at age 25-30 when surveillance would begin, a recommendation that would avoid discrimination in *shiddukhim* as many women would already be married at this age.[115] He writes that because genetic testing is straightforward and without risk, and because those who test positive face a 70% chance of being diagnosed with cancer during the course of their lives, BRCA testing falls under the commandment, "*ve-nishmartem me'od l-nafshotekhem.*" Rav Professor Steinberg states that BRCA testing does not violate the prohibition against searching after the future because the danger of carrying a BRCA mutation is known and common. He writes that ultimately *pikuaḥ nefesh,* the opportunity to

---

114 http://curiousjew.blogspot.com/2007/01/yu-medical-ethics-genetic-screening.html; https://www.yutorah.org/lectures/lecture.cfm/730940/rabbi-mordechai-i-willig/catching-cancer-before-it-catches-you-medical-and-halachic-implications-of-brca-gene-testing/.

115 Personal communication with Rav Professor Steinberg occurred on January 2019. The forthcoming edition of *Ha-Refua K-Halacha* has not yet been published

save lives, overrides all other concerns regarding any potential arguments against BRCA testing.

In 1997, Rabbi Moshe Tendler was quoted in a personal communication as strongly opposing population-based testing for BRCA because he feared that a positive test result would cause anxiety and discrimination, especially in *shiddukhim*.[116] Over the last 22 years, several subsequent publications have cited this original article and reiterated Rabbi Tendler's strong objection to BRCA testing in Ashkenazi women without a family history of breast or ovarian cancer. In fact, as recently as May 2017, Dr. Daniel Eisenberg wrote, "Rabbi Moshe Dovid Tendler, chairman of biology at Yeshiva University, once described genetic testing for BRCA genes as an issue of 'tyranny of knowledge.' He rightly stated that when information causes anxiety, but offers no way to reduce that anxiety, it controls us. In the case of screening for the BRCA genes, where no absolutely reliable diagnostic tool exists, the patient is faced with the prospect that she may develop breast or ovarian cancer, diseases which she cannot guard against without radical prophylactic surgery."[117]

Rabbi Moshe Tendler has since modified his position on BRCA testing for all Ashkenazi women.[118] His earlier concerns regarding testing were only that the mere act of undergoing genetic testing could make *shiddukhim* difficult and thus he advised his students to be tested in Israel, rather than in America, so as to keep people from knowing that they had done it. However, he now declares, "I am in full support of BRCA testing for all Jewish women, not just Ashkenazi women, and you can quote me on that. I believe that today it is a חיוב דאורייתא. It is an absolute *halakhic* requirement to do the testing since we have the means to respond to a positive test. It's not just finding out and not being able to do anything about it." In fact, he does not think that women should delay testing until the age of 25–30 when surveillance can begin. He recommends that women undergo BRCA testing as soon as they are married. "If you are old enough to get married, you are old enough to know what your genetic future holds for the next 20–30 years. There are enough cases of it (cancer) occurring in your twenties and thirties for the test to be done and provide valuable information." The obligation to undergo BRCA testing is so strong that Rabbi Tendler believes there is no situation in which one is permitted to refuse BRCA testing. Only the *gedolei Yisrael* of the past, such as Yosef *ha-tzadik,* who achieved such a high level of spirituality that G-d performed miracles for him on a daily basis, can rely on *Hashem* for

116 Mosenkis, "Genetic Screening for Breast Cancer Susceptibility."

117 http://www.aish.com/ci/sam/Genetic_Screening_for_Breast_Cancer_Genes.html.

118 Personal communication, Rabbi Moshe Tendler, January 16, 2019, Israel.

cure. "A person does not have that individual right unless he is of the stature of Yosef *ha-tzadik*. Anyone less than Yosef *ha-tzadik* is criticized by our *ḥakhamim* for failure to take advantage of whatever can be helpful to him. There is a חיוב of a person to help himself. G-d allowed it in the laws of nature for us to be vaccinated to prevent disease, for us to do testing so that we can control disease, then you are required to do so. Period." Rabbi Tendler's endorsement of BRCA testing for *all* Jewish women is unequivocal and unconditional.

Rabbi Yuval Cherlow has also stated that all Ashkenazi women must undergo testing. "If an individual Ashkenazi woman asked me if she should undergo BRCA testing, I would tell her absolutely. I would tell her to run. If testing were only being done on *Shabbat*, she may undergo testing on *Shabbat*. The larger question is whether we as a Jewish society should fund such testing."[119] As more modern *poskim* become aware of the medical benefits of population-based testing for all Ashkenazi women, I believe that the number of rabbinic leaders who obligate testing will increase.

Future Directions

In the United States, The BFOR Trial (Breast Cancer Founder Research Study) is offering free BRCA testing to 4,000 Ashkenazi men and women in four U.S. cities.[120] Study participants register via their smartphone or computer, complete an online education module, provide their informed consent electronically, and have their lab test order sent directly to a local Quest Diagnostics Patient Service Center to which the participant then goes to supply a DNA sample. The participant's primary care physician or a BFOR cancer genetics specialist will provide test results, follow-up genetic counseling, and order additional genetic testing if appropriate. Most health insurance covers intensive screening or risk-reducing surgery for those found to carry a BRCA mutation.

Canada launched the Screen Project in March 2017 to offer BRCA testing to all women and men 18 years of age or older.[121] It uses a guided direct-to-consumer approach through the study's web site (http://www.thescreenproject.ca/) to enroll individuals. A team of genetic counselors contacts all individuals with a mutation in person or by

119 Personal communication, Rabbi Yuval Cherlow, February 19, 2019, Israel.

120 https://www.bforstudy.com/release.

121 Akbari, M.R., Gosjka, N., Narod, S.A. "Coming of Age in Canada: A Study of Population-Based Genetic Testing for Breast and Ovarian Cancer," *Current Oncology* [S.l.], v. 24(5) (Ontario: 2017) pp. 282–283.

telephone to discuss their options for cancer prevention and to facilitate a referral to a local genetic clinic for long-term follow-up. The cost of this BRCA genetic test is 165 Canadian dollars.

On January 17, 2020, the Israel Ministry of Health announced that it will include BRCA testing for Ashkenazi women in the basket of health services.[122] In the United States, the organization, "1 in 40," has petitioned the National Comprehensive Cancer Network, a non-profit alliance of 28 leading cancer centers devoted to creating clinical practice guidelines and standards for clinical policy in cancer care, to recommend BRCA testing for all Ashkenazi women regardless of family history. Future studies will determine the feasibility of BRCA testing for all Ashkenazi women and the appropriate management of Ashkenazi men and non-Ashkenazi populations.

Conclusion

"To identify a woman as a carrier only after she develops cancer is a failure of cancer prevention,"[123] writes Mary Claire King. Dr. Kenneth Offit, chief of the clinical genetics service at Memorial Sloan Kettering Cancer Center in New York, who discovered one of the most common BRCA gene mutations for Ashkenazi Jews, estimates, "In the [Ashkenazi] Jewish community, where these mutations are quite common, we think that probably 90% of people who could be tested have not been tested."[124]

BRCA testing identifies women at increased risk of cancer who will benefit from surveillance, chemoprevention, and risk-reducing surgery. That limiting BRCA testing to women with a family history of cancer fails to identify more than 50% of carriers provides a compelling scientific argument for testing *all* Ashkenazi women. The *halakhic* argument for BRCA testing of all Ashkenazi women derives from the obligation to ward off disease and the reality that the information obtained from testing can be used not only to prevent disease but also to save lives. Recognizing this reality, several modern *poskim* believe that BRCA testing for all Ashkenazi women is *pikuaḥ nefesh*, which overrides any other consideration. A growing number of rabbinic leaders in the United States and Israel endorse and even require BRCA testing for all Ashkenazi women. ☙

---

122 https://www.health.gov.il/NewsAndEvents/SpokemanMesseges/Pages/17012020_1.aspx.

123 King, "A Population Based Screening for BRCA1 and BRCA2."

124 https://www.timesofisrael.com/new-study-on-cancer-risk-in-ashkenazi-jews-aims-to-be-model-for-genetic-testing/.

Outlawed Visitors on al-Haram al-Sharif: Jews on the Temple Mount during the Ottoman and British rule of Jerusalem, 1517–1967

By: F. M. LOEWENBERG*

"The 144-dunam al-Aqsa Mosque/al-Haram al-Sharif is a place of worship and prayer for Muslims only," according to Zaid Lozi, Secretary-General of the Jordanian Ministry of Foreign Affairs.[1] This statement that the Temple Mount in Jerusalem is exclusively a Muslim holy site is not new, but merely repeats what has been a basic position of the Arab world for many centuries. Because of this belief non-Muslims were prohibited for centuries from going up on the Temple Mount. It is widely believed that no Jew ascended the Temple Mount in the 450 years prior to the Israel army's capture of East Jerusalem in 1967.[2]

While there are many reports of Jewish activities on the Temple Mount in the millennium prior to the Ottoman conquest of Jerusalem in 1517,[3] after that date the ascent of Jews and all other non-Muslims was strictly prohibited. An unsubstantiated folktale has it that the Western Wall was awarded to the Jews as a place of Jewish prayer in compensation for any rights they previously had on the Temple Mount.

Actually, the prohibition of Jews from going up to the Temple Mount was in effect already prior to the Ottoman conquest. Rabbi Oba-

---

* I want to thank Rav Elisha Wolfson who in his recent book *Har Habayit k-halakhah* (Jerusalem: Divrei Shir, 2018) drew my attention to several rabbis who went up on the Temple Mount in the 1920s.

1 Jordan parliament calls for expelling Israeli envoy, *Jerusalem Post,* 19 August 2019.

2 See, for example, Gedalia Meyer and Henoch Messner, "Entering the Temple Mount—in Halacha and Jewish History," *Ḥakirah,* 2010, vol. 10, pp. 29–72, esp. pp. 64-65.

3 See, for example, Meir Loewenberg, "A Synagogue on Har Habayit in the 7th Century: Dream or Historical Fact?", *Ḥakirah,* vol. 21, Summer 2016, pp. 253–262.

F. M. Loewenberg is professor emeritus at Bar Ilan University's School of Social Work. Since his retirement his research interests have focused on the history of the Temple Mount and the Western Wall. His writings have been published in *Middle East Quarterly, Ḥakirah, Segula, Nonprofit & Voluntary Sector Quarterly,* and *Journal of Jewish Communal Service.*

diah of Bertinoro, the famous Mishnah commentator (born in Italy in 1445) settled in Jerusalem in 1488, that is, almost thirty years before the Ottoman occupation of Jerusalem He wrote in one of his letters from Jerusalem:

> No Jew is allowed to enter the site of the Holy Temple. Even though the Muslims frequently have wanted to employ Jews who are skilled in wood work and metal work to work on the Temple Mount, these Jews have refused to enter these areas because of their uncleanliness.[4]

Similarly, one of Rabbi Obadiah's students wrote in 1495 that no Jew would enter the place of the Temple because this was forbidden by *halakha* "and in any event, the Muslims would not permit [any Jew] to enter their holy place."[5] In other words, there were two reasons that Jews did not enter the Temple Mount—Jewish law forbids their going up on the Temple Mount in a state of ritual defilement and the Muslim rulers of the country did not allow a non-Muslim to enter the sacred areas.

Alongside the *halakhic* prohibition of entering the Temple Mount there appeared to be another *halakhic* tradition that permitted the ascent to the Temple Mount to specified areas. This is evident from a responsa of the chief rabbi of Jerusalem in the 16th century, Rabbi David ben Shlomo Ibn Zimra (1479–1573), known as the Radbaz, who wrote that in his day all of the city's Jews regularly went up to the Temple Mount in order to view the entire Temple ruins and pray there. He added that "we have not heard or seen anyone object to this."[6] It is not clear whether this ruling was written in the last decades of the Mamluk era or during the first years of the Ottoman rule, but it is obvious that in these years Jews did not hesitate to ascend the Temple Mount to offer their prayers.

---

4 Ya'ari, Abraham. *Igarot Eretz Yisrael* (Eretz Yizrael Letters). Tel Aviv, 1943. [Hebrew], pp. 98–103.

5 Ya'ari (1943), p. 173.

6 Responsa of the Radbaz, v.2, no. 691. For the full text and a critical analysis of this ruling see Sagiv, Tuvya. "Ha-knissa l-Har Ha-bayit—T'shuvat Ha-Radbaz" [Entering the Temple Mount—the Decision of the Radbaz], pp. 46–81 in *Kumo v'Na'aleh,* ed. Yehuda Shaviv. Alon Shvut: Machon Tzomet, 2003 [Hebrew]. See also Wolfson (2018), pp. 59–89 for another critical analysis.

Ottoman conquest of Jerusalem in 1517

Ever since Ottoman Sultan Mehmed II conquered Constantinople in 1453 the Ottoman Empire was considered the preeminent power in the eastern Mediterranean. In the following century further conquests in the Balkans and the Middle East resulted in a vast expansion of the Ottoman Empire.

Many Jews had joined the Ottoman army when it was about to conquer Jerusalem. Among the Jewish soldiers were professionals with much experience who occupied senior posts in the army's medical corps, planning division and supply corps. Sultan Selim I had promised the heads of the Jewish community that after the conquest of Jerusalem he would permit them to renovate all of the Jewish holy places in the Holy Land, except those places that were also holy to Islam — first and foremost in this excluded list was the Temple Mount!

Selim's successor, Suleiman I the Magnificent, was the longest reigning ruler of the Ottoman Empire, ruling from 1520 until his death in 1566. He was among the most prominent monarchs of 16th-century Europe and conquered many Christian strongholds in Europe, including Belgrade, Rhodes and most of Hungary — his advance was stopped in 1529 when he failed to conquer Vienna. Subsequently he turned his attention towards consolidating his gains in the Middle East. In 1536 he rebuilt the walls of Jerusalem which had remained in ruins since the 13th century. Suleiman's positive attitude toward the Jews of Jerusalem persuaded many European Jews, especially those who had been expelled from Spain and Portugal a generation earlier, to settle in the Holy City of Jerusalem. Suleiman no doubt had his own reasons for encouraging Jewish immigration, but many believe that he did so because he wanted to limit the influence of the Arab population. Whatever his reason, Jerusalem's Jews benefited from his benevolence toward them.

In the last decades of the Mamluk regime the Jewish population of Jerusalem declined from 250 families in 1481 (as reported by Meshulam da Volterra) to 76 in 1488 (as reported by R. Obadiah of Bertinoro). While conditions improved greatly after Bertinoro took over the community's leadership, the real growth occurred only after the Ottomans captured the city in 1517. The census of 1525-26 listed 199 Jewish families, compared with 119 Christian families and 616 Muslim families. A census 13 years later reported 224 Jewish families and 19 bachelors. In the 1553-54 census there were 324 Jewish families and 13 bachelors.

Even though nine years later only 237 Jewish families and 12 bachelors were enumerated, the long-term trend was a growing Jewish population.[7]

Subsequent Ottoman rulers invested great effort and funds to rebuild Jerusalem, but they did little to keep the Dome of the Rock and the Al-Aksa Mosque in good repair. The weeds and grass that are visible between the stone flooring in an 1875 photo suggest that few Muslims came to the Temple Mount during those years.[8] There are no records of important Muslim clerics or kings praying on the Temple Mount nor is there any evidence that great crowds of Muslims came to worship on the Mount during the four hundred years of Ottoman rule (1517–1918).[9]

Outlawed visitors on the Temple Mount

For more than three hundred years the official policy was that everyone who was not a Muslim was forbidden to enter the Temple Mount; almost all of those who disobeyed and were caught visiting the mountain were executed, unless they were categorized as feeble-minded or drunkards. The London Literary Gazelle of June 1818, for example, published the following letter that describes the experiences that a "Prussian Traveler" had in Jerusalem:

> The Turks told us, that it was certain death for any Christian to be found in the interior of the mosque. They related to us that many years ago a Christian obtained a *firman* of the Grand Seignior to examine the interior, and having arrived at Jerusalem he presented his document to the *Bey*, who told him that he certainly was bound to respect the *firman* of Constantinople, and that therefore he was at liberty to enter the temple. After remaining for some hours in the interior, and having fully satisfied his curiosity, the Christian wanted to quit the place, but he found the door locked, and was informed that the *firman* gave him permission to go in, but not to come out again. The *Bey* kept him shut up till night came on, and then caused his head to be cut off, and his body to be buried beyond the walls of Jerusalem.

We have found no evidence whether this incident actually took place, but it does illustrate what contemporary Christians believed or

7 Salo Wittmayer Baron, *A Social and Religious History of the Jews,* 2nd ed., revised and enlarged (Philadelphia: JPS, 1980) vol. 18, p. 206.

8 This picture can be found at http://www.lib.uchicago.edu/e/su/mideast/photo/155-85.jpeg

9 Manfred R. Lehmann, "The Moslem Claim to Jerusalem is False," *Algemeiner Journal,* August 19, 1994.

what the Muslim authorities wanted non-Muslims to think. Shor compiled a list of Christians who had visited (with — or more rarely — without permission) the Temple Mount during the Ottoman period.[10] He dismissed the idea that any Jews would ascend the mountain because this was prohibited by Muslim law, as well as by Jewish religious law.

Nevertheless, there is no doubt that throughout this period of over 400 years some Jews did visit the Temple Mount furtively—some to pray, some to observe, and some for other reasons. Most of these visitors left no record of their visit so that we do not know how many there were. Occasionally there is a short reference to such a visit in a sacred book or in the Muslim court records that refer to the proceedings against those few Jews who were caught by the ruling authorities on the Temple Mount. We have no way of knowing whether the list of "outlawed" Jewish visitors includes all or only a part of those who did go up on the Temple Mount. Most probably there were many others who did not leave a record, whose records have been lost, or who were not caught.

In the mid-16th century, Rabbi Zechariah al-Zahari (c.1519–c.1585), one of the most famous Jewish poets from Yemen, visited Jerusalem. After travelling to India, the Middle East, and spending many years in Safed, he returned to his native Yemen around 1567. Describing his short stay in Jerusalem, he laconically wrote that "I walked on the Temple Mount." Soon after his return home he was imprisoned together with most of Sana's Jewish community by the authorities who suspected them of sympathizing with the Ottoman Empire, the country's bitter enemy. It was in prison that he wrote his famous book, "The Book of Morality," a rhymed prose narrative, which was based in part on his extensive travels and contains the statement cited.[11]

In 1551 a group of Jewish men, accompanied by six Jewish women, was caught on the roof of a Muslim school, next to and overlooking the Temple Mount. They were brought before the Muslim court. The evidence presented to the judges suggested that the men were drunk. What particularly upset the judges was that from this roof there was a walkway directly to the Al Aqsa Mosque. After weighing all the evidence, the judges decided to forbid all Jews from "looking at the Temple Mount."

---

10 Natan Shor, "Forbidden Visits on the Temple Mount," *Kardum* 21–23, 1982, pp. 90–96. [Hebrew].

11 Abraham Ya'ari, *Massa'ot Eretz Yisrael* (Travels to Eretz Yisrael) (Tel Aviv, 1976) [Hebrew], p. 207; Adena Tanenbaum, "Of a Pietist Gone Bad and Des(s)erts Not Had: The Fourteenth Chapter of Zechariah Aldahiri's *Sefer hamusar*," *Prooftexts* , Vol. 23, No. 3 (October 2003), pp. 297–319.

The men also received lashes as punishment for looking at the Mount. Another group of Jews was caught at the same place three years later and also received lashes.[12] Evidently these men received a "light" punishment because they did not actually enter the Temple Mount but merely looked at it. From reading a number of such court records, covering several centuries, it almost seems that the Muslim judges considered that any Jew who ascended the Temple Mount, despite the strict prohibition, must have been drunk, mentally deranged, or insane.

Later in the 16th century, the body of Yakov ben Yosef, a Jew, was found in a well on the Temple Mount. He had been murdered by unknown persons. At first the judges of the Muslim court tried to pin the murder on one or more Jews, thus suggesting that surreptitious visits by Jews on the Temple Mount were not unknown at that time. The judges, however, were unable to obtain sufficient evidence to reach such a conclusion. No one was ever charged with this murder.[13]

Rabbi Joseph Mitrani (1568–1639), known as the Mahari"t, wrote in his *Kuntres Ha-bayit* that he had "the privilege to go up on the Temple Mount in Jerusalem."[14] Rabbi Mitrani's visit, as well as those of other rabbis (see below) suggests that the rabbinical prohibition was not universally accepted.

A complete ban on access to the Temple Mount by non-Muslims remained in effect until the end of the Crimean War (1853–1856). Yet, "accidents" did happen. One morning in 1833 when the Muslim guards opened the Temple Mount they found a young Jew who had spent the night on the mountain. "He had made great havoc among the costly lustres, lamps, lanterns, and the like—whatever, in fact, he was able to destroy. But it was speedily perceived that he lacked reason, and was not much less than downright crazy." The Muslims dragged him off the mountain, threw him into prison and beat him mercilessly all day long, "thinking it a religious duty to ill-use him." They asked Mahmud Ali Pasha of Egypt, the ruler of the land, to approve the usual punishment, burning him at the stake, but the answer to their request was not what they had expected. Ali Pasha wrote that the guards of *Haram al-Sharif* [The Noble Sanctuary, the Arabic name for the Temple Mount] were responsible; and greatly deserving of punishment, in so carelessly execut-

12 Amnon Cohen, *Jews in Moslem Religious Courts: 16th century* (Jerusalem: Ben Tzvi 1993) [Hebrew], document 104 of 4 May 1551, pp. 114-15 and document 107 of 19 May 1554 of p. 117.

13 Cohen (1993), document 194 of 20 October 1585, p. 183.

14 Wolfson (2018), p. 92, citing R. Chaim Alfandri, *Sefer Derekh Ha-kodesh* 10:3.

ing the duties of their office; and that the Jew should be set at liberty, since the sacred law which interdicts the entrance to the mountain to a non-Muslim, under punishment of death, that is, to be burnt, is inapplicable in the present instance, because the Jew is also circumcised, and is thus somewhat akin to a Muslim; that he could not indeed be permitted to enter freely the sanctuary; nevertheless he is not liable to the death penalty.[15]

For centuries armed guards kept non-Muslims away. A mid-19th-century book describes this complete closure as follows:

> On all sides of the temple place, are seen Mahomedan dervishes, who come from Barbary, in Africa … armed with spears, standing sentinel day and night, to prevent any profane person, i.e., anyone but a Mahomedan, from entering on this holy spot.[16]

How complete this barring of non-Muslims was can be seen by the following story that appeared in an 1858 book on Jerusalem, written by James Turner *Barclay* (1807–1874) the first missionary of The American Christian Missionary Society to Jerusalem:

> It is well known that every kind of handicraft avocation is regarded as degrading by all classes of Moslems; and hence when the clock of the Mosk needs repairing, they are compelled, however reluctantly, to employ a Frank. But in order to have a clean conscience in the commission of such an *abominable piece of sacrilege* as the admission of an *infidel* upon the sacred premises, they adopt the following expedient. The mechanic selected being thoroughly purged from his uncleanness by ablution *a la Turc,* a certain formula of prayer and incantation is sung over him at the gate. This being satisfactorily concluded, he is considered as exorcised, not only of Christianity (or Judaism, as the case may be), but of humanity also; and is declared to be no longer a man but a donkey. He is then mounted upon the shoulders of the *faithful,* lest, notwithstanding his depuration, the ground should be polluted by his footsteps; and being carried to the spot where his labors are required, he is set down upon matting within certain prescribed limits; and the operation being performed, he is carried back to the gate, and there, by

15 Joseph Schwartz, *Geography of Palestine,* trans. I. Leeser (Philadelphia, 1850) pp. 417-418. This story does not appear in the 1900 Hebrew edition edited by Lunz. I do not know the reason for this omission.

16 Schwartz (1850), pp. 262-3.

certain other ceremonies, he is duly *undonkeyfied* and transmuted into a man again![17]

It is not clear whether this description refers to an event that occurred in the 19th century or earlier; it may even be that this story is apocryphal.

Temple Mount open to Non-Muslims

As the power of the Ottoman Empire waned in the 19th century, a few very important persons were able to obtain exceptional permission to go on the Temple Mount. Among these was Sir Moses Montefiore who was accompanied on his first visit in 1855 by James Fine, the British consul in Jerusalem. The critical turning point came as a result of the Crimean War (1853–1856) which was fought between an alliance of England, France and the Ottoman Empire against Russia. This war was part of a long-running contest between the major European powers for influence over territories of the declining Ottoman Empire. The more specific cause for this conflict was France's attempt to force the Ottoman Empire to recognize it as the "sovereign authority" in the Holy Land, a claim that was disputed by the Russian Czar.[18] One of the many consequences of the defeat of Russia was the opening of the Temple Mount to all visitors, no matter what their religion — a concession that was insisted upon by the victorious British Empire. In the Treaty of Paris, signed on 30 March 1856 at the end of the Crimean War, the Ottoman Empire agreed that the Temple Mount would be open to non-Muslims daily (except on Fridays). However, until 1910 each visitor was required to obtain an admission ticket which was issued only after a specified amount of money was paid to the official who issued this document.

In response to this new policy the rabbis of Jerusalem once again issued a public decree prohibiting all Jews from going up to the Temple Mount. As Meyer and Messner noted, "By the time the Muslims lifted the prohibition during the 19th century, the tradition to not ascend to Har Habayit was firmly entrenched in the Jewish world."[19] Any Jew who dared to ignore this decree faced a violent response from the Jewish community, including being put under the ban. Nevertheless, there were

---

17 J.T. Barclay, *The City of the Great King* (Philadelphia: J. Challen and Sons, 1858) p. 483. Schwartz (1850, p. 425) confirms this procedure, but notes that no Jewish craftsman was willing to enter the Temple Mount "on account of want of purification."

18 Trevor Royle, *Crimea: The Great Crimean War, 1854–1856* (Palgrave Macmillan, 2000).

19 Meyer and Messner, 2010, p. 65.

Jews who ignored this decree and did go up. As noted above, Sir Moses Montefiore had visited the Temple Mount already in the summer of 1855, prior to the signing of the peace treaty. Montefiore, an observant Jew, was aware of the rabbis' opposition to anyone visiting the Temple Mount, but thought that he could overcome their ruling if he would arrive at the site in a closed cabin, in what is known in halakha as "a box, a cabinet, or a tower." In this way, he thought that he would not be in violation of the prohibition to ascend the Mount in an impure state. Nevertheless, his visit caused a vehement reaction from Jerusalem's Jews who pelted him with stones when subsequently he visited a synagogue. Some of the rabbis put him under the ban, prohibiting any social or commercial contact with him; this ban was removed only after he solemnly promised that he would not repeat such a visit.

Dr. Ludwig August Frankel, Ritter von Hochwart, an Austrian poet and secretary of the Vienna Jewish community, came to Jerusalem in 1856 for the purpose of opening the Lemel School, the first Jewish school in Jerusalem where secular subjects were to be taught. He was very much aware that the rabbis and traditional leadership of the Old Yishuv were opposed to his school.[20] He also was acquainted with the stringent rabbinical prohibition against visiting the Temple Mount, yet he could not deny his curiosity. Not wanting to antagonize the very Jews whose children he was trying to attract to his new school, he scheduled his visit on a Saturday morning when the streets of the city would be empty of all pious Jews who at that hour would be at prayer in the synagogue. Thus he hoped to escape detection and the fury of Jerusalem's Jews.[21]

Despite the rabbinical prohibition, Jews yearned to be in contact with the holy places on the Temple Mount. Thus, the Po'alei Tzedek Society announced in 1874 that it had purchased a house overlooking the site of the Holy Temple and was planning to open a synagogue there. The house, however, was outside the proscribed area of the Temple Mount so that those worshipping there were not be affected by the rabbinical prohibition. Another example of Jewish yearning for the Temple Mount is a report that Rabbi Yehoshua Leib Diskin (1817–1898), the rabbinical leader of the Old Yishuv, lived only in houses that

---

20 Dovid Rosoff, *Where Heaven Touches Earth* (Jerusalem, Guardian Press, Feldheim, 2004) pp. 236-237 discusses the Orthodox opposition to this educational innovation.

21 Frankel's visit to the Temple Mount, as well as some of those listed in the following pages, was documented in Dotan Goren's thesis, a summary of which appears at http://www.e-mago.co.il/Editor/history-1728.htm.

faced the Temple Mount so that there would never be a thirty-day period when his eyes did not catch sight of the Mount, yet he steadfastly refused to go up on the Temple Mount because of halakhic reasons.

Baron Edmond Benjamin James de Rothschild (1845–1934) was known as "HaNadiv HaYadu'a" (Hebrew for "The Known Benefactor" or "The Famous Benefactor") because of his generous donations that lent significant support to the Zionist institutions during the early decades of the Return to Zion. He went on the Temple Mount during his visit to Jerusalem in April 1887 and again on later visits, even though he was made aware of the opposition of the rabbis to such visits. After his last visit to Jerusalem and the Temple Mount in February 1914 Rabbi Abraham Isaac Kook (1865–1935), then chief rabbi of Yaffo, issued a stringent rebuke to the Baron for failing to adhere to the rabbis' ruling against visiting the Mount.

Theodor Herzl (1860–1904), the father of the Zionist political movement, came to Jerusalem in October 1898 in order to meet with German Kaiser Wilhelm II whose support he sought for the Zionist enterprise. He wanted to visit the Temple Mount but decided to respect the feelings of the Jerusalem Jewish community, even though he himself was a completely secular Jew. He, therefore, only viewed the Temple Mount from the roof of the Tiferet Israel Synagogue in the Old City. In his utopian novel *Altneuland* (1902) he described the erection of a secular Third Temple, but did not locate this building on the Temple Mount.

Baron de Rothschild and Dr. Ludwig Frankel were not the only Jews who visited the Temple Mount in the years before World War I. The Hebrew-language newspaper *Hamoriah* reported in 1914 that many Jews from the "New Yishuv," in other words, many secular Jews, openly visited the Temple Mount, walked from one gate to the other and even entered the various buildings, though all of this was forbidden by the rabbis. In 1913, Rabbi A.Y. Kook, when he was chief rabbi of Yaffo–Tel Aviv, wrote to the administration of the new Herzliya Gymnasium, asking them not to take their students onto the Temple Mount when they took their annual class trip to Jerusalem.

Though the rabbis consistently tried to prevent Jews from entering the Temple Mount, an ever-increasing number of visitors ignored their decrees. They, as well as a large number of Christian pilgrims, went up to the sacred mountain. Despite the growing number of pilgrims from all over the world, the Muslims seemed to have done little to maintain the Temple Mount or the buildings located on it. When the British army conquered Jerusalem in 1917, it found the Temple Mount in a state of complete neglect. The Dome of the Rock and the Al-Aqsa Mosque were almost on the point of collapse.[22]

British occupation and the Mandatory government, 1917–1948

Jerusalem's mayor surrendered the city to the British army on December 9, 1917. Two days later General Sir Edmund Allenby entered the city as its first Christian conqueror since the Crusades. He was greeted by the city's Jewish inhabitants who had high hopes and saw him as their savior, but these hopes soon turned into disappointment. The army of occupation seemed unaware of the recently issued Balfour Declaration. For example, it ruled that from now on the official languages of the country were to be English and Arabic.[23]

General Allenby tried to demonstrate his government's goodwill to all inhabitants of the city. Standing on the steps of the Tower of Herod, he announced that even though Palestine was now under military occupation, "every sacred building, monument, holy spot, shrine, traditional site, endowment, pious bequest, or customary place of prayer of whatsoever form of the three religions will be maintained and protected according to the existing customs and beliefs of those to whose faith they are sacred."[24] He reported to his superiors that the Temple Mount had been placed "under Moslem control, and a military cordon of Mohammedan [Indian Muslim] officers and soldiers has been established around the mosque. Orders have been issued that no non-Moslem is to pass within the cordon without permission of the Military Governor and the Moslem in charge." This order, of course, cancelled the policy that had been in effect for sixty years and permitted free access to the Temple Mount to everyone, Muslims as well as non-Muslims.[25] This order was strongly protested by many Christian groups in England that were determined to strengthen the Christian presence in Jerusalem. As a re-

---

22 Menachem Elon, Temple Mount Faithful - Amutah Et Al v. Attorney-General, Inspector-General of the Police, Mayor of Jerusalem, Minister of Education and Culture, Director of the Antiquities Division, Muslim WAQF - In the Supreme Court Sitting as the High Court of Justice [September 23, 1993]; English translation in Catholic University Law Review, 45, 3 (Spring 1996), pp. 866–942 at p. 888.

23 Robert W. Nicholson, *Managing the Divine Jurisdiction: Sacred Space and the Limits of Law on the Temple Mount (1917–1948)*, p. 9.

24 "Proclamation of General Allenby," in Charles F. Horne (ed.), *Source Records of the Great War*, vol. V (Boston: Stuart Copley Press, 1923) p. 417, archived at https://archive.org/details/sourcerecordsofg05char/page/n. 9.

25 Nicholson, p. 21.

sult three months later the British Cabinet commanded Allenby to cancel this order and permit once again free access to the Temple Mount for everyone.[26] This "new" policy remained in force for more than ten years.

The British army enforced military rule until 29 September 1923. The military was replaced by the civilian British Mandate over Palestine, under the general supervision of the League of Nations. The mandatory government continued the previously established policies with respect to the Holy Places. Not long after the 1929 Arab riots against the Jews, the Mufti of Jerusalem Haj Amin al-Husseini closed the Haram to all non-Muslims. The British mandatory government evidently condoned this closure order as far as it was directed against Jews who were barred from the Temple Mount for the next 38 years.[27]

There is a widespread belief that the Temple Mount was of little importance or interest for Jews during the 20th century. Religious Jews stayed away because their rabbis severely prohibited entering the sacred precincts. And most secular Jews just were not interested. Chaim Weizmann, president of the Zionist Organization, for example, moved the "Temple" from the Temple Mount to Mount Scopus, the next mountain over, where he was instrumental in building the Hebrew University.[28]

In the years following World War I, the Jerusalem rabbis continued to prohibit going up to the Temple Mount. Rabbi A. Y. Kook, now the Ashkenazi chief rabbi of the Holy Land, did not revoke the prohibition, preferring to leave things as they were. He explained a number of times that Jews were not permitted to go up to the Mount because the exact location of the holy sites could not be determined.[29] His successor, Rabbi Yizchak Isaac Halevi Herzog (1888–1959), testified in 1938 before the British Partition Committee that Jews were not allowed to go onto the Temple Mount until the Messiah came.

---

26 *War Cabinet, Eastern Report* no. 61, Mar. 27, 1918, CAB/24/145.

27 Uri Kupferschmidt, *The Supreme Muslim Council: Islam Under the British Mandate in Palestine* (Leiden: E. J. Brill, 1987) p. 237.

28 Norman Rose, *Chaim Weizman—A Biography* (NY: Penguin Books, 1989) p. 126.

29 See, for example, *Mishpat Cohen,* p. 202 – H. Beit Habechira, par. 96. In his ruling Kook followed most medieval and contemporary halakhic codes—for example, Rabbi Abraham Gombiner (c. 1633–c. 1683) wrote that "one who enters nowadays the place where the Temple used to stand incurs the punishment of excision (*karet*)" (*Magen Avraham* OḤ 561.2). Rabbi Yisrael Meir Kagan, known as the Chofetz Chaim (Poland, 1838–1933) used the very same words in his authoritative legal commentary *Mishna Berurah* (561.5).

Yet some Jews continued to go up on the Temple Mount. While most religious Jews followed the Chief Rabbis' ruling, secular Jews were not the only ones who ascended. Rabbi Shmuel Horowitz, a leader of the Breslever community in Jerusalem, described his going up on the Temple Mount in the 1920s. On Sukkot 5685 (1924) he and others of his group walked up to the Temple Mount "as far as it is permitted for *tamei meitim* to walk." They said various prayers, but not from a prayer book because the Arab guard did not permit them to open a prayer book. On one occasion they were able to organize a circle dance on the Temple Mount while singing sacred melodies. He reported that they continued to go up on the Temple Mount for some years, but later certain areas that in the past were open were now closed for Jews. Still later [presumably in 1929] Jews were prevented from entering the Temple Mount altogether and were permitted only to look upon it from afar.[30]

Rabbi Jacob Nissan Rosenthal (1924–2010), born and educated in Jerusalem, served for many years as Chief Rabbi of Haifa. He was in close contact with all the Torah giants of his generation. In his *Mishnat Yaakov,* a commentary on Maimonides, he wrote that it is possible for a Jew to visit the Temple Mount nowadays (*Beit Habechira* 7.1-2). According to his primary student, Rabbi Shlomo Amar, Chief Rabbi of Israel (2003–2013) and currently Chief Rabbi of Jerusalem, Rabbi Rosenthal went up on the Temple Mount in the years before the establishment of the State of Israel because he and other rabbis had an established tradition informing them which places on the Temple Mount Jews were allowed to visit and which were prohibited.[31]

Prior to the War of Independence which established the State of Israel, General David Shaltiel (1903–1969), the commanding general of the Haganah, the Jewish underground forces in the Jerusalem sector,

---

30 Wolfson (2018), pp. 102-3, no source given.

31 R. Avi Kahana, "93rd birthday of the late R. Jacob Nissan Rosenthal" [Hebrew], archived at https://har-habait.org/articleBody/7723. Wolfson 2018, p. 103, n.13, cites an undated comment by R. Amar, confirming that his rabbi, R. Jacob Nissan Rosenthal, as well as other rabbis, did go up onto the Temple Mount in the past because they had a tradition about the permitted places. When he, R. Amar, issued his decree prohibiting going up on the Temple Mount, he first contacted his rabbi to explain to him why he felt it necessary to prohibit something that his rabbi himself practiced. He explained that he issued his prohibition because nowadays most Jews were no longer aware of the tradition of permitted areas and would therefore mistakenly enter areas of the Temple Mount that are prohibited to them. Rabbi Rosenthal responded that he agreed with his ruling.

consulted with Rabbi Herzog, the chief rabbi of the Holy Land, about the forthcoming war. The rabbi instructed the general that if his forces captured the Temple Mount, they should make every effort to expel all of the enemy forces — but once they had accomplished this, they should leave the Temple Mount as quickly as possible because of the holiness of the place.

Jordanian occupation and annexation of Jerusalem (1948–1967)

Following the 1948 War of Independence, the Jordanian army occupied East Jerusalem, including the Old City and all of its Christian and Jewish holy places. For nineteen years no Jew was allowed to approach the Temple Mount or the Western Wall. This absolute ban was strictly enforced, despite provisions in the Jordanian-Israeli Armistice Agreement that called for "… free access to the Holy Places and cultural institutions and use of the cemetery on the Mount of Olives…."[32] The Temple Mount and the Western Wall were hermetically sealed for any Jewish visitors, no matter what their nationality.[33]

Summary

For almost 340 years the official policy of the Ottoman Empire was that the Temple Mount be accessible only to Muslim worshippers. In earlier times provisions were made for Jews to go up on the Mount either freely or occasionally (or at times, not at all), but now the rule was that any Jewish presence was proscribed. Nevertheless, the attachment of Jews to site of the destroyed Temples, the holiest site in Judaism, was so strong that illicit or forbidden ascents continued to occur throughout this period. We have combed the relevant literature to bring a number of examples of these. We suspect that there were many more.

Postscript

For almost two thousand years until 1967, foreign rulers decided whether or not Jews were permitted to go up on the Temple Mount. The situation changed radically after the Israeli victory in the Six Day War. From

---

32 Israel-Jordan Armistice Agreement of 3 April 1949, Article 8, archived at https://mfa.gov.il/mfa/foreignpolicy/mfadocuments/yearbook1/pages/israel-jordan%20armistice%20agreement.aspx

33 Shmuel Berkowitz, *The Temple Mount and the Western Wall in Israeli Law* (Jerusalem: The Jerusalem Institute for Israel Studies, 2001) p. 13.

that day on, the Temple Mount came under the jurisdiction of the State of Israel, the Jewish State.

As a result of the Israeli government's decision in 1967, the general public, including Jews and Christians, were now allowed to visit the Temple Mount (but not allowed to pray there) without hindrance. Many visitors have taken advantage of this permission. Initially most religious Jews followed the instructions of the Chief Rabbinate which prohibited Jews from entering the Mount because nowadays no Jew is ritually fit to do so. A small (but over time, increasing) number of rabbis have followed Rabbi Goren's plea to permit Jews to enter those areas on the Temple Mount that did not require complete ritual purity.

Many appeals have been made to Israel's Supreme Court to permit Jews to pray on the Temple Mount. Despite the 1967 Law for the Protection of Holy Places which allows free access and freedom of worship to all religions everywhere, Jews and Christians are prohibited from praying on the Temple Mount, ostensibly to ensure public order. As Justice Menachem Elon, Deputy Chief Justice of the Supreme Court, explained, this prohibition was created because "the Temple Mount possessed extraordinary sensitivity that has no parallel anywhere."[34]

The final chapter in this story still has not been written. ☙

---

34 Elon (1993); Yoel Cohen, "The Political Role of the Israeli Chief Rabbinate in the Temple Mount Question," *Jewish Political Studies Review,* 11 (1-2), 1999, pp. 101–126.

Tehillat Hashem and Other Verses Before *Birkat Ha-Mazon*

By: ZVI RON

In this article we investigate the origin and development of saying various Psalms and selected verses from Psalms before *Birkat Ha-Mazon*. In particular, we will attempt to explain the practice of some Ashkenazic Jews to add Psalms 145:21, 115:18, 118:1 and 106:2 after Ps. 126 (*Shir Ha-Ma'alot*) and before *Birkat Ha-Mazon.*

Psalms 137 and 126 Before *Birkat Ha-Mazon*

The earliest source for reciting Ps. 137 (*Al Naharot Bavel*) before *Birkat Ha-Mazon* is found in the list of practices of the Tzfat kabbalist R. Moshe Cordovero (1522–1570). There are different versions of this list, but all versions include the practice of saying *Al Naharot Bavel.*[1] Some versions specifically note that this is to recall the destruction of the Temple,[2] some versions state that the Psalm is supposed to be said at the meal, though not specifically right before *Birkat Ha-Mazon*,[3] and some versions state that the Psalm is only said on weekdays, though no alternative Psalm is offered for Shabbat and holidays.[4] Although the exact provenance of this list is not clear, the parts of it referring to the recitation of Ps. 137 were already popularized by 1577.[5]

The mystical work *Seder Ha-Yom* by the 16th century Tzfat *kabbalist* R. Moshe ben Machir was first published in 1599. He also mentions saying *Al Naharot Bavel* at a meal in order to recall the destruction of the

---

1 Moshe Hallamish, *Kabbalah in Liturgy, Halakhah and Customs* (Ramat Gan: Bar Ilan University Press, 2000), pp. 349, 353 (Hebrew).

2 Hallamish, p. 349, MS 1691, item 13.

3 Hallamish, p. 349, MS 1961, item 13.

4 Hallamish, p. 353, MS 1955, item 22.

5 Hallamish, p. 347.

Zvi Ron received *semikhah* from the Israeli Rabbanut and his PhD in Jewish Theology from Spertus University. He is an educator living in Neve Daniel, Israel, and the author of *Sefer Katan ve-Gadol* (Rossi Publications, 2006) about the big and small letters in Tanakh, and *Sefer Haikkar Haser* (Mossad Harav Kook, 2017) about the variable spellings of words in Tanakh.

Temple, and adds that "on Shabbat and holidays, when sorrow and sighing should not be mentioned, mention verses of the comfort of Zion and Jerusalem and the Psalm 'When the Lord brought back those that returned to Zion' (*Shir Ha-Maalot*, Ps. 126)."[6]

The recitation of *Al Naharot Bavel* before *Birkat Ha-Mazon* was next included in the work *Seder Ha-Shulḥan* by R. Naftali ben David Zecharia, published in 1603, as the introductory part of a small bencher, making it the earliest bencher to include this custom.[7] There he writes that the custom is based on the *Zohar* in *Terumah* 157b which states, "One who has pleasure at his table, and has pleasure from the food, should remember and worry about the holiness of the Holy Land and the Palace of the King which is destroyed; and on account of the sorrow which he experiences at his table along with the same joy and feasting which is there, The Holy One, Blessed be He, will consider it as if he built His House and built all of the ruins of the Temple, fortunate is his lot."[8]

This practice was then included in *Shnei Luḥot Ha-Brit* by R. Isaiah Horowitz (Shelah ha-Kadosh, c.1555–1630), first published in 1648 by his son. He puts together all the elements previously seen, bringing the quote from the *Zohar* as the source of the idea, and explains, "We recite the Psalm 'By the rivers of Babylon' (*Al Naharot Bavel*, Ps. 137) before *Birkat Ha-Mazon*…and on Shabbat and holidays we recite the Psalm 'When the Lord brought back those that returned to Zion' (*Shir ha-Ma'alot*, Ps. 126)."[9]

This idea was quoted in the name of Shelah by halachic authorities already in the 1600s, *Magen Avraham* (*Oraḥ Ḥayyim* 1:5)[10] and *Eliah Rab-*

---

6 Moshe ben Machir, *Seder Ha-Yom* (Venice: 1599), p. 29b. Some *kabbalists* already refrained from reciting Ps. 137 from Friday afternoon; see Moshe Hallamish, *Kabbalistic Customs of Shabbat* (Jerusalem: Orchot, 2006), p. 49, note 21 (Hebrew); *Mishna Berura* 267:1.

7 Abraham Berliner, *Ketavim Nivcharim, vol. 1* (Jerusalem: Mossad Harav Kook, 1969), p. 31; Yissachar Jacobson, *Netiv Bina, vol. 2* (Tel Aviv: Sinai, 1987), p. 134. Note that R. Naftali ben David Zecharia only brings the custom to recite *Al Naharot Bavel*, not *Shir ha-Ma'alot.* On R. Naftali, see Reuven David Gershon and Moshe David Shvicha, "Seder Ha-Shulḥan l-Rabbi Naftali" in *Birkat Menachem* (Cleveland: Machon Nahor Safra, 2007), pp. 77–79.

8 R. Naftali ben David Zecharia, *Birkat Hamazon* (Venice: 1603), p. 13a. *Al Naharot Bavel* is brought there on pp. 16a-16b.

9 R. Isaiah Horowitz, *Shnei Luḥot ha-Brit* (Jerusalem: Machon Shaarei Ziv, 1993), *Shaar ha-Otiot, Kuf – Kedushat ha-Akhila, siman* 88, p. 369.

10 R. Avraham Gombiner in his *Magen Avraham* often includes *kabbalistic* works as halakhic sources, see Chaim Tchernowitz, *Toldot Ha-Poskim vol. 3* (NY: 1947) p. 172.

bah (181:9), popularizing it outside of mystical circles. *Magen Avraham* was in turn quoted in *Mishna Berura* (*Oraḥ Ḥayyim* 1:11). For this reason, popular works often attribute the origin of this practice to Shelah.[11]

Other Psalms were suggested to fulfill the purpose of recalling the Temple. For example, for Shabbat and holidays, Maharshal says to recite Ps. 87,[12] and R. Yaakov Emden writes that Ps. 122 is recited.[13] Different Psalms were suggested in other *kabbalistic* sources.[14] Still, Ps. 137 and 126 proved to be the most popular. Even so, many early prayer books and benchers did not include any Psalms before *Birkat Ha-Mazon*, demonstrating that it was not a universal custom.[15] For various reasons, some persisted in omitting *Al Naharot Bavel*[16] and even *Shir ha-Ma'alot*.[17]

---

11 See for example, Eliyahu Munk, *Olam haTefilot – vol. 1* (Jerusalem: Mossad Harav Kook, 1992), p. 227; Macy Nulman, *The Encyclopedia of Jewish Prayer* (Northvale: Jason Aronson, 1996) 304n2; Nosson Sherman, *Zemiros and Bircas Hamazon* (Brooklyn: Mesorah Publications, 1998), p. 260.

12 R. Menachem Mendel Landa, *Siddur Tzluta d–Avraham,* vol. 2 (Tel-Aviv: Grafika, 1961) p. 389.

13 R. Yaakov Emden, *Amuddei Shammayim* (1962 facsimile edition), p. 23b.

14 Avraham Landa, *Siddur Tzluta d-Avraham,* vol. 2 (Tel Aviv: 1961) p. 495. Ps. 87 was chosen for this purpose among Karlin-Stolin Chassidim, Yaakov Yisraeli, *Beit Karlin-Stolin* (Tel Aviv: Keren Yaakov v-Raḥel, 1982) p. 90.

15 Although the earliest bencher was published before the time of Shelah (Prague: 1515), even much after, these Psalms were not included. For example, they are not found in *Birkat Ha-Mazon* (Amsterdam: 1723); *Birkat Ha-Mazon k-Minhag Ashkenaz u-Polin* (Frankfurt am Main: 1727); Yitzchak Stanov, *Siddur Vayeater Yitzhak* (Berlin: 1785), p. 151a; *Birkat Ha-Mazon* (Dyhernfurth: 1811); Naftali Hertz Ha-Levi, *Siddur ha-Gra* (Jerusalem: 1895), p. 157b.

16 In certain circles it is rare to find people who say *Al Naharot Bavel* before *Birkat Ha-Mazon*, see Pinchas Ben Harush, *Mei Pinḥas* (Ashdod: 2011) 134n13. Some only said it on the eve of the Ninth of Av, see Aharon Pinchuk, *Mateh Aharon* (Jerusalem: 1980) p. 17. R. Shlomo Zalman Auerbach is also reported to not have said *Al Naharot Bavel*. See Shlomo Aviner, *Piskei Shlomo, vol. 1* (Beit El: Sifriat Chava, 2013) p. 89. R. Zvi Yehuda Kook replaced *Al Naharot Bavel* with *Shir Ha-Ma'alot*, which according to R. Yaakov Ariel, *rav* of Ramat Gan, is something that many in Israel do. See Mordechai Zion, *Kum Hithalekh b-Aretz* (Maale Adumim, 2015) p. 394. Regarding Chassidim who do not say Ps. 137, see the oft repeated anecdote regarding Reb Hillel Paritcher (1795–1864) in *R. Hillel m-Paritch–Sippurim* (Heichal Hanegina, 2015) pp. 56–57; *Kovetz Sippurim*, vol. 2 (Brooklyn: Beit Midrash Lubavitch, 1988), *siman* 63, p. 45. On the Chassidic custom, reported in the name of the Baal Shem Tov, to always say *Shir Ha-Ma'alot* instead of *Al Naharot Bavel*, see the comprehensive discussion in Yosef Lowy, *Minhag Yisrael Torah vol. 1* (Brooklyn, 1994) 1:4, pp. 43–44; Also Natan Perlman, "Minhag Rabboteinu sh-Ein Omrim ha-Piyut Dvai Haser," *Kovetz Beit Aharon v-Yisrael*, vol. 180, Elul 5771 (2011) 155n28; Meir Yisrael,

We can now understand the development of this custom. At first it was noted that one should recall the destruction of the Temple during the meal, and reciting Ps. 137 was used to fulfill this. Since this Psalm was considered sad and thus inappropriate for Shabbat and holidays, a different Psalm was chosen to fill this role on those festive days.[18] The Psalms then moved to being said immediately before *Birkat Ha-Mazon*. These Psalms do not have any particular connection to *Birkat Ha-Mazon* specifically,[19] and they were given a specific location just to ensure that they would be said during the meal and not forgotten. However, there is a natural connection between these Psalms and parts of *Birkat Ha-Mazon*, as the second blessing of *Birkat Ha-Mazon* (*Birkat Ha-Zan*) is focused on thanking God for the Land of Israel, and the third blessing (*Birkat Neḥama*) focuses on Jerusalem and the Temple, ideas central to Psalms 137 and 126, so it was reasonable to view them all as one extended unit.

Additional Verses Before *Birkat Ha-Mazon*

Some people say additional verses after Ps. 126 before *Birkat Ha-Mazon*, the most prevalent being Ps. 145:21 (תהלת ה' ידבר פי ויברך כל בשר שם קדשו לעולם ועד, My mouth shall speak the praise of the Lord; and let all flesh bless His holy name forever and ever) and Ps. 115:18 ואנחנו נברך יה

Birkat Ha-Mazon Ha-Mevoar (Bnei Brak: Keter Chaim, 2011) p. 144; Levi Yitzchak Raskin, *Seder Birkat Ha-Mazon* (London, 2013) 4n3. See also Zev Goldberger, *Darkhi ha-Yashar v-ha-Tov* (1910) p. 23b who reports that R. Zvi Hirsch Friedman of Lesko (d. 1874) always said *Shir Ha-Ma'alot* before *Birkat Ha-Mazon*, even on weekdays.

17 It is reported that R. Chaim of Volozhin would not say *Shir Ha-Ma'alot*, as it is still referring to exile and so not appropriate for Shabbat; Avraham Halevi Horowitz, *Orkhot Rabbeinu, vol. 1* (Bnei Brak, 1991) p. 115. The Ḥatam Sofer said neither Psalm; Yehuda Nachshoni, *Rabbenu Moshe Sofer* (Jerusalem: Mashabim, 1981) p. 441, *siman* 75. Regarding Chassidim who do not say Ps. 126, see Eliezer Brandwein, *Degel Maḥane Yehuda* (Brooklyn, 2011) 360n26; Eren Moshe Margalit, *Haggadat Likutei Sfat Emet* (Or Etzion, 2009) 201n129. See also *Rebbe Velvel* (Bnei Brak: 2003) p. 335.

18 See Moshe Hallamish, *Kabbalistic Customs of Shabbat* (Jerusalem: Shalem, 2006) p. 354 (Hebrew).

19 See Moshe Barzam, *Imrot Moshe* (Bnei Brak: 2004) p. 134, *siman* 3; Natan Einfeld, *Minchat Natan – Aggada* (Bnei Brak: 2007) p. 48; Moshe Shlezinger, *Zimrat ha-Levi* (Zikhron Meir: 2010) p. 27, *siman* 3. Attempts have been made to show a conceptual connected between these two chapters of Psalms and *Birkat Ha-Mazon*. See for example, Yitzchak Etshalom, "Al ha-Dim'a ve-al ha-Rina – Iyyun b-Mizmor 126," *Meggadim* vol. 42 (2005) pp. 58–59.

מעתה ועד עולם הללו יה, But we will bless the Lord from this time forth and forever, Hallelujah). This is often reported as the Ashkenazic custom.[20] What is the source for this addition?

The earliest reference to reciting these particular verses before *Birkat Ha-Mazon* is found in the work *Sha'ar ha-Mitzvot* by the Tzfat kabbalist R. Chaim Vital (1542–1620).[21] There he reported that R. Isaac Luria (the Ari) told him that certain verses should be said after washing *mayim aharonim* and before *Birkat Ha-Mazon*.[22] First Ps. 67 should be recited in its entirety. This is followed by Ps. 34:2 (אברכה את יהוה בכל עת תמיד תהלתו בפי), which functions to banish the forces of evil (*sitra ahra*) present at the table, then Eccl. 12:13 (סוף דבר הכל נשמע את האלהים ירא ואת מצותיו שמור כי זה כל האדם), Ps. 145:21 and 115:18, and the end of Ezekiel 41:22 (וידבר אלי זה השלחן אשר לפני ה'). Thus, these two verses popularly recited are actually the middle part of the Ari's *kabbalistic* pre-*Birkat Ha-Mazon* prayer.

This Lurianic practice was also reported by R. Meir Poppers (c. 1624–1662),[23] who wrote many works based on the teachings of R. Isaac Luria. It was later noted by the prominent Sefardic authorities R. Yosef of Baghdad (*Ben Ish Chai*, 1832–1909)[24] and R. Yaakov Ḥayyim Sofer (*Kaf ha-Ḥayyim*, 1870–1939).[25] This entire pre-*Birkat Ha-Mazon* recitation is found in many prayer books and benchers, particularly those reflecting Sefardic practice.[26] Some sources are particular not to add any other Psalms or verses to the ones listed by Ari.[27]

Note that all of the customs to say Psalms and verses before *Birkat Ha-Mazon* originated with Tzfat kabbalists in the 1500s: Ari, R. Moshe Cordovero, R. Chaim Vital and R. Moshe ben Machir. While the recitation of Psalms mentioned by Cordovero, Moshe ben Machir and Shelah

---

20 Avigdor Unna, "Customs of the Jews of Germany", in Asher Wasserteil, ed., *Yalkut Minhagim* (Jerusalem: Ministry of Education, 1996), p. 71.

21 This book is the fifth of the *Shemoneh Shearim*, which as a whole are sometimes referred to as *Etz Ḥayyim*.

22 R. Chaim Vital, *Sha'ar ha-Mitzvot* (Jerusalem: 1905), *Ekev*, p. 45a.

23 R. Meir Poppers, *Or Tzadikkim* (Warsaw: 1889), p. 59, *siman* 23, item 35. This book was first published in Hamburg, 1690.

24 *Ben Ish Ḥai*, *Shlaḥ*, first year, *siman* 15.

25 *Kaf ha-Ḥayyim*, 157:22.

26 *Zmirot Shabbat v-Seder Birkat Ha-Mazon* (New York: Otzar Hasefarim, 1968), p. 30; Michael Peretz, *Siddur Ohalei Shem* (Jerusalem: 2007), p. 255; Zvi Yevrov, *Birkat Ha-Mazon im Biur Mimaran Hagraḥ Kaniefsky* (Bnei Brak, 2009), p. 4; *Siddur Kavvanat ha-Lev* (Machon Shira Chadasha, Elad, 2014), p. 423.

27 See Baruch Cohen, *Barukh Ha-Shulḥan,* vol. 4 (Bnei Brak, 1986) 50n25 there.

is focused on a remembrance of the destroyed Temple, those chosen by Ari, Ps. 67 and the five verses, are focused on the theme of blessing, praising God and an awareness of His Presence.[28] The current custom of reciting two of these verses before *Birkat Ha-Mazon* can understood to be a remnant of the custom of Ari, appended to the end of the Psalm that R. Moshe ben Machir said to recite.[29] Thus it is a kind of amalgam of both *kabbalistic* practices. This development of different versions of additional mealtime prayers would then parallel the development of the *Kabbalat Shabbat* service, where Cordovero and Ari each chose additional Psalms to be recited as *Kabbalat Shabbat*, our current practice being a combination of both customs.[30]

Some sources suggest that these verses function to fulfill the obligation to say words of Torah at a meal,[31] but that was not the original intent expressed in the first sources to mention these practices. In fact, works which give lists of verses to say in order to fulfill saying words of Torah at a meal give entirely different verses from the ones brought in the name of Ari.[32] Shelah also discusses the idea of saying words of Torah at the meal, but as distinct from the Psalms said to remember the Temple. He specifically mentions that ideally Psalms should not be used for this purpose, and if Psalms are used, as in the case of unlearned people, they should pick something having to do with the meal.[33]

---

28 R. Shem Tov Gagin, *Keter Shem Tov* (Jerusalem: 1960), vol. 1, 141n188.

29 See Daniel Goldschmidt, *Yeshuat Daniel* (Modiin Illit, 2013) p. 264, *siman* 185n1.

30 Moshe Hallamish, *Kabbalah in Liturgy, Halakhah and Customs* (Ramat Gan: Bar Ilan University Press, 2000), p. 319 (Hebrew).

31 See *Avot* 3:3. Seligman Baer, *Seder Avodat Yisrael* (Rodelheim: 1901), p. 553; R. Shem Tov Gagin, *Keter Shem Tov* (Jerusalem: 1960), vol.1, p. 141, note 188; Eliyahu Munk, *Olam ha-Tefilot, vol. 1* (Jerusalem: Mossad Harav Kook, 1992), p. 227. See also *Arukh ha-Shulḥan*, *Oraḥ Ḥayyim* 170:1, who states that even *Al Naharot Bavel* and *Shir ha-Ma'alot* can function as the words of Torah at a meal, although actual Torah study is preferable.

32 See Yechiel Michel Epstein, *Kitzur Shnei Luḥot ha-Brit* (Amsterdam: 1721) p. 23b. This became popularized by being included in Abraham Sperling, *Sefer Ta'amei ha-Minhagim u-Mekorei ha-Dinim* (Lemberg, 1928) p. 23a. For the development of the practice to be careful about saying words of Torah at a meal, see Ze'ev Gries, *Safrut ha-Hanhagot* (Jerusalem: Bialik Institute, 1989) pp. 18-22 (the upshot of which is quoted in Daniel Sperber, *Minhagei Yisrael, vol. 2* (Jerusalem: Mossad Harav Kook, 1991) pp. 46–47) and Daniel Sperber, *Minhagei Yisrael, vol. 3* (Jerusalem: Mossad Harav Kook, 1994) pp. 162–165.

33 R. Isaiah Horowitz, *Shnei Lchot ha-Brit* (Jerusalem: Machon Shaarei Ziv, 1993), *Shaar ha-Otiot, Kuf – Kedushat ha-Akhila*, p. 385.

Additional pre-*Birkat Ha-Mazon* verses are found in other works,[34] for example, a list of ten verses to be said before those of Ari, which are "a *segulah* that one will not lack sustenance all the days of his life,"[35] the two verses (Lev. 26:5 and Ex. 23:26) which R. David of Lida reported that the great men of Jerusalem would say before the five verses of Ari,[36] and the verses brought in *Kitzur Shnei Luḥot ha-Brit* that were traditionally recited both after completing a *masekhet* and also after completing a meal.[37] However, those of Ari proved to be the most popular.

The Two Verses

The question is: why were only these two verses retained from the five that Ari said should be recited? There is no clear explanation for this found in the literature,[38] but when certain factors are taken into account, possible explanations can be theorized.

First of all, these two verses are much more familiar to people than the other three in the group of verses, as they form the ending of *Ashrei*, recited three times a day during prayers. The addition of Ps. 115:18 to the end of *Ashrei* is already noted in the first siddur, *Seder Rav Amram Gaon*, where it is explained that this was done so that *Ashrei* will end with "Halleluyah" like the parts of *Pesukei d-Zimra* which follow.[39] If any verses were to survive out of a list to be recited, it would be this very familiar duet.

Another factor is seen in the *Shulḥan Arukh* of Ari, where it says to recite the four verses, and then discusses holding the cup of wine, and then says that one should recite the end of Ezekiel 41:22 just before placing the cup in his right hand.[40] This version of the custom was pop-

34 Moshe Hallamish, *Kabbalistic Customs of Shabbat* (Jerusalem: Orchot, 2006), pp. 354, 355 (Hebrew); Adin Steinzaltz, *ha-Siddur ve-ha-Tefilla* (Tel Aviv: Yediot Acharonot, 1994), p. 266.

35 Eliyahu Ha-Cohen, *Shevet Mussar* (Jerusalem: 1989), 31:37, pp. 442–443; *Siddur k-Minhag Polin* (Ostroh: 1876) p. 95a; *Siddur Otzar ha-Tefillot* (Vilna, 1911) vol. 1, p. 474.

36 David ben Aryeh Leib of Lida, *Divrei David* (Brooklyn: Tiferet Baḥurim d-Bobov, 2006) p. 16, *siman* 77.

37 Yechiel Michel Epstein, *Kitzur ha-Shelah* (Zikhron Tzaddikim Edition) pp. 43–44.

38 Yitzchak Satz, David Yitzchaki, David Salmon, eds., *Birkat Ha-Mazon l-Moreinu Ha-Rav Shabbtai Sofer* (Toronto: Otzreinu, 2002), p. 2, note 1.

39 Shlomo Goldschmidt, ed., *Seder Rav Amram Gaon* (Jerusalem: Mossad Harav Kook, 2004), p. 9.

40 *Shulḥan Arukh shel Rabbeinu Yitzḥak Luria* (Frankfort: 1691), p. 34b. These instructions are also found in Daniel Reimer, ed., *Siddur Tefillat Ḥayyim* (Beitar:

ularized by being quoted in *Eliah Rabbah* (183:7). The custom is also described that way also in the popular *Likutei Maharikh*.[41] We can see from these sources that the Ezekiel section was considered a somewhat distinct element, separated from the other four verses.

Many sources have the Ezekiel verse separated from the others, describing it as being recited after *mayim aḥaronim* while the four others are said before,[42] even though R. Chaim Vital reported that Ari said all should be recited after *mayim aḥaronim*.[43] Probably this verse alone was shifted by some to after *mayim aḥaronim* to minimize any perceived interruption between *mayim aḥaronim* and *Birkat Ha-Mazon*.[44]

Once the Ezekiel verse was considered a separate unit, we find that it was completely omitted in some prayer books and benchers, with no explanation offered.[45] Another reason to leave out the Ezekiel section is that it is not a full verse, and recitation of incomplete verses is avoided.[46]

Thus, the group of verses to be said before *Birkat Ha-Mazon* can be viewed as a unit ending with Ps. 145:21 and 115:18, with Ezekiel 41:22 coming after on its own, if at all. Additionally, since the *Shulḥan Arukh*

Tzrur Ha-Hayyim Publications, 2004) p. 108, a siddur based on the teachings R. Chaim Vital received from R. Luria.

41 Yisrael Chaim Friedman, *Likkutei Maharikh,* vol. 1 (Jerusalem, 2013) p. 506, first published in 1900.

42 Yaakov Emden, *Siddur Ya'avetz, Amudei Shamayim* (Altona, 1745), p. 296b; *Siddur Tefilla im Likutei Torah* (Vilna: Romm, 1912); Moshe Yair Weinstock, *Siddur ha-Geonim v-ha-Mekubalim v-ha-Ḥassidim,* vol. 18 (Jerusalem: 1981) pp. 90–91; Levi Bistritzky, *Siddur Sha'ar Menaḥem* (Tzfat: Ḥasdei Lev, 2008) pp. 283, 127; *Birkat Ha-Mazon v-Sheva Berakhot* (Brooklyn: Empire Press) p. 2; *Megillat Esther u-Birkat Ha-Mazon* (Brooklyn: Empire Press) p. 54. The Chabad custom is to recite this verse after *mayim aḥaronim,* see Yehoshua Mondshein, *Otzar Minhagei Chabad, Nissan Iyyar Sivan* (Jerusalem: Heikhal Menaḥem, 1996) p. 189.

43 R. Chaim Vital, *Sha'ar ha-Mitzvot* (Jerusalem: 1905) *Ekev*, p. 45a. See also Lior Rosenruas, *Birkat ha-Shulḥan* (Bnei Brak, 2011) p. 113, 4:7. The ruling of Ari was not universally accepted, and some sources indicate that all the verses should be said before *mayim aḥaronim.* See, R. Avraham Ḥayyim Naeh, *Ketzot ha-Shulḥan* (Jerusalem: 1928) p. 29b, vol. 2, *siman* 43:1.

44 Levi Yitzchak Raskin, ed., *Siddur Rabbenu ha-Zaken* (Brooklyn: Kehot, 2004), 365n2 and 366n9; Levi Yitzchak Raskin, *Seder Birkat Ha-Mazon* (London: 2013) 3n2.

45 Israel Ricardo, *Tefillat Kol Peh* (Amsterdam: 1993), p. 184; Yitzchak Satz, David Yitzchaki, David Salmon, eds., *Birkat Ha-Mazon l-Moreinu Ha-Rav Shabbtai Sofer* (Toronto: Otzreinu, 2002) p. 4; Chanoch Vidislefsky and Aryeh Leib Pepper, eds., *Birkat Ha-Mazon–Pninei Maharal* (Ashdod: Mechon Maharal Tzintz, 2010) p. 8.

46 This is the reason R. Shmuel Aharon Yudelvitz (1907–1979) omitted the part from *Ezekiel.* See Shalom Meir Wallach, *Meilo shel Shmuel* (Bnei Brak: 1998) p. 275.

of Ari has this verse associated with lifting the cup for *Birkat Ha-Mazon*, and other sources have it recited after *mayim aḥaronim*, people who did not do these things prior to *Birkat Ha-Mazon* may have left out the verse associated with these practices. In fact, some siddurim preface the recitation of Ezekiel 41:22 with directions that can be understood as instructing one to say this verse only if *Birkat Ha-Mazon* is being said over a glass of wine.[47]

Another verse that could be considered a distinct element is Ps. 34:2, which R. Chaim Vital writes functions to remove the *sitra aḥra* that is present at the table, "and in order to banish it you must say '*hav lan v-navarich*'...that is why we say אברכה את ה' בכל עת."[48] Based on this, when people say "*rabbotai nevarech*" as is customary today, Ps. 34:2 may not be necessary,[49] and so this verse would also be omitted.

Furthermore, some sources indicate that some people only recited some of the Ari verses rather than all of them.[50] Additionally, it is not difficult to imagine a scenario where the first verses in the group were said quietly and only the last two aloud, in the style of Ashkenazic *pesukei d-zimra*, thus focusing attention on these two verses to the exclusion of others that came before. Based on this understanding, the current Ashkenazic recitation of Ps. 145:21 and 115:18 is a remnant of the five verses given by Ari.

Another Two Verses

Some benchers add two additional verses to Ps. 145:21 and 115:18, Ps. 118:1 (הודו ליהוה כי-טוב: כי לעולם חסדו), Give thanks unto the Lord, for He

---

47 See for example, Menachem Mendel Landa, *Siddur Tzluta d-Avraham,* vol. 2 (Tel Aviv, 1961) pp. 495–496, אם מברכים על הכוס, מוזגים קודם ואח"כ נוטלין הידים ואומרים: וידבר אלי זה השלחן אשר לפני ה'.
Yechezkel Bing, *Siddur ha--Rashash* (Bnei Brak: Divrei Shalom, 2009) p. 79, כשיש לו כוס, יקח הכוס בידו ויאמר: וידבר אלי זה השלחן אשר לפני ה'.
See also Yitzchak Satz, David Yitzḥaki, David Salmon, eds., *Birkat Ha-Mazon l-Moreinu Ha-Rav Shabbtai Sofer* (Toronto: Otzreinu, 2002), 2n2 at the end.

48 R. Chaim Vital, *Sha'ar ha-Mitzvot* (Jerusalem: 1905) *Ekev*, p. 45a.

49 Yitzchak Satz, David Yitzchaki, David Salmon, eds., *Birkat Ha-Mazon l-Moreinu Ha-Rav Shabbtai Sofer* (Toronto: Otzreinu, 2002) 2n2. In Chizkiya Dachbash, *Tiklal* (Shami) (Rosh Ha-Ayin, 2005) p. 706, the instructions are to say the verse when there is no *zimmun*. See the discussion of omitting the *zimmun* when reciting this verse in *Or Torah*, Elul 5762 (2002), vol. 12 (418), *siman* 138, pp. 788-792.

50 See Shushan Hacohen, *Perach Shushan* (Jerusalem, 1977) p. 17 in the biographical section, where only Ps. 34:2, Eccl. 12:13 and the end of Ezekiel 41:22 are said.

is good, for His mercy endures forever) and Ps. 106:2 (מי ימלל גבורות ה' ישמיע כל תהלתו, Who can express the mighty acts of the Lord, or make all His praise to be heard). No source is ever provided for the recitation of these particular verses.[51] For example, the verses appear in *Siddur Aliyot Eliyahu*, a modern day siddur which is intended to represent the rulings of the Vilna Gaon and *Mishna Berura*; however, no references are brought there as to the source or reason for their inclusion.[52]

The addition of these two verses is generally referred to as a German custom.[53] It should be noted that Joseph Juspa Hahn included the recital of *Al Naharot Bavel* and *Shir ha-Maalot* before *Birkat Ha-Mazon* in his book *Sefer Yosef Ometz*, an important collection of the customs of the Frankfurt am Main community.[54] This work was completed around 1630, before *Shnei Luḥot ha-Brit* was published, although it was only published afterwards in 1723.[55] This attests to the early acceptance of the practice of saying *Al Naharot Bavel* and *Shir ha-Ma'alot* among German Jews. However, there are no early references to these additional verses.

In *Seder Zemirot Yeshurun*, a work meant to represent the German Ashkenazic tradition, three different versions of this custom are brought. In all versions, two additional verses are added after *Shir ha-Ma'alot* and Ps. 145:21 and 115:18, the difference is which two verses are said and in what order. In one version, Ps. 118:1 and 106:2 are recited. The other has Ps. 106:2 followed by Ps. 150:6 (כל הנשמה תהלל יה הללויה, Let everything that hath breath praise the Lord, Hallelujah). The Amsterdam custom reported there has the order switched; Ps. 150:6 is said

---

51 Shlomo Riskin, *Around the Family Table* (Jerusalem: Urim Publications, 2005), p. 12; *The Koren Birkon* (Jerusalem: Koren Publishers, 2010) p. 153; Natan Zvi Yarom, *Birkat Ha-Mazon Be-mechitzat ha-Ḥafetz Ḥayyim* (Moddin Illit: Mechon Mishnat ha-Ḥafetz Ḥayyim, 2014) p. 5; Aaron Perlov, *Birkat Ha-Mazon–Karnei Hod* (Jerusalem: 2014), p. 9; *Birkon Koren–Shir Zion Edition* (Jerusalem: Koren, 2016) p. 178. Regarding the Tunisian custom to say Ps. 118:1 before *Birkat Ha-Mazon* on holidays, see David Setbon, *Alei Hadas* (Kiryat Sefer: 2010) p. 586, *siman* 13.

52 *Siddur Aliyot Eliyahu* (Jerusalem: Machon Aliot Eliyahu, 2013) p. 141. When contacted, the various bencher and siddur editors replied that although they do not know the source of these verses, they included them because they are commonly said. This response is illustrative: לא מצאתי כעת מקור פסוקים האחרים, אבל היות שדשו בו רבים לא נמנענו מלהביאם.

53 Yitzchak Satz, David Yitzchaki, David Salmon, eds., *Birkat Ha-Mazon l-Moreinu Ha-Rav Shabbtai Sofer* (Toronto: Otzreinu, 2002) 2n1.

54 Joseph Juspa Hahn, *Sefer Yosef Ometz* (Frankfurt am Main, 1723), p. 21b, *siman* 154.

55 Dean Phillip Bell, *Jewish Identity in Early Modern Germany: Memory, Power and Community* (NY: Routledge, 2016) pp. 48–49.

first, followed by Ps. 106:2.[56] In this work as well, no sources are given for the recitation of these verses.[57]

This custom is brought without any source in the contemporary work *Otzar Ta'amei Ha-Minhagim*, with the explanation that these particular verses may have been chosen because each parallels one of the four blessings of *Birkat Ha-Mazon*. Ps. 145:21 and the first blessing both contain the phrase "all flesh" (כל בשר), Ps. 115:18 and the second blessing both have the term "we" (אנחנו) referring to blessing or thanking God, Ps. 118:1 and the third blessing both contain the phrase "forever" (לעולם), and Ps. 106:2, which refers to "all the praises" (כל תהלתו), parallels the multiple descriptions of praise accorded to God in the fourth blessing (מלכנו, אדירנו, בוראנו, גואלנו).[58] Some of these connections are clearly forced, as the terms "we" (אנחנו) and "forever" (לעולם) are fairly common in liturgical contexts.

The kabbalistic work *Ḥemdat Yamim* gives extensive and detailed lists of Psalms and verses that are to be recited before *Birkat Ha-Mazon*, with different selections based on the day and time. For example, on Shabbat night a selection of verses is said followed by Ps. 87,[59] Shabbat day the Psalms are 121, 45, 24, along with the verses from the night meal,[60] with different selections from Psalms for *seuda shlishit*.[61] Holidays have their own Psalms as well, for example, on Purim Ps. 98 is to be recited before *Birkat Ha-Mazon*.[62]

For *Rosh Ḥodesh*, the verses chosen begin with the letters that spell out the Hebrew word Adonay in its "*milui* (filled)" form. For example, the first letter of the word, *alef*, is divided into the three letters that spell the word *alef*: *alef*, *lamed*, *peh*. Then each of these letters is itself spelled out, *alef* becomes *alef*, *lamed*, *peh*; *lamed* becomes *lamed*, *mem*, *dalet*; *peh* becomes *peh*, *heh*. A verse is chosen beginning with each letter of this expanded spelling. In this list of verses, Ps. 106:2 (מי ימלל) is the verse for

---

56 Shlomo Hofmeister, *Seder Zemirot Yeshurun* (Vienna: Yeshurun, 2016) p. 57.

57 Personal queries to the editor of *Seder Zemirot Yeshurun* went unanswered. The additional verses are also found in the new edition of the German prayer book, Joseph Scheuer, ed., *Siddur Schma Kolenu* (Basel: Morascha Verlag, 2000), p. 106, but not in early editions.

58 Shmuel Gelbard, *Otzar Taamei Haminhagim* (Petach Tikva: Mifaal Rashi, 1996) pp. 105–106.

59 *Ḥemdat Yamim*, vol. 1 (Bnei Brak: Machon Ḥemdat Yamim, 2011) p. 192.

60 *Ḥemdat Yamim*, vol. 1 (Bnei Brak: Machon Ḥemdat Yamim, 2011) p. 291.

61 *Ḥemdat Yamim*, vol. 1 (Bnei Brak: Machon Ḥemdat Yamim, 2011) p. 332.

62 *Ḥemdat Yamim*, vol. 2 (Bnei Brak: Machon Ḥemdat Yamim, 2011) p. 347.

the *mem* in the middle of the *lamed*, and Ps. 118:1 (הודו) appears as the verse for the *heh* at the end of the *peh* of *alef*. Furthermore, Ps. 145:21 (תהלת) also appears here as the verse for the *tav* from the spelled out *dalet*.[63]

Ḥemdat Yamim is a *kabbalistic* work of unclear authorship first published in Turkey in the early 1730s under the auspices of R. Israel Yaakov Algazi. For years, the book was the subject of much controversy stemming from allegations that it represents Sabbatean ideas. This controversy continues to this day. However, the current state of scholarship seems to understand that the work is a collection of customs and practices based on the students of Ari, often brought without attribution, and is not necessarily a Sabbatean work.[64] Thus there is a *kabbalistic* source for reciting these verses before *Birkat Ha-Mazon*. However, this cannot be the source of the addition of the two verses, as *Ḥemdat Yamim* instructs that they are for *Rosh Ḥodesh*, not for other occasions, and furthermore they appear in a very long list of verses, the rest of which are not recited.

Possible Explanations: Melodies and Zionism

A possible explanation for the addition of two verses may be indicated by the fact that although there are variations in the verses and order of the verses among German and Amsterdam customs, in all cases it is totals four verses added to Psalm 126. This has led to speculation that the additional verses are connected to the tunes used for *Shir Ha-Ma'alot* among German Jews. Many of the popular Ashkenazic *Shir ha-Ma'alot* tunes work well with a song divided into four line stanzas. Once two of the Ari verses are added, the tune no longer fits well, and an addition of two more verses would make the tune fit nicely.[65] This would be the reason that although different verses are added in different Ashkenazic communities, it is always two more verses that are added to the standard two. Why these particular ones?

It is documented that the German Jewish community had distinct tunes for *Shir Ha-Ma'alot* for different holidays, special Shabbatot and certain times of year.[66] These tunes were not only used for *Shir ha-Ma*

---

63 *Ḥemdat Yamim*, vol. 2 (Bnei Brak: Machon Ḥemdat Yamim, 2011) p. 51.

64 See Moshe Fogel, "The Sabbatean Character of Ḥemdat Yamim: A Reexamination," *Jerusalem Studies in Jewish Thought* 16:2 (2001): pp. 365–422.

65 See Steve Epsten, "The Source of the Addition of Tehillat Hashem after Shir ha-Maalot" (Heb.) in *Chiddushei Torah@NDS*, vol. 12 (2011) 163n16.

66 Yaakov Rothschild, "Shabbat Zemirot of the Jews of Southern Germany and the Customs Connected to Them," *Duchan* 7, 1964, p. 100 (Hebrew). For a list

'alot, but also for other liturgical elements on that Shabbat, for example, *Lekha Dodi*.[67] The *Shir ha-Ma'alot* tunes for Sukkot, Pesach and Shavuot were often the same tunes used for the responsive sections of *Hallel* said on those days, which includes the refrain ליהוה כי-טוב: כי לעולם חסדו הודו.[68] Thus, among German Jews, there was a natural connection between *Shir ha-Ma'alot* and *Hodu*: they shared the same tune on festivals. Therefore, if melodically a verse should be added to make the *Shir ha-Ma'alot* tune fit, this would seem to be a very appropriate verse. These tunes even outlasted their original liturgical context].

> By the second half of the twentieth century, when many German Jewish liturgical traditions fell into oblivion, the original melodies of the festive *piyyutim* were no longer performed in synagogue services. Therefore the survival of these melodies as a marker of liturgical time remained alive through their continuous practice in the domestic sphere among families of German origin.[69]

Ps. 106:2 (מי ימלל גבורות יהוה ישמיע כל תהלתו) is also a reasonable verse to add to make up a four verse stanza, as it indicates that in our recitation of these verses we have in no way said all the praises due to God. This verse is also appended to *Anim Zemirot* where it serves a similar function.[70]

Another popular explanation for the addition of these verses is that they were chosen to stress that God should be praised irrespective of any connection of returning to the Land of Israel. Thus, the verses were

---

with sound samples, see Naomi Cohn-Zentner, "Shir Ha-Ma'alot–the Umbilical Cord Between Liturgical and Domestic Soundspheres in Ashkenazi Culture," July 2014, Jewish Music Research Center, Hebrew University, http://www.jewish-music.huji.ac.il/content/shir-hama%E2%80%99alot-umbilical-cord-between-liturgical-and-domestic-soundspheres-ashkenazi-culture.

67 Uri Aharon, "Melodies for Shir Hamaalot in Frankfurt Am Main," *Duchan* 16, 2005, pp. 296–297 (Hebrew); Yair Goldreich, "Sidrei Tefilla ba-Kehilla," *Shnot Ḥayyim* 2007, p. 71, detailing the practices of the Mekor Ḥayyim community in Petach Tikvah, following the Frankfurt am Main customs.

68 Aharon, pp. 302–304.

69 Naomi Cohn-Zentner, "Shir haMa'a lot – the Umbilical Cord Between Liturgical and Domestic Soundspheres in Ashkenazi Culture," July 2014, Jewish Music Research Center, Hebrew University, http://www.jewish-music.huji.ac.il/content/shir-hama%E2%80%99alot-umbilical-cord-between-liturgical-and-domestic-soundspheres-ashkenazi-culture

70 See Elchanan Adler, *Zvi Tifara* (Passaic, 2017) p. 145.

added as an "anti-Zionist" expression, to lessen the focus on Israel found in *Shir ha-Ma'alot.*

We saw that the *kabbalistic* addition of Psalms 137 and 126 to the meal was to emphasize "the holiness of the Holy Land and the Palace of the King" (*Zohar, Terumah* 157b), themes already found in the second and third blessings of *Birkat Ha-Mazon.*[71] *Shir ha-Ma'alot* in particular, with its description of actually returning to the Land of Israel especially resonated with the early Zionists. Rav Kook noted that the "secret" behind reciting this Psalm before *Birkat Ha-Mazon* is to demonstrate a yearning to come to Israel, thus tapping into the *shefa* (bounty) of the Land of Israel even when eating food from outside of Israel.[72] Connections were also made between *Shir ha-Ma'alot* and the national anthem of Israel, the *Hatikvah.* It has been reported many times that early Zionists would sing *Shir ha-Ma'alot* before *Birkat Ha-Mazon* to the tune of *Ha-Tikvah,*[73] and there were authorities who opposed this.[74] The exchange of melodies worked both ways, it is reported that Bialik wanted to use Yossele Rosenblatt's tune for *Shir ha-Ma'alot* for *Ha-Tikvah* after hearing

---

71 See Avi Erlich, *Ancient Zionism: The Biblical Origins of the National Idea* (NY: Free Press, 1995) p. 14.

72 Abraham Isaac Kook, *Orot Ha-Kodesh* vol. 3 (Jerusalem: Mossad Harav Kook, 1950) p. 295. See on this Moshe Tzuriel, *Otzrot ha-Raya,* vol. 3 (Rishon Letzion: Yeshivat Hesder Rishon Letzion, 2002) p. 362; Chaim Drukman, *Netiot Ha'aretz* (Kfar Darom: Makhon ha-Torah v-ha-Aretz, 2004) p. 185.

73 See for example, Yaakov Efrati, *Vavim l-Amudim,* vol. 3 (Jerusalem, 2002), 153n1; Michael Englishman, *163256: A Memoir of Resistance* (Ontario: Wilfrid Laurier University Press, 2007) p. 4; Joseph Reider, "Secular Currents in Synagogal Chant in America (1918)," in Jonathan L. Friedman, ed., *The Value of Sacred Music* (Jefferson: McFarland & Company, 2009) p. 146; Raymond Apple, *Let's Ask the Rabbi* (AuthorHouse, 2011) p. 140. Ps. 126 sung to the tune of *Hatikvah* became part of the *Yom Ha-Atzmaut* evening service, right from the very first *Yom Ha-Atzmaut,* see R. Maimon, "Pirkei Zikhronot al ha-Tzionut," *Sinai* vol. 34 (1953) p. 277. See also, *Seder ha-Tefilot v-ha-Hodiot* (Jerusalem: Ministry of Religion, 1952) p. 9 and Shmuel Katz, ed., *ha-Rabbanut ha-Reishit l-Yisrael: Shivim Shana l-Yisoda* vol. 2 (Jerusalem, 2002) p. 839.

74 R. Avraham Weinfeld, *Lev Avraham, part one* (Brooklyn: Balshon, 1977) *siman* 133, pp. 229–230. This was vehemently opposed in the Neturei Karta literature, as expected, see *Mishmeret Ḥomoteinu* vol. 8 (1956) p. 37 (5). See the description of a dispute that broke out over singing *Shir Ha-Ma'alot* after a meal to this tune on the first Yom Ha-Atzmaut in Miriam Sperber, *mi-Sippurei ha-Savta* (Jerusalem: 1986) p. 143.

him sing it on a trip to Israel.[75] *Shir ha-Ma'alot* was even suggested to be the national anthem instead of *Ha-Tikvah*.[76]

It is reported that Rabbi Dr. Mordechai Halevi (Markus) Horovitz (1844–1910), the Hungarian born Orthodox rabbi of Frankfurt from 1878–1910, although regarded among the most prominent *Protest Rabbiner* against organized Zionism,[77] would sing the first stanza of *Ha-Tikvah* after *Shir ha-Ma'alot*.[78] Also, it is reported among some Amsterdam Jews that *Ha-Tikvah* was sung at the end of the Shabbat meal.[79]

Even with these connections, there is no documentation that verses were ever added after *Shir ha-Ma'alot* specifically to mitigate any Zionist message, and historically this explanation cannot be accurate as two of these verses were added already in the 1600s.[80]

The Purpose of Additional Verses

There may be another explanation for the added verses. They all have a common theme; they talk about praising God. This might not seem particularly special, but note that *Al Naharot Bavel* and *Shir ha-Ma'alot* were instituted to recall the destruction of the Temple. They refer either to the destruction of Israel at the hands of the Babylonians or the future redemption, but not specifically to praising God.

We have records of other verses and Psalms said by different communities right before *Birkat Ha-Mazon*. For example, Ps. 34:2 (אברכה את ה' בכל-עת תמיד תהלתו בפי, I will bless the Lord at all times; His praise shall continually be in my mouth) and Neh. 9:5 (ויברכו שם כבדך, ומרומם על כל ברכה ותהלה, Let them bless Thy glorious Name, that is exalted above all blessing and praise) among some Yemenites,[81] or Ps. 33 among

75 Shmuel Rosenblatt, *Yossele Rosenblatt* (2007) p. 248.

76 Goel Rappel, *Moreshet Am v-Aretz* (Tel Aviv: Yediot Acharonot, 2002) p. 134.

77 Matthias Morgenstern, *From Frankfurt to Jerusalem* (Leiden: Brill, 2002) p. 18.

78 Mordechai Halevi (Markus) Horovitz, *Rabbanei Frankfurt* (Jerusalem: Mossad Harav Kook, 1972) p. 340, in the additional material added by Joseph Unna after the passing of R. Horovitz. On this work and this description of R. Horovitz, see the review by Ernest Simon in the Joseph Unna memorial volume, *Zikhron Yosef* (Kfar Haroeh, 1983) p. 498.

79 Suzanne Mehler Whitley, *Appel is Forever: A Child's Memoir* (Detroit: Wayne State University Press, 1999) p. 25.

80 See the discussion in Steve Epstein, "The Source of the Addition of Tehillat Hashem after Shir ha-Ma'alot" (Hebrew) in *Ḥiddushei Torah@NDS*, vol. 12 (2011) pp. 161–163, particularly note 16.

81 Yitzchak Mualem, *Agadata d-Pischa* (Beitar Illit: Machon Ohalei Avraham Yaakov, 2003) p. 120. Regarding the various Psalms and verses added into the

the Skolye Chassidim,[82] and Ps. 111 and 121 among some Jews of Amsterdam.[83] All of these have the common element of blessing or calling out to God.

The idea that it is particularly important to recall that in reciting *Birkat Ha-Mazon* one is thanking and praising God is specifically noted in a number of sources, most popularly with the statement of R. Yitzchak Meir Alter (1799–1866), the first Ger Rebbe. He stated that "if a person eats before God and then recites *Birkat Ha-Mazon* and known before Whom he is blessing, and thanks the One who gave him the food, there are no greater words of Torah than this."[84] We have seen that some sources relied on the verses said before *Birkat Ha-Mazon* to fulfill the idea to say words of Torah at the meal. Those verses are even more significant when they also remind us that God is the source of our food and it behooves us to praise and thank Him for that. In fact, many of the verses prescribed by Ari fulfill this purpose as well. The recitation of these four verses after *Shir Ha-Ma'alot* would therefore not necessarily be a conscious selection of two verses from Ari along with two additional verses, but rather another collection of verses referring to praising God, two of which happen to be the same as two verses of Ari.[85]

This is the explanation offered by R. Yosef Tzvi Halevi Dunner (1913–2007), regarding the various additional verses recited by German and Amsterdam Jews after *Shir Ha-Ma'alot.* He was a graduate of the Hildesheimer Rabbinical Seminary in Berlin and Chief Rabbi of East Prussia before moving to England and ultimately serving as head of the

---

Yemenite liturgy before *Birkat Ha-Mazon*, see Moshe Gavra, *Meḥkarim b-Siddurei Teiman* (Bnei Brak: HaMakon l-Ḥeker Ḥakhmei Teiman, 2010) p. 365; Moshe Gavra, *ha-Tiklal ha-Madai ha-Mehudar* (Bnei Brak: Ha-Makhon l-Ḥeker Ḥakhmei Teiman, 2012) p. 365.

82 Yissachar Ringel, *Adir Ba-Marom* (Brooklyn: Makhon Tal Orot, 2003) p. 231, *siman* 509.

83 Yehuda Brillman, *Minhagei Amsterdam* (Jerusalem: Makhon Yerushalayim, 2001) p. 235, 2:3.

84 Yoetz Kim Kadish Rakocz, *Siaḥ Sarfei Kodesh* vol. 3 (Bnei Brak, 1989) item 16, p. 16; Yehuda Leib Levin, *Ḥidushei ha-Rim* (Jerusalem: Nachliel, 1965) p. 300. This idea is brought in many sources, see for example, Yehuda Arye Leib Heina, *Likutei Yehuda, Dvarim* I (Jerusalem, 1972) p. 68; Elchanan Printz, *She'elot u-Teshuvot Avnei Derech* vol. 7 (Jerusalem, 2014) p. 85.

85 It is interesting to note, *le-havdil*, that among Lutherans, the blessing before the meal includes selections from Ps. 145, and the thanksgiving after includes selections from Ps. 106, indicating that these Psalms are particularly meaningful in the context of praising God at a meal. See Frank Senn, "Lutheran Spirituality" in his *Protestant Spiritual Traditions* (Eugene, OR: Wipf and Stock, 200) p. 37.

Union of Orthodox Hebrew Congregations. A family member reports that once at a meal R. Dunner explained that in his father's family

> they were accustomed to say Ps. 150:6 (כל הנשמה תהלל יה הללויה) and other verses, and today it is customary to say Ps. 145:21 (תהלת ה' ידבר פי ויברך כל בשר שם קדשו לעולם ועד) and others, but the point of all these verses is the same, to awaken us to understand and feel that we are coming to bless and thank the Holy One Blessed be He.[86]

We can now understand that there were different verses and Psalms used by various communities to fulfill the dual function of words of Torah at a meal and a reminder that we are now blessing God. Which verses to add varied, and may have been chosen either with or without regard to the verses of Ari. The particular number of four verses popular among the German and Amsterdam Jews is probably related to the tunes used for singing *Shir Ha-Ma'alot*. ☙

86 *Kol ha-Torah*, vol. 65 (Nissan 5768, 2008), p. 173.

THE NEW APPROACH
TO VIEW THE ANCIENT
We are delighted to announce the start of the most exciting Tanakh project in generations!
תנ״ך קורן ארץ ישראל
THE KOREN
TANAKH
OF THE LAND
OF ISRAEL
Using the latest discoveries from the worlds of archeology, Egyptology, Ancient Near Eastern Studies, Language & Linguistics and much, much more, we bring the text to life and show the subtle beauty of the words of God and the prophets as they applied to the people both then and today.
The full text is beautifully presented alongside the all new translation by Rabbi Lord Jonathan Sacks.
FOR MORE INFORMATION OR TO ORDER VISIT
WWW.KORENPUB.COM
OR YOUR LOCAL JEWISH BOOKSTORE
AVAILABLE NOW
THE SUSAN AND ROGER HERTOG EDITION OF EXODUS
THE KOREN TANAKH OF THE LAND OF ISRAEL
EXODUS • שמות

Rabbi Joseph B. Soloveitchik
Confrontation and Other Essays
Rabbi Joseph B. Soloveitchik
The Lonely Man of Faith
Rabbi Joseph B. Soloveitchik
On Repentance
Rabbi Joseph B. Soloveitchik
Halakhic Morality
Essays on Ethics and Masorah
Rabbi Aharon Lichtenstein
By His Light
Character and Values in the Service of God
Rabbi Aharon Lichtenstein
Return and Renewal
Reflections on Teshuva and Spiritual Growth
Rabbi Yehuda Amital
When God Is Near
On the High Holidays
Faith Shattered and Restored
Rabbi Eliezer Berkovits
Faith After the Holocaust

את הביטוי "גם מתמול גם משלשם" כאומר "תמיד הייתי מגמגם."[35] קושי הדיבור של משה הוא חדש ונבע מהזעזוע שעבר עליו בימים האחרונים. (או שהוא גמגום שמשה כבר חווה בעבר ועכשיו חזר).

טבעו של גמגום זה הוא שכאשר הלחץ והזעזוע חולפים – חולף גם הגמגום.[36] כשמשה רכש יותר בטחון ביכולתו – נעלם הגמגום, ולא היה צורך ב"מתווך" בינו לבין פרעה ובינו לבין העם. משה בסוף ימיו נשא נאום בן שלושים ושלושה פרקים ללא קושי, ולכן, במעמד הר סיני:

מֹשֶׁה יְדַבֵּר וְהָאֱלֹהִים יַעֲנֶנּוּ בְקוֹל. (שמות, יט, יט)

---

35 כך הבינו מספר מפרשים. רמב"ן כתב: ועל דרך הפשט יאמר כי אני כבד פה גם מתמול גם משלשום, כי מנעורי הייתי כבד פה, אף כי עתה כי אני זקן.

36 השיפור יכול להיות מהיר ודרמטי. עיין ב:
John Van Borsel, “Acquired stuttering: differential diagnosis,” *Ghent University, Ghent, Belgium Veiga de Almeida University, Rio de Janeiro, Brazil*, www.asha.org/events/convention/handouts/2011/borsel/.

ה' ביקש ממשה לנתק את עצמו בפעם השלישית מכל הידוע והאהוב לו. האם הוא צריך לוותר על חייו הנעימים עבור אנשים, שההכרות היחידה שלו עמם היתה שלילית? האם הוא נדרש לוותר שוב על הווה בטוח עבור עתיד מעורפל ומסוכן? זכרונות ילדותו, עת נקרע לראשונה מחיק אמו, ולאחר מכן, כאשר הוא נאלץ לברוח מצרים, צפו ועלו אל המודע. קשה היה למשה להכיל את כל מה שעובר עליו. אולי לכן הבינו המפרשים (על פי המדרש) כי השיחה בין משה לאל נמשכה שבעה ימים, למרות שבפרקים ג' וד' היא נראית כשיחה אחת קולחת.[33]

אפשר להניח שלמשה היו בעיות דיבור שיכלו לנבוע שני גורמים שונים, הקשורים זה בזה:

א. הצורך ללמוד שפות שונות ולהסתגל לתרבויות שונות. גמגום נפוץ יותר בין ילדים רב לשוניים (bilingual, multilingual). משה היה צריך ללמוד לדבר בשלוש שפות שונות.[34]

ב. החוויות הטראומטיות שעבר: הניתוק הראשון מהוריו, הניתוק מבית פרעה ואמו המאמצת, והדרישה האלוהית לעזוב את משפחתו ולשוב מצרימה כדי להתעמת עם מיטיביו לשעבר.

יתכן כי הגמגום הראשון של משה עבר עוד לפני שיצא אל אחיו. אולם הזעזוע שעבר בסנה, המחזה, דיבור של ה' אליו, וביחוד הדרישה לחזור למצרים – החזירו את משה אל תקופות הטראומה הקודמות וגרמו לחזרה של אפיזודת הגמגום. משה הרגיש שהוא חוזר אל אותו עולם שהוא חשב שהוא ניצל ממנו, ולכן התחנן:

> בִּי ה'! לֹא אִישׁ דְּבָרִים אָנֹכִי גַּם מִתְּמוֹל גַּם מִשִּׁלְשֹׁם גַּם מֵאָז דַּבֶּרְךָ אֶל-עַבְדֶּךָ כִּי כְבַד-פֶּה וּכְבַד לָשׁוֹן אָנֹכִי.

להבנתי, דברי משה "גם מאז דברך אל עבדך" משמעם כפשוטם – אני כבד פה "<u>מאז</u>" – מהרגע שהתחלת לדבר אלי, ודיבורך זה הוא הגורם לכבדות פי ולשוני. אין צורך להבין

---

33 מדרש רבה...לא איש דברים אנכי וגו.' אמרו חכמים: שבעה ימים קודם היה הקב"ה מפתה למשה שילך בשליחותו ולא היה רוצה לילך, עד מעשה הסנה, הדא הוא דכתיב: לא איש דברים אנכי - חד, מתמול - שנים, גם– שלשה, משלשום - ארבעה, גם– חמשה, מאז - ששה, דברך- שבעה.

34 Gerald McDermott, "Was Moses a stutterer?" available at https://www.firstthings.com/web-exclusives/2013/09/was-moses-a-stutterer. John Van Borsel, Elise Maes, Sofie Foulon "Stuttering and bilingualism: A review," *Journal of Fluency Disorders*.
See also, Yairi and Seery "Foundation and clinical application," *Pearson,* 2015 https://1642598126.rsc.cdn77.org/testbankonly/pdf/Stuttering-Foundations-and-Clinical-Applications-2nd-Edition-Yairi-Test-Bank.pdf.

כל החוויות הטראומתיות שתוארו כאן יכלו לגרום למשה לגמגם. יתכן שהגמגום היה זמני ונעלם כאשר משה חזר לחוות תקופה של שקט ונחת.

במדין זכה משה לארבעים (או ששים) שנה של מנוחה, בהן התגבר על חוויות ילדותו הקשות. אך כאשר רעה את צאן חותנו, הוא שוב עבר זעזוע, אולי הקשה בחייו:

> וַיֵּרָא מַלְאַךְ ה' אֵלָיו בְּלַבַּת-אֵשׁ מִתּוֹךְ הַסְּנֶה וַיַּרְא וְהִנֵּה הַסְּנֶה בֹּעֵר בָּאֵשׁ וְהַסְּנֶה אֵינֶנּוּ אֻכָּל : וַיֹּאמֶר מֹשֶׁה אָסֻרָה-נָּא וְאֶרְאֶה אֶת-הַמַּרְאֶה הַגָּדֹל הַזֶּה מַדּוּעַ לֹא-יִבְעַר הַסְּנֶה: (שם, ג, ב וג)

משה הסתקרן וניגש לראות מה פשר התופעה העל טבעית הזאת, אך אז:

> וַיִּקְרָא אֵלָיו אֱלֹהִים מִתּוֹךְ הַסְּנֶה וַיֹּאמֶר מֹשֶׁה מֹשֶׁה וַיֹּאמֶר הִנֵּנִי : וַיֹּאמֶר אַל-תִּקְרַב הֲלֹם שַׁל-נְעָלֶיךָ מֵעַל רַגְלֶיךָ כִּי הַמָּקוֹם אֲשֶׁר אַתָּה עוֹמֵד עָלָיו אַדְמַת-קֹדֶשׁ הוּא : וַיֹּאמֶר אָנֹכִי אֱלֹהֵי אָבִיךָ אֱלֹהֵי אַבְרָהָם אֱלֹהֵי יִצְחָק וֵאלֹהֵי יַעֲקֹב וַיַּסְתֵּר מֹשֶׁה פָּנָיו כִּי יָרֵא מֵהַבִּיט אֶל הָאֱלֹהִים. (שם, ד – ו)

המחזה כל כך הפחיד את משה, עד שהוא הסתיר את פניו כדי לא לראות אותו. הזעזוע שעבר על אדם שבעשרות השנים האחרונות חי חיים אידיליים ושקטים, ולפתע מתעמת עם מציאות מהממת כל כך, השולטת על הטבע עצמו, היה מעבר למה שיכולתו האינטלקטואלית והרגשית יכלה להכיל. כיצד לא יושפע משה קשות על ידי ארוע זה?

> וַיֹּאמֶר ה' רָאֹה רָאִיתִי אֶת-עֳנִי עַמִּי אֲשֶׁר בְּמִצְרָיִם וְאֶת-צַעֲקָתָם שָׁמַעְתִּי מִפְּנֵי נֹגְשָׂיו כִּי יָדַעְתִּי אֶת-מַכְאֹבָיו : וָאֵרֵד לְהַצִּילוֹ מִיַּד מִצְרַיִם וּלְהַעֲלֹתוֹ מִן-הָאָרֶץ הַהִוא אֶל-אֶרֶץ טוֹבָה וּרְחָבָה אֶל-אֶרֶץ זָבַת חָלָב וּדְבָשׁ אֶל-מְקוֹם הַכְּנַעֲנִי וְהַחִתִּי וְהָאֱמֹרִי וְהַפְּרִזִּי וְהַחִוִּי וְהַיְבוּסִי : וְעַתָּה הִנֵּה צַעֲקַת בְּנֵי-יִשְׂרָאֵל בָּאָה אֵלָי וְגַם-רָאִיתִי אֶת-הַלַּחַץ אֲשֶׁר מִצְרַיִם לֹחֲצִים אֹתָם: (שם, ז – ט)

האם הבין משה את דברי ה'? – אינני בטוח. עובדה היא שלמרות שה' הבטיח לו "ושמעו לקולך" (שם, יח), הוא שאל "והן לא יאמינו לי ולא ישמעו בקולי" (שם, ד, א) אולי הוא היה מפוחד מדי לקלוט את דברי ה'.

יש להניח שמשה תמה מדוע ה' מספר לו כל זאת. מה הוא יכול לעשות? בפעם האחרונה שהוא הציל עברי <u>בודד</u> ממכהו המצרי – כמעט עלה לו הדבר בחייו. הסכנה לחייו הגיע אליו מצידם של עברים אחרים. מדוע העברים בכלל ראויים להצלה ממצרים?[32] אז מגיעה ההפתעה:

> וְעַתָּה לְכָה וְאֶשְׁלָחֲךָ אֶל-פַּרְעֹה וְהוֹצֵא אֶת-עַמִּי בְנֵי-יִשְׂרָאֵל מִמִּצְרָיִם. (שם, ד – ו)

---

32 עיין רש"י לפרק ב, יד, ד"ה אכן נודע הדבר "ומדרשו".

וַיִּפֶן כֹּה וָכֹה וַיַּרְא כִּי אֵין אִישׁ וַיַּךְ אֶת-הַמִּצְרִי וַיִּטְמְנֵהוּ בַּחוֹל. (שם, יב)

משה ראה את אכזריות המצרי, ותמה: המצרים מועטים, והעברים רבים,[29] מדוע לא יעזרו העברים לאחיהם המוכה? (מובן המילים "וירא כי אין איש" , כאשר המקום היה הומה מאנשים, הוא ראה שלא היה איש שההין לעצור את המצרי[30]) משה הרג את המצרי וטמן אותו בחול. תוך שניות הפך משה מנסיך מצרי מכובד לרוצח עברי, מבוקש על ידי האיש שגדלו כבן.

עבור משה זו היתה טראומה כפולה. הראשונה: ההכרה שאחיו מעונים ומושפלים עד שהם לא מעיזים לבא לעזרת אחיהם המוכה. השניה: השינוי הקיצוני במעמדו החברתי והמשפטי. מי יכול לעבור חוויה כזאת מבלי שיושפע נפשית?

משה חשב שקבורת המצרי תגן עליו, העברים ודאי לא "ילשינו" על מי שהציל עברי מוכה! קל לתאר מה שהרגיש למחרת:

וַיֵּצֵא בַּיּוֹם הַשֵּׁנִי וְהִנֵּה שְׁנֵי-אֲנָשִׁים עִבְרִים נִצִּים וַיֹּאמֶר לָרָשָׁע לָמָּה תַכֶּה רֵעֶךָ: וַיֹּאמֶר מִי שָׂמְךָ לְאִישׁ שַׂר וְשֹׁפֵט עָלֵינוּ הַלְהָרְגֵנִי אַתָּה אֹמֵר כַּאֲשֶׁר הָרַגְתָּ אֶת-הַמִּצְרִי?! (שם, יג)

העובדה ששני עברים מסוגלים, בתוך הקטל והסבל מסביבם להכות זה את זה, היתה מקוממת. אולם תגובת המכה לתוכחתו של משה, היכתה אותו בתדהמה. הוא התיחס להריגת המצרי כלא מוצדקת! משה אינו גיבור, כי אם פורע חוק! משה היה המום ונבוך: האם זהו העם שלי, עבורו בגדתי בפרעה? האם אנשים אלו ראויים להגנה?!

וַיִּשְׁמַע פַּרְעֹה אֶת-הַדָּבָר הַזֶּה וַיְבַקֵּשׁ לַהֲרֹג אֶת-מֹשֶׁה וַיִּבְרַח מֹשֶׁה מִפְּנֵי פַרְעֹה וַיֵּשֶׁב בְּאֶרֶץ-מִדְיָן וַיֵּשֶׁב עַל-הַבְּאֵר. (שם, טו)

שוב נקרע משה מסביבתו הטבעית. הוא נאלץ לברוח למדין. עם הגיעו למדין הוא הושיע את בנות יתרו מרועים שבאו לנשלן ממי הבאר, (שם, טז ויז) ונשא את בתו של יתרו לאישה. השם גרשום שנתן לבנו, "כי אמר גר הייתי בארץ נכריה" (שם, כב) מבטא את געגועיו לארצו – מצרים.[31]

---

29 היחס היה קרוב לאחד למאה: הנוגשים, שהיו מצרים, היו אחראים על מספר שוטרים (כנראה עשרה) והשוטרים, שהיו יהודים, היו ממונים על מספר עבדים. נמצא שעל כל נוגש מצרי היו כמאה עברים, ואולי יותר, אם נמנה את השוטרים. במדרש תנחומא סימן ט: היה אותו נוגש עשוי על ק"כ אנשים...

30 כך כתב ב"הכתב והקבלה" כאן.

31 גם יוסף לא שכח את ארצו. הוא קרא לבכורו מנשה "כי נשני אלהים את כל עמלי ואת כל בית אבי, לבנו השני קרא אפרים "כי הפרני אלהים בארץ עניי". מצד אחד ה' השכיח ממנו את צרותיו ואת בית אביו, ומצד שני, קורא לארץ בה הוא משנה למלך "ארץ עניי".
שמות רבה, פרשה לג: דרך הצדיקים לשום שם לבניהם לענין המאורע. ביוסף מהו אומר (בראשית מא, נא-נב) ויקרא שם הבכור מנשה, ואת שם השני קרא אפרים, כדי להזכיר את הנסים שעשה הקב"ה עמו. אף משה קרא שם בנו גרשום, על הנס שעשה לו ה', שגר היה בארץ נכריה והצליחו הקב"ה משם.

היא שמה אותו בתיבה (סגורה! בת פרעה היתה צריכה לפתוח אותה (שמות ב,ו) הילד היה על הנהר מספר שעות בודד ומפוחד, ואין פלא שכאשר בת פרעה פתחה את התיבה, היא ראתה "נער בוכה" (שם). היא אימצה את התינוק לבן, ושכרה את אם הילד להניק אותו. את שתי שנותיו הראשונות בילה הילד בחיק אמו האוהבת, שהקנתה לו כל מה שהיה מסוגל להשיג, בעיקר את השפה העברית. אחר שנתיים, עבר משה את טראומת הפירוד והניתוק הראשונה בחייו. אמו הביאה אותו אל בת פרעה, ואת עשרים (או ארבעים)[25] השנה הבאות בילה בבית פרעה, לומד שפה חדשה, מנהגים חדשים ותרבות אחרת. משה גם היה צריך ללמוד שתי שפות בעת ובעונה אחת.

שנים עברו, ומשה גדל ו"יצא אל אחיו" (שם, יא)

אבן עזרא כתב כי אחיו אלו הם אחיו המצרים - משה בשלב זה לא ראה את עצמו כעברי. רש"י, בעקבות המדרש,[26] הבין כי אלו אחיו העברים.

הפסוק ממשיך: "וירא בסבלותם". להבנת אבן עזרא, סבלות המצרים,היא העבודה עליה היו אחראים, (בדומה למה שאמר פרעה למשה ואהרון "לכו לסבלותיכם". (שם, ה, ד)[27]

קל להבין את הזעזוע שעבר על משה, בראותו לראשונה את העבודה המפרכת והתנאים המשפילים בהם היו שרויים אחיו.

אולם עכשיו יעבור משה זעזוע גדול יותר, שישנה את מהלך חייו, את זהותו ואת גורלו:

וַיַּרְא אִישׁ מִצְרִי מַכֶּה אִישׁ-עִבְרִי מֵאֶחָיו. (שם, ב, יא)

לפי אבן עזרא, שהמילה "אחיו" בתחילת הפסוק מתיחסת למצרים,[28] משה עבר טלטלה אדירה: תוך שניות הוא הרגיש שהוא אח לעברים ולא למצרים. אדם לא עובר חויה כזאת ללא השפעה על מצבו הנפשי. גם לפי המדרש ורש"י, היתה החוויה הזו מטלטלת. משה לא היסס:

[באור הביטוי "יולדת למקוטעין" הוא שבלידות בחדש השביעי התינוק נולד בתחילת החדש, ולא בסופו. יבמות מב., נידה כז. ועוד].
במציאות, אין הדבר כך. מאמרים רבים נכתבו על דברי חז"ל בנושא הרפואה, והאם נשתנו הטבעים מאז. יעוין לדוגמא במאמר "השתנות הטבעים" מתוך: אנציקלופדיה הלכתית רפואית, כרך ב', ירושלים תשנ"א 1991 (ליקט ערך והעיר: פרופ' אברהם שטינברג) גם הרב אברהם קרליץ (החזון איש) כתב (יורה דעה סימן קנ"ה, סעיף ד) כי נשתנו טבעים אלו היום.

25 מדרש רבה, שמות פרשה א, כז: ויהי בימים ההם ויגדל משה, בן עשרים שנה היה משה באותה שעה, ויש אומרים בן ארבעים.

26 שמות רבה, פרשה א, כז: ...וירא בסבלותם מהו ויראה? שהיה רואה בסבלותם ובוכה ואומר: חבל לי עליכם, מי יתן מותי עליכם, שאין לך מלאכה קשה ממלאכת הטיט, והיה נותן כתפיו ומסיע לכל אחד ואחד מהן.

27 רש"י: לכו לסבלתיכם - לכו למלאכתכם שיש לכם לעשות בבתיכם. אבל מלאכת שעבוד מצרים לא הייתה על שבטו של לוי, ותדע לך שהרי משה ואהרן יוצאים ובאים שלא ברשות.

28 (שמות ב, יא): ויצא אל אחיו - המצרים, כי בארמון המלך היה.

גמגום זה מצוי בעיקר בשנות ההתפתחות של הילדים, ועובר בהדרגה. אולם משה גמגם כאשר היה בן שמונים, דבר נדיר מאד (אם כי מצוי יותר בין בנים מאשר בין בנות).[20]

כבר הערנו כי אין שום עדות כי משה היה מגמגם לפני שהוא עמד בסנה.

הגמגום הנורולוגי (Neurogenic stuttering) נגרם בדרך כלל על ידי פגיעה במוח, כתוצאה מתאונה, שבץ או שמוש יתר בסמים. [21] אפשר לשלול על הסף אפשרויות אלו כאשר מדובר במשה.

הגמגום הפסיכולוגי (Psychogenic stuttering), הנדיר מבין שלושת הסוגים, נגרם על ידי מאורעות טראומטיים שהשפיעו נפשית על המגמגם. [22] היד קרא לו Hysterical stuttering. בין המאפיינים של גמגום זה הם, בין היתר שהוא בדרך כלל זמני בלבד (דיל, 1982).

באומגרטן ודאפי כתבו:

> ברור שגמגום יכול להתפתח כתוצאה מקשיים פסיכולוגיים אצל מבוגרים שלא נחשדה או אובחנה אצלם מחלה נורולוגית. (תרגום שלי)[23]

ברצוני לטעון כי גמגומו של משה אכן היה שייך לקבוצה השלישית. משה נולד אחר שפרעה גזר להשליך לנהר כל בן שנולד. משה נולד בתחילת החדש השביעי להריון, ואמו החביאה אותו שלושה חדשים, בתנאים שלא עוזרים להתפתחות בריאה.[24] לאחר שלושה חדשים,

---

20 Nayerossadat Nouri, Nargesossadat Nouri Hossein Abdali, Meisam Shafie, and Hamid Karimi "Stuttering: Genetic updates and a case report," *Advanced Biomedical Research,* available at https://www.ncbi.nlm.nih.gov/pmc/articles/PMC3507011/
בושל וסומר מצאו כי כאשר הגמגום מתמיד אל שנות הבגרות, דבר נדיר יחסית, שעור המגמגמים בין הגברים הוא פי שלוש מאשר אצל נשים. המאמר הוא:
Christian Büchel and Martin Sommer, "What Causes Stuttering?" *PLOS Biology* 17 Feb 2004
ד"ר הדס הרמתי *גמגום אצל מבוגרים* כותבת כי גברים מהווים 80% מבין המגמגמים המבוגרים: .Available at http://www.hadas-haramati.co.i/2015/08/

21 Fidias E. Leon-Sarmiento, Edwin Paez, Mark Hallett, "Nature and nurture in stuttering: a systematic review on the case of Moses," https://link.springer.com/content/pdf/10.1007/s10072-012-0984-2.pdf. Luc De Nil, Catherine Theys, "Advances in Our Understanding of Adult Neurogenic Stuttering," *The Stuttering Foundation* (Summer 2012).

22 Henry Head, "The diagnosis of Hysteria," *British Medical Journal*, May 27 1922.

23 John Baumgartner and Joseph R. Duffy "Psychogenic stuttering in adults with and without neurologic disease," *Mayo Clinic* https://mayoclinic.pure.elsevier.com/en/publications/psychogenic-stuttering-in-adults-with-and-without-neurologic-dise.

24 רש"י (שמות ב, ג) ולא יכלה עוד הצפינו - שמנו לה המצריים מיום שהחזירה, והיא ילדתו לששה חדשים ויום אחד, שהיולדת לשבעה יולדת למקוטעין, והם בדקו אחריה לסוף תשעה:

...אני כבד פה גם מתמול גם משלשום, כי מנעורי הייתי כבד פה, אף כי עתה כי אני זקן. וגם מאז דברך היום אל עבדך, כי לא הסירות כבדות פי בצוותך אותי ללכת אל פרעה לדבר בשמך...

אולם לא ראינו כי משה התקשה בדיבורו כאשר גער בעברים הניצים, או כאשר דיבר בביתו של יתרו, או אחר הדברים האלו. אם משה אכן גמגם, מה גרם לגמגום זה?

ככלל, אנו מבחינים בשלושה סוגי גמגום:[16]

א. גמגום שמקורו בגנים

ב. גמגום נורולוגי

ג. גמגום פסיכולוגי

הסוג הראשון, נקרא בשפה המקצועית (בין היתר Developmental stuttering) מצוי בעיקר אצל ילדים בגיל צעיר. לא תמיד ידועות הסיבות לגמגום, אולם שכיח שבמשפחה ישנו יותר מאשר מגמגם אחד,[17] מה שתומך בהשערה כי יש לגמגום מקורות גנטיים.

מחקרים הראו, למשל, שהגמגום שכיח יותר בילדים שנולדו מנשואי קרובים.[18] נישואין כאלו מקטינים את ה"סל" הגנטי, ועושים מחלות תורשתיות יותר שכיחות.[19]

לענייננו – אמו של משה היתה דודתו של אביו. האם זה היה הגורם לגמגום של משה?

---

16 Christian Büchel and Martin Sommer, "What Causes Stuttering?" *PLoS Biology* available at| http://biology.plosjournals.org.
Psychogenic Stuttering: Definition & Characteristics, study.com
"A Case of Psychogenic Acquired Stuttering: 'A Solution in Search of an Explanation'," available at http://isad.isastutter.org/.

17 Christian Büchel and Martin Sommer, "What Causes Stuttering?" *PLoS Biology,* 2004 available at http://biology.plosjournals.org.

18 Fidias E. Leon-Sarmiento, Edwin Paez, Mark Hallett, "Nature and nurture stuttering: A systematic review on the case of Moses." See https://link.springer.com/content/pdf/10.1007/s10072-012-0984-2.pdf.

19 סטטיסטיקה של משרד הבריאות בישראל מראה כי נשואי קרובים בין ערבים מוסלמים ונוצרים, דרוזים ובדואים הם בשעורים גבוהים מאד. שכיחות הנשואים בין בני דודים ראשונים נעה בין 21% אצל ערבים נוצרים ו-35% בין בדואים בנגב. סך כל הנישואים בין קרובים בקרב הבדואים בנגב הוא 67%! (54% בין הדרוזים) המקור למספרים אלו הוא:
https://www.health.gov.il/PublicationsFiles/Inbred_genetic_disease.pdf
להבנה מפורטת של הקשר בין נשואי קרובים וגמגום, נא לעיין במאמר שמצאתי מאד מועיל:
Dennis Drayna and Changsoo Kang, "Genetic approaches to understanding the causes of stuttering," *Journal of Neurodevelopmental Disorders,* 2011 Dec; 3(4), pp. 374–380.

ממך. מהם אומרים להרגו, מהם אומרים לשרפו. והיה יתרו יושב ביניהן, ואומר להם: הנער הזה אין בו דעת, אלא בחנו אותו והביאו לפניו בקערה זהב וגחלת, אם יושיט ידו לזהב, יש בו דעת והרגו אותו, ואם יושיט ידו לגחלת, אין בו דעת, ואין עליו משפט מות. מיד הביאו לפניו, ושלח ידו לקחת הזהב, ובא גבריאל ודחה את ידו, ותפש את הגחלת והכניס ידו עם הגחלת לתוך פיו ונכוה לשונו, וממנו נעשה כבד פה וכבד לשון.

כווית הלשון והשפתיים (ילקוט שמעוני: ותבער קצת שפתיו ושפת לשונו) עשויה לגרום לאי יכולת לבטא את אותיות השפתיים והלשון, ואכן, רבינו בחיי (שמות ד,י)[14] הביא דעה זו:

וכתב רבינו חננאל מה שהזכיר שני דברים כבד פה וכבד לשון, יורה כי משה רבינו לא היה צח הדבור באותיות זשרס"ץ שהן אותיות השינים, זהו שאמר: "כי כבד פה", גם לא באותיות הלשון שהם אותיות דטלנ"ת, ועל זה אמר "וכבד לשון"

כמו הדעות הקודמות, גם שיטת המדרש לא עולה בקנה אחד עם זה שלא נראה כי משה סבל מקשיי דיבור אחר יציאת מצרים, ולא היה צריך את עזרתו של אהרון כדי להתקשר עם העם. למעשה שמתאר המדרש אין גם שום מקור בכתובים עצמם.

הנרי גרפינקל[15] מתאר את הטראומה הפסיכולוגית שעבר משה במעמד אותו מתאר המדרש:

קל לדמיין כיצד, כאשר התחיל המשפט, נתג מלודיה קצבית, והצופים, בעיקר פרעה, נתמלאו בדאגה ובתחושה מבשרת רעות. משה, שלפי מקורות מסוימים היה בן שלוש בלבד, היה חייב להרגיש שדרמה חזקה ומפחידה מתרחשת. המתח הגבוה, המוזיקה הפועמת והפחד שלו עצמו, כל אלו ככל הנראה הביאו אותו למצב של מעין טרנס. (התרגום שלי).

לדעתו, יתכן כי הנזק שנגרם אז למשה הקטן היה בעיקרו פסיכולוגי, ולא פיזי! מה שמביא אותנו אל הדעה הרביעית:

דעה רביעית: משה היה מגמגם

זו היא דעתו של רש"י (ד, י):

כבד פה - בכבידות אני מדבר, ובלשון לעז בלב"א [גמגמן].

מה גרם לגמגום זה של משה? מתי הוא התחיל? לפי רמב"ן (שם), כאשר משה אומר "גם מתמול גם משלשום", כוונתו היא שהוא סבל מקשיי דיבור מנעוריו ועד עתה.

---

14 גם אבן עזרא ואחרים הביאו אפשרות זאת.

15 Henry Garfinkel, “Why did Moses stammer? and, was Moses left-handed?” *JR Soc. Med.* May 1995, 88 (5) pp. 256 – 257. Available at .https://www.ncbi.nlm.nih.gov/pubmed/7636817

ב. מדוע אהרון, ולא משה, נבחר להיות לכהן גדול? אילו משה היה מגמגם בלבד הוא לא היה פסול, אין זאת אלא שהיה לו מום פיזי נראה לעין שפסל אותו.[10]

ההנחה שלמשה היה מום פיזי מצויה כבר ברמב"ן ובאברבנאל. גם מדרש שכל טוב טוען כי היה למשה מום חיצוני, אלא שהמדרש[11] אומר:

> איני יכול לדבר צחות, לשון פלטין, דהיינו לשון מלכות. ומה כבד פה וכבד לשון? חוט יש שמושך מן הפה ללשון מתחתיו, ומכביד את הלשון מלמהר לדבר צחות...

המום אותו מתאר המדרש הוא Ankyloglossia, הידוע בשם הפופולרי Tongue tied – זהו מצב בו חוט המחבר את הלשון לתחתית הפה קצר מהרגיל, ולכן מקשה על הדיבור ועל האכילה, בעיקר על הבליעה.[12]

אבל אם למשה היתה שפה שסועה, שתיקונה מחייב התערבות חירורגית שלא היתה מצויה בימיו, כיצד משה דיבר לאחר מכן ללא בעיה המוזכרת בתורה? ואת הבעיה שמתאר המדרש ניתן היה לפתור באמצעים שהיו קיימים בימי משה (ניתן לחתוך מעט את החוט המקשר את הלשון לחיך) ומשה לא היה צריך לסבול ממום זה כל חייו.

3. דעה שלישית, משה נכווה בפיו

זוהי דעתו של המדרש[13] שמספר:

> **ותבאהו לבת פרעה וגו'**... והיה פרעה מנשקו ומחבקו, והוא נוטל כתרו של פרעה ומשימו על ראשו,... והיו שם יושבין חרטומי מצרים, ואמרו : מתיראין אנו מזה, שנוטל כתרך ונותנו על ראשו, שלא יהיה זה אותו שאנו אומרים שעתיד ליטול מלכות

להם, למחרת, כאשר התעמת עם העברים. ראה ילקוט שמעוני, סימן קסו: ויהי בהיות הילד בבית המלך בבגדי ארגמן לבושו, ויגדל בקרב בני המלך...

10 נניח לעובדה שלוין הבין כי מום פוסל אדם רק מלשמש ככהן גדול, דבר שאיננו נכון כלל. (עיין רמב"ם הלכות ביאת המקדש פרק ו הלכה א) או להנחה כי משה היה פסול לעבודה. אולם בחומש שמות, וגם בחומש ויקרא, מסופר כי משה שימש בכהונה בשבעת הימים הראשונים של שמונת ימי המילואים! עיין שמות לט וויקרא ח. לדעת רבים מחכמינו, משה היה כהן גדול כל ארבעים השנה שבני ישראל היו במדבר. עיין זבחים קא: אמר רב: משה רבינו כהן גדול וחולק בקדשי שמים היה, שנאמר: מאיל המלואים למשה היה למנה. בהמשך, (קב.) השאלה אם משה היה כהן או לא היא מחלוקת תנאים: וחכמים אומרים: לא נתכהן משה אלא שבעת ימי המלואים בלבד; ויש אומרים: לא פסקה כהונה אלא מזרעו של משה, שנאמר: [דה"י א, כג, יד] ומשה איש האלהים בניו יקראו על שבט הלוי.

11 מהדורת בובר.

12 https://www.mayoclinic.org/diseases-conditions/tongue-tie/symptoms-causes/syc-20378452 עיין במידע כאן.

13 שמות רבה, פרשה א, כ"ו, עיין גם בילקוט שמעוני, סימן קס"ו.

גם פילון האלכסנדרוני כתב שהבעיה של משה לא היתה רפואית. לדעתו משה טען כי רהיטת הלשון של בני אדם אינה מספיקה כדי לבטא את דברי ה'. (מעניין שמשה עדיין ביקש שה' ישלח מישהו אחר).[3]

זיגמונד פרויד טען[4] שמשה לא היה עברי אלא מצרי, ולכן הבין את טענת משה, "כי כבד פה וכבד לשון אנכי" כפשוטה: איני יודע את שפת העם אליו אני נשלח!

דעה זו היא דעת מיעוט (קטן) בין מפרשי התורה, רובם הבינו כי למשה היתה איזו שהיא בעית דיבור, ולא של אי ידיעת השפה.

בנוסף, לא נראה כי למשה היו אילו בעיות שפה. הוא הוביל את שירת הים, הביא לבני ישראל את התורה, ואף נשא נאום ארוך לקראת סוף ימיו.

את טענתו של רשב"ם כי אי אפשר לנביא להיות בעל מום, סתר הר"ן בדרשותיו[5] ובאר מדוע בחר הקב"ה דווקא אדם עם קשיי דיבור להוציא את העם ממצרים ולתת להם את התורה.[6] מכיון שכך, נעבור לדעה השניה, שהיה למשה מום פיזי נראה:

2. דעה שניה: למשה היה מום פיזי

ג'פרי טיגאי,[7] בהסתמך על נתוח המילים "כבד" ו"ערל" בעברית, ערבית, אקדית ושומרית, כתב כי מונחים אלו מתיחסים לבעיה רפואית (כמו גמגום או בעיה רפואית אחרית) או בלשנית, היינו חוסר הבנת הלשון או היכולת להתבטא בצורה נכונה. (כפי שאכן הבינו רשב"ם ובעלי בריתו)

ס. לוין[8] טוען כי למשה היה שפה שסועה או חיך שסוע (Cleft lip or palate). הוא מבסס את דבריו בין היתר על הטענות הבאות:

א. כיצד ידעו העברים הניצים, למחרת היום בו היכה משה את המצרי, את זהותו? אין זאת אלא כי היה למשה מום שהקל על זיהויו.[9]

---

3 .Philo, “On Abraham. On Joseph. On Moses” (Harvard University Press) p. 319 .www.hup.harvard.edu › Loeb Classical Library › Philo

4 .Sigmund Freud, *Moses and Monotheism*, 1939 pp 53 -54

5 בדרוש השלישי (עמ' צ"ז והלאה במהדורת מוסד הרב קוק, ירושלים 2003) והחמישי (עמ' קע"ה שם).

6 גם אבן עזרא לשמות שם כתב: והאומר ששכח לשון מצרים איננו נכון. עיין בטענתו שם.

7 Jeffry H. Tigay, “‘Heavy of Mouth’ and ‘Heavy of Tongue’ on Moses’ Speech Difficulty,” *Bulletin of the American Schools of Oriental Research* .No. 231 (Oct., 1978), pp. 57-67

8 S. Levin, “The speech defect of Moses,” *Journal of the Royal Society of Medicine*, volume 85, October 1992.

9 אבל הגיוני יותר לומר כי מה שזיהה את משה היו בגדיו המלכותיים – שנראו מרחוק יותר משפה שסועה, הנראית רק מקרוב ומזוית מסויימת! משה לבש את אותם הבגדים, או דומים

"כבד פה וכבד לשון" – הצעות להסבר

מאת: אבנר טלר

אחת הסיבות שנתן משה לסרובו ללכת אל פרעה, היתה:

> בִּי אֲדֹנָי לֹא אִישׁ דְּבָרִים אָנֹכִי גַּם מִתְּמוֹל גַּם מִשִּׁלְשֹׁם גַּם מֵאָז דַּבֶּרְךָ אֶל-עַבְדֶּךָ כִּי כְבַד-פֶּה וּכְבַד לָשׁוֹן אָנֹכִי. (שמות, ד, י)

כאשר ה' שלח את משה בשנית אל פרעה, הוא טען:

> הֵן בְּנֵי-יִשְׂרָאֵל לֹא-שָׁמְעוּ אֵלַי וְאֵיךְ יִשְׁמָעֵנִי פַרְעֹה וַאֲנִי עֲרַל שְׂפָתָיִם. (שם, ו, יב)

מפרשי התנ"ך, ואף חוקרים ומדענים בני ימינו ניסו לבאר את כבדות הפה והלשון של משה. ופה אסקור את הדעות השונות שנאמרו בענין, ואוסיף הסבר חדש.

1. דעה ראשונה: למשה לא היתה בעיה רפואית

רשב"ם[1] לא מאמין כי למשה היה מום:

> וכי איפשר נביא אשר ידעו השם פנים אל פנים וקיבל תורה מידו לידו היה מגמגם בלשונו?! (על שמות, ד, י)

ולכן באר:

> איני בקי בלשון מצרים בחיתוך לשון, כי בקטנותי ברחתי משם ועתה אני בן שמונים. (על שמות, ד, י)

גם העמק דבר (שם)[2] הבין כי משה לא דיבר על מום פיזי:

> ...דלשוני הולך בכבדות, ויש מי שאפילו אינו כבד פה ואינו מדבר בלעגי שפה, מ"מ אין לו כח בלשונו להוציא אמרי שפר מכח אל הפועל...

---

1 גם חזקוני כתב שמשה טען כי שכח לשון מצרי.

2 לדעתו משה טוען שאינו רהוט בדבורו, הוא לא נואם טוב, ובכך דעתו שונה משל רשב"ם.

אבנר טלר למד בישיבת הרב עמיאל (הישוב החדש) ואחרי כן כתשע שנים בישיבת איתרי. היה חברותא עם הרב צבי קושלבסקי, וכחמש שנים עם הרב מרדכי אלפנט זצ"ל. בשנת תשמ"ג התחיל ללמד בישיבה דפלטבוש, וכעשר שנים שמש כראש מחלקת התנ"ך.

שההגשמה של העיקר הזה לא תהיה כל כך קלה גם מצד הבית דין וגם מצד הערכאה. אדרבא בתי הדין הורגלו וטענו במשך עשרות בשנים ש"קנס שהייה" הוא כפייה ישירה על הגט ופוסל את הגט ושאי אפשר לקבלו. גם הערכאות כבר הורגלו בדבר והן אף חושבים שסכנת הכפייה על הגט מהווה גם סכנה של הפרת חוק ההפרדה בין המדינה החילונית והדת ויש סכנה שהן כבר מקבלות את המושג הזה באופן מוחלט. עכשיו יצטרכו בתי הדין להפוך עורם ולמצוא הצדקה משכנעת ומספיקה להתפתחות הזו שהיא הכרחית להבטיח את העתיד של קידושין ונישואין כדת משה וישראל בצרפת. הפיתרון הכללי הזה קל מאוד להתקין, יש רק להתחשב בדרך עיונית ולהתייעץ עם רבנים בני סמכא על הבעיה ההלכתית כדי שהפיתרון הנבחר יתאים לדיני התורה ולחוקי המדינה וכך, בלי מכשול, הוא ימצא חן בעיני אלוקים ואדם. ❧

לאו דווקא, אלא עד שכופין אותו ליתן כתובה. וכמו שכופין אותו ליתן גט יכפה לזון."[43] במילים אחרות ובדרך יותר ברורה: הרשב"א לא הבין כמו הרב יצחק הזקן "כופין" ממש אפילו בשוטים, אבל עוררים אותו לתת גט בלי כפייה גופנית על ידי שכופים אותו לתת כתובה וכמו כן כופים אותו לזון. הרי שהבעל חייב ליתן מזונות לאשתו בשלב הזה כאשר מבקשים על הגט ומותר לכפות את תשלום הכתובה והמזונות ואין זה כפייה על הגט.

ובדרך דומה נזכיר הפסקא:"אמר רב, האומר איני זן ואיני מפרנס יוציא ויתן כתובה[44] ומסיקים: עד שכופין אותו להוציא, יכפוהו לזון," והכפיה לזון אינה כפיה ישירה הפוסלת את הגט.

לכן, בשלב זה, הבית דין צריך להטיל מזונות מורחבים על הבעל הסרבן, ואם אינו זן כופים אותו לזון (אבן העזר סימן קנד סעיף ג'). עכשיו היות שהערכאה לא יכולה לפסוק מזונות בעד המסורבת גט שהרי היא כבר מגורשת בגירושים אזרחיים, אין לנו דרך אחרת מלתבוע נזק שהייה בעד הנזק הנפשי והנזק הגופני שהיא סבלה וסובלת עוד. הבית דין מעריך את הקנס החודשי הזה למזונות שמגיעים לה וברור שאף אחד לא יעלה על דעתו או יעיז לומר שהטלת המזונות על הסרבן מהווה כפייה על הגט. כללו של דבר השתדלנו בעד הראיון להצדיק את ה"קנס שהייה" של הערכאה האזרחית כתחליף למזונות "מעוכבת מחמתו להינשא". ברור שצריך שייפסק סכום סביר שאינו חורג ממזונות מוגדלים. לכן צריכה התובעת לתבוע קנס חודשי בגין נזק העיגון, בגובה זהה למזונות מורחבים המגיעים לה לפי פסק והערכת הבית דין.

4. מסקנה

היצעתי שלושה נימוקים מדוע "קנס שהייה" לא יפסול את הגט.

לאור נימוקים אלה אין הצדקה שבית הדין יתנה את התביעה הנזיקית בכך שתתייחס לעבר דווקא. דרישה זו גורמת שהתביעה לפני הערכאה מתעכבת בכמה שנים עד שהתביעה לפיצוים תגיעה לסכום משמעותי. הרבה יותר יעיל להגיש תביעה לפיצוים מיד אחר שהבית דין הוציא את הכתב סירוב והיתיר לאישה לפנות לערכאה האזרחית ולבקש מן הערכאה פסק דין של "קנס שהייה" המתאים לסכום סביר שאינו חורג ממזונות מוגדלים. זה ימנע את הצורך לתבוע את הנזק בדרך חוזרת. הסרבן יחליט לתת את הגט קודם שהפיצוי יגדל וכן נצליח לקצר באופן משמעותי את אורך העיגון של הנשים.

כאשר סוף סוף אזכה לשכנע את הרבנים היושבים על מדין בצרפת שבדרך עיונית "קנס שהייה" אינו כפייה ישירה על הגט ואינו פוסל את הגט וכך אפשר לשפר את סדר נתינת הגט באופן משמעותי ולקצר אורך זמן העיגון במקרים היותר קשים, אני מפחד

---

43 חידושי הרשב"א על מסכת כתובות ס"ג ע"ב וס"ד ע"א.

44 כתובות ע"ז ע"א.

רמ״א:״ודווקא שחלה תוך הזמן. אבל הגיע הזמן ולא כנסה ואחר כך חלה, חייב במזונותיה אף על גב דהשתא הוא אונס.״

נמצא שהדברים קל וחומר: אם הארוסה, שעוד לא נכנסה לחופה ועוד אין לה תנאי כתובה ואין עוד לבעל מעשה ידיה ומציאתה, אפילו הכי חייב במזונותיה במצבים המפורטים מפני שהיא אגידה בו והיא מעוכבת מחמתו להינשא לאחר, מסורבת גט שהיא אשתו, והיא מעוכבת להנשא מחמתו על אחת כמה, חייב בעלה לזון אותה ואין לו זכות במעשה ידיה ובמציאתה.[41] למרות שהיא לא נותנת לו את מעשה ידיה, כמו שקורה במקרה הארוסה או האשה שהתקוטטה עם בעלה וברחה לבית אביה, היא לא הפסידה את מזונותיה.[42]

לכן חיוב המזונות נובע מהיותה אגידא בו ומעוכבת להנשא מחמתו והוא לא נובע עוד מחיוב הבעל לזון את אשתו וכך אפשר לדייק מדברי רש״י במסכת כתובות צ״ז ע״ב: ״בחייו: משום דמעוכבת בשבילו להנשא.״ יש לשים לב שרש״י כתב כן דווקא ביודעין והוא לא כתב שכל עוד שאינה גרושה לחלוטין יש לה מזונות מפני שהיא עוד אשתו. ולכן נראה לדייק מדבריו שיש לה מזונות משום שהיא מעוכבת בשבילו להנשא אבל אין לה שאר תנאי כתובה ולכן אין לבעל עוד זכות במעשה ידיה.

ואף על פי כן אין הבעל זוכה במעשה ידיה ולכן אין הבעל יכול להתנות את תשלום מזונותיה בקבלת מעשה ידיה במצב מגורשת ואינה מגורשת והמקרים הדומים כמו שמוכח מהמקרים שהבאנו למעלה, הארוסה או האשה שהתקוטטה עם בעלה ואינה דרה עמו והמניעה ממנו, שהבעל חייב לזון אותה אף על פי שאינו זוכה במעשה ידיה. אחרת היו השולחן ערוך והרמ״א צריכים להדגיש את זה.

סוף דבר, דברי הרשב״א דלהלן לא צריכים סעד או חיזוק: ״ואי קשיא לך אמאי דאמרינן דכל היכי דאמר רבנן יוציא ויתן כתובה, כופין משמע, איכא למימר כופין אותו

---

41 ראה למעלה. ראה ש״ע אה״ע סימן פ״ד.

42 מה שהיה כבר היה אבל מכאן ולהבא מומלץ לרווחא דמלתא כמו שכבר הצעתי במקום אחר (צהר מ' שנת התשע"ו, עמ' 275) להחתים בכל מקרה את הבעל בין הקידושין לנישואין על שטר סילוק ממעשה ידיה של האשה, נכסיה הנוכחיים ואלו שיפלו לאחר הנישואין, פירותיהן ופירי פירותיהן וגם ירושתה. שטר הסילוק הזה מוזכר ברמב״ם, הלכות אישות פרק כ״ג, בש"ע אבן העזר סימן צ"ב וסימן ס"ט סע' ז' ובשו"ת נודע ביהודה, מהדורא תניינא ס' צ"ח ובשו"ת הרדב"ז, חלק ד' סימן אלף רס"א. הנודע ביהודה מדגיש שיסודי לרשום בשטר שהוא נחתם בין הקידושין והנישואין. השטר הזה יתקן את המצב הנובע מן ההסכמים הנוכחיים בישראל, שבהם מוותר הבעל על מעשה ידיה של אשתו בזמן הפירוד, שזה נראה מלאכותי ובעייתי. השטר הזה יתאים את המסגרת ההלכתית למסגרת החברתית והמציאות המודרנית והחוק האזרחי. ובנידון של האישה הגרושה בצורה אזרחית ומסורבת גט הוא ישפר את המצב ההלכתי של האשה. אבל זה נראה להיות לרווחא דמלתא. שימו לב שקודם הכרזת הגירושין האזרחיים יכול הבעל לטעון שאין המצב מצב של סרבנות גט והגורם של המצב הוא חוקי המדינה. ולכן אפשר להכריחו לשלם מזונות בדיני ישראל רק על ידי הוכחה שהוא האחראי של ההפרדה שהרי עודה נשואה. אחר הכרזת הגירושין האזרחיים היא עוברת למעמד מסורבת גט.

נימוק ג

האישה המורדת: מעמד ההלכתי של האישה בין ההפרדה לבין הכרזת הגירושין האזרחיים והוצאת הכתב סירוב.

אף על פי שרבינו תם אסר לכפות את הגט, ברור שהבעל מחויב לגרש את אשתו ואסור לו לעגנה. אחרת איך היה הוא כותב בסוף התשובתו[38] לגזור באלה חמורה את הרחקותיו.

יש שרוצים לטעון שאין מזונות למורדת לפי מה שמובא במסכת כתובות ס"ד ע"א: "ומשהינן לה תריסר ירחי שתא אגיטא ובהנך תריסר ירחי שתא לית לה מזוני מבעל."

הרבה מפרשים הבינו שהפסקה הזו מתייחסת למורדת הטוענת מאיס עלי וביניהם רש"י, הרשב"א והרא"ש[39] ורבינו ירוחם.[40] הרמב"ם מצידו הולך בשיטתו לפיה כופים את הגט לאלתר במקרה המורדת מטעם מאיס עלי והתקנה של השניים עשר חודשים חלה רק במקרה המורדת מטעם בעינא ליה ומצערנא ליה. לכן יש מבוכה ביחס לתקנה של שניים עשר חודשים: על מי היא חלה? האם היא בת תוקף בזמן הזה שהרי משום המבוכה והספקות, ודאי היא לא פשטה ולא נתקבלה על כל ישראל. איך שיהיה חשוב להבין שמדובר בתקנה שהייתה בת תוקף במשך זמן מוגבל, דהיינו שנה מהתחלת זמן המרידה. אבל אחר סוף השנה המצב חזר לעיקר הרגיל והכללי שיש לה מזונות במסגרת חיובי האיש לאשתו לפי ההלכה.

גרושה ואינה גרושה, מסורבת גט, מעוכבת להינשא: מעמד ההלכתי של האישה אחר הוצאת הכתב סירוב.

נפסק בשולחן ערוך אבן העזר סימן צג סעיף ב':"האישה שהיה לה ספק גירושין...בחיי בעלה יש לה מזונות עד שתתגרש גירושין גמורים." ועוד מובא ברמ"א בש"ע אה"ע סימן ע' סעיף י"ב: "אם הייתה לה קטטה עם בעלה ולא מתדר לה עמו והמניעה ממנו ולותה למזונות, צריך לשלם."

ובסימן נ"ו סעיף ג' כתב המחבר: "הגיע זמן שנתנו לאיש ולא נשאה, נתחייב במזונותיה אף על פי שלא כנס. ואם עכבו אונס שחלה... אינו חייב לזונה." וכתב

38 ספר הישר, חלק התשובות, סימן כד.

39 אולם רבינו תם כתב בספר הישר, חלק התשובות סימן ב"ד שכלתו של רב זביד מרדה מטעם בעינא ליה ומצערנא ליה ומה שמשהינן לה למורדת תריסר ירחי שתא, הוא לאחר כרוז והמלכה אבל למאיס עלי ליכא שהייה. אבל בספר הישר חלק החידושים, סימן ד' כתב אחרת: במאיס עלי לא הויא מורדת אבל מורדת דמשהינן תרסר ירחי שתא אגיטא אחר הכרזה, אולי תחזור וכלתו של רב זביד מרדה מטעם דמאיס עלי כדמוכח מהפסידה בלאותיה.

40 ראה למעלה.

את סברתו כך: יש להבחין בין רצונו של הבעל לנתק את הקשר עם אשתו ובין רצונו להפיק תועלת ממתן הגט. לפי סברת הרב משה פיינשטיין, אפילו אם כופין אותו לוותר על התועלת הזו שהוא רצה להפיק מנתינת הגט, רצונו לגרש את אשתו מכשיר את הגט והגט שריר וקיים. אכן האונס לא היה על רצונו לגרשה אלא על רצונו להפיק תועלת מן הגט.

בתור שיקול והעמקה אפשר להבחין בין הרשב״א[34] המכשיר גט הכפוי על ידי שכופים אותו לקבל תועלת כספית לבין הר״מ פיינשטיין שמכשיר גט כאשר כופים אותו לתת את הגט ולוותר על התועלת הכספית בתנאי הכרחי שהוא רוצה להשתחרר ממנה.[35] אולי ההבדל ביניהם נובע מזה שהרשב״א לא נוקט את החרם של רבינו גרשום ולכן צריכים לתת לבעל תועלת כספית ממשית. אבל הר״מ פיינשטיין בא על סיפוקו על ידי התועלת הנובעת מנתינת הגט שמאפשרת לבעל להשיא מחדש. אבל הוא מתון ודורש את הביטחון שהבעל רוצה להשתחרר ממנה. כך שאולי אין סתירה ממשית ביניהם. גם מעניין להזכיר את התשובה סימן קכו מתשובות רבי חיים אור זרוע[36] שגם הוא נקט בחרם דרבינו גרשום, שכתב ביחס לבעל שאסרו אותו ואחר כך שיחררו אותו והסכימו שהוא יתן גט תמורת קבלת סכום כסף, שאפילו אם לא נותנים לו בסוף את הסכום המוסכם, אפשר שהגט כשר. נדמה שדעתו ממש זהה לדעתו של הר״ם פיינשטיין.

אנחנו היום במצב הלכתי חדש שלא היה קיים בעבר. האיש והאשה מגורשים גירושים אזרחיים ביוזמת הבעל או לפחות בהסכמת הבעל.[37] בית הדין הוציא כתב סירוב כך שהמקרה דומה למקרה של מורדת הנותנת אמתלא לדבריה ואין לחוש שמא נתנה עיניה באחר ובנוסף הבעל רוצה לעגנה. ראינו שבמקרה כזה מותר לבית דין לכפות את הגט אלא שהוא נעדר סמכות ורשות לכפות את הגט. הוא רק יכול להשען על הערכאה האזרחית ולהשתמש בה כביכול כזרועו. ואפילו אם יטעון הטוען ש"קנס השהייה" שהערכאה מטילה על הסרבן היא כפייה על גט, אין בכך כלום שהרי אנחנו במצב המתיר כפייה. אכן אפשר לומר שכל המצבים, חוץ מאלו שבם הערכאה מכריזה על הגירושין למרות התנגדות הבעל, מצדיקים כפיית גט ולכן אין סיבה להימנע מ״קנס שהייה״. על כן יש לדרוש מבתי הדין שידונו בכל מקרה לגופו, ובמצבים המתאימים, בנוסף על כתב הסירוב, יתירו לאישה לפנות לערכאה האזרחית בלא להמתין שלוש שנים, כפי שהסברנו. וכך תפעול הערכאה כמקלו של בית הדין. כל ההצדקות הקודמות נחוצות רק אם מעריכים את ה״קנס שהייה״ לאונס על הגט, לכן ראו עוד בסעיף הבא טענה חשובה משכנעת.

---

34 תשובות הרשב״א חלק ד׳ סימן מ׳, בה המחבר, לפי ההבנה המקובלת, פוסק שקנס המקובל מרצונו החופשי של הבעל, הוא אונס גמור הפוסל את הגט. הרשב״א הוא היחיד הפוסל את גט זה. אף על פי כן, הרשב״א פוסק שגט זה הניתן בכפייה יוכשר על ידי מתן סכום כסף לבעל.

35 הסתירה ביניהם גלויה. הרשב״א מכשיר את הגט הכפוי על ידי שכופים אותו לקבל סכום כסף. הרב פיינשטיין מכשיר (בתנאים מסוימים) את הגט הכפוי אף על פי שכופים אותו לוותר על סכום הכסף שהוא רצה להפיק מן הגט.

36 הוא היה בקשר מכתבי עם הרשב״א ושאל ממנו. בתשובה הזו, הוא לא נתן טעם לדבריו.

37 עקרונית ייתכן מצב שבו הערכאה מכריזה על גירושין למרות התנגדות הבעל. ראו הערה 13.

שתסתמך על מנהגכם [לפסוק כמו הרמב״ם, הלכות אישות פרק י״ד הלכה ח׳] בעת הזאת לכופו ליתן גט לזמן...״

הרי אפילו הרא״ש שבאופן עקרוני מתנגד לכפיית גט במקרה של מורדת הטוענת מאיס עלי והוא, כמו רבו המהר״ם, מסתייג מאוד מבחינה עקרונית מכפיית גט אפילו אם נתנה אמתלא משכנעת למאיסותה. אבל במקרה מעשי הוא היה פחות קיצוני והוא ציווה את השואל, הרב יעקב אלפסי, לחקור ולבדוק אם יש ממש בטענתה. ואם היא צודקת והוא רוצה לעגנה אז הוא פוסק שיש לכפות אותו לתת גט.

ויש לנו עוד עדות שניה, אבל היא עקיפה, בעניין עמדת המהר״ם, בדברי הרב אברהם[29] אבן טוואה[30]:

״הדעת השישי: אף על פי שאין כופין האיש לגרש אפילו באומרת מאיס עלי, משום דחיישינן שמא נתנה עיניה באחר, מכל מקום אם נתנה אמתלא לדבריה, כופין אותו לגרש וזה דעת הר״ם מרוטנבורק ז״ל וכתבו הרא״ש בפסקיו. אבל היה מחרים על מי שלמדה ונתן לה עצה למרוד על בעלה כדי להוציא הנדוניא...״[31]

שוב ראיתי שרבינו ירוחם בן משולם מפרובינציה[32] כותב במקרה זהה לחלוטין לנידון שלנו: ״וכתב מורי הרב אברהם בן אשמעאל כי נראה לו שאישה שאמרה לא בעינא ליה, יתן לי גט וכתובה והוא אומר אנא נמי לא בעינא לך אבל איני רוצה ליתן גט, מסתברא דאין דנין אותה כמורדת להפסידה כלום מעיקר כתובה ונדוניא אלא מיהו משהינן לה תריסר ירחי אגיטא דילמא הדרי בהו.[33] לאחר שנה כופין אותו לגרש והפסידה תוספת [כתובה] וכל מה דיהיב לה מדיליה דאדעתא למשקל ולמיפק לא יהיב לה.״

מצבן של נשים מסורבות גט בצרפת אחרי שנתגרשו בגירושין אזרחיים, זהה למצב שדן בו הרב אברהם בן אשמאעל, תלמידו של הרשב״א שגם הוא היה תחת השפעת המהר״ם והחמיר הרבה, וסבר, אף על פי כן, שיש לכפות את הגט כאשר היה משוכנע מאמיתות טענות האישה ושכל רצונו של הבעל הוא רק לעגן אותה.

גם חשוב להזכיר את סברת הרב משה פיינשטיין בשו״ת אגרות משה, אבן העזר, חלק שלישי, סוף סימן מ״ד. שם הוא הביא סברה חדשה וחשובה להכשיר גט אף באונס שלא כדין ושל עכו״ם. והוא כתב בענוותנותו ״שאף שהיא סברה גדולה, אין לסמוך עליה לבד אבל לצרף אותה לעוד טעם דוודאי היא סברה גדולה לצרף.״ אפשר להציע בקצרה

---

29 רב באלג׳יר במאה השש עשרה, הוא היה נין ונכד לרבי שמעון בן צמח, דור שישי להרשב״ץ.

30 ספר תשב״ץ: חוט המשולש, חלק רביעי, הטור השלישי, סימן ל״ה.

31 ממש כדברי הרא״ש בתשובה כלל מ״ג, סימן ח׳. ראה הקטע למעלה.

32 ספר אדם וחווה, נתיב כ״ג, חלק ח׳. הוא היה תלמידם של הראש ושל הרב אברהם בן אשמעאל שהיה תלמידו של הרשב״א.

33 רבינו ירוחם מתייחס כאן לפיסקא בגמרא כתובות צ״ד ע״א: ״ומשהינן לה תריסר ירחי שתא אגיטא ובהנך תריסר ירחי שתא לית לה מזוני מבעל.״ ראה להלן.

ואף הרא״ש כתב על רבו רבי מאיר בן ברוך מרוטנבורג, המהר״ם: ״ורבי מאיר בעסקי מורדת, בעניין הממון היה דן בדינא דמתיבתא שיתנו לאשה כל מה שהכניסה אבל לא היה כופה לגרשה...״[27]

אם כן רואים שהמהר״ם והרא״ש, בעקבות רבינו תם, היו חוששים לעורמה ולנתינת עיניה באחר ולא היו כופים את הגט ואף היו זהירים מאוד בחלוקת הנכסים. עמדה זו היא בהתאמה עם התשובות של המהר״ם המתייחסות לבעיית המורדת: ראה סי׳ רכח, תמב, תמג, תתקמו, תתרכא (דפוס פראג).

אבל כנראה עמדתם של המהר״ם ושל הרא״ש התפתחה והשתלשלה קצת. אכן נעיין בתשובה סימן תנ״ה מתוך אוסף התשובות של מהר״ם וחביריו, ירושלים תשע״ב שההדיר פרופסור שמחה עמנואל על פי כתבי יד. המהר״ם כתב: ״אם היא תביא ראיה לדבריה בעדים שהלז אמת, אז ישבו הבית דין וידקדקו מה דינן של אלו, אם יוציא ויתן כתובה או לא.״ רואים שהמהר״ם היה מוכן לחייב את הבעל להוציא ולתת כתובה אם טענות האשה היו מוצדקות ואמיתיות, ולא היה חשש לעורמה. אבל השאלה היא מה הוא תוקף המושג ״יוציא ויתן כתובה״ בדברי המהר״ם, כלומר מה היא כוונתו בשימושו במילים אלה. בעלי התוספות כבר עוררו את השאלה במסכת כתובות ע׳ ע״א בד״ה יוציא ויתן כתובה: ״נראה לר״י [רבי יצחק הזקן] דבכל הנך דקתני במתניתין יוציא, היינו שכופין אותו דכיוון דשלא כדין עביד, כופין אותו להוציא...״ סביר שדעת המהר״ם הייתה כמו דעתו של הרב יצחק הזקן, שהיה רבו של רבו. תוקף המושג ״יוציא ויתן כתובה״ נבחן גם בשולחן ערוך אה״ע סימן קנד סעיף כ״א: כל אלו שאמרו להוציא, כופין אותו אפילו בשוטים ויש אומרים שכל מי שלא נאמר בו בגמרא בפירוש כופין להוציא אלא יוציא בלבד, אין כופין בשוטים אלא אומרים לו, חכמים חייבוך להוציא ואם לא תוציא מותר לקרותך עבריין.״ לכאורה השולחן ערוך לא הכריע, אולם הרמ״א כתב שראוי להחמיר. איך שיהיה, אין אנחנו מעוניינים פה בפסק הלכה אלא שאנחנו רוצים להבין את דברי המהר״ם, וסביר להבין מתוך דבריו שבמקרה שאין לחשוש לעורמה, המהר״ם היה כופה, כפשוטו, את הסרבן לתת גט.

לתלמידו של המהר״ם, הרא״ש הייתה עמדה דומה. הוא היה בוודאי מן היותר מחמירים והוא חשד שכל אישה הטוענת מאיס עלי, נתנה עיניה באחר וחפצה בו יותר מבעל נעוריה. והוא כותב:[28] ״האם נשלים תאוותה ונכוף האיש שהוא אוהב אשת נעוריו, שיגרשנה חלילה וחס לשום דיין לדון כן.״ אבל הוא גומר את תשובתו כך: ״הרי כתבתי לך בעניין כפית גט מורדת. אומנם בנידון זה סיפר לי אחיה אמתלאות שנותנת למרידתה ואתה דיין בדבר הזה, תחקור על הדבר אם יש ממש בדבריה. ואם דעתו לעגנה, ראוי

27 תשובות הרא״ש, כלל ארבעים ושלושה, סימן ח׳.

28 תשובות הרא״ש: כלל מ״ג, סימן ח׳: תשובה לחכם יעקב אלפסי.

הגרושין האזרחיים כאשר אי אפשר עוד לדבר על מזונות לפני הערכאה. אבל לפי נקודת מבט של הבית דין, מדובר על תשלום מזונות מורחבים המגיעים לאשה במצבה של גרושה ואינה גרושה.[25]

הדרך היחידה לשפר את המצב היא לאפשר לאישה לתבוע את הפיצוים מיד אחרי שבית הדין הוציא כתב סירוב ופסק דין לכפיית גירושין כלומר זמן קצר אחר הכרזת הגירושין האזרחיים, כאשר אי אפשר עוד להפוך את המצב, בלי לחכות שלוש שנים עד שהפיצוים יגיעו לסכום משמעותי המצדיק את התביעה. ולכן צריכה האישה לתבוע קנס שהייה, כלומר שהיא צריכה לתבוע סכום פיצוים לחודש או ליום שיחול לכל אורך תקופת העיגון. נבדוק עכשיו את המושג "קנס שהייה" ונשווה אותו לקנס מאסר או להפקעת רשיון עבודה שבתי הדין הישראליים מפעילים. יש יתרון "לקנס שהייה" על הקנסות האחרים המוזכרים לעיל, מפני שהוא לא מוטל, באופן פורמלי, כדי לכפות את הגט אלא כדי לפצות את האישה בגין הסבל שנגרם לה. הסרבן יכול לשלם,[26] כמו שמשלמים דמי שכירות, ולשמור על אשתו. אף על פי כן הסרבן יודע שהקנס יפסיק כאשר הוא יתן את הגט. במיוחד "קנס השהייה" יפסיק להצטבר עם מסירת גט כשר אבל מה שהוא כבר חייב לא יימחק באופן אוטומטי. לכן "קנס השהייה" אינו חמור יותר מהפקעת רישיון עסק ואין צריך לומר מעונש מאסר ואינו כפייה על הגט יותר מן האמצעים האלו שבתי הדין הישראלים מפעילים, אדרבא. להפך הוא יכול לשלם את הקנס ולשמור על אשתו כאשר סכום הקנס הוא לא מוגזם, מחריב והרסני. ועוד שנתינת הגט לא פוטרת אותו מהקנס על העבר שכבר נפל בחלקה של האישה. לעומת זאת עונש המאסר והפקעת רשיון עסק הם יותר קרובים לכפייה גופנית מפני שהם יורדים לחייו. והוא הדין גם כן בהפקעת הדרכון או רשיון נהיגה שבהרבה מקרים גם הן יורדות לחייו.

כללו של דבר, "קנס שהייה" יהיה הרבה יותר יעיל ממה שנוהג היום. הוא יחסוך כמה שנות עיגון למסורבות גט והוא פחות תקיף מאמצעי הכפייה המופעלים בארץ ישראל כמו הפקעת רשיון עבודה ונהיגה או עונש מאסר והוא מהווה כפייה עקיפה על הגט. סוף סוף הוא אינו כפייה ישירה על הגט, הוא רק הוצאה חודשית מאותו סדר גובה כמו המזונות שהוא היה צריך לשלם כדי לשמור עליה.

נימוק ב

כידוע רבינו תם והבאים אחריו התנגדו לכפיית גט במקרה של המורדת הטוענת מאיס עלי כמו שמובא בתוספות, מסכת כתובות ס"ג ע"ב, בד"ה אבל אמרה מאיס עלי לא כייפינן לה.

---

25 ראה עוד להלן בנימוק ג'.

26 במקרה עונש מאסר אי אפשר לומר כן ולכן האונס חמור יותר.

כידוע רבינו תם התנגד בתוקף לכל כפית גט במקרה של מורדת. לכן אסור לכפות את הבעל בשוטים או בדרכים קשות או על ידי נידוי ושמתא. אבל חשוב להעיר שגם אונס ממון הוא אונס לכל דבר ופוסל את הגט.[22] רבינו תם התיר רק ללחוץ עליו באופן עקיף על ידי מה שמכונה "הרחקות של רבינו תם". מדובר על אמצעים סבילים ושליליים: לא לעשות לו שום טובה, להתעלם ממנו ולהתנהג כאילו לא היה קיים.[23] אולם בתי הדין הישראליים, אחר שהם פסקו חיוב לתת גט, כופים את הבעל הסרבן בדרכים פחות סבילות ויותר פעילות כגון איסור יציאת מן הארץ והפקעת הדרכון, הפקעה של רשיון נהיגה או אפילו של רשיון עסק (לעסק הטעון רישיון) ואפילו עונש מאסר, כלומר אמצעיים פחות סבילים ויותר פעילים מההרחקות המקוריות של רבינו תם. בחברה של ימי הביניים, בזמנו של רבינו תם, ההרחקות היו מסכנות את חיי הסרבן המוטל כביכול בחרם עובדתי, אף על פי שרבנו תם אסר חרם מוחלט. בחברה הנוכחית כמעט אי אפשר להביא לבידודו של הסרבן באופן יעיל. לכן האמצעים הנוספים שבית הדין מפעיל, מנסים להחזיר את יעילות ההרחקות המקוריות כמו שהיו פועלות בראשיתן. אף על פי שהאמצעים החדשים הם יותר פעילים ויותר אלימים ומתרחקים מכוונתן של ההרחקות של רבינו תם שהיו סבילות לגמרי אבל הם נשארים בגדר כפייה על הסרבן ואינם כפיה על הגט ממש אלא אך רק על דבר אחר.

בצרפת אי אפשר להפעיל אף אחד מאמצעים אלה. הדרך היחידה היא להפעיל על ידי הערכאה האזרחית את תביעת הפיצויים בגין הנזק הגופני והמוסרי שהאישה סובלת. ואף על פי שהנזק הזה, שהוא ממשי ולא דימיוני, אינו קיים במשפט העברי[24] ומטעם זה יש להחשיב אותם שלא כדין. אבל לפי ההצעה שהיציענו, הפיצוים בעד הנזק שהאשה סבלה מפני סירוב בעלה לתת לה גט, הם רק הלבשה משפטית כדי לאפשר פרעון ממשי אחר

22 הדבר נלמד מהמעשה דפרדיסא, ראו בבא בתרא מ׳ ע״ב. ראו חידושי הרשב״א על מסכת בבא בתרא דף מ׳ ותשובות הרשב״א חלק ד׳, סימן מ׳ שם הוא מתייחס לפירושם של הר״ח והראב״ד על הא דפרדסיא. ראו ש״ע חו״מ סימן ר״ה סעיפים א׳ ו ז׳. ראו גם רמב״ם, הלכות מכירה פרק י׳ הלכות א׳ ו ד׳. ומפני זה, יש דיינים בארץ הנתרעים מלהפעיל את הסנקציות שהחוק מאפשר. ראה לדוגמה: גט מעושה, ר׳ יוסף גולדברג ירושלים תשס״ג. אבל בתשב״ץ ח״א ס״א הוא מסתפק אי הוי עישוי ובתולדות אדם וחווה, חלק חווה, נתיב ארבעה ועשרים, ממש בסוף חלק א׳ באישה שגנבה שטרי חובות, ר׳ ירוחם מסיים: ולפי עניות דעתי הגט גט.

23 הרחקה אחת המפורסת על ידי הרמ״א בש״ע אה״ע סימן קנד סעיף כ״א היא שלא לקוברו כלומר לא לקוברו בקבר ישראל. הצעד הזה יעיל מאוד אם הוא מתואם כהלכה ומפורסם ואם החברה ממלאת אחריו. תפקיד הציבור הוא יסודי. רבינו תם היה גוזר באלה חמורה על הציבור היהודי. ומכאן תשובה לכל אלה שטוענים שלבייש את הסרבן מהווה אונס על הגט שאי אפשר לקבלו. ולא היא, אדרבא האונס הנגרם על ידי הבושה לא חמור יותר היום ממה שהוא היה בזמנו של רבינו תם כאשר הוא היה מכריז באלה חמורה נגד הסרבן והוא לא חמור יותר ממה שהוא היה בימי הריב״ש והרשב״ץ כאשר הם היו ״כופים על הכתובה ומבקשים על הגט.״ הרי שאונס מעט כזה לא פוסל את הגט ואפילו מותר להפעיל אותו לכתחילה. למה לא משתמשים בשני האמצעים המועילים האלה?

24 ובכל זאת אין להחשיב אותו לאלימות (גנבה, הפחדה).

כבר מוצא פסק דין לכפיית גט.[21] לאור זאת, אציע להלן שלושה נימוקים הלכתיים שניתן להצדיק בהם הטלת "קנס שהייה".

נימוק א.

21 לפי המקובל משכו הרבנים והבתי דין את ידיהם מן הכפייה למתן גט כמו שנובע מן המימרה התלמודית "אין מעשין אלא לפסולות" (כתובות ע"ז ע"א). אלא כאשר אין סיכוי להתפייסות ולשלום בית, אז הגירושין הם הפיתרון היחיד והבית דין צריך להתערב ולשכנע את הצד המעכב. ובלית ברירה, לפעמים הבית דין נמצא מול בעיות ותוצאות סרבנות נתינת הגט או סרבנות קבלת הגט והוא כמו מוכרח בהסתייגות לכפות את הגט. יש שני מקורות הלכתיים עיקריים המתירים ומצדיקים את הכפייה של הגירושין כאשר הפירוד מתארך בלי שום סיכוי להתפייסות. המקור הראשון הוא תשובה מהרב חיים פלאג'י, שו"ת חיים ושלום, חלק ב', סימן קי"ב, התשובה האחרונה של הספר. בסוף התשובה המוסרית הזו הוא כותב: "והנני נותן קצבה וזמן לדבר הזה, דאם יארע איזה מחלוקת בין איש לאשתו וכבר נלאו לתווך השלום ואין להם תקנה, ימתינו עד זמן י"ח חודשים ואם בינם לשמים [כמו שמים ביני לבינך (משנה נדרים י"א, י"ב) כלומר (ראו תוספות על אתר) כמה דשמיא רחיקין מן ארעא, כך ההיא איתתא רחיקא מן ההוא גברא (ירושלמי נדרים ל"ט ע"ב בדפוס וילנא)] נראה לב"ד שלא יש תקווה לשום שלום ביניהם, יפרידו הזווג ולכופם לתת גט עד שיאמרו רוצה אני כדבר האמור ותמצא מ"ש בזה בספר החסידים. כ"ז כתבתי לכבוד הש"י ותורתו הקדושה. הצעיר חיים פאלג'י ס"ט."
הרב עובדיה יוסף זצ"ל בשו"ת יביע אומר, (אבן העזר חלק ג' סימן י"ח) הסתפק בביאור כוונת הרב פלאג'י שאפשר שדבריו המוסריים אינם כפשוטם של דברים. אבל יש סעד גדול לדברי הרב חיים פאלג'י בשו"ת איגרות משה (יורה דעה חלק ד', סימן ט"ז אות ב') שכתב בקצרה, בדיוק כמותו: " ובדבר איש ואשתו שזה הרבה שנים שליכא שלום בית, וכבר שנה וחצי דרים במקומות מופרדים. וכבר ישבו בית דין חשוב ולא עלה בידם לעשות שלום בינהם...אז מדין התורה באופן כזה מוכרחין להתגרש ואין רשות לשום צד לעגן, לא הבעל את אשתו ולא האשה את הבעל, בשום עיכוב מצד תביעת ממון".
המקור השני הוא פסקו של רבינו ירוחם (הוא היה ראשון, תלמידו של הרא"ש, ראה להלן הערות 31 ו 32 ובקטע שעליו מתייחסות שתי ההערות): "וכתב מורי הרב אברהם בן אשמעאל כי נראה לו שאשה שאמרה לא בעינא ליה, יתן לי גט וכתובה והוא אומר אנא נמי לא בעינא לך אבל איני רוצה ליתן גט, מסתברא דאין דנין אותה כמורדת להפסידה כלום מעיקר כתובה ונדוניא אלא מיהו משהינן לה תריסר ירחי אגיטא דילמא הדרי בהו. לאחר שנה כופין אותו לגרש והפסידה תוספת [כתובה] וכל מה דיהיב לה מדיליה דאדעתא למשקל ולמיפק לא יהיב לה." בתי הדין בישראל בשנים האחרונות משתמשים רבות בשיטתו של רבינו ירוחם לפסוק חיוב בגט לבני זוג כששניהם מורדים ואינם מעוניינים זה בזה, אז כופים או על כל פנים מחייבים את הבעל לגרש את אשתו. הרבנים אוריאל לביא, אב"ד ירושלים (עטרת דבורה, עמ' 636) וחיים שלמה שאנן, אב"ד תל אביב (עיונים במשפט, אה"ע חלק א' סימן כ"ח) נוקטים הדעה שאם בית הדין נוכח שהאשה לא רוצה בבעלה והבעל לא רוצה באשתו יש לחייב בגירושין את בן הזוג המסרב להתגרש אחר פירוד של שנה, שבו מתברר לבית הדין שאין סיכוי לחזרה לשלום. ואין מוטל על בית הדין לברר מה הגורמים שהביאו לכך. בדיוק כדברי הרב רבינו ירוחם. המקרה של רבינו ירוחם זהה לחלוטין לנידון שלנו בפרט ולמצב החיים המודרניים בכלל. אחרי הגירושין האזרחיים וחלוקת הנכסים, אנחנו באמת בשלב האחרון שאין לו כמעט שלב שווה בישראל ובצדק אפשר לומר שבשלב הזה יש לכפות את הגט.

שלוש שנים אחר הגירושין האזרחיים כמצב של עיגון המאפשר לסמוך על המושג בדיעבד או אפשרות שלישית לפיה סביר יותר להניח שהבית דין הצרפתי פוסק מזונות מוגדלים בעד האשה, שהיא מגורשת (נפרדת ועזובה ועוד יותר כאן, מגורשת לפי החוק האזרחי) ואינה מגורשת (בדיני ישראל).[19] אבל הדרך היחידה המאפשרת לגבות אותם מן הבעל, היא להלביש אותם בלבוש חדש ולכנות אותם באופן רשמי, "פיצוים". וכך נוכל להעריך את הכפייה, כדין והגט יהיה כשר לכל הדעות כמו שמומלץ לכתחילה בדיני הערווה החמורה.

3. הצעה כללית לקיצור זמן העיגון של מסורבות הגט

חשוב להעיר שאפילו אם הכפייה לפיצוים הייתה נחשבת לכפייה ישירה למתן הגט היה אפשר להצדיק את האסטרטגיה ולהכשיר את הגט. אכן אנחנו נמצאים אחר הגירושין האזרחיים, בית הדין כבר הוציא סמוך אחר הגירושין האזרחיים, כתב סירוב נגד הסרבן אחר שהוא דחה את ההזמנות להופיע לפני בית הדין ונתק סופית את הקשרים עם בית הדין. הכתב סירוב מתיר לאישה להגיש תביעה נגד בעלה הסרבן. עקרונית היה צריך הבית דין להוציא פסק דין לכפיית גירושין בד בבד עם הוצאת הכתב סירוב. צריך לדעת שלפי מדיניות החוק הצרפתי, הערכאה מוציאה בדרך כלל פסק דין לגירושין אזרחיים מתוך הסכמה הדדית ורק באופן יוצא מן הכלל פסק דין לגירושין כתוצאה של תביעה חד צדדית לגירושין בגין אשמה של הצד הנגדי. וזה עומד בניגוד למצב הקודם כאשר הייתה קיימת רק אפשרות של תביעה חד צדדית לגירושין בגין אשמה של הצד הנגדי. זאת אומרת שבמצב הנוכחי הבעל רוצה או לפחות מסכים לגירושין[20] האזרחיים ולפירוד ובהכרח סירובו לתת גט לא נובע מרצונו לשמור על אשתו. אדרבה הוא לא רוצה אותה אבל הוא רוצה לעגן אותה להרע לה ולצער אותה, כדי לנקום ממנה או כדי בסוף, כאשר המצב בשל לביצוע, לסחוט סכום משמעותי ממנה או לפחות לבטל את התועלת והפיצוים שהערכאה מעניקה לה. עכשיו הם התגרשו לפי הערכאה האזרחית ואי אפשר עוד להפוך את המצב ובכל זאת הוא לא רוצה לתת לה גט אבל רוצה לעגן אותה ולסחוט אותה. במצב כזה לא היה עוד שום בית דין ישראלי פוסק המלצה, מצווה או חיוב לגרש אבל הוא היה

---

19 על הביטוי הזה, ראו במיוחד בבא מציעא י"ב ע"ב ובבא בתרא מ"ז ע"ב ועוד במקומות אחרים בש"ס בבלי וירושלמי. על הצדקת חיוב המזונות ראה להלן בנימוק ג'.

20 פרט למצב של גירושין הנובעים מתביעה חד צדדית של האישה בגין אשמת בעלה. במצב זה המבט ההלכתי הוא הרבה יותר מסובך ואף בעייתי. והוא חורג מן המסגרת של המאמר. במקרה שיש לאשה טענות מספיקות לתבוע את בעלה לדין האזרחי בגין אשמה חמורה, צריכה היא להתייעץ תחילה עם עורך דין רבני מומחה כדי שתבטח שבית הדין יוציא פסק דין לכפיית גירושין. אחרת היא בסכנה עיגון סופי.

כעישוי כדין. אכן, אף על פי שחישוב הפיצוים האלה לא קיים במשפט העברי (מפני שהם מתייחסים בחלקם הגדול לנזקים מוסריים וסובייקטיביים שנגרמו לאשה והם בגדר "גרמא"), היה אפשר להחשיב אותו "כעישוי כדין" מפני הכלל של "דינא דמלכותא דינא".[16] אבל הדבר יותר מסובך מפני שכמה גדולים הגבילו את השימוש בכלל הזה ולא קבלו אותו בדברים של בין אדם לחברו.[17] אם כן, בהוצאה לפועל של האסטרטגיה של בית הדין, אנחנו נשארים במצב של כפייה בדבר אחר ובלתי תלוי למתן הגט. אבל דרך הכפייה היא שלא כדין, מפני שעל אף שאסור לגרום נזק לחברו, אין תשלום בעד הגרם בדיני ישראל. ולכן הגט כשר רק לפי הריב״ש ומקצת פוסקים כמו הר״ם פיינשטיין. אני מניח שהבית דין של פריז הושפע על ידי התשובה של הר״מ פיינשטיין[18] שיצתה לאור באותו פרק זמן, הדנה במזונות שהערכאה היטילה על הבעל, וסמך עליה. לכן אני רואה שלוש אפשרויות: הראשונה שהבית דין פסק כמו שיטה זו מפני שהר״ם פיינשטיין פסק לקולה, בדיעבד ואף לכתחילה שדהגט כשר. השנית שהבית דין העריך את המצב שתי או

במילים: ״והגט אינו מעושה אלא מרוצה״: מדבריו נראה שגם אם כפוהו שלא כדין על עניין אחר ונתרצה לתת גט, אין זה אונס...

ג. הרב משה פיינשטיין כתב באגרות משה אבן העזר תשל״ד, סימן קל״ז על אודות בעל ואשתו שהתגרשו לפי הדין האזרחי והיות שהוא לא רצה לתת לה גט, הערכאה צוותה אותו לשלם מזונות מוגדלים לאשה שהייתה עוד אשתו בדין ישראל. הבעל לא מילא את חובתו והערכאה שמה אותו במאסר. בסוף הסכימה האשה לוותר על התביעה כך שהוא יוכל לצאת ממאסרו, בתנאי שהוא יתן לה גט. האם הגט מעושה? הרב פסק שהגט כשר בדיעבד ואף לכתחילה. העובדה שהערכאה שמה את הבעל במאסר, כלומר שהכפייה הייתה שלא כדין לא פוסלת את הגט, כנראה העיקר הוא שלא כפו על הגט, ובלבד שהאונס הוא לפחות לפי דינם ואינו שרירותי ושהסכום היומי הוא באותו סדר גודל כמו זה שהבית דין היה פוסק, אחרת היה אונס על הגט, וזה החלטה דומה לזו של הריב״ש.

לאמיתו של דבר, התקשתי להבין את דרכם של בתי הדין הצרפתיים מפני שני פסקים שליליים שנשלחו לצרפת בשנת תש״ם: מנחת יצחק חלק ח, סי׳ קלו ושבט הלוי חלק ה׳ ס׳ ר״י. אחר העיון מוודאים שנוסח השאלה לא ברור ולא נכון והתשובות מיוסדות על הנחה שגויה. בשאלה כתוב ש״אם יגרשנה יפטר מתביעת ממון״ וזה מתמיה. הרי מה נפשך: אם הקנס מתייחס לנזק העבר אז נתינת הגט לא מבטלת אותו ואם הקנס יבוטל אחר נתינת הגט קודם זמן קבוע, אז די לחקות עד עבור אותו הזמן ואז חוזרים למצב הראשון. ראו פתחי תשובה על ש״ע אה״ע סי׳ קלד סע׳ ד סוף אות ט, לעיל בהערה 10. לכן התשובות האלו לא מכריעות.

16 ראה דינא דמלכותא דינא באנציקלופדיה תלמודית. יש מן הראשונים שסוברים שלא אמרו דינא דמלכותא דינא אלא בדברים שהם לתועלת המלך או היום לתועלת הממשלה, כגון המיסים. אבל יש שסוברים שהכלל הזה הוא גם בתוקף בדברים שאינם לתועלת הממשלה אלא בין אדם לחברו. אבל מכל מקום אין זה אלא בדברים שאינם נגד דין תורה. כך כתבו הש״ך (שיפתי כהן, הרב שבתי כהן) חושן משפט סימן ע״ג סעיף ל״ט והחזון איש חושן משפט, ליקוטים סימן ט״ז אות א׳ ועוד כמה אחרונים אחריהם.

17 ושניהם יהודים.

18 אבן העזר סימן קל״ז. ראה לעיל הערה 15.

התפיסה אינה כדין ומה בכך? הטענה המשכנעת של הריב״ש היא שהרי לא היה תפוס כדי שיגרש והיא בת תוקף גם בתביעה שלא כדין. הרב המבקר מטעם המוציא לאור טוען שהתפיסה הייתה בעד חוב שהוא כדין. אחר בקשת המחילה, אני לא מבין מהיכן הוא מדייק את הדבר. ״היו נושין בו ממון והיה תפוס בבית הסוהר״. כל מה שאנו יודעים עוד ״שלא היה תפוס כדי שיגרש״. בוודאי החוב היה בר תוקף בדיני המדינה כך שהיה אפשר לתפוס אותו. אבל אין שום הנחיה שהחוב היה בר תוקף בדיני ישראל. אדרבה, אולי מדובר בחוב שרירותי בעד בעל משרה. אבל העיקר הוא שהוא היה תפוס ללא קשר עם מסירת הגט, בעד חוב כדין ישראל או לא. ומה בכך? אם קרובי אשתו הציעו לשלם את חובו אם הוא יתן לה גט פיטורין, הגט מרוצה. וברור שהדין לא היה משתנה אילו המשא ומתן בין קרובי האשה ובעלה היה מתקיים עובר לתפיסתו בבית הסוהר או אפילו קודם שעמד בדין הערכאה ואפילו אם קרובי אשתו היו בעלי חובו. הרי לנו ראיה שכפייה על דבר אחר, ללא קשר עם נתינת הגט, על אף שהיא שלא כדין, לא פוסלת את הגט. מכל מקום, אפילו אם החוב הוא כדין, המאסר מעביר אותנו לכפייה שלא כדין. אבל עכשיו נעיין עוד בתשובה אחרת של הריב״ש, בסימן רל״ב הקרובה לנידון שלנו. כמתואר שם, בחור קידש נערה במירמה ושלא בפני עשרה, בניגוד להסכמת הקהילות שאין לקדש אלא בפני עשרה. כתוצאה מכך, ציווה הרב לתופסו במאסר. לאחר מכן הסכים הבחור לגרש את ארוסתו ואף נתן לה גט, אחר שביטל אותו ומסר מודעה בפני שני עדים (בנפרד) בטענה שהוא חבוש במאסר כדי לכפות אותו לתת גט ולכן הוא אנוס והגט פסול. הריב״ש דן בצדדיה של שאלה זו ובין דבריו כותב כך: ״מכל מקום בנידון זה שאי אפשר לדעת זה [סיבת המאסר, מטרתו ומשך תפישתו] אלא מפי הרב מה הייתה כוונתו, הנה הבעל נאמן יותר כיון שהאמינוהו חכמים. ועוד שהרי זה היה תפוש לעינינו ויודע שכשיגרש יתירוהו ממאסרו. אם כן הרי הוא כאילו נאנס לגרש, כיון שמסר מודעה קודם לכן מחמת זה האונס. **ואף על פי שאונס זה אין מספיק לבדו לבטל הגט מדין גט מעושה, היכא שלא מסר מודעה מתחילה, כיון שלא נתפש על שיגרש, מכל מקום כשמסר מודעה מתחילה, אף אם נאמר שאין מסירת מודעה מועלת אלא ע״י אונס, אפילו הכי קצת אונס מועיל להחשיב המודעה, אף על פי שאינו אונס גמור מצד עצמו.״**

יש לשים לב שגם במצב הזה הבחור נכלא מפורשות משום שעבר על הסכמת הקהילות ולא כדי לכפותו לתת גט. אבל קשה להגיד שמאסרו היה כדין וכך נראה באמת מתוך דבריו של הריב״ש שהכפייה הייתה שלא כדין. אבל הריב״ש היה מכשיר את הגט, אם לא המודעה, מפני שאין ראיה ברורה, שקנס המאסר היה מכוון לכפות את הגט.

אנחנו שוב רואים שכפייה בדבר אחר שלא כדין אינה פוסלת את הגט אף על פי שהיא קצת אונס המועיל להחשיב המודעה. הנידון דומה מאוד לנידון שלנו. בנידון דידן הבעל לא נאסר אבל נושים ממנו פיצוים על העבר מפני שזה הדרך היחידה שהחוק מאפשר. והרי אנחנו במצב של כפייה על דבר אחר ואף אם הכפייה היא שלא כדין, אינה אונס מספיק כדי לפסול את הגט. כך נראה פשטם של דברי הריב״ש לפי השכל הישר ויש עוד להוסיף שהריב״ש היה פוסק מצוין בעל השפעה עצומה על המחבר רבי יוסף קארו שהעיד בשם מורו ר׳ יעקב בירב, שהוא היה סומך על תשובות הריב״ש יותר מעל פוסקים אחרים.

עכשיו אם מישהו ירצה להתווכח עימי ולהאשים אותי בהבנה מוטעית את דברי הריב״ש, הנה יגעתי ומצאתי סעד לדברי.

א. הרב הדיין יהודה ווארבורג כתב בספרו ״רביניק אוטוריטי״ (באנגלית) חלק א, עמוד 144, הערה 140: שכמה פוסקים סבורים שאפילו אם הבעל היה במאסר מפני חוב שלא כדין ישראל או שהמאסר לא היה כדין ישראל, הגט כשר, והוא מתייחס לתשובת הריב״ש סימן קל״ז.

ב. הרב הדיין חגי איזירר במאמר: ״אונסא דנפשיה״ בממונות, בעונשין ובגיטין, שורת הדין ה׳, עמודים רצ״ח עד שט״ו, כתב בעמוד ש״י על דברי הריב״ש סימן קל״ז על הקטע הנגמר

ראינו שבית הדין מדגיש שהתביעה תהיה אך ורק על הנזק המתייחס לעבר והוא אוסר לתבוע על העתיד, עד תום עילת הנזק.[14] נימוקו של בית הדין הוא בוודאי שתביעה על העתיד תהיה עישוי ישיר על הגט בעוד שתביעה על העבר אינה תביעה למתן הגט אלא תביעה על הנזק שסבלה האישה והוא בגדר אונס בדבר אחר שהרי נתינת הגט אינה פוטרת את הבעל מתשלום הפיצוים ולכן העישוי הוא על דבר אחר. ואם יטען הטוען שאכן אחר שהסרבן ישלם בגין הנזק על העבר יישאר איום על העתיד, שהרי בעוד שלוש שנים תוכל האשה לתבוע שוב את הנזק של השנים הנוספות שעברו. התשובה היא שאנחנו מול סכנה רחוקה, שהרי יש הרבה ספיקות בדבר: האם האישה תתאושש ותשים נפשה בכפה ותתבע פעם נוספת, האם האישה תרצה שוב להתדיין בערכאות ולא תתייאש, האם תרצה ותוכל לעמוד בהוצאות העורך דין והסדרים המשפטיים ובעיקר האם תוצאות התביעה יהיו חיוביות כמו בפעם הראשונה. כנראה שסכנה זו היא סכנה רחוקה ושפיר אמרינן שהעישוי הוא בדבר אחר ולא על מתן הגט. ועוד הוכחה מכרעת נוספת מהניסיון שהענקת הפיצוים על העבר על ידי הערכאה אינה איום, אפילו עקיף, על מתן הגט: הסרבן לא רוצה את אשתו אלא הוא רוצה רק להקניט אותה. מיד כשהוא כפוי לשלם לה פיצויים על העבר, ובלי להתחשב רגע באפשרות של גזר דין עתידי אפשרי, הוא מוכן לתת את הגט כתמורה לוויתור על הפיצויים הנוכחיים. הרי זו ראיה שהוא רוצה לעכב את גיטה בשיטנה כל זמן שאין לו שום נזק. אבל הוא לא מוכן לסבול הוצאות, מה שתהיינה. ולכן הוא באמת לא מתחשב כלל בסכנה הרחוקה. מה שחשוב לו הוא להשתמט עכשיו מן ההוצאות הנוכחיות, הקרובות והבטוחות. ואם כן בצדק יש להחשיב את התביעה על פיצויי העבר כתביעה על דבר אחר ולא על מתן הגט.[15] בנוסף על כך, היה אפשר לכאורה להחשיב את התביעה

של עישוי על דבר אחר, לא קשור לגט, עקרונית הגט כשר. אבל אם העישוי הוא "שלא כדין", כלומר נגד הדין, למשל כשמפחידים אותו להפסידו ממון או על ידי גניבה, יש לחשוש הרבה יותר שהעישוי נעשה בדרך שרירותית, אך ורק כדי לכפות אותו בעקיפין לתת את הגט, כמו שאמרו בגמרא בבא מציעא ק"א ע"ב: "לנקטיה בכובסיה דלשבקיה לגלימא" , ובמקרה כזה הגט פסול לפחות לפי כמה פוסקים אבל אין זה מוסכם.

14 קנס שהייה בגין איחור במימושה של החלטה משפטית או במילים אחרות: קנס יומי בגין אי מימוש של החלטה משפטית. בצרפתית: astreinte, באנגלית: Daily fine for delay in performance of contract.

15 אם התביעה היא שלא כדין המגמה הנוכחית היא להחשיב את הגט כמעושה. אבל זה לא מוסכם. ראו בתשב"ץ ח"א ס"א, שם הוא מסתפק במקרה שהאשה גנבה חפציו, אי הוי עישוי ובתולדות אדם וחווה, חלק חווה, נתיב ארבעה ועשרים, ממש בסוף חלק א' באשה שגנבה שטרי חובות, ר' ירוחם מסיים: ולפי עניות דעתי הגט גט. ראו גם פתחי תשובה על אה"ע ס' קלד סע' ד' אות י"א ובמיוחד בד"ה וכן מעשים בכל יום שאשה לפעמים מצירה להבעל בגזילת ממון ובשאר דברים ומחמת זה מגרש ואין מי שחש לגט מעושה עכ"ד [על אף שיש כאן, כמו במקרים הקודמים, כפייה עקיפה ואפילו ישירה על הגט]. אבל ראו במיוחד ריב"ש ס' קכ"ז בד"ה: והרי זה כמי שהיו נושים בו ממון והיה תפוס בבית הסוהר...והגט אינו מעושה אלא מרוצה. לכאורה (רמב"ם, מלווה ולווה פ"ב ה"א ושו"ת הריב"ש ס' תפ"ד) עונש

אחר פסק הדין וחיוב הבעל בתשלום פיצויים לאשתו הבעל, שכל רצונו להכאיב ולעגן או לסחוט את אשתו, מתרצה לתת את הגט בתמורה לוויתור של אשתו על הפיצויים, או לפחות על חלק מהם.

התהליך כולו הוא איפוא ארוך ביותר. כלומר: משך הזמן מן ההפרדה עד הגירושים האזרחיים ועד הגשת התביעה לפיצוים ועד פסק-דין הערכאה ועד נתינת הגט יכול להימשך מחמש עד שמונה שנים, ולפעמים עוד יותר כאשר הבעל אבד כל היגיון ומוכן להיות נודד ונרדף כדי לגרום סבל לאשתו. המצב הזה הוא ניסיון קשה מייגע וגורם סבל, שיכול להרוס את חייה של האשה, המונע אותה מלהבריא והמשדד מערכות-חייה.

2. מבט הלכתי על האסטרטגיה של הבית דין.[12]

לכאורה, אפשר להצדיק את האסטרטגיה הזו, המופעלת באמצעות הערכאות הצרפתיות על ידי העיקרון הנזכר, שמותר לעשות עישוי "בדבר אחר". הריב"ש בתשובותיו סי' קכ"ז וסי' רל"ב וכן הרשב"ץ בתשובותיו: תשב"ץ חלק א' סי' א' תמכו בעיקרון הזה. אולם יש לעיין בשתי נקודות: ראשית, האם העישוי נעשה כדין, כלומר בדרך מותרת, בלי עשיית עבירה ואיסור, ושנית האם אנחנו באמת במצב של עישוי בדבר אחר בלי עישוי ישיר על הגט עצמו? אחרת אנחנו כופים על הגט, ובמקרה כזה יש עישוי על הגט שלא כדין, כלומר עישוי במקום שאין הדין נותן לכפות את הגט.[13]

אפשרויות: מתן הגט או תשלום הנזק אין כאן כפייה אם משלימים את תנאי הערה 9 למעלה.

12 אני לא טוען שבית הדין המציא את האסטרטגיה הזו, להפך. אבל אני מכנה אותה: אסטרטגיה של הבית דין מפני שהיא מתוארת ומומלצת בחוברת שפרסמו הארגון ויצ"ו והקונסיסטואר עם הקדמה של הרב הראשי של הקונסיסטואר ונשיא בית הדין כך שבוודאי בית הדין תומך בה. ברור שהאסטרטגיה הזו היא תוצאה של התפתחות עמדת בתי המשפט הצרפתיים כלפי הגדרת אשמתו של הבעל הסרבן. בעבר הוגדרה אשמתו של הבעל כ'הפרת זכויות', בצרפתית: « abus de droit », באנגלית: « violation of right ». כלומר שימוש בלתי חוקי לטובתו של ההלכה המעניקה לו את הזכות לתת את הגט לרצונו. אבל הגדרה זו חִייבה את מסורבת הגט להוכיח את כוונתו של בעלה לשעבר לפגוע בה. עליה היה מוטל להוכיח שאין לבעל שום תועלת מוצדקת להשתמש בזכותו הדתית לא לתת לה גט ושכל כוונתו של הבעל היא רק לפגוע בה, לעשות לה עוולה או לגרום לה נזק. חובת ההוכחה הייתה מוטלת עליה. המגמה הנוכחית היא להזניח את המושג של 'הפרת זכויות' ולהפוך את חובת ההוכחה עליו. עכשיו הוא צריך לתת הצדקה רצינית ומשכנעת להמנעותו לתת את הגט. אחרת הדרכתו היא עשמה. כך שנטל הראיה שהיה על האישה, מוטל כעת על הבעל. העיקרון הוא שבית המשפט, מפני חוקי חילונות בתי המשפט, לא מוסמך להתערב בנתינת הגט ואין לו רשות לכפות את הבעל לתת את הגט. כל מה שבית המשפט מוסמך לעשות הוא להטיל עונש על הבעל הסרבן בגין הנזק העובדתי והנזק המוסרי שהוא גרם לאשתו.

13 יש להיזהר מאוד בשימוש בביטוי "עישוי כדין" ו "עישוי שלא כדין". בשו"ע אבן העזר סי' קל"ד המשמעות היא עישוי המותר או עישוי האסור הפוסל את הגט מפני שהדין נותן שמותר או אסור לכפות את הגט, ראו המשנה האחרונה בפרק שביעי של מסכת כתובות. בספרות השו"ת משמעות הביטוי יכולה להיות, במקרה של עישוי בדבר אחר שלא קשור ישירות לגט, עישוי שנעשה בדרך מותרת לפי הדין או עישוי הנעשה בדרך אסורה לפי הדין. אכן במקרה

סירובו של הסרבן להתדיין לפני הבית דין או לציית לו. רק מסמך זה המעיד על סרבנותו של בעלה לשעבר לתת לה גט פיטורין יאפשר לה להגיש תביעה נגד הסרבן. ברור שהאסטרטגיה הזו דורשת משך זמן מספיק מאז שהערכאה נתנה פסק-דין של גירושין אזרחיים מפני שרק משך זמן זה ייחשב על ידי הערכאה לצורך חישוב הפיצויים. כך שיש צורך לפחות למשך זמן מזערי של שלוש שנים בין הגירושים האזרחיים ובין הגשת תביעת הנזיקין. אני מניח שבתי הדין הרבניים[8] הצרפתיים מצדיקים דרך זו בנימוק, שתביעת פיצוים[9] על הנזק ממנו סבלה האישה בעבר אינה בגדר כפייה על הגט אלא על דבר אחר,[10] כלומר כפייה על התוצאות של היעדר גט בעבר. אין זו כפייה ישירה על הגט, שהרי הבעל יכול לבחור לשלם את הפיצויים ולהמשיך לעגן אותה.[11]

את הנתבע בפני כל ערכאה אחרת. וכן עשוי המסמך הזה גם לשמש אמצעי בידי בית הדין הרבני לכפות על הנתבע שיסכים להתדיין לפני בית הדין ולמלא אחרי פסק הדין. על פי השולחן ערוך, במקרה של סירוב לדון בדין תורה, רשאי בית הדין גם לנדות את הסרבן ואף להורות שלא לצרפו למניין עד להסכמתו להתדיין. במקרה של סרבנות גט יש להיזהר מאוד כדי למנוע כל חשש של גט מעושה. לפיכך, במקרה הזה, המיוחד במינו, אסור לנדות את הסרבן אבל אפשר להפעיל כנגדו את ההרחקות של רבינו תם.

8 למרות מאמצים חשובים לא הצלחתי לקבל מאף אחד מן חברי הבתי דין הצרפתיים הצדקה הלכתית מספקת לנוהג הזה שהם תומכים בו, ולכן אני מוכרח להציע הצדקה עצמית סבירה מתקבלת על הדעת, אם אפשר, לכתחילה, אחרת בדיעבד. הקורא כבר ראה איך המצב הרבה יותר קשה ומסובך מהמצב בארצות הברית ואין צריך לומר מהמצב בישראל.

9 אני מבקש מהקורא מעט סבלנות שהרי אי אפשר לבחון את כל הבעיות בבת אחת. ברור שהתביעה צריכה להיות מוצדקת ושווה לכל. תביעה שרירותית או קנס ״לפי מידה״ שפקד רודן או פקיד בעל השפעה, אף על פי שהם באופן רשמי לא קשורים למתן הגט, עלולים להיות כפייה על הגט. בכל זאת אני כותב את זה בהסתייגות שהרי הריב״ש בסימן רל״ב היה מכשיר את הגט על פי הטעם הרשמי אף על פי שקנס המאסר היה שרירותי, אם לא שהבעל מסר מודעה נגדו (ראו להלן הערה 15). כנראה פיתרון הסתירה הוא שכל זמן שהקנס הוא על דבר אחר ואי אפשר להוכיח בוודאות שהיטילו אותו בכוונה כדי לכפות את הגט, אין קנס זה אונס גמור הפוסל את הגט. ראו ניתוח התשובה בהערה 15. בדרך כלל אם התביעה היא כדין תורה אין בעיה והגט כשר ואם היא שלא כדין תורה אבל לפי הדין האזרחי אז הדבר תלוי במחלוקת. ראו להלן הערה 15.

10 יש אונס אחר, אף על פי שהוא אונסו בגופו אינו אונסו לגרש, אלא שאונס אותו לעשות דבר אחר. והוא מעצמו כדי להנצל מאותו אונס מגרש מעצמו. וזה אינו קרוי כפייה כיוון שלא כפו אותו ממש להוציא. תשב״ץ חלק א׳, סימן א׳, עמוד ח׳, תחתית עמודה ב׳, תשב״ץ חלק א׳ מכון ירושלים תשנ״ח, העורך הראשי: הרב יואל קטן. ראו גם פתחי תשובה על ש״ע סי׳ קלד סע׳ ד׳ סוף אות ט׳: בד״ה אומנם אם התחייב עצמו בקנס כשלא יגרש לזמן קבוע ונתחרט ולא רצה לגרש עד שעבר הזמן, ממילא כשעבר הזמן נתחייב בהקנס אפילו אם יגרשנה שוב דהא חיוב הקנס חל תיכף כשהגיע הזמן ולא גירש וא״כ הב״ד יכולין לתובעו כדין בהקנס והוי כמופין אותו לשלם חובו וכשמגרש להיפטר מחובו לא הוי גט מעושה כמ״ש הרשב״ץ הנ״ל עכ״ד.

11 אם נתינת הגט הייתה מבטלת את תביעת הפיצוים אז יש קשר ישיר יותר בין התביעה ומתן הגט. התביעה עודדת את הבעל לתת את הגט. כאשר הבעל שומר על ברירה חופשית בין שתי

יורק המתנה את הגירושין האזרחיים בהסרת כל מניעה דתית לשחרורו של בן הזוג ההוראה האחרונה הזו מונעת פיתרון מהיר ומועיל נגד סרבנות גט. אדרבא, הוראה זו מסבכת באופן חמור את המצב. אכן, במצב כתיקונו, כאשר הבעל משתף פעולה, הוא נותן את הגט לאשתו לפני בית הדין, ואחר כך הגט נשאר שמור אצל בית הדין עד לאחר הכרזת הערכאה על הגירושין האזרחיים. רק אז האשה מקבלת תעודה מבית-הדין המאשרת שהאשה גרושה על-פי דין.[4] באופן זה הרווחנו שאם בינתיים היא מתייחדת עם מישהו אחר, היא לא תעבור על איסור אשת-איש והנולדים האפשריים לא יהיו ממזרים. אבל מפני חוק הצפרתי, רק אחר הכרזת הערכאה על הגירושין האזרחיים הבית דין נותן את התעודה הזו לאשה וקורע את הגט כנהוג. לכן היא לא תוכל לקבל קידושין לפני קבלת התעודה, כלומר רק אחר הגירושין האזרחיים. אולם במקרים קשים של סרבנות, המצב הרבה יותר מסובך. אכן, כל עוד שהערכאה האזרחית לא נתנה פסק-דין של גירושין אזרחיים, הסרבן יכול לטעון שאסור לו לתת גט. ואחר כך, כאשר הערכאה כבר הוציאה פסק-דין המאשר את הגירושים האזרחיים, יכול הסרבן להתעקש ולהתנות את מתן הגט בוויתור האשה על כל מה שהשופט פסק לזכותה. או גרוע יותר, הוא יכול להתעלם מן הבית דין ולא לענות להזמנותיו ולהיעלם לגמרי. ועוד, בגלל חוק ההפרדה, לא יכולה האשה להבטיח את מתן הגט[5]. ואף אם הערכאה הייתה קובעת בפסק הדין את חיוב[6] הבעל לתת גט לאשתו, הרי שהדבר היה יוצר מצב של לפחות ספק גט מעושה.

אם לאחר שבית המשפט פוסק ומכריז על הגירושין האזרחיים של הזוג, הבעל עוד מסרב לתת לה גט, כי אז עורכי הדין של האשה משתמשים באסטרטגיה, שבית הדין תומך בה, והיא היחידה שהחוק הצרפתי השאיר להם: הם תובעים לדין את הסרבן שמסרב לציית לבית הדין, ואין צריך לומר במקרה שהסרבן מסרב להופיע לפני בית הדין, והם דורשים ממנו על-יסוד סעיף 1382 של החוק האזרחי הצרפתי פיצוים עבור כל משך הזמן, אחר הכרזת הגירושין האזרחיים, שהאישה נשארה עגונה וגלמודה, בלי אפשרות להינשא. חשוב לשים לב שבשלב הזה יש לבית דין פיקוח מלא על המצב מפני שהוא צריך לתת אישור לאשה כדי שתוכל להגיש את התביעה המשפטית הזו נגד בעלה הסרבן. הרי האשה לא יכולה להגיש את תביעתה בלי שבית הדין יתן לה תעודת סירוב[7] המעידה על

הגירושין האזרחיים ולכן אין כאן עונש מפורש.

4 לא ברור לי אם הנוהג הזה הוא רשמי או שזה ביצוע פנימי המוסתר מן הרשויות ולכן טוב להשאר שתקן.

5 כמו שמקובל בארצות הברית.

6 התחייבותו העצמית או הבטחתו של הבעל לתת גט פיטורין לא בעייתית שהרי רק השבועה או קבלת קנס דומות לאונס. בכל זאת ראה שולחן ערוך, אבן העזר סימן קנ״ד, סדר הגט סעיף י״ד.

7 תעודת סירוב או כתב סירוב הוא פסק דין אשר בא בתגובה לסירובו של הנתבע להתדיין בפני בית דין על פי דין תורה. בכתב הסירוב מודיע בית הדין הרבני כי הנתבע מסרב להופיע לפני בית הדין או שהוא מסרב להתדיין בפני בית הדין או לציית לו ולפיכך רשאי התובע לתבוע

סרבנות גט: *המצב באירופה בכלל ובצרפת בפרט.* *הצעה לקיצור זמן העיגון של מסורבות גט*[1]

מאת: יוסף יצחק איידלר

1. המצב הנוכחי בצרפת

לפי חוק ההפרדה בין המדינה החילונית והדת (כל הדתות בכלל, אבל הדת הנוצרית בפרט) המדינה לא מכירה בנישואים הדתיים ובגירושין הדתיים. לא זו בלבד, על פי החוק בצרפת אסור לרבנים הרשמיים לסדר חופה וקידושין קודם הנישואין האזרחיים,[2] וכמו כן אסור להם לסדר גירושין קודם הגירושין האזרחיים.[3] בניגוד לחוק הגט של מדינת ניו

1 אני מודה לפרופ' ברכיהו ליפשיץ (שיצא לגמלאות, אוניברסיטה העברית ירושלים) שקרא את הטיוטה הראשונה והעיר הערות חשובות, לפרופ' עמחי רדזינר (אוניברסיטה בר אילן) שהסב את תשומת ליבי למסמכי כנס הדיינים אדר התשע"ו. ראה בקישור http://www.rbc.gov.il/DocLib1/Kenes2016.pdf, ולפרופ' ליליאן ונה מפריז, חוקרת בתחום ההלכה ומסייעת לנשים מסורבות גט, שיידעה אותי על פרטים חשובים בנוגע למציאות בצרפת. אני גם מודה בלבביות לד"ר מיכאל ויגודה, ראש היחידה למשפט עברי, משרד המשפטים, מדינת ישראל, שקרא את הטיוטה האחרונה אחר שתוקנה ביסודיות והסכים עם טענת המאמר בדרך כלל, עשה הערות חשובות ושיפר את הלשון. חרף עזרתם של כל אלה, כל האמור במאמר הוא על אחריותי הבלעדית.

2 ראה החוק הפלילי הצרפתי, סעיף 21-433, הקובע שהעובר על החוק ייענש בשישה חודשי מאסר וקנס של 7500 פרנקים צרפתיים חדשים.

3 העיקרון הזה מקובל על הכל אבל כנראה אינו כתוב בפירוש בחוק. כמו כן אין בחוק הפלילי הצרפתי סעיף מקביל לסעיף הקודם כאשר רב צרפתי עובר על החוק ומסדר גט קודם

יוסף יצחק איידלר בהכשרתו המקצועית הוא מהנדס אזרחי (בגמלאות). במשך עשרות בשנים הוא ניהל משרד הנדסה בבלגיה (משרד המתמחה ביציבות מבנים וחישובי סטטיקה), תכנן בנייני מגורים מלונות בתי חולים, בנייני תעשיה, מאגרים ומגדלי מים. הוא למד תורה אצל אביו הרבני ר' אליעזר איידלער ז"ל, איש עסקים שהוסמך להוראה בצעירותו על ידי הרב שלמה זלמן ברויאר בפרנקפורט והגאון רבי מאיר יחיאל הלוי זצ"ל האדמור ואבד"ק אוסטרובצה. במשך כמה עשרות שנים למד והתמחה בנושאי אסטרונומיה יהודית וזמני היום בהלכה. חיבר את הספר החדשני "הלכות קידוש החודש על פי הרמב"ם" ספרייתי תשנ"ו, ספר שפתח צוהר לרבים בהבנת סוגיות מורכבות בהלכות קידוש החודש שעד כתיבת הספר היו בבחינת אוצר חתום גם ליודעי ח"ן.
הוא כתב מאמרים רבים בנושא האסטרונומיה היהודית בימי הביניים, הלוח העברי, מקורו, התפתחותו, עתידו ותכונותיו המתמטיות בכתבי-עת *בד"ד* (אוניברסיטת בר-אילן) וכתב העת *חקירה* (פלטבוש, ניו יורק). ההדיר, העיר והוציא לאור כמה מחיבוריו החשובים של רבי רפאל הלוי מהנובר גדול חכמי התכונה היהודית של המאה ה 18- בשנים האחרונות הוא כתב כמה מאמרים בנושא הסכם קדם-נישואין וסרבנות גט בכתב-עת תורני *צהר* ועכשיו הוא עומד לפרסם (במקביל למאמר זה) מאמר נוסף בשם "חשש לדעת יחיד במקום עיגון" בכרך מ' של כתב-עת תורני *תחומין*.
חלק ממאמריו ופרסומיו מצויים ברשת בקישור- www.ajdler.com/jjajdler/index.html.

חקירה

כרך כ"ח – שנת תש"פ

תוכן עניינים

סרבנות גט: המצב באירופה בכלל ובצרפת בפרט.
הצעה לקיצור זמן העיגון של מסורבות גט
מאת: יוסף יצחק איידלר ....ה

"כבד פה וכבד לשון" – הצעות להסבר
מאת: אבנר טלר .... כג

חקירה

כרך כ"ח – שנת תש"פ